EXISTENCE IN BLACK

Routledge
New York and London

EXISTENCE IN BLACK

An Anthology of Black Existential Philosophy

Edited and with an Introduction by

Lewis R. Gordon

Published in 1997
by Routledge
29 West 35th Street
New York, NY 10001

Published in
Great Britain by
Routledge
11 New Fetter Lane
London EC4P 4EE

Copyright © 1997 by
Routledge
Printed in the
United States of America
on acid-free paper.

Library of Congress Cataloging-in-Publication-Data
Existence in Black:
    an anthology of Black existential philosophy/
    edited, with an introduction by Lewis R. Gordon
        p. cm.
    Includes bibliographical references and index.
    ISBN 0–415–91451–5 (cl).—ISBN 0–415–91450–7 (pb)
    1. Afro American Philosophy   2. Existentialism
    3. Liberty—Philosophy   I. Gordon, Lewis R.
    (Lewis Ricardo), 1962–   .
B936.E85   1996
191'.089'96073—dc20   96-24896
                                       CIP

CONTENTS

CONTENTS

DEDICATION

[W]e have had to fight, and still do, for that very visibility which also renders us most vulnerable, our Blackness. For to survive in the mouth of this dragon we call america, we have had to learn this first and most vital lesson—that we were never meant to survive.

—Audre Lorde

The first premise of all human history is, of course, the existence of living human individuals.

—Karl Marx

Was my freedom not given to me then to build the world of the You?

—Frantz Fanon

ACKNOWLEDGMENTS

THIS WORK was a difficult project. It would have been an uncompleted project but for the support of the following people. First, Ms. Christina Boyd, Ms. Pamela Connelly, Ms. Elizabeth Smith, and Ms. Beth Turner provided nearly all of the clerical support needed for its completion. T. Denean Sharpley-Whiting provided much-needed dialogue on its early structure and she proofread a version of the entire manuscript. Lisa Anderson, M. Shawn Copeland, Paget Henry, Joy James, William Jones, Maurice Natanson, and Gary Schwartz provided support, both intellectually and spiritually, in more ways than they may have imagined. So, too, in many ways, did most of the contributors to this volume.

I would like to thank Leonard Harris and Robert Bertolet, chairpersons of, respectively, African-American Studies and Philosophy at Purdue University for their support over the past few years. In addition, I would like to thank my Purdue colleagues Floyd Hayes III, Carolyn Johnson, William McBride, Jacqueline Martinez, Martin Matuštík, Calvin O. Schrag, Renée T. White, and Charlene Zeigfried for the ongoing, stimulating discussions of existential issues. At Routledge, Maureen McGrogan, her former assistant Alison Shonkwiler, and her subsequent assistant Meghan Dailey deserve special thanks for the care they added to the project and the patience with which they encouraged each of its steps.

I would also like to thank some of the individuals and organizations who have provided places and support for the presentation of black existential thought over the past few decades: the Black Caucus of the American Philosophical Association, the Sartre Societies of North America and Europe, the Radical Philosophy Association, the Society of Feminist Philosophers, the Society of Africana Philosophy, and the African Studies Association. Individuals to whom special thanks are in order are William R. Jones, Bob Stone, Betsy Bowman, Iris Marion Young, Sandra Bartky, Karsten Struhl, Linda Bell, Debra Bergoffen, and Robert Bernasconi. Among historical figures without whom there would not be the set of ideas that comprise this volume are David Walker, Maria Stewart, Frederick Douglass, Edward Blyden, Anna Julia Cooper, Alexander Crummell, W.E.B. Du Bois, Jose Marti, Alain Locke, Ida B. Wells-Barnett, Ella Baker, Paul Robeson, Claudette Jones, Frantz Fanon, Richard Wright, Martin Luther King, Jr., Malcolm X, Walter Rodney, C. L.R. James, and many, many more. I would also like to extend a special thanks to Angela Davis for the encouragement and support she has given me over the past year. She helped put more into focus than she may have realized.

Three of the articles have appeared elsewhere but either copyright or right of reprint is the authors': A short version of "Existential Dynamics of Theorizing Black Invisibility" appeared in The Proceedings of the National Association of African-American Studies (1994). I thank NAAS for permission to reprint that material. Sartre's contribution is a translation of his essay, "Retour des Etats Unis: Ce qui j'ai appris du problème noir," which originally appeared in *Le Figaro* (16 June 1945). I thank Arlette Elkaïm-Sartre, executor to Sartre's estate, and Éditions Gallimard for permission of translation and reprint. "Nietzsche on Blacks" appears by courtesy of William Preston, who holds the 1995 copyright for that essay.

Finally, there are Lisa, Mathieu, and Jenny, as well as Pat, Sylvia, Gertrude, and Lola, whose love is reason enough always to go on.

Lewis R. Gordon
Providence, Rhode Island
July 1996

CONTRIBUTORS

Ernest Allen, Jr., teaches in the W.E.B. Du Bois Department of Afro-American Studies at the University of Massachusetts at Amherst. He is author of numerous articles on African-American nationalism.

Robert Birt teaches Philosophy at Morgan State University. He is author of a number of articles on Africana Philosophy and Existentialism.

Bernard R. Boxill is Pardue Professor of Philosophy at the University of Carolina at Chapel Hill. He is well known for his work on blacks and social justice. He is author of *Blacks and Social Justice* (Rowman and Littlefield).

George Carew teaches Philosophy at Spelman College, where he specializes in Political Philosophy and Africana Philosophy.

Bobby R. Dixon taught Philosophy at Kent State University, where he specialized in Continental Philosophy, Critical Theory, and Africana Philosophy. **G.M. James Gonzalez** is a doctoral candidate in Philosophy at the State University of New York at Binghampton. Her specializations are aesthetics, feminist theory, and postcolonial theory.

Lewis R. Gordon teaches Africana Philosophy and Contemporary Religious Thought at Brown University where he is also a member of the Center for the Study of Race and Ethnicity. He is the author of *Bad Faith and Antiblack Racism* (Humanities Press), *Fanon and the Crisis of European Man: An Essay on Philosophy and the Human Sciences* (Routledge), and *Her Majesty's Other Children* (Rowman & Littlefield). He is also co-editor of *Fanon: A Critical Reader* (Blackwell) and *Black Texts and Textuality: Constructing and De-Constructing Blackness* (Rowman & Littlefield).

Floyd W. Hayes III teaches Political Science and African-American Studies at Purdue University. He is author of numerous articles on public policy and political theory. He has published in numerous journals of politics and African-American studies, and he is editor of the anthology, *A Turbulent Voyage: Readings in African American Studies* (Collegiate Press). He is currently working on a book, tentatively titled *African-American Cynicism: Cultural Crosscurrents in a Postindustrial-Managerial Polity*.

Paget Henry is Director of Afro-American Studies and Professor of Sociology at Brown University. He is also a member of Brown's Center for the Study of Race and Ethnicity and former president of the C.L.R. James Society. He has written numerous articles on the political economy of the Caribbean and African and Afro-Caribbean philosophy, and he is the author of *Peripheral Capitalism and Underdevelopment in Antigua* (Transactions) and co-editor of *C.L.R. James' Caribbean* (Duke UP).

Patricia Huntington teaches Philosophy at American University in Washington, DC. Her work focuses on feminist theory, philosophy of existence, and theories of liberation. She is currently writing a book on Heidegger, Irigaray, and Poststructuralism (SUNY UP).

Joy Ann James teaches in the Department of Ethnic Studies at the University of Colorado at Boulder. She is author of numerous articles on the intersection of gender, race, and class and state violence. She is co-editor of *Spirit, Space, and Survival: Black Women in (White) Academe* (Routledge) and author of *Resisting State Violence in US Culture* (U. Minnesota Press) and *Transcending the Talented Tenth* (Routledge). She is currently editing an Angela Davis Critical Reader and an Angela Davis Primary Reader for Blackwell Publishers.

Clarence Sholé Johnson teaches Philosophy at Spelman College. He has also taught at Marianapolis College in Montreal, Canada, and Fourah Bay College, the University of Sierra Leone in West Africa, specializing in the philosophy of David Hume; his publications have appeared in major scholarly journals such as *The Journal of Philosophical Research, Dialogue: Canadian Philosophical Review, The Southwest Philosophy Review* and *Metaphilosophy*.

Bill E. Lawson teaches Philosophy at the University of Delaware. He specializes in Ethics, Political Philosophy, and Africana Philosophy (particularly in the 19th century). He is editor of *The Underclass Question* (Temple UP) and coauthor of *Between Slavery and Freedom* (Indiana UP). He is currently editing a volume of philosophical essays on Frederick Douglass.

Howard McGary teaches Philosophy at Rutgers University. He has also taught at the University of Arizona, the University of Illinois at Chicago, and Oxford University. He specializes in Africana Philosophy, Ethics, and Political Philosophy. He is coauthor of *Between Slavery and Freedom*, and he serves on the editorial boards of the *Philosophical Forum, Encyclopedia of Ethics*, and *Social Identities*.

Roy D. Morrison II taught Philosophy at Wesley Theological Seminary in Washington, DC. He specialized in Epistemology and Philosophy of Science. He is the author of *Science, Theology and the Transcendental Horizon* (Scholars Press).

William A. Preston is a Political Theorist with specializations in Marxism, Nietzsche, and French Political Thought. He is author of a forthcoming book, *Nietzsche as Anti-Socialist: Prophet of Bourgeois Ennoblement*.

Jean-Paul Sartre is one of the major European twentieth-century philosophers of existence and arguably the most influential philosopher of the 20th century. His work as a philosopher and activist are well known. He is the author of many books, including *Being and Nothingness, Critique of Dialectical Reason, Nausea*, and *The Family Idiot*. He was offered and turned down the Nobel Prize for Literature. **Gary Schwartz** teaches classics at Lehman College of the City University of New York and he is Director of the Lehman Scholars Program. He also teaches courses on African-American, Brazilian, and Australian literatures. He is currently composing a collection of critical essays on film.

Robert St. Martin Westley is Associate Professor of Law and Jurisprudence at Tulane Law School. He has just completed his first book, *White Normativity: Race and the Rights of Groups*.

T. Denean Sharpley-Whiting teaches French and African-American studies at Purdue University. She is co-editor of *Fanon: A Critical Reader* (Blackwell), *Spoils of War: Women, Cultures, Revolutions* (forthcoming) and author of two forthcoming books, *Black Venus: Sexualized Savages, Primal Fears and Primitive Narratives* (Duke UP), and *Fanon and Feminisms: Theory, Thought, Praxis* (Rowman & Littlefield).

Naomi Zack teaches Philosophy at the State University of New York at Albany. She specializes in Epistemology, Existentialism, and Critical Race Theory. She is author of *Race and Mixed Race* (Temple UP) and *Bachelors of Science: 17th Century Identity, Then and Now* (Temple UP), and editor of *American Mixed Race* (Rowman and Littlefield) and *Race/Sex: Their Sameness, Difference, and Interplay* (Routledge).

NOTE ON THE TEXT

THIS IS a long volume, which necessitated editorial and stylistic decisions that will not make any self-respecting environmentalist shudder. The welfare of trees and economic realities of making the volume affordable demanded economy of expression and citation wherever possible. As a result, I have eliminated citations that are obvious. The bibliography has also been sparing on obvious terms (e.g., the word "University Press" and "Publishers" have been omitted).

INTRODUCTION

Black Existential Philosophy

Lewis R. Gordon

FOR MANY black people, when the question of their blackness is raised, there is but one challenge from which all the others follow. It usually takes the form of another question: What is to be done in a world of nearly a universal sense of superiority to, if not universal hatred of, black folk? Or, to paraphrase W.E.B. Du Bois from *Darkwater:* What is to be understood by black suffering?

It is this question that animates a great deal of the theoretical dimension of black intellectual productions. It is what signals the question of liberation on one level and the critique of traditional, read "European," ontological claims on another. Together they inaugurate black liberation thought and black critical race theory. The former finds its fountainhead most poignantly in Frederick Douglass. His answer in 1857 was straightforward:

> The whole history of the progress of human liberty shows that all concessions yet made to her august claims, have been born of earnest struggle. This struggle may be a moral one, or it may be a physical one, and it may be both moral and physical, but it must be a struggle. Power concedes nothing without demand. It never did and it never will.

The ontological question was examined by many philosophers and social critics of African descent in the nineteenth century, including such well-known and diverse figures as Martin Delany, Anna Julia Cooper, and W.E.B. Du Bois. It wasn't until the 1940s, however, that self-avowed existential examinations of these issues emerged, and they emerged ironically through a European philosopher—namely, Jean-Paul Sartre.

Sartre stands as an unusual catalyst in the history of black existential philosophy, for he serves as a link between Richard Wright and Frantz Fanon (undoubtedly the two most influential revolutionary black existential "men of letters" of the twentieth century) on the one hand, and the historical forces that came into play for the ascendence of European Philosophy of Existence in the American academy on the other hand. These forces provided a context for the academic work of African-American philosophers like William R. Jones, who wrote his dissertation on Sartre, and Angela Y. Davis, who focused on French existentialists as an undergraduate and studied for her doctorate with Herbert Marcuse. Marcuse was very critical of Sartre's work, which he misunderstood on a number of fundamental levels, but his explorations into one-dimensionality and questions of liberation were brought to more concrete dimensions in the black experience by Davis.[1] Black academic philosophers who have also been influenced by Sartre's work, by way of either Sartre himself or by philosophers like Frantz Fanon or Merleau-Ponty, also include Robert Birt, Bernard Boxill, Robert Gooding-Williams, Tommy Lott, Lucius T. Outlaw, Thomas S. Slaughter, Robert Westley, Naomi Zack, and myself.

Our reference to Sartre raises the question of what is here meant by the particular black context that occasions this volume. We will at times use the term *Africana philosophy* to describe our philosophical context. According to Lucius T. Outlaw ([1992–3]: 64), "Africana philosophy" can be regarded as

> a "gathering" notion under which to situate the articulations (writings, speeches, etc.), and traditions of African and peoples of African descent collectively, as well as the subdiscipline- or field-forming, tradition-defining or tradition-organizing reconstructive efforts, which are (to be) regarded as philosophy. However, "Africana philosophy" is to include, as well, the work of those persons who are neither African nor of African descent but who recognize the legitimacy and importance of the issues and endeavors that constitute the disciplinary activities of African or African American philosophy and contribute to the efforts—persons whose work justifies their being called "Africanists."

Using the qualifier "Africana" is consistent with the practice of naming intellectual traditions and practices in terms of the national, geographic, cultural,
racial, and/or ethnic descriptor or identity of the persons who initiated and
were/are the primary practioners—and/or are the subjects and objects—of the
practices and traditions in question (e.g., "American," "British," "French,"
"German," or "continental" philosophy).

Although the category of the black is broader in scope than the category
Africana, that distinction will not be of great consequence here since Africana philosophy constantly raises the question of blackness (Lott [1992–3] and Gordon
[1995a]: Part III). Returning to Sartre, then, it will be an error to construct Africana
academic existential philosophy as a fundamentally Sartrean or European-based
phenomenon. For although there are Africana philosophers who have been influenced by both Sartre and European thought, for the obvious reason that there has
been no place "outside" of Western/European civilization from which to raise
questions about existence in the twentieth century, it will nevertheless be fallacious
to assume that that influence functions as the "cause" instead of a consequence.
Africana philosophers already have a reason to raise existential questions of liberation and questions of identity, as we've already suggested, by virtue of the historical fact of racial oppression manifested most vividly in the European and Arabic
slave trades and the European colonization of the African continent and the entire
world of color. What those events brought about was not only a period of intense
suffering for black peoples, but also the hegemonic symbolic order of Western civ-
ilization(s) itself, a symbolic order whose "place" for the black, if you will, has been
fundamentally negative as far back as the Middle Ages and antiquity. There is much
debate on this issue, especially in light of postmodern scholarship that locates such
phenomena in the modern era. The problem is that there are texts in the Middle
Ages and antiquity that refer not only to the black, but also to the black in very
negative terms (see Baltazar [1973]). Africana philosophers' choice of European
thinkers through whom to consider these questions is therefore already existentially situated. To place European thinkers as "cause" would be to place the proverbial cart before the horse.

There is, however, a distinction that should here be borne in mind. We can
regard *existentialism*—the popularly named ideology—as a fundamentally European
historical phenomenon. It is, in effect, the history of European literature that bears
that name. On the other hand, we can regard *philosophy of existence* (the specialized
term that will also sometimes be referred to in this volume as *existential philosophy*)
as philosophical questions premised upon concerns of freedom, anguish, responsibility, embodied agency, sociality, and liberation. Unlike fashionable standpoint
epistemologies of the present, philosophy of existence is marked by a centering of
what is often known as the "situation" of questioning or inquiry itself. Another
term for situation is the lived- or meaning-context of concern. Implicit in the exis-

GORDON

3

tential demand for recognizing the situation or lived-context of Africana people's being-in-the-world is the question of value raised by people who live that situation. A slave's situation can only be understood, for instance, through recognizing the fact that a slave experiences it. It is to regard the slave as a value-laden perspective in the world.

Given our conception of philosophy of existence, it is clear that the history of Africana philosophy—at least from David Walker's *Appeal to All Colored Citizens of the World* to Cornel West's Kierkegaardian call for keeping *faith* and Toni Morrison's tragic questions of identity and ethical paradox in the Present Age (in both her *Playing in the Dark* and *Beloved*)—has its own unique set of existential questions. We find a constant posing of the teleological question of black liberation and the question of black identity in the midst of an antiblack world. The irony is that, as Fanon has shown, one cannot in critical good faith raise the question of the black without raising these accompanying existential questions (1952/1967).[2]

What this is to say is not that Africana philosophy is existential in the sense of reducing it to philosophy of existence. It is to say that the impetus of Africana philosophy, when the question of the black or the situation of black people is raised, has an existential impetus. That Africana philosophy cannot, and should not, be reduced to existential philosophy is paradoxically because of a central dimension of philosophy of existence itself: The question of existence, in itself, is empty. Philosophy of existence is therefore always a conjunctive or contextualized affair. It must, in other words, be situated. This is because, for complex reasons that will become evident to the reader, the sine qua non of an existential philosophy is the paradoxical incompleteness of existential questions. Consider the famous existential credo of existence preceding essence. If the epistemic correlate of essence is conceptualization, then the theoretical or conceptual domain is always situated on what can be called the reflective level. The reflective dimension of situated life always brings in an element of concrete embodiment of relevance. What this means is that theory, any theory, gains its sustenance from that which it offers *for* and *through* the lived-reality of those who are expected to formulate it. Africana philosophy's history of Christian, Marxist, Feminist, Pragmatic, Analytical, and Phenomenological thought has therefore been a matter of what specific dimensions each had to offer the existential realities of theorizing blackness. For Marxism, for instance, it was not so much its notion of "science" over all other forms of socialist theory, nor its promise of a world to win, that may have struck a resonating chord in the hearts of black Marxists. It was, instead, Marx and Engels' famous encomium of the proletarians' having nothing to lose but their chains.[3] Such a call has obvious affinity for a people who have been so strongly identified with chattel slavery.

Academic Africana existential philosophy has oscillated from time to time on the centrality of the liberation question. In the 1980s and 1990s, for instance, one will find priority placed on the identity question. The concern has taken many euphemisms, particularly in terms of questions of culture and ethnicity, but in the end, it usually amounts to the ever-infamous "race question." This consequence is a function of an historical fact: race has emerged, throughout its history, as the question fundamentally of "the blacks" as it has for no other group. It is not that other groups have not been "racialized." It is that their racialization, if we will, has been conditioned by a chain of being from the European to the subhuman—on a symbolic scale, from the light to the dark. As we have already noted, it is not that Africana philosophy has been the only situated reality of blackness, but instead that it has been the only theoretical reality that is fundamentally conditioned by the question of blackness.[4] The link between Africana philosophy of existence and the question of race is pronounced on the critical race theoretical problem of human designation.[5] What Africana critical race theory has shown is that the situation of blacks cannot be resolved by philosophical anthropologies that place the human being as a consequence of essential properties of valuative determination. Race issues are not primarily issues, in other words, of chromosomal make-up nor simply morphological appearance. Race issues, as Alain Locke has shown through a number of essays on values and identity, are issues by virtue of the values placed upon what has been interpreted as "given." Thus, in spite of biophysical evidence, "world history," beyond black struggles for significance, questions the humanity of black peoples. As Fanon has so provocatively put it, black defiance to black dehumanization has been historically constituted as *madness* or social deviance.[6] Blackness and, in specific form, *the black* thus function as the breakdown of reason, which situates black existence, ultimately, in a seemingly nonrational category of faith. Blacks live on, as Dostoyevsky might say, in spite of logic. It is the plight of, in other words, *the damned of the earth*. In the face of unreason, the nihilistic chasm yawns open with particular force as a conundrum of black existence. The black stands as an existential enigma. Eyed, almost with suspicion, the subtext is best exemplified by the question: "Why do they go on?"

One can readily see why such European existentialists as Jean-Paul Sartre and Simone de Beauvoir were particularly interested in the situation of blacks.[7] Their philosophies of existence, premised upon a critical encounter with bad faith, requires an understanding not only of bourgeois or ruling-class self-delusions of *Angst*, but also the force of *their* circumstances (as de Beauvoir might put it) as social realities of those upon whose labor their society drew its luxuries.[8]

"Why do they go on?" placed in the context of the black is easily reformulated, simply, as, "Why go on?"

It is, as Albert Camus has so well noted, *the* question (1942/1955). If there are readers who may be suspicious of our peculiar invocation of the question of suicide here on questions of race, they need only consider that the question of whether blacks commit suicide was treated with such seriousness by psychiatrists in the first half of the twentieth century that Fanon had to address the question in *Peau noire, masques blancs* (*Black Skin, White Masks*) in the midst of a *philosophical*

GORDON

argument. Blacks, it was believed, were incapable of committing suicide because, supposedly like the "rest" of the animal kingdom, they lacked enough apperception or intelligence to understand the ramifications of their situation. This reasoning was based on the supposition of what a "true" human being *would do* if treated as blacks are treated.[9]

This question of continuing to live on is connected to a controversial theme of all existential thought. It goes like this: There is a sense in which none of us has ever chosen to be born into this world and possibly any imaginable world. Yet, in our decision to live on, we live a choice which requires our having been born—in a word, our *existence*. In the context of blacks, the implication is obvious. No one chooses to have been born under racial designations, but the choice to go on living, and especially choices that involve recognizing one's racial situation, has implications on the meaning of one's birth. It transforms itself into a subjunctive choice to have been born. Applied to groups, it is the question of whether certain groups "should" have existed. The racist sentiment on this issue is summarized well by the antiblack racist Henry Ward Beecher, when he remarks that

> Were Africa and the Africans to sink to-morrow, how much poorer would the world be? A little less gold and ivory, a little less coffee, a considerable ripple, perhaps, where the Atlantic and Indian Oceans would come together—that is all; not a poem, not an invention, not a piece of art would be missed from the world. (from Cooper [1988]: 228)

Antiblack racism espouses a world that will ultimately be better off without blacks. Blacks, from such a standpoint, "must" provide justification for their continued presence.

So, why go on?

Africana philosophers have issued quite a number of responses to this question, and the reader will find that such an effort guides the discussions that comprise Parts II ("The 'Situation'") and IV ("Black Existence and Black Liberation") of this volume.

In the course of any effort to describe a philosophical position there will always be people who, in the tradition of old, demand names. Who, in other words, are black existential philosophers? The problem is made particularly acute by virtue of there being both black existential philosophies and black philosophers of existence, the first category of which is broader than the second. Although there are many philosophers who have contributed to black existential philosophy, not all are *black* existential philosophers, as we see in Sartre's contribution to this volume, and among black philosophers, not all are existentialists, as we see in Roy Morrison II, who regarded himself as an epistemological philosopher of science (see R. Morrison [1994]). Further, the problem is exacerbated by the conjunctive dimension of existential philosophy, which makes suspect any unequivocal assertion of

6

GORDON

individuals' being black existentialists. There are, for example, black existential Christians, black existential Marxists, black Existential Nationalists. Thus, for example, Cedric Robinson's characterization of Richard Wright as living a journey from Communism to Existentialism to Black Nationalism is inaccurate because of Black Nationalism's being a concrete instantiation of a form of existential position. Black Nationalism is, after all, committed to approaching the world through the situation of black people (Robinson [1983]: chap. 11). Black Power demands, among its values, first and foremost the recognition and valuing of black people as sources of value. That being said, we can consider black existential thinkers in two ways.

First, there are theorists whose positions have an existential dimension, *among other dimensions*, and who may not have formally defined themselves as existentialists. These individuals fall under the designation of philosophers *of* existence. These individuals are existentialists in the way that Europeans like Søren Kierkegaard, Friedrich Nietzsche, Fyodor Dostoyevsky, Martin Heidegger, Franz Kafka, Martin Buber, and even Herbert Marcuse are studied in existentialism courses in spite of their never having *claimed* to be existentialists and, in some cases, having even claimed *not* to be existentialists.[10] Given our considerations of what is involved in raising both the question of black suffering and the classical encounter with nihilism—that is, the struggle involved in deciding to go on—black existential thinkers of this type include such diverse figures as Frederick Douglass, Anna Julia Cooper, W.E.B. Du Bois, Zora Neale Hurston, Alain Locke, Aimé Césaire, Angela Y. Davis, Toni Morrison, Cornel West, bell hooks/Gloria Watkins, Joy Ann James, and nearly all of the central figures in black liberation and black womanist theology (by virtue of their point of focus in biblical interpretation being similar to many black Marxists' point of focus in Marxian interpretation).

We find examples of existential dimensions in Douglass' thought throughout his work but especially in his conception of struggle and his interpretation and various efforts to develop a theory behind the significance of his decision to fight against his abusers, especially in the case of the slave-breaker Covey. A discussion of that effort is provided in this volume by Bernard Boxill, in his essay, "The Fight with Covey." For Cooper, an excellent example is her provocative essay, "What Are We Worth?," which can also be interpreted as her articulation of the conditions of responding to, "Why go on?," in her classic volume, *A Voice from the South*. There she addresses the implications of demanding a race of people to justify their right to exist—in a word, their "worth." The Du Boisian story is a complex one that is articulated through the course of essays in this volume, but see especially his articulation of "the race problem" in *The Souls of Black Folk*, and note also, in his last autobiography, *Soliloquy on Viewing My Life From the Last Decade of Its First Century*, his description of the turning point of his political consciousness. Hurston, too, will require discussion that is well beyond the scope of an introduction. But for a sample, see her discussion of religion in her *Dusk Tracks on a Road*. For Locke, see especially his essay, "Values and Imperatives," in *The Philosophy of Alain Locke*, where

Locke defends, among a number of theses, the view of values as "lived"—that is, *valuing*. Aimé Césaire is well known for his posing questions of black existence through the lens of what he coined *négritude*. We have already mentioned Angela Y. Davis. A developed discussion of Davis' work can be found in the *Angela Davis Reader*, edited by Joy Ann James. Similarly, we have already mentioned both Morrison and West. Discussions of both are included in essays by Joy James on the former and Clarence Sholé Johnson on the latter in this volume. hooks/Watkin's existential positions are influenced by the work of Paulo Freire, as she attests in most of her work, but one can argue that her centering of liberation and identity questions are already rooted in black existential philosophy. Her affinity with Freire's work is, in other words, animated by the same concerns as black liberation theologians are animated by certain sections of the Bible and black Marxists by certain sections of Marx's opus. Every one of hooks' works substantiates this claim. And for James, see her books *Transcending the Talented Tenth* and *Resisting State Violence in U.S. Culture*, as well as her edited volume, *Spirit, Space, and Survival: Black Women in (White) Academe* (a text which has become a sort of "Bible" for many academic intellectuals of color).

We can also consider black existential philosophers and social critics among those who have taken an openly admitted existential identity as philosophers of existence, those who were and those who are, in other words, "out of the closet." Those include Richard Wright, Léopold Senghor, Frantz Fanon, Ralph Ellison, James Baldwin, William R. Jones, Thomas F. Slaughter, Jr., Lucius T. Outlaw, Naomi Zack, Tsenay Serequeberhan, and myself. Wright and Fanon are discussed in a number of essays in this volume. Léopold Senghor's role in the négritude movement is a well-known example of the Kierkegaardian, Heideggarian, and Sartrean links (Senghor [1964]; and Masolo: 42–5). Ellison's existential thought is well known, particularly in terms of his classic *Invisible Man* and his collection of essays on literature, politics, and culture, *Shadow and Act*. There are numerous instances in Baldwin's writings, but a primary example is *The Fire Next Time*. For Jones, there is his classic critique of Black Theology, *Is God a White Racist?* Slaughter is most known for his Fanonian article, "Epidermalizing the World: A Basic Mode of Being Black." Lucius T. Outlaw has defended the place for not only Africana philosophy and critical theory in American academic philosophy, but also existential phenomenology. Through a number of important articles he has issued what is ultimately an *existential* critique of the socialconstructivists in critical race theory—that such constructivists fail to articulate the most relevant dimensions of the *lived*-realities of race and racism (see Outlaw [1990]). Zack's positions can be found in her book *Race and Mixed Race* and her anthologies *American Mixed Race* and *Race/Sex*. And for Serequeberhan, who takes an existential hermeneutical approach to African philosophy by way of Fanon, Almicar Cabral, and Hans-Georg Gadamer, see his outstanding volume, *The Hermeneutics of African Philosophy*. This list is not, I should stress, an exhaustive list, and it is not necessarily the case that each of these thinkers converge on the same set of values. For instance, although all ultimately "humanists," Wright's (middleperiod), Baldwin's, and Zack's works take a more individualistic turn, whereas Wright's (early and later), Fanon's, Jones', Serequeberhan, and my own works are situated in what may be called black existential revolutionary thought along contextual communalist lines.

I should also like to stress that not all of the contributors to this volume are black existentialists in any sense. This volume raises questions of black existential philosophy, and in that regard, some of the individuals who have something to say of value on that subject are also those who are most critical of it, or at least suspicious of an existential philosophy premised upon what Fanon calls *l'expérience vécue du Noir*—the lived-experience of the black. Such is the case.

And so we begin.

NOTES

1 See, e.g., Davis (1983b) and Bobby Dixon's and Robert Birt's discussions in this volume. For Marcuse's views of Sartre, see Marcuse (1972), and for a criticism of Marcuse's interpretation of Sartre, see Gordon ([1995a]: 26–27).

2 For discussion, see Judy (1996) and Gordon (1995b; 1996a; 1996b).

3 This is not to say that those other concerns are not relevant. For the classic statement on the subject as it pertains to blacks, see Robinson (1983).

4 Other groups have functioned as points of darkness, but only temporarily so. For discussion, see T. Lott (1992–3) and Gordon ([1995a]: Parts II and III).

5 This question of human designation has led, ironically, to defenses of humanism throughout nearly all of Africana philosophy. See, e.g., West (1982 and 1993a) and even a standpoint epistemological black feminist theorist like Patricia Hill Collins (1990). See also Norman Allen (1991).

6 See especially the first part of the collection of essays that comprise Fanon (1979/1967b), as well as his discussions of psychopathology in (1952/1967a).

7 One finds allusions in the Sartrean corpus as early as his first novel *Nausée* (1938), but see his 1945 essay in Part II of this volume.

8 On these issues, see Catalano (1986), Charmé, L. Bell, and Gordon (1995a).

9 For some discussion of this reasoning, see Preston in Part III of this volume (below) and Gordon ([1995a]: 153).

10 See, e.g., Heidegger, where especially the humanistic dimensions of work like those that emerge out of the Sartrean tradition are held suspect. And even Martin Buber has denied being an existentialist (see Friedman [1991]: intro.). See also the discussions on Postmodernism and Black Existence in this volume, Part IV.

CONTEXTUALIZING BLACK PHILOSOPHIES OF EXISTENCE

part I

AFRICAN AND AFRO-CARIBBEAN EXISTENTIAL PHILOSOPHIES

Paget Henry

TO THINK seriously about Caribbean philosophies of existence, we must broaden this notion to include the existential experiences and attitudes of cultures other than those of the West. In every culture we find a wide variety of attitudes toward existence. We find attitudes of positive fatalism or negative fatalism, attitudes of world affirmation or world negation. If these attitudes toward existence constitute the primary data of existential philosophizing, then Caribbean existential philosophy must be constituted around the systematic formulation and evaluation of our attitudes toward existence in the region. The primary purpose of this chapter is to show that in spite of being very unevenly thematized, there is an underlying continuity in our existential situations and their discursive formulation.

In our earliest and most basic formulation, we inherited from Africa very ecstatic, life-affirming and participatory attitudes toward spiritual existence.

Those attitudes included a very deep respect for the power of deities and ancestors. They were formulated largely in the dramatic discourses of ritual, whose performances were the primary means of interacting with our deities and ancestors. Ritual and other discourses were empowering mediations against a specific type of non-being: the anxiety of fate.

This complex of African attitudes toward existence was slowly transformed through syncretization with Christianity. It adopted in varying degrees the latter's ethical salvational attitudes to spiritual life. The drama of spiritual existence no longer revolved around ritualized interactions with the deities. Rather, it now centered around the individual's difficult struggle for moral excellence. This was an anguished struggle because of powerful temptations from the world, the flesh and the Devil to do wrong. The anxious stain of guilt displaced the anxiety of fate as the primary form of spiritual non-being in spite of which existence had to be affirmed. The individual's only chance of overcoming temptation and guilt was assistance from a God who had to be reached primarily through faith and not rituals.

Finally, this complex of Afro-Christian attitudes toward existence was radically historicized by the experiences of slavery and colonial domination. These imperial projects racialized the Afro-Caribbean identity and imprisoned it in degraded images of its black color. Existential resistance was now socio-historical and ceased to be primarily spiritual in nature. The anxiety of racial negation was the new form of non-being that displaced the anxieties of fate and guilt. Developing a revolutionary capability marks the high point of Caribbean responses to the historical and racial fetters of this negating dimension (among many) of colonialism. In the twentieth century, these struggles with imperialism and racism have been the dominant factors in our attitudes toward existence. Using Fanon as a base, we will examine a variety of responses to this historicizing of Caribbean existential philosophy.

The reader may find problems at the outset with my claim to continuity among these three existential situations because of the cleavages that exist on the discursive level. In spite of this common struggle against nonbeing, the producers of these discourses did not recognize each other's humanity in these efforts. Christian discourses did not recognize African religious discourses and consequently obscured the connections between them. Socio-historical discourses openly rejected Christian ones, producing patterns of fissures and concealments. Each remained trapped in its own existential situation. We will therefore have to examine the consequences of these discontinuities for the growth and development of Afro-Caribbean existentialism, and more generally regional philosophy. In particular, I will argue that these fissures and cleavages have retarded the processes of creolization that are vital for a strong Afro-Caribbean philosophy.

EXISTENTIAL PHILOSOPHIES AND EXISTENTIAL SITUATIONS

By existential philosophy, I mean the systematic formulation by an individual or group of an ongoing consciousness of its existence that is first concretely realized in everyday interactions and practices. This consciousness of existence is determined in part by the long-term constraints and possibilities experienced in specific life situations. These existential standpoints are as basic a set of coordinates of philosophical discourses as the epistemological, ontological, or ethical standpoints. They may not always be explicitly thematized, but they cannot be completely avoided by any fully articulated philosophical position.

The human capacity for self-consciousness points to our existence as ego-centered subjects who are capable of experiencing ourselves as finite sites of agency in relation to the surrounding world. It is the fate of this capacity for agency that is crucial for our attitudes toward existence. How significant are its actions? How capable? How effective? Through its sense of agency, an individual or group makes an estimate of its chances for successful self-assertion or strategic intervention vis-à-vis its environment. Success or failure in such undertakings are important determinants of existential attitudes.

Although experiences of agency vary widely across cultures, this capacity has for the most part been forged in practical interactions with three broad domains of existence into which human life is inserted: the material world of outer nature, the human world of social life, and the spiritual world of inner nature. For a human, being-in-the-world is to be simultaneously engaged in self-preserving activities on all three of these planes as each confronts the human self with unique threats of non-being. How these planes are discursively constructed, the emphasis we place on one over another, and our different responses to the resistance of these planes are some of the factors that make for different existential situations.

Our insertion into the material world challenges us to gain effective measures of control over the natural environment. We need to be able to extract food and to counter droughts, floods, heat, cold, and sickness if we are to live well. However, these natural forces operate with an indifference to human agency that is often frightening and overpowering. To maintain agency in the face of these impersonal forces, human beings have developed a variety of discourses—dramatic, empirical, scientific—to increase their control over material nature. The significance of these discourses is their varying abilities to decode the inscriptions governing the impersonal functioning of nature and to rewrite them in codes that increase human agency. In other words, discursive decoding and recoding generate empowerment, which in turn affects a people's sense of ease or unease about natural existence.

Our insertion into the human world of social life challenges us to intervene practically in social processes so that they do not negate but enhance human agency. The social world is communicatively structured and is maintained by reified norms and institutional power. Because of its communicative structure, it is often quite personal. However, its reified norms and power structures often make it appear impersonal and hence nature-like. But, it is not natural. The non-being with which social structures threaten the human self is different from that of material nature. Agency against these normative and institutional structures require the decoding of their impersonal, nature-like appearance and their rewriting in codes that reveal their roots in ordinary communication and social action. Such decodings have been attempted in mythic, humanistic, and social scientific discourses. So here, too, the lived sense of agency is also in part dependent upon the decoding and recoding capabilities of available discourses.

Insertion into inner nature establishes us in a spiritual order that has been experienced as both personal and impersonal. The spirituality of inner nature does not fit neatly into the codes we use to describes outer nature or the social world. Yet we attempt to grasp it largely through metaphorical appropriations of these codes. On the plane of inner nature, we experience our agency as being either in conflict or cooperation with other sites of agency that are believed to be of a higher order. Non-being is spiritual and not social or material in origin. Hence the tasks of existence are determined by the actions and counter actions of these higher agents that have been constructed in a variety of ways. Human agency vis-à-vis these forces is also discursively mobilized. Spiritual orders have been recoded in mythic, ritual, religious, humanistic, and social-scientific discourses. In some of the latter, inner nature is treated as illusory projections of social and material processes and therefore nonexistent. Again, these different recodings make available different levels of agency, and hence different existential situations.

Although qualitatively different, the existential significance of these three domains is that they are the media in which human agency confronts the conditions of its possibility and nonpossibility. Consequently the unique consciousness of existence that a culture lives and affirms will be shaped by its responses to the constraints and possibilities available on these planes. Further, cultures tend to emphasize one plane over another, although capacities for intervention in all three areas are usually developed. India is a good case of a culture that emphasizes inner nature. The modern West exemplifies a case of emphasis on outer nature, while traditional Africa is a good case of balance between the planes.[1] These differences both reflect and shape different existential situations, which, when systematized, gives rise to different existential philosophies.

The variety of available existential philosophies further increases when we take into account the different discourses in which these existential situations may be formulated. We have seen that these range from the dramatic to the scientific. Together with the different emphases that cultures place on the three domains, these discursive differences help us to understand some of the general features of existential situations and some of their important differences.

Philosophical formulations of existential situations usually employ intensive phenomenological descriptions of individual cases. Fanon quotes Jaspers to the

effect that "what is important in phenomenology is less the study of a large number of instances than the intuitive and deep understanding of a few cases" (Fanon
[1967a]: 169). Further, in these descriptions it is fairly standard to focus on the self-
positing and defensive capabilities of the ego, its capacity for bad faith, inauthenticity, etc., as it struggles to establish its agency. Such in-depth understanding of single cases makes it phenomenologically possible to transfer the general features of
this understanding to many other cases. Consequently, Fanon's existentialism is
very much in this tradition.

Yet, given the oral and collective nature of the early centuries of Afro-Caribbean
life, this methodology is not the most appropriate for analyzing the existential situations of that period. Much more appropriate are Alfred Schutz's phenomenological descriptions of anonymous, typified, collective situations or ethnographic
descriptions of collective beliefs and practices. Lewis Gordon has recently pointed
out the importance of Schutz's approach for instances such as these (see Gordon
[1995b]). In cases of shared beliefs and other typified situations, the collective
aspects of subjectivity eclipse the more individual ones. Discursive empowerment
overshadows the defensive strategies of the ego. Thus the drama of individual
agency is played out against a backdrop of collective symbols and practices in
which it is imperatively inscribed. Because of the greater weight of these collective
dimensions in both the African and Afro-Christian heritages, our approach will
make extensive use of both the Schutzian and ethnographic strategies in radically
historicized forms.

17

FOUNDATIONS OF AFRO-CARIBBEAN EXISTENTIALISM

Although grounded in the African experience, relocation in the Caribbean disrupted the discursively mediated equilibria that Africans had established between
human agency and the imperatives of outer nature, inner nature, and social life.
Consequently, Afro-Caribbeans were forced to establish new balances in relations
with these three planes. Achieving these new balances established Afro-Caribbeans
in a new and independently centered existential situation for which they found
themselves responsible. That is, they were confronted with new modes of non-
being against which agency had to be secured. Preserving and discursively empowering the agency that subjects in this new situation had been able to realize were
the constituting activities of a new and distinct existential practice.

Because of its independence of geography, inner nature was not experienced
differently as a direct result of physical relocation. On the contrary, Africans
brought their religious constructions of inner nature with them to the Caribbean.
Consequently, there was little or no spiritual pressure to change the inner aspects
of the new (Caribbean) mode of being-in-the-world, or its African coding. It was
still a realm of gods, goddesses, and ancestors who determined the spiritual constraints and possibilities on human agency. The real pressure for the new spiritual

HENRY

balances that were established came from an imperial Christianity that carried a different coding of inner nature.

In the domain of outer nature, a new terrain had to be named, coded and assimilated. Hence the changes in the natural dimensions of the new Afro-Caribbean existential situation. However, given the colonial order of Caribbean societies, these new relations with nature were mediated primarily through European economic demand, European technology, and other discursive practices.

In the area of social life, new patterns of normative reification and institutional domination had to be decoded and recoded. The norms and institutions of plantation capitalism and of racism had to be discursively reduced to their roots in ordinary communication and social interaction between people. Thus, the changes in the social aspects of the new mode of being-in-the-world were also quite dramatic. As we will see, these changes produced a radical historicizing of Afro-Caribbean existential discourses.

Within the scope of one paper, we cannot examine in detail the contributions of all three domains to the new mode of world insertion and the resulting sense of agency. Because of their greater significance we will focus on two: the spiritual and social domains. However, before leaving the material domain, it is important to note that slavery and colonialism left the region without an indigenous technological discourse. Consequently, we are still unable to mediate effectively between our natural environment and the supplying of popular needs, which must also be done at internationally competitive standards. This absence of technological empowerment in relation to both the environment and the global market has produced attitudes of dependence and defeatism. These are persistent existential orientations that reflect important dimensions of our mode of being-in-the-world.

THE AFRICAN ROOTS

The African roots of Afro-Caribbean existentialism are both structural and representational. The dominance of inner nature, the ways in which it influenced human actions, its basic patterns of organization were all important structural characteristics inherited from Africa. On the representational level, these African roots are to be found in the mythic, religious, genealogical, and ritual discourses that were used to code the spiritual happenings and demands of inner nature, and to empower human agency in the face of these occurrences and pressures. Both of these aspects of the African view of inner nature were crucial for the new existential situation that emerged in the Caribbean.

In precolonial Africa, the world of inner nature was not radically separated from that of outer nature. The latter was seen as a manifestation of the former. Hence the two were inextricably connected. Yet, like the two sides of a coin, they were different. Inner nature had a personal, agential quality to it that outer nature did not. Further, inner nature was not accessible through the senses like outer nature.

The primary condition for its accessibility was the silencing or displacing of the everyday ego-centered self. In this state of ego dissolution, inner nature reveals itself and its connections to humans in varying degrees of detail. These details depend in part upon the receptivity of the individual. Such disclosures are not available to the ego-active, observational states in which we encounter outer nature. Thus the epistemology of spiritual knowledge was very different from that of everyday empirical knowledge.

Among the distinctive features of African religions which Afro-Caribbeans inherited were their techniques for displacing the ego, and in general creating space for the revelations of inner nature. Ego displacement was facilitated by the rhythms of the drums. Invitations to the deities of inner nature to fill the space left by ego displacement also went out on customized drum rhythms. Each deity had his/her own rhythm. Hence there was a musical, polyrhythmic structure to the interactive framework that mediated relations with inner nature. This polyrhythmic pattern continues to be a vital part of jazz, calypso, and other musics of the diaspora. In addition to ego displacing, knowledge of inner nature was also achieved through divining and the use of oracles.

From knowledge accumulated in these epistemic frameworks, traditional Africans developed a complex view of inner nature and their relations to it. It was constructed as a hierarchy of gods, goddesses, spirits, and ancestors who were sites of agency capable of opposing human actions. There was usually a creator god at the apex of this hierarchy, with lesser deities being in charge of various parts of creation, including the human self-formative process. This amounted to a divine administration that governed creation, whose authority and capacity for action penetrated even the minutiae of human self-formation. African deities were thus both immanent and transcendent.

African societies displayed great variation in the manner and the extent to which this religious worldview was discursively elaborated. Among the Ashanti and the Yoruba, the above spiritual hierarchy and its relationships to creation were elaborately thematized. The creator god and the lesser deities were clearly identified with details of their lives narrated in myth. The ancestors and the lineage ties that were important to them, were celebrated and thematized in the genealogical discourses. Further, a complex body of rituals linked these mythic, religious and genealogical elaborations of the underlying worldview to the practical interactions with the deities and ancestors. Because of this extensive thematizing, the Yoruba gods and goddesses, such as Shango, Ogun, Obatala, Legba, Yemoja, Oshun, Oya, are particularly well known (Soyinka: 1–36).

In other African societies like the Tellensi, the discursive elaboration of this lived-worldview was not as extensive. The deities and the ancestors are all there, but strikingly absent are the narratives that make up the myths of the Yoruba. As late as the 1930s, discursive elaboration among the Tellensi occurred primarily in the dramatic performances of rituals (Fortes [1945]: 171–7). (On a recent field trip

19

HENRY

to Tellensi communities, I was able to confirm that this comparative absence of myths continues into the present.) Thus, depending on how complex the discursive elaboration of founding worldviews or images of existence were, inner nature was coded in terms of some combination of ritual, mythic, religious, or genealogical discourses.

Given this construction of the world of inner nature, its existential significance was to be found in the way it supported, regulated, constrained, or negated human agency. In the most general terms, Africans made the relations between deities and human beings analogous to those between a higher order regulatory principle and a lower one. There was a cosmic order to be recognized and its daily maintenance was the responsibility of the gods and goddesses. Hence the antagonism between human beings and deities.

Gods and goddesses had the power to intervene in the creative process, if necessary, to ensure the smooth functioning of creation. Within the framework of these broad regulatory responsibilities, the deities also shared in the power of fate, even though they were also subject to it. Fate is a regulatory principle between subjects with different capacities for creation and agency. The notion of fate poses very starkly the basic problem of religious action: the coordination of divine and human wills without the loss of autonomy by the latter. Because of the imperative element in these relationships, they are often made analogous to the control and guidance that parents or monarchs exercise over their children or subjects. Such analogies are important as they may be bases for coding another aspect of the divine—human relations.

Like parents, the deities were considered to be wiser and more knowledgeable about creation than human beings. But in spite of their lesser knowledge, human beings were capable of acting with a measure of autonomy in relation to the deities. This included the ability to violate knowingly or unknowingly the rules of the established cosmic order. Hence the problem of coordination. To manage this problem, the deities were seen as being able to control, punish, support, guide, or compensate for the excesses of the human will. Thus the notion of fate entailed the punitive and corrective powers of deities and ancestors but not the elimination of human autonomy.

Within this framework of fateful regulation, African deities and ancestors exercised even more precise control over human activities. They exercised this control through the influence of predestiny. A strong belief in predestiny existed in varying degrees of elaboration among the Ashanti, the Tellensi, the Yoruba, the Ndembu, and many other African cultural groups. Like fate, the notion of predestiny raises the central coordinating problems of spiritual regulation. In predestinarian thinking, a divinely authored script for an individual's life has been filed somewhere in spiritual space. This individual, more rooted in social space, is very likely to be unaware of this script and its implications for his/her life. Consequently, this individual could easily embark on a life project that is at odds with the contents of this divine script. What are the deities and ancestors to do with such an individual? How will they get him/her to fulfill the script they authored?

In carrying out their responsibilities for human destinies, African deities had many powerful instruments through which they could achieve such corrections of human behavior. The primary instruments used were prescriptions and prohibitions, joys and afflictions, sickness and health, success and failure, birth and death, anxiety of fate and certitude of fate, sacrifices and sacred laws. These were intermediary mechanisms that constituted important channels of divine agency. In varying combinations, they constituted a complex and powerful system of behavior regulation.

Inserted in this complex world of inner nature, the African was like an individual walking through a minefield. The odds were that he/she would set off many explosions, because of limited knowledge of the terrain. Given this high probability of breaking the rules of inner nature, it was extremely difficult to run a surplus on one's accounts with the deities. One was always indebted to them, and thus the object of punishments, sickness, or misfortune. Hence the strong need in traditional Africa for relief from the anxiety of fate. This sense of being perpetually in debt to the deities, being enmeshed in their scripts, their systems of punishments, and constraint was an important aspect of the existential situation of traditional Africans.

For example, among the Tellensi, the destiny of an individual was shaped by a constellation of spiritual forces (Fortes [1959]: 15–26). One was the spiritual guardian of the individual. The identity of this guardian is usually ascertained through a diviner soon after the individual's birth. When acknowledged and ritually recognized, the guardian will work for the health and success of the individual. If ignored, he/she may block the most strenuous efforts of the individual to achieve health and success.

The destiny of a Tellensi is also determined by the life plans that his/her soul outlined to the creator god before physical birth. In this prebirth discourse with the creator, the soul may take a positive or negative attitude toward human existence. However, it could not refuse the earthly sojourn. This was the script that was filed in spiritual space. A negative attitude on the part of the soul was considered negative prenatal destiny, while a positive one was welcomed as good prenatal destiny. Like helpful or unhelpful spiritual guardians, good or bad prenatal destinies were seen as important determinants of failure and success in life.

Third and finally, the outcome of a Tellensi life was also shaped by the actions of other deities and ancestors whose pleasure or displeasure was aroused by the agency of the individual. The ordinary Tellensi was for the most part unaware of these constellations of spiritual forces that were shaping his/her life. They were usually recognized or discovered through the help or resistance they offered to individual choices and actions. Health and success in life were not achieved without their cooperation and approval. The popular Ghanaian saying *Gye Nyame* ("except God") captures very nicely this dependence of ego capability, agency, and

21

the success of personal choices on spiritual approval. These are important keys to the religious dynamics of the existential situation of traditional Africa.

Fortes reports the interesting case of Kunyaamba. When he began farming at about age sixteen, Kunyaamba became quite ill. On consulting a diviner, the parents were informed that it was the boy's great grandfather and grandfather "demanding to be accepted as his destiny" (Fortes [1959]: 20). They also imposed on him the taboo that he should not eat any of the grains he produced, which Kunyaamba clearly resented. He was temporarily cured of his illness, but soon became even more seriously ill. Divination revealed that the ancestors were angry at his defiance and were now insisting that he give up farming completely. This he did and went to work outside of his village.

What is striking in this case is the powerful restraining hand of the ancestors. Kunyaamba is clearly and effectively blocked in his efforts to choose himself and his career. Illness and anxiety of fate were the primary instruments of ancestral restraint. They brought his self-positing to a halt and turned it in a new direction. This heavy handiness of the ancestors elicited from Fortes compares with the situation of Job.

Kunyaamba's situation was not a rare or isolated one. My interviews with Tellensi religious leaders revealed similar experiences of spiritual heavy handedness on the way to choosing and realizing themselves as holy men. Many simply wanted to be carpenters and farmers. The typicality of these spiritual intrusions are further indicated by the rituals that the Tellensi and other African cultural groups have established for addressing them. Victor Turner's studies of rituals of affliction among the Ndembu of Zambia are very insightful from the existential point of view. To be afflicted among the Ndembu was to be "caught" by a spiritual agent of some sort (Turner [1967]: 11). Such a spiritually inhibited individual felt him/herself to be the object of a personalized prohibition. If a man, he might experience misfortune in hunting; if a woman, reproductive difficulties. In short, agency or ego capability in a particular area was immobilized to some degree.

To be relieved of his/her affliction, the individual had to be the initiate in a ritual of affliction in which the demands of the immobilizing agents were recognized, discussed and subsequently implemented. It is important to note that these rituals of affliction were educative and reconciliatory in nature. This was the weighty side of interpersonal relations with the deities. To encounter their "no," or to be "caught" by them is to experience the negating of one's capacity for agency. Autonomy and self determination are temporarily reduced to naught, and the individual is threatened with ego collapse. In these moments of extreme negation, "coefficients of adversity" are at their highest. By defining conditions of nonpossibility, these coefficients established the negative extremities of the African existential situation.

The positive extremities of this mode of being-in-the-world were defined by three spiritual conditions. First was good prenatal destiny. Second was the cooperation and blessings of the deities. Third was the practice of rhythmically induced ego displacement. This added a participatory dimension to the life of inner nature. In situations governed by these principles, the African individual discovered the conditions of his/her possibility. This type of cooperation and participation empowered individuals and confirmed them in their choices. Ego agency is available, and one feels at home and at ease in the universe. In these moments of strong affirmation we can speak of high coefficients of facility.

On balance the African response to this existential situation was a positive one. It was able to affirm and empower agency in spite of anxieties of fate. Existence was grounded in an ordered cosmos, which had a specific niche for human beings. Negativities were not arbitrary occurrences, but punitive/corrective responses to human disruptions of the cosmic order. Participation in the life of the deities produced an attitude of ecstatic mysticism toward spiritual existence. The deep joy that Africans derived from this spiritual participation is quite nicely captured in the Afro-American expression for these practices—"getting happy." In sum, we can describe the African attitude toward spiritual existence as joyous mysticism. However, this was not a world-rejecting mysticism.

This attitude of ecstatic mysticism with its underlying coefficients of adversity and facility was the important legacy that Africans passed on to Afro-Caribbeans. As we will see, it continued for a long time to define their existential situation after the exposure to Christianity. Today, in spite of Christianization, this African legacy continues to be a living stream of discursive activity both in the diaspora and on the continent. In the Caribbean, its spiritual concerns have found new formulations in writers such as Wilson Harris. On the continent, similar developments can be seen in the work of philosophers like Alex Kagame and Kwame Gyekye, and writers such as Wole Soyinka and Chinua Achebe. But our next task must be an examination of the impact of imperial Christianity on this African inheritance.

THE CHRISTIAN ROOTS

As already noted, relocation in the Caribbean disrupted the discursively mediated equilibria that Africans had established between their capacity for autonomous action and the spiritual order of inner nature. Achieving new balances in relation to this domain was one of the factors that established Afro-Caribbeans in a new and unique experience of existence. Disruption of the spiritual balances achieved by Africans was primarily the result of pressure from Christian missionaries and not from spiritual changes that were specific to the Caribbean environment.

The Christian coding of inner nature was monotheistic and focused on ethical salvation, with a strong emphasis on belief as opposed to spiritual participation. The relationships between it and the African coding were imperial, antagonistic, and racist in nature. The unequal competition resulted in processes of asymmetrical syncretism in which the Afro-Caribbean constructions of agency changed significantly. Agency was now inscribed in a salvific project of moral excellence in which

23

HENRY

sin, the world, and the devil had to be overcome through faith in the creator God. This shift in agency also produced changes in the coefficients of adversity and facility as the spiritual terrain shifted from a polytheistic and participatory pattern of organization to a monotheistic and ethical salvational one.

Relocation in the colonial societies of the Caribbean subjected African codings of inner nature to four distinct processes of creolization: inter-African syncretism, native Caribbean and African syncretism, Afro-Christian syncretism, and the expanded politico-ideological dimensions these syncretized religious beliefs had to develop in response to colonial domination. Inter-African syncretism resulted from the mixing of Africans from different cultural groups. This produced a merging and/or eliminating of deities but little or no change in the basic pattern of coding inner nature. The merging of deities was made possible by the fact that gods and goddesses from different cultural groups were quite similar in attributes and functions, in spite of having different names. Native Caribbean deities were also incorporated but more often as new members of the pantheon. In this complex reshuffling, the names of deities from dominant cultural groups were the ones that were retained. The dominance of Yoruba deities in Haitian Voodoo illustrates this pattern.

The deities that survived these inter-African and native Caribbean processes of syncretism were subject to a third round of syncretism with Christian saints and the Trinity. As in the case of inter-African syncretism, similarities between African deities and Christian saints made Afro-Catholic syntheses possible. Identifications between deities and saints varied over time and place. Thus in Cuban Santeria, Ogun, god of iron and war, has been identified with both St. Peter and St. John. Lega, god of crossroads, is identified with the devil, while Shango, god of thunder, is considered a masculine St. Barbara (Bisnauth: 165).

Haitian Voodoo is another old and well established Afro-Catholic syncretic religion. In it, Legba was merged with St. Anthony, Damballah with St. Patrick and Erzille with Mater Dolorosa (Simpson [1970]: 248–9). In addition, a god unique to Haiti, Papa Pie, is also worshipped as St. Peter. In Trinidadian Shango, similar syncretic patterns are found. Both African and Trinidadian deities are identified with Catholic saints. Shango is also St. John, Obatala is St. Benedict, while Osain is also St. Francis (Simpson: 17–19). In these Afro-Catholic syntheses, the African deities were able to survive in this challenging environment. Through the dominance of these deities, the polytheistic and participatory features of the African coding were able to survive and resist ethical salvational restructuring.

In Afro-Protestant syntheses, the absence of saints reduced the possibilities for similar processes of merging. Syncretism could therefore only take place with the Trinity. Consequently, in these synthesis there are more marked changes in the African coding of inner nature. The case of the Jamaican movement known as Revival, which dates back to at least the late nineteenth century, is particularly instructive. In it, the African deities survive in form and spirit but not in name. The central deity of Revival is the Christian creator God. Like his African counterpart,

24

HENRY

he is not involved in everyday affairs. Consequently, he does not come to Revival services to possess the faithful in states of ego suspension. His son Jesus attends, but he too does not possess the faithful. However, the Holy Ghost both attends and possesses. In addition to the Holy Ghost, Biblical characters such Mark, Luke, Daniel, Moses, and Elijah would also attend services and possess the faithful. Here, the polytheistic and participatory structure of African religion has imposed itself on the Protestant narrative.

Because of the paucity of the data, we do not know how widespread these types of Afro-Protestant syntheses were in the 18th and 19th centuries. In the 20th century, the more common syncretic pattern has been one in which possession is only by the Holy Ghost. On a more thematic level, Afro-Caribbeans most likely found echoes of their predestinarian beliefs in early Protestantism. This common theme together with the more emotional spirituality of Protestantism may help to explain its appeal to Africans.

Our fourth and final creolizing tendency was the politico-ideological responses of religious practioners to the oppressive condition of slavery and colonialism. These consisted of giving greater prominence to the aggressive deities, and greater visibility, if not importance, to Obeah or "black magic." The rise of Petro in contrast to Rada rites in Haitian Voodoo illustrates this pattern of creative resistance to political pressure. Petro rites arose in the Maroon communities of ex-slaves who had fled the plantations for the more inaccessible hills. In spite of this difference in social setting, Petro and Rada rites share the same deities. However, in Petro ceremonies, the gods and goddesses manifested themselves in their more angry and aggressive aspects (Bisnauth: 170). Thus a much more angry Ogun (god of iron and war) became central to Petro rites. The prominence of Shango (god of thunder) in the Yoruba religions of Trinidad point to a similar pattern of creative resistance. Thus in both Voodoo and Shango, creolization included a definite politicization of religious practices. However, this politicization did not significantly alter the ecstatic and polytheistic codings of inner nature inherited from Africa.

These in brief are some of the syncretic processes through which African and European religion impacted on each other. In the early centuries, African codings dominated the resulting creole formations. By the start of the postslavery period this pattern began to reverse itself, however, as efforts at Christianizing intensified. In the Catholic colonies, Christianizing began with European settlement but was rather superficial. In the Protestant colonies, it began much later with arrival of the Moravians and Methodists between 1730 and 1760. This work got off to a slow start as it initially encountered strong resistance from slave owners and local colonial states (Henry 1985: 61–3). This resistance turned into strong support in the postslavery period, which gave a major boost to the colonial churches. The latter were essentially overseas departments of denominational churches in Europe that were tightly controlled by ministers who were sent from Europe. Out of these churches came Afro-Caribbeans whose Christianity was highly Europeanized and bore only slight traces of the African (for example, Coptic) heritage. The latter was now concentrated in the independent churches and the syncretic religions.

This gradual shift toward Christianity produced significant changes in the ways Afro-Caribbeans experienced inner nature. It changed radically their understanding of spiritual existence, the measure of human autonomy, agency's relation to it, and their overall attitude toward existence. Inner nature ceased being a spiritual field in which authority was delegated to gods and goddesses and became one that was divided between two powers: God and Satan. These were the two spiritual powers to which the human self-formation was subject and hence were its primary links with inner nature. The Christian self was posited in terms of the will to moral perfection, in spite of Satan and the temptations of the world. Thus the anxiety of guilt became the new form of non-being to which it was vulnerable. This self asserted its freedom from the demands and authority of gods and goddesses. The departure of these deities also marked the fall of the crucial notions of fate and destiny. In the Christian coding, only Satan had the power to hinder the affirmation of this moral self and threaten it with ego collapse. It was the coefficients of adversity (guilt) and facility experienced in this new struggle that increasing colored Afro-Caribbean attitudes toward existence.

THE HISTORICIST ROOTS

Behind the steady rise of Christianity in the above creolizing of religious practices was a growing European capability for historical action. This capability dramatically transformed the social context of Afro-Caribbean life, and the way in which it shaped existential situations and attitudes. It enabled Europeans to dominate Afro-Caribbeans in unprecedented ways. The preservation of subjectivity and the exercise of agency had to be secured against a new adversity. This adversity is what Lewis Gordon calls the evading of black humanity by European enslavers and colonizers (Gordon [1995a]: 94–103). To be was to be despite this racial negation. This was the new source of non-being that would historicize existential thinking in the region. European evasion of Afro-Caribbean humanity was maintained and justified by the racializing of Afro-Caribbeans. The latter were transformed into "Negroes," men and women whose "essence" was their black color. The struggle against this dehumanization as opposed to that with the deities was the shift in existential awareness that marked the ascendancy of the historicist phase.

Historical action differs from religious action in the many ways in which it makes human beings the authors and directors of their self-formative processes. It is not concerned with harmony between deities and humanity, but with making social life conform to the projects of elite classes. This model of action is in tension with the open, religious constructions of the self in which the deities penetrated and controlled human agency. The self of historical action is a more closed entity, one which has been severed from inner nature and asserts its freedom from the latter's influence. Thus historical action is a very different kind of action from religious action. It generates different capacities for agency and requires different attitudes toward existence.

If historical action sustained the European practice of evading black humanity, then it was also an increased capability for this type of action that sustained Afro-Caribbean attempts at reasserting black humanity. Thus, as the colonial order of Caribbean societies crystallized, Europeans and Afro-Caribbeans were increasingly locked into a historically structured game of imperial and anti-imperial struggle. As this conflict came to dominate the Afro-Caribbean consciousness, it also historicized the latter and separated it from its Afro-Christian mythic and religious moorings.

This historicization can be seen in the tradition of thought that extends from Love, Blyden, Padmore, and Garvey through James, Césaire, and Fanon, and into the present. Although the importance and necessity of an increased historical capability were widely recognized, the response to it was quite mixed. In Blyden, historical action retained a significant Christian coding. In James, it came closest to the secular model outlined above. In Wilson Harris, historical action is confronted with its inability to create genuinely new projects without the spirituality of inner nature. Although there is much on the evasion of black humanity in these works, it is in Fanon that the existential significance of this problem is most explicit.

For Fanon, the aspect of African identity that became central to the European construction of "the Negro" identity was the African's black color ("the black"). African social and cultural practices—whether beliefs, dress, dance, politics or economics—were all eclipsed by this lived-experience of the black, of his or her "blackness." This emphasis on blackness resulted in the racialization or "epidermalization" ([1967a]: 13)[2] of Afro-Caribbean identity, while at the same time elevating the symbolic meanings of blackness to the status of primary cultural signifiers.

In European discourses, black skins came to symbolize everything that white Europeans were not or did not want to be. In the white eye of the European, the Afro-Caribbean as Negro became a black, a phobogenic object with multiple layers of psychosocial determination.[3] A phobogenic object is a stimulus to anxiety. This phobogenic identity and the resistance it elicited from Afro-Caribbeans were the new psychoexistential formations that would eclipse the Afro-Christian ones. For Fanon, these new formations marked the crucial "substitution of the exploiter" for the "ontological relations of forces" ([1967a]: 186) that dominated precolonial societies and established the salience of religious and philosophical ontologies.

At the most basic layer of this phobogenic construction, "the Negro symbolized the biological danger" ([1967a]: 165), the eruption of instincts that civilized people had placed under control. Strength, physicality, athleticism, brutishness, and sexual prowess were all important symbols of Negro identity. "In Europe," Fanon writes, "the Negro has one function: that of symbolizing the lower emotions, the baser inclinations, the dark side of the soul" ([1967a]: 190). The Negro also sym-

27

HENRY

bolized evil and ugliness: good/evil, beauty/ugliness, white/black were inter-changeable binaries in European discourses on race. The basic layers of this phobo-genic reconstruction of Afro-Caribbean identity were so negating in their claims, that they made the practice of evading black humanity an easy one.

In Fanon's view, these layers of the racialized identity were projections onto Afro-Caribbeans of repressed contents in the European psyche. Underlying these projections was the scapegoat mechanism through which we get rid of something unacceptable in ourself by attributing its origin to some one else. Thus "the imago of the Negro" that constructed him/her as physical, biological, and brutish has its roots in the repressed underside of white identity. Fanon describes this mechanism as follows:

> In the remotest depth of the European unconscious, an inordinately black hollow has been made in which the most immoral impulses, the most shameful desires lie dormant and as every man climbs up toward whiteness and light, the European has tried to repudiate this uncivi-lized self, which has attempted to defend itself. When the European civilization came into contact with the black world, with those savage peoples, everyone agreed: Those Negroes were the principle of evil. ([1967a]: 190)

The "imago of the Negro" in the European mind was not exhausted by these layers of projective determination. To the black phobogenic object was added those of the enslaved and colonized subject. These additional layers of the Negro identi-ty were rooted in the system of labor extraction adopted by Caribbean plantation capitalism. This system extracted surplus labor from racialized Afro-Caribbeans in the extremely repressive modes of slavery and black wage laborers. These exploita-tive practices required both physical and symbolic violence. Hence the additional symbolic layers that also defined Negro identity. As symbol, the slave inscribed the negro as a workhorse or an animal to be exploited. Hence it provided its own bases for evading black humanity. As property, the slave had no rights and worked from sunrise to sunset for no pay.

As colonized subject, the blackened Afro-Caribbean was denied the right to self-rule. Thus a yawning political chasm separated colonizer and colonized. In Fanon's view, the colonial world was "a world cut into two. The dividing line, the frontiers, are shown by barracks and police stations" ([1963]: 38). In short, to be colonized was to be reduced to a political zero. The addition of these enslaved and colonized dimensions to the already phobic ones completed the "overdetermined" imago of the Negro in the mind of the European. They also completed the bases for the evading of black humanity.

The core of Fanon's existential thought is to be found in his descriptions of the lived-experiences of Afro-Caribbeans who have encountered this imago and its

HENRY

evasive practices in a dominant white society. The confrontation with such monstrously distorted images of self poses in the most fundamental way the problem of human negation of selfhood, agency, and autonomy of Africans as human beings.

Fanon begins his existential-phenomenological description of exposures to the imago with the reactions they produce in the black psyche. Because of the institutional power of this overdetermined imago, "when the Negro makes contact with the white world a certain sensitizing action takes place. If his psychic structure is weak, one observes a collapse of the ego" ([1967a]: 154). Against this imago, black ego-genesis becomes a Sisyphusian struggle. In the face of the reality defining power of European historical action, the racialized Afro-Caribbean had little or no "ontological resistance" ([1967a]: 110). Only through increasing their capacity for historical action would Afro-Caribbeans be able to stop the repeated defeats of their attempts at autonomous self-projection.

Fanon speaks of an "existential deviation" that results from the internalizing of this imago by the Afro-Caribbean. He/she becomes a changed person. The whole psyche is reorganized to contain the resulting psychoexistential complex, of which the above deviation is a part. At its worst, this complex causes the Afro-Caribbean to deny his/her blackness and to identify with whiteness.

The existential deviation that Fanon examines with such brilliance is the vulnerability of the Negro identity to ego collapse and consequent exposure to the zone of non-being that borders its extremities. Ego collapse and non-being in these cases are not spiritual in origin. They are not work of the gods, but the work of the colonizer. This persistent vulnerability is examined through phenomenological descriptions of the dialectical moves made by the Negro spirit as it attempts to establish itself against formidable historical odds. However, in contrast to Hegel's phenomenology, this is a downward spiraling dialectic in which the Negro spirit encounters not absolute Truth, but the overwhelming power of European discourses and institutions to maintain the imago, and to counter all attempts at autonomous self-projection.

Fanon begins this dialectical aspect of his descriptive phenomenology with the defensive responses that the besieged Afro-Caribbean ego initiates against the intrusions of the imago: "and then the occasion arose when I had to meet the white's eyes. An unfamiliar weight burdened me. The real world challenged my claims" ([1967a]: 110). These challenges were made against Fanon's claims to being a human being. Fanon's first response is an attempt to assert his humanity through a bodily construction of his identity. By showing that the movements of his limbs were like those of other human beings, he hoped to prove his case. But that was not to be. All it took to destroy this physiological move was a communicative gesture based on the imago: "Look, a Negro!" This gesture was negating because behind it "there were legends, stories, history and above all historicity" ([1967a]: 112). These media enshrined this symbol that had just defeated his physiological move: "I thought that what I had in hand was to construct a physiological self, to

29

HENRY

balance space, to localize sensations, and here I was called on for more" ([1967a]: 111). Like sense certainty in Hegel's dialectic, Fanon's opening move ended in an ego collapse that left him at the door of non-being.

Determined not to be defeated and eager to escape the anguish of non-being, Fanon undertakes another attempt at self-projection. He will assert himself as a "black man":

> What! When it was I who had every reason to hate, to despise, I was rejected? When I should have been begged, implored, I was denied the slightest recognition? I resolved, since it was impossible for me to get away from an *inborn complex*, to assert myself as a BLACK MAN. ([1967a]: 115)

As a black man, Fanon introduces the white to the outstanding blacks—Aimé Césaire, Marion Anderson, and others. But besides adding their achievements to his, the imago persists undiminished. Further, these outstanding blacks were all objects of discrimination. On demanding an explanation for this treatment, Fanon was initiated into the realities of color prejudice. The irrationality of the practice destroyed all the attempts at black self-projection and returned Fanon to his anguished state.

Still refusing to be deterred, the next move in this struggle against the imago is toward rationality: "I intended to rationalize the world and show the white that he was mistaken" ([1967a]: 118). Fanon based this rational projection of self on the findings of science: "*In vivo* and *in vitro* the Negro has been proved analogous to the white: the same morphology, the same histology. Reason was confident of victory at every level" ([1967a]: 119). But even here, too, Fanon was forced to abandon this rational move. For, despite this abstract acknowledgement of black humanity, the phobogenic imago continued to be the bases for dealing with real Afro-Caribbeans.

Because he refused to be a Negro, Fanon's anxious dialectic continued to move, seeking possibilities in the irrational and then in a rummage through the African past. But liberation from being determined by the other was not to be found. At the end of *Black Skin*, the tragic outcome of Fanon's dialectic is an amputated ego that leaves the individual grasping for selfhood somewhere between nothingness and infinity. From this point onward Fanon will rely less on the elementary ontological structure of consciousness to produce the possibilities for overcoming the power and domination of the imago. The being of the latter and the consequences of its looks all seemed to be rooted in another plane—the historico-political domain. The secrets of Negro existence were not to be found in descriptions of the basic ontological powers of Afro-Caribbean consciousness. Rather, they were to be located in the colonizer's violent substitution of "the principle of reciprocal exclusivity" ([1963]: 39) for interactive reciprocity between blacks and whites.

Consequently, Fanon moved away from individual attempts at authentic self projection as strategies for liberation. In *The Wretched of the Earth*, Fanon's existential dialectic made its celebrated turn towards history and its most sustained engagement with Marxism. Historical action, and in particular revolutionary action, became the only real way out. Fanon's existential philosophy confronted in full its latent historicism. In other words, the substitution of the exploiter for the gods in Caribbean colonial societies established a phase of black existence in which agency and humanity could no longer be secured primarily through spiritual or ontological action.

Only the historical struggle for decolonization could end the downward spiralling of the above dialectic, explode the imago, and restore existential authenticity. "Decolonizing, as we know, is a historical process...[It] is the veritable creation of new men. But this creation owes nothing of its legitimacy to any supernatural power; the 'thing' which has been colonized becomes man during the same process by which it frees itself" ([1963]: 36–7). Here Fanon's existential philosophy breaks with its phenomenological ontology of consciousness and adopts a sociohistorical one. The socio-historical constitution and capabilities of consciousness displace (not replace) the selfpositing, onto-existential activities of consciousness as possible counters to the ego instabilities of racial domination. Fanon is here brandishing a new weapon against these racial threats of non-being. To counter them, he will now strategically direct or redirect the violence of historical action at the being of the colonizer. It is the coefficients of adversity and facility experienced in this struggle that have been primary determinants of our existential situation for most of the 20th century.

31

As noted earlier, Fanon was not the first or the only Caribbean theorist to make this turn toward historicism. We can see it also in Padmore and James. Fanon's importance here is that he makes the linkages with existential situations more explicit than any other. However, from a philosophical standpoint, it is precisely the relationship Fanon established between existentialism and historicism that has been a major source of debate. Differences over this issue are important for an understanding of the present state of Caribbean existential discourse.

For example, Wilson Harris has written some very important criticism of the tradition of historical writing in the region. While conceding the importance of historical action in any modern anticolonial project, Harris insists that we be historical without becoming prisoners of history. The historicizing of consciousness is a strategic move that is necessary for dealing with a particular problem. It is an error to imprison consciousness in this limited posture. Such a forced limiting is itself a new form of inauthenticity that can only lead to the disappointment of failed projects. These failures results from the inability of closed historical projects to imagine new possibilities or compensate for their intrinsic limitations. Harris' concern is with the creative possibilities that are excluded by the closed posture that the self assumes in historical action. Hence his fear that Caribbean historians

HENRY

and historical actors "have conscripted the West Indies into a mere adjunct of imperialism, and (have) overlooked a subtle and farreaching renascence" (W. Harris: 20).

What is this renascence that the historicists have overlooked? It is the streams of creative activity that are capable of establishing new and modern meanings by building on those produced by the older African, Christian, and East Indian traditions. Harris notes that "it has taken us a couple of generations to begin—just begin—to perceive, in this phenomenon, an activation of subconscious and sleeping resources in the phantom limb of dismembered slaves and gods. An activation which possesses a nucleus of great promise—of a far-reaching new poetic synthesis" (W. Harris: 20). Here the difference with Fanon's positions becomes very clear. For Harris, there is a poetics of consciousness that resists historicization. Its symbolic and naming capabilities provide history with original meanings, without becoming subject to history. New names, new values, new gods are the products of new poetic syntheses between conscious and unconscious. These are intentional activities that historical action cannot replicate or force to conform to its imperatives. In Harris, this "vertical drama" of a poetic union between a historicized consciousness and an ahistorical unconscious takes precedence over the "horizontal drama" of history. Thus, unlike Fanon, Harris' strategy is that of dissolving the imago through the power of poetics to redefine identity by establishing new relations between consciousness and subconsciousness. However this type of solution would require relinquishing the closed self of historical action for a more open one that is relinked to inner nature, now coded as a poetic unconscious. Here the power, creativity, and integrity of a supplemented consciousness to resolve its existential crises and resist determination by the other are preserved.

A similar defense of the internal capabilities of a relatively autonomous consciousness to break the spell of the imago can be seen in the work of Lewis Gordon. Like Harris, Gordon's point of departure is the creative and self-constituting capabilities of consciousness. However, his analysis proceeds via a phenomenological ontology of consciousness and not a poetics. Gordon's ontology approaches consciousness through its possibilities for Sartrean bad faith. In bad faith, we take anguished flights from the anxiety of moments of indeterminacy that both initiate and puncture our projects of selfhood. In it, we attempt to be more determined than we in fact are. Hence it is an attempt to evade an inherent freedom that is a basic fact of human existence. In bad faith, the truth is expendable. It comes in a distant second to the need to evade freedom. Thus lying to oneself, to others, and about others are necessary moves for the individual in bad faith.

Gordon links the evasion of black humanity that marks our historicist period with the evasive behaviors of bad faith that derive from his phenomenological ontology of consciousness. From the perspective of bad faith, racism is a set of discriminatory attitudes and practices toward a specific group that provides the racist with a false layer of determinacy against the anguish of indeterminacy or non-being. Racism then becomes a form of existential exploitation as opposed to a form of economic exploitation as suggested by the historicists. The surpluses being extracted by this form of exploitation are ontological—semblances of determined presence, of full positivity, to provide a sense of secure being.

For Gordon, the racist is "a figure who hides from himself by taking false or evasive attitudes toward people of other races. The antiblack racist is a person who holds these attitudes toward black people" (Gordon [1995a]: 94). Using this ontological code, Gordon reexamines many of the well recognized positions and attitudes of antiblack racists. For example, he reads black bodies, white bodies, black antiblackness, the exoticism of blacks, and effeminacy in terms of this ontology of consciousness that is centered around bad faith. The result is a novel onto-hermeneutics of antiblack racism.

By now the important difference with Fanon should be clear. While recognizing the importance of history in the modern period, Gordon defends the importance of ontological action for the recovery of blacks from the imago and the evasions it has made possible. "The cure" for the inauthenticity of bad faith is ontological action that enables the individual to live with the fact that his/her being is the product of a free choice. This action is available in the practice of existential psychoanalysis which encourages continuous self-reflection on the processes by which we choose ourselves moment by moment (Gordon [1995a]: 61). With this reassertion of ontology, Gordon is suggesting that historical action cannot by itself eliminate racism or the imago through which it functions. As long as whites are in bad faith and phobogenic constructions of blacks provide needed reinforcements of ego determination, antiblack racism will be with us. Thus, like Harris, there is a vertical drama of consciousness that is coding racism in ways that resist historical action. Here the drama is the movement from bad faith to critical good faith. This is the ineliminable ontological condition for exploding the phobogenic imago. In short, the intentionality of consciousness retains a greater self liberating capability than in Fanon.

Establishing the continuities between Afro-Caribbean existential discourses has been my primary concern rather than defending my historical approach to these discourses. However, this point of view does raise some questions for Gordon and Harris that are very relevant. Is there a relation between the vertical dramas of consciousness and historical developments such as the movements from traditional African to Afro-Christian and then to historical existentialism? Can the former achieve their goals independent of the latter type of activity? Can bad faith become critical good faith, or consciousness and the unconscious achieve new poetic syntheses without progressive historical mediations? These are difficult questions raised by the positions of Gordon and Harris.

If consciousness, as a condition for historical action, remains to some degree outside of history, then it at least has a diachrony or a horizontal drama of its own. What does it mean historically and diachronically that the deities of traditional

33

HENRY

African religions become archetypal forces in the poetics of Harris and Soyinka, and completely disappear in the Marxism of James?[4] Are these transformations historical, diachronic, or both? Although moving to different beats, history and diachrony must affect one another. Thus I would argue for a line of meaningful determination linking socio-historical activity to diachronic transformations of consciousness such as those we have examined. If this is the case then the diachrony of consciousness cannot be fully understood solely in terms of its inherent capabilities for self-definition, bad faith, poetic unions with the unconscious, or religious unions with divinity. To these must be added the impact of socio-historical mediations.

Other important contributors to this debate are Sylvia Wynter who takes a categorical approach to consciousness, Aimé Césaire, Edouard Glissant, and Derek Walcott, who share Harris' poetic approach to consciousness. But in spite of the differences in how they view consciousness, these writers share an assessment of its creativity and power to transform existential situations that is quite different from the historicists. Thus the contemporary picture of Caribbean existential discourse is quite complex, with many positions and differences still in need of more extensive debate.

CONCLUSION

From our survey of Caribbean existential discourses, it should be clear that this is a rich body of thought with both hidden and open lines of continuity. The three existential situations that I have described are indeed quite different. In each, agency was confronted by a different form of non-being: anxieties of fate, guilt, and racial negation. The continuities between the existential philosophies they have produced are neither simple nor linear. This should be clear from the fact that African codings persisted in the Christian period, that historicist tendencies were on the rise in the Christian, and that both African and Christian codings have continued into the historicist period. In addition to the linear aspects, we saw some of the hidden dialectical connections among the existential positions of the present period. Consequently, this continuity is more than just linear. There are also complex dialectical relations that link some of the different positions, particularly those of the historicist period.

Along with these connections, there are some important discontinuities that need to be pointed out if we are to have a balanced view of Afro-Caribbean existential philosophy. Between Fanon's existentialism and the African and Christian ones that preceded it, there is really little or no exchange. Between Christian and African existentialism there has been a lot of dogmatic assertions and denials, but no real exchange. These cleavages are not only indicative of the discontinuous aspects of Caribbean existential discourse, but also of Caribbean philosophy as a whole.

HENRY

Elsewhere I have shown that these schisms plaguing the discipline have their roots in the intellectual tradition that emerged in the colonial period (Henry [1996]). Within this tradition, there could be no dialogue between African and European philosophers. The former were slaves and the latter slavemasters. The philosophies of both could not have equal weight. In fact, there was a complete disenfranchising of African philosophy. It did not exist. Hence there is the pattern of no dialogue with it—a pattern that continues to this day. This is clearly not a healthy situation. It creates artificial blockages and inert spaces on the Caribbean philosophical imagination which maintain its fractured state.

Consider the fruitful exchanges that could take place between the religious ontology of consciousness that informs traditional African existentialism and the poetic and phenomenological ontologies of Harris and Gordon. To the vertical dramas of the latter, we can add the drama of achieving harmony between the wills of deities and human beings that characterizes religious action. What would bad faith mean in a religious ontology of consciousness that is rooted in this harmonizing of wills? Are the anguished flights from destiny, the deities and ancestors forms of bad faith? If they are, what do the deities and freedom have in common that human beings flee or pursue them in anguish? What are the different models of selfhood that go with these different ontologies of consciousness, and are they contradictory or complimentary? How does Kunyaamba's experiences of ego collapse compare with Fanon's? These are some of the exchanges that have been artificially blocked by the invisibility of African philosophy within the Caribbean intellectual tradition. (In another paper, I have tried to raise, though not answer, some of these same questions regarding a genuine exchange between traditional African philosophy and the Caribbean historicist tradition [Henry (1993): 17–36].)

Similar patterns of denial and invisibility have also stood in the way of meaningful exchanges between the African discourse of fate and the Christian struggle for salvation. The similarities or points of convergence suggested by the patterns of syncretism described earlier have never really been the basis for serious exchange in which both sides hoped to learn from each other. Although different, both share a religious ontology of consciousness that is rooted in the vertical drama of achieving harmony between humans and deities. These are potentially fruitful exchanges that have been blocked by the social relations and patterns of communication that were established in the colonial period.

These and other cleavages must be overcome if Caribbean existentialism is to be fully aware of itself and embrace its own historical formation. Special attention must be given to the African roots of this discourse, as they have been grossly overlooked in the past. Stronger links need to be established with existential thinking in contemporary Africa. In my view, Afro-Caribbean existential philosophy will not achieve the self-consciousness it requires without a fuller coming to terms with its African roots. In doing so, it will not only creolize itself, but also the larger discourse of Caribbean philosophy.

35

HENRY

NOTES

1 Although Cartesianism, with its focus on the *Cogito*, may seem like a focus on the "inner nature," it should be born in mind that Descartes' aim was to develop a secure philosophical foundation for the natural sciences; his goals were, in other words, geared toward securing the theoretical study of the external world.

2 All references are to Fanon unless otherwise noted.

3 For more discussion of the black as phobogenic, see Gordon (1996b) and Judy (1996).

4 Some of Gordon's writings also suggest a position of revolutionary existentialism that incorporates both a focus on black identity and historical liberation. See, e.g., his discussion of tragedy and mediations ([1995b]: chap. 4) and his discussion of law and revolutionary struggle (1994b).

SELF-TRANSFORMATION IN AMERICAN BLACKS

The Harlem Renaissance and Black Theology

Roy D. Morrison II

BLACK AMERICANS have pursued self-maintenance and self-transformation in a number of ways that involved the leadership of many illustrious individuals. The Civil Rights Movement and the leadership of Martin Luther King, Jr., immediately come to mind. However, we will focus on another well-known aspect of black engagement in self-transformation, namely, the projection of a new identity for blacks. This notion of a "New Negro" was conceived and promoted primarily by blacks who were employing autobiography, novels, theology, occasionally philosophy, and especially poetry.

The term North Atlantic Theology refers to the forms of Christianity practiced in Europe and in North America. African slaves were brought to Jamestown, Virginia in 1619. Consequently, by the beginning of World War I in 1918, American blacks had been under the influence of North Atlantic Theology and its eschatology for almost three hundred years. The term *eschatology* means the study of the last things. It pertains to the end of individual human lives, and it pertains to the end of human history. It includes a projection of future vindication and fulfillment in objective places and events that are beyond natural, empirical history. Eschatology, in this sense, is a matter of nonrational faith. Consequently, it is frequently designated as "pie-in-the-sky" theology.

North Atlantic Christianity has played a very important role in black Americans' efforts toward self-maintenance and toward self-transformation. When a community recognizes that adequate empirical, historical solutions to their problems are highly probable, they may construct pictures of supernatural, eschatological solutions that preserve their dignity and help them to avoid the conclusion that history is absurd. Such an eschatological solution seems to complete history and is sometimes accorded a higher degree of reality than the empirical world.

Arnold J. Toynbee describes this thought process as "transcendentalizing" when he interprets the Judaic expectation that their salvation would come from above through the appearance of the Son of Man or the Son of God. In the New Testament, Jesus the Christ and St. Paul prophesy the imminent return of the Messiah and the conclusion of natural history. Albert Schweitzer and Fyodor Dostoyevsky have poignantly reminded us that this unfulfilled eschatology is a major stumbling block for logical thinkers, and that it is the major intellectual problem of the Christian faith (Schweitzer: 111). Nevertheless, eschatologies and theologies do not persist because they are logical, or because they are objectively real. Rather, they live because of the functions they perform for a human community—whether it is delineated by race, class, or culture.

Consequently, eschatologies and their parent theologies are not abandoned simply because they fail to correspond with reality. In fact, in some cases, an eschatology is employed to help a community escape from reality, or to cope with negative reality, or to assist in self-transformation so that the social entity can eventually overcome destructive aspects of reality. Paul Tillich has observed that religious symbols can lose their power. This is also true of an eschatology that has enshrined the hopes and aspiration of a downtrodden people. Moreover, an eschatology that once was effective in assisting self-maintenance may, in a different century, be irrelevant for the task of self-transformation.

Black American slaves found themselves in a situation of political powerlessness. Postemancipation blacks had social and economic inferiority imposed upon them by Jim Crow laws and racism. In many cases, they internalized such negative notions and came to regard themselves as innately inferior to whites. Christianity taught them that they were sinners, that they should obey their masters, and that their reward would be received in heaven.

In this situation, blacks sought self-maintenance through religion. Three major factors here were faith, theism, and eschatology. By theism we mean the belief in a personal, loving, cosmic parent-God who guarantees justice and fulfillment either in this world or in the next. Such a god is understood to communicate with human beings in sentences and to intervene, miraculously, in human affairs—often in response to prayer.

The theistic notion of God has undergone various forms and fortunes in the history of Western ideas. On one hand, Homer's *Iliad* depicts Zeus as immediately sending a great eagle in response to Priam's prayer for safe passage to Achilles' camp. On the other hand, in the 20th century, Albert Schweitzer, Albert Einstein, and Paul Tillich reject supernaturalism and also the notion of divine intervention in human affairs. Black Theology sustains a critique of the theistic notion of God, but does not totally relinquish it. This critique focuses on God's justice and his concrete intervention on behalf of his black suppliants; however, it has implications that affect the existence of a personal God.

As slaves and after the emancipation, a large percentage of blacks became Baptists and developed a religion characterized by highly emotional praying, preaching, and shouting. This religion provided a sense of self-worth and a sense of access to transcendent reality. They could talk directly to God. They believed that once a week, at least, they could actually feel the power of God's holy spirit. The religion also provided catharsis and a kind of anesthesia. Both of these functions were extremely important when salvation could only come after death and when God Himself had indefinitely postponed any effective historical intervention on their behalf.

The Christianity that was donated to black slaves rationalized their subhuman status by presenting it as the will of God—a part of His inscrutable plan for human history. People of dark skin were expected to find adequate solace in the supernatural optimism of St. Paul whose advice included the following points: (1) We will understand it better by and by, (2) Nothing, absolutely nothing will separate us from the love of God, and (3) Jesus will return very soon.

Within the preceding introduction, our observation will be as follows: In the 20th century, the religion of supernatural faith, theism, and eschatological postponement has been subjected to critical reassessment by a small stream of thinkers who pursue black self-transformation. This ongoing critique has produced powerful new approaches to theology. Reflections on this movement reveals that radical theological reconstruction is one of the indispensable pathways to black self-transformation.

The proponents of these new approaches progressively make the following argument: North Atlantic slave religion programmed the traditional black community with religious taboos, artificial guilt, a sense of racial inferiority, and a psychology of acquiescence that was built, in part, upon imaginary eschatology. Blacks must deprogram themselves from the *methods* and the internalized *constraints* of North Atlantic Theology if they are to achieve liberation and self-transformation.

CAUSE FOR THE DEMAND FOR SELF-TRANSFORMATION

It is worthwhile to list some of the issues and circumstances that have provoked the radical critique set forth in the preceding two paragraphs:

(1) The barbaric lynching and race riots which occurred against the backdrop of legally sanctioned and religiously tolerated racial segregation. The lynching event explicitly or implicitly thematizes a great deal of Negro Renaissance poetry. Remarkably, the lynching event (or an equal atrocity) emerges quite powerfully in William Faulkner's *Yoknapatawpha County* (Faulkner: 439f). For a number of years, up through the 1930s, the inexpressible terror of lynching was encaustically programmed into the mentality of Southern and Northern blacks and it decisively inhibited their optimism toward the possibility of self-transformation. Employing the records of the *Chicago Tribune*, the National Association For the Advancement of Colored People states that there were 3,224 documented lynchings between 1889 and 1918. Seventy-eight and two-tenths percent of the victims were black.[1]

(2) The two World Wars which gave many thousands of blacks a glimpse of other cultures and a tragic hope for more freedom and socio-economic mobility in America.

(3) The problem of cosmic and social and national identity.

(4) The emergence of modern methods and thought patterns. These include Freudian depth psychology; scientific method and consequent technologies in communication and transportation; the higher criticism in biblical studies; critical philosophy, as in Immanuel Kant; and the romantic European philosophies and theologies that explicitly reject supernaturalism and traditional theism.

(5) The radical reinterpretation of classical Christian theology in European and American Ph.D. programs. In other words, the perspectives of many current Ph.D. programs in theology avoid the notion that Christianity's doctrines, miracles, and theistic God are objectively real. In many instances, the philosophical notions of realism or of objectivity are not employed when constructing or interpreting theology.

(6) The continuing emergence of a small cadre of black intellectuals. Whether poets, novelists, sociologists, theologians, or philosophers, they insist that black human beings have a right and an obligation to create their own theologies. One can no longer assume that theology flows exclusively from white human beings to black ones. If there must be a theological enterprise, it must include the perceptions, critiques, and aspirations of black human beings. Most importantly, these thinkers insist that their theologies and religious symbols have as much *validity* and *authenticity* as those invented by white North Atlantic Theology.

(7) The problem of theological *method*. Anti-intellectualism and taboos against critical thinking were built into classical North Atlantic Theology. Specifically, the slaves were not to judge God on the basis of logic or on his empirical behavior. Now, however, some black liberation theologians insist that claims made on behalf

of God's morality and intervention must be past the test of empirical verification or be quietly abandoned.

(8) The perception that—relative to its own classical concepts, and relative to the nonwhite peoples of the earth—North Atlantic Theology is in a state of methodological and moral bankruptcy.

SELF-TRANSFORMING INDIVIDUALS

A striking example of individual black self-transformation is found in an autobiography published in 1892. Titled *The Life and Times of Frederick Douglass*, the work is a graphic narration of the experiences of a slave who was repeatedly subjected to savage beatings by his Christian masters, who nevertheless taught himself to read and write, and who eventually became an advisor to Abraham Lincoln as well as Consul General to the Republic of Haiti. Those who still think that slavery was benign can find a corrective education here. With critical detachment, Douglass skeptically notes the lack of correlation between the professions and the practices of the Christian slave holders. More importantly, he notes the disparity between the theological picture of God and the chronic absenteeism of God in the slave situation. Theologically speaking, Douglass advises his colored brothers to stop "strutting about in the old clothes of the masters." Instead of depending on "faith," supernaturalism, and the "Almighty," he argues for *self-transformation* achieved through "self-reliance, self-respect, industry, perseverance, and economy" (Douglass [1962]: 479–80).

W.E.B. Du Bois wrote his Harvard University Ph.D. dissertation in 1896 on the suppression of the African slave trade. In this and other works, he applied the tools of sociology to study causes and conditions in the Western slave trade and in black neighborhoods of Philadelphia. In 1903, eleven years after Douglass' autobiography, Du Bois published *Souls of Black Folk*. There, he sensitively elaborated the poignant "twoness" of black Americans—the split identity and the inner tensions resulting from the attempt to be a black human being and, simultaneously, to play the subservient role demanded by America's racism in contradiction to its democratic and Christian ideals. Also in that volume, he uttered his most quoted and most tragically prophetic sentence: "The problem of the Twentieth Century is the problem of the color line" (Du Bois [1969]: chap. 2). Later, Du Bois helped found the Niagara movement which eventually became the National Association for the Advancement of Colored People (NAACP). Of equal importance was his long editorship of the *Crisis*, a periodical which treated various aspects of America's color problem.

Official America was highly displeased by the emergence of this new, self-transforming attitude exhibited by blacks. In response to a Senate resolution on October 17, 1919, the U.S. Attorney General prepared a report addressing *Radicalism and Sedition among the Negroes as Reflected in Their Publications*. Black leaders, including Du Bois, were charged, among other things, with the following

41

activities: (1) an ill-governed reaction toward racerioting, (2) threatening retaliation in connection with lynching, and (3) the more openly expressed demand for social equality, a demand which includes the "sex problem." The document includes the following comment on the Negro pursuit of self-transformation:

> Underlying these more salient viewpoints is the increasingly emphasized feel-ing of a race consciousness, in many of these publications always antagonistic to the white race and openly, defiantly assertive of its own equality and even superiority…The sense of oppression finds increasingly bitter expression…Defiance and insolently racecentered condemnation of the white race is to be met with in every issue of the more radical publications…(Wagner: 156)

There occurred a brutal and bloody race riot in Atlanta, Georgia, in 1906. In response, Du Bois composed a poem titled "Litany at Atlanta." This poem exhibits some of the reverent, suppliant, conversational theism of the Old Testament Psalms. Like some of the Psalms, it inquires of God's inscrutable timetable, "How long, O Lord?" Like the Forty-Fourth Psalm (verses 12–26), it reproaches God for failure to rescue his own people from violent enemies. Remarkably, however, this litany goes beyond the classical Christian complaints that arise when God has failed to intervene. With tragic, almost rebellious intensity, he beseeches God to hear the cries of black people and to speak. He briefly entertains the notion that God might be dead. Then he makes the following appeal:

> Sit not longer blind, Lord God, deaf to our prayer and dumb to our dumb suf-fering. Surely Thou, too are not white, O Lord, a pale, bloodless, heartless thing! But whisper—speak—call, great God, for Thy silence is white terror to our hearts! (Du Bois [1920]: 27)

The poem does not merely raise the question of God's justice, it symbolically identifies an inactive, silent God with terror, heartlessness, and with the skin color *white*! In this litany, then, there appears a major and enduring leitmotif of black protest literature, namely, the notion that the God of North Atlantic Theology is a white God, who, therefore, is innately incapable of experiencing concern for the plight of black people. This pitiful but empirically defensible conclusion is deci-sively operative for the Black Theology movement of the 1970s.

On the other hand, Du Bois also wrote powerful passages and essays portraying God as black—thus asserting the hope that God, ultimately, does understand and identify with black people. In another context, Du Bois actually calls for the birth of "the black Christ."[2] It should be noted that despite his criticisms and anguish, he retained his faith in his inherited notion of God.[3] This deliberate oscillation in the assignment of skin color to God occurs repeatedly in the poetry of the Negro

Renaissance and, later, in the work of the black theologians. The thoughts of Douglass and of Du Bois are remarkable for the strong, comprehensive element of ethical humanism that they embarked. This respect for humanity and justice prompted them both to speak out for the civil rights of women. Obviously, they both were ahead of their time.[4]

The movement known as the Harlem Renaissance is generally dated from World War I to World War II. It was a time of great ferment and a small group of black writers, centered in Harlem, New York City, pursued self-transformation by writing some of America's most remarkable poetry. Only two of the major Negro Renaissance poets will be treated here. First, there is the remarkable career of James Weldon Johnson, who served as secretary of the NAACP for fourteen years. He is perhaps best known for composing "Lift Every Voice and Sing," a song that came to be known as the Negro National Anthem. This great hymn contained a stirring expression of black racial pride submerged under a remarkable blend of American patriotism and faith in the supernatural, theistic god of slave Christianity.

Research reveals, however, that the public image of Johnson differed sharply from his private philosophy and concealed his true feelings. Put bluntly, "Lift Every Voice and Sing" was composed at a time when black requests for justice were quite unlikely to be heard, or even tolerated, if they were not dutifully prefaced by declarations of uncritical patriotism and religious faith. As a consequence, the sophisticated French historian of the black poets, Jean Wagner, concludes that Johnson was wearing the "mask" of the oppressed, for the sake of conformity, survival, and diplomacy (Wagner: 358–65). Far from being unique, Johnson's behavior in this regard simply dramatizes a pattern of self-maintenance that was employed to some degree by many blacks, well over into the second half of this century.

In his autobiography, *Along This Way*, Johnson includes an account of a situation in which he narrowly escaped being lynched (pp. 165–9). Also, at the end of that work, he elaborately explains that he did not hold the philosophy of life that millions of blacks believed him to hold when they sang his music or read his book of poetic sermons titled *God's Trombones*. Instead, he states his agreement with "those scientists and philosophers who hold that the universe is purposeless." He also explicitly rejects the possibility and the significance of possessing knowledge about a personal God (pp. 413–4). Thus, Johnson seeks self-transformation through the social, economic, and legal changes promoted by the NAACP. He also seeks transformation by liberating himself from dependence upon the traditional theism of black folk religion.

Our second Harlem Renaissance figure is the lyrical and provocative poet, Countee Cullen. The adopted son of a rigid, fundamentalist Methodist minister, Cullen was deeply religious and exceptionally talented. At the same time, he was enigmatic and tormented by problems concerning his parentage, his personal identity, and American racism. He continued to believe in the immortality of the soul

43

MORRISON

while raising profound questions regarding the justice and righteousness of God in the face of evil in the world.

His struggle to achieve self-transformation were individual, racial, communal, secular, and religious. Jean Wagner correctly observes that Cullen carried a multiple load of shame. He interpreted his birth and his adoption as enshrouded in sin and shame; he felt judged by God because of these situations. He felt shame that he was dehumanized on the basis of his color by white America and, at times, he longed to escape in death. While carrying these burdens, he continued to believe in the Christian God to whom he traced the ultimate responsibility for all things—including his own plight. This tendency is clearly revealed in the often quoted lines from "Yet Do I Marvel":

> Inscrutable His ways are, and immune
> To catechism by a mind too strewn
> With petty cares to slightly understand
> What awful brain compels His awful hand.
> Yet do I marvel at this curious thing:
> To make a poet black, and bid him sing!

In his attempt to transform himself and achieve control over the negations in his life, Cullen takes several interesting steps. First, he seeks, at times, to change the connotations of blackness. Black comes to connote beauty, victimization, and other virtues. The color white, in such contexts, becomes a symbol for "evil, violence, and brutality, and also for hypocrisy, ugliness, and perversity" (Wagner: 319).

Second, most important in Cullen's poetry is the theme of Christ as symbol and as reality. There is prolific variation in his terms and connotations. Somewhat like the alternating portrayals of Christ in W.E.B. Du Bois, Cullen sometimes paints a white Christ who is a symbolic ally of white racist oppression. In other passages, Christ is pictured as one who is black, crucified, as mystically identified with a black lynch victim, and consequently as one who is an enemy of the white lynch mob.

Third, and somewhat astonishingly, Cullen sometimes mystically merges his own identity with that of the black Christ. This step may be seen as a quest for spiritual transcendence and, simultaneously, a desperate striving for self-transformation. Unfortunately, however, such antithetical pictures of Christ in Negro Renaissance poetry reflect not only the private pain of the poets, they reflect the contradictions in Christianity itself, as practiced by the white Christians. Jean Wagner observes that this contradiction became inevitable once the white man "decided he could at the same time abase his fellow man to the level of an object and proclaim himself to be a Christian, affirming that his deed was the will of God and understanding, into the bargain, to evangelize those he had enslaved" (Wagner: 330f).

Perhaps Cullen's crowning creation was a poem of 963 lines titled "The Black Christ." Its themes include racism, lynching, and the radical controversy between faith and doubt in regard to Christian theism. Jim is the strong willed, skeptical son who is lynched. His mother represents uncritical faith. Somewhat like the conflicting viewpoints in Dostoyevsky's Grand Inquisitor Scene, Cullen's protagonists argue their positions throughout the poem while, simultaneously, the conflict rages in Cullen's own mind and heart. After his death by lynching, Jim suddenly reappears in a state of miraculous resurrection. With a mixture of contrition, remorse, and gratitude, Cullen apparently resolves his doubt and also achieves union with Christ, with God, and with the bereaved Mother's faith commitment ([1929]: 107–9). Consequently, within the poem, Cullen's effort toward self-transformation culminated in a mystical spiritualizing of the problems that had caused his suffering. While "The Black Christ" remains a landmark in the Negro Renaissance, it tended to alienate Cullen from the masses.

By the beginning of the 1970s, there had emerged a small group of black scholars who held PhD's and who taught academic theology. Of these, we shall mention two. First, James Cone, more than anyone else, broke certain long-standing taboos in America, in North Atlantic Theology, and in black folk religion. He freely expressed his rage and (in a powerful autobiographical sketch) documented some of its causes (Cone [1975]: 1–15). He identified the political and controlling social roles of theology and issued a dramatic, iron-fisted proclamation that defined a black theology and combined it with a demand for black (political) power. He identified Christ's mission with the *empirical* liberation of black people and declared that Christ and God were "symbolically" black.

Most remarkable was his decision to participate in an established form of protest which is known as theocide. This means the killing of the *idea* of a God who oppresses or otherwise dooms persons to suffering and dehumanization. In "The Ugliest Man" scene of *Zarathustra*, Friedrich Nietzsche had insisted that the classical theistic God must be killed because he deprived human beings of their subjectivity; he knew everything and could peer into the dirtiest nooks and crannies of our minds—leaving no privacy, and thus making it impossible to be a person.

Paul Tillich, one of the great white theologians of the 20th century, had incorporated and reiterated Nietzsche's declaration in his *Courage to Be*. Then, in 1969 and 1970, the black theologian James Cone declared that, "If God has made the world in which black people *must* suffer, and if he is a God who rules, guides, and sanctifies the world, then he is a murderer" (Cone [1969]: 124). In a different work, Cone argues that if God is a murderer, "we had better kill him" (Cone [1970]: 59f).

Cone had thus broken two taboos of American theism: First, a human being should never sit in judgment on God's morality because of his empirical behavior. Second, no black person should ever dare to criticize the empirical morality of the white supernatural God that the white slave masters had given him. Like other human beings caught in a transitional period, Cone has been accused of oscillation and even contradictions. What is important, however, is that his notion of self-transformation is not compromised by the old taboos, or by any other inherited social or theological constraints. He seeks complete, empirical liberation, and history can now never erase that a *black* theologian has publicly recommended the murder of the God who practices racism.

Our second black theologian is William R. Jones. Jones is probably the only member of that family of thinkers who employs critical philosophical analysis to make a critique of the internal structures of traditional black religion. His work focuses on the issues of God's goodness in a world saturated by evil. The technical term, *theodicy*, means the study of the question as to how God can be righteous while permitting so much evil in the world. Theodicy is the point of departure or the causal agent for all black theology. American black theology emphasizes ethical problems raised by God's *performance* in history (see Gordon [1995a]: Part IV; and Henry's contributions to this volume). In other words, when all the technical terminology and all the apologetic arguments have been explored, black theology asks what, if anything, does God actually *do* for black people?

Jones goes farther than any of his colleagues in pursuing this issue because he gives philosophical attention to the question of *methodology* in this context. Taking one of his cues from Jean-Paul Sartre, Jones declares that "God is the sum of his acts" ([1973]: 10–15). This assertion specifies a new method for doing theology. God is not what blacks have been programmed to believe that he is. God is only that which his historical acts on our behalf reveal him to be. We have been taught that God has all knowledge, all power, that he is absolutely righteous, and that he loves all human beings equally. In Jones' theological method, one would not assign such lofty attributes to God a priori, or on faith; rather, one would assign these characteristics to God only insofar as they are merited by God's actual behavior toward black people. God would not receive gratitude and praise for the things that he has not yet done. Moreover, we should not seek to conform to the Bible and to classical Christian faith. Instead, we should inquire what, if anything, Christian thought can do to meet the needs of black people. This stance did not win very many friends, black or white, for Jones. He grasped the central critique of liberation theology and proceeded to its logical conclusion.

Others have made these points mildly and occasionally, but many were threatened by Jones' relentless consistency. For Jones, self-transformation involved freedom from theism, from superstition, and freedom from logical inconsistency. It should be noted that these points make radical demands upon blacks themselves— as well as upon the white population.

Alain Locke edited a book entitled *The New Negro* in 1925, in which he speaks of "metamorphosis," a "transforming psychology," and a "positive self-direction" exhibited by the new Negro of the Harlem Renaissance. He also cites a greater desire for "objective and scientific appraisal," instead of the previous sentimentality. As we have seen, the black theologians of the 1970s have pursued Locke's vision and have unflinchingly probed the role of folk religion in the internal self-limitation of American blacks.

In conclusion, then, the emergence of the "New Negro" presupposed reconstruction of traditional attitudes. Albert Einstein declined to believe in a God who punished those whom he had created. He also insisted that the categories of traditional philosophy (and science) must be removed from "Mt. Olympus" and brought down to earth so that we could make them serviceable (Einstein [1946]: 2; [1961]: 142). Just as Einstein argued that our categories must be brought down from the transcendental level of Platonic and Kantian idealism, the figures of the Harlem Renaissance and Black Theology frequently argued that the solutions to the problem of black liberation and fulfillment must be brought down to earth and addressed at the level of historical reality. They insist that blind faith and supernatural myths are not adequate responses to the deprivations and absurdity that sometimes occur in history. Stated more bluntly, this means that blacks must first save themselves from the debilitating effects of their inherited folk religion if they are to achieve liberating self-transformation.

NOTES

1 NAACP: 7. See also Wells-Barnett 1969: 173. A table of blacks lynched annually from 1882 to 1899 (a total of 2,533 reported cases) is provided on 46–7.

2 "Bid the Black Christ Be Born!" in the poem, "The Riddle of the Sphinx" (Du Bois [1920]: 54).

3 Du Bois' credo: "I believe in God,…in the Negro Race,…in the Devil and his angels,…Finally, I believe in Patience" ([1920]: 3–4).

47

4 "The Damnation of Women" (Du Bois [1920]: 163–186). See also, "The Call," 161–2.

ON THE READING OF RIDDLES

Rethinking Du Boisian "Double Consciousness"

Ernest Allen, Jr.

chapter 3

ALMOST A century ago W.E.B. Du Bois posited the claim that African Americans had internalized a set of powerful, mutually incompatible ideals. The conundrum resulting from this internalization, he believed, threatened to sabotage the struggle for full democratic rights and economic equality within the United States. "One ever feels his twoness," wrote Du Bois, "—an American, a Negro; two souls, two thoughts, two unreconcilable strivings..." (Du Bois [1969]: 45). This and other equally dramatic assertions were set forth in a pair of essays publicly presented within months of each other in 1897: "The Strivings of the Negro People" (Du Bois [1897]: 194-8),[1] destined to become the initial and most memorable chapter of *The Souls of Black Folk* some six years later, and "The Conservation of Races," second in a series of occasional papers issued by the newly formed American Negro Academy (Du Bois [1970a]: 250–62). Du Bois' lyrical plaint of "two souls dwelling in one" has been endlessly echoed over the years by sympathetic commentators, but in ret-rospect it seems that Du Bois himself was never altogether forthcoming as to what, exactly, those conjoined, inhospitable ideals were. In both *The Souls of Black Folk* and "Conservation of Races" he spoke of "Negro strivings" and "Negro ideals" which, even in his most analytically grounded passages, he failed to define. Typically such notions were embedded within an ambiguous mass of dualistic references— "twoness," "second sight," "double consciousness," "double aims," and the like— which, in a confused brew of allegory and concept often seemed to point to the same meaning.[2]

In contrast to a commonly accepted notion that in these works Du Bois set forth a broadly defined issue of "cultural conflict" (in the sense that African Americans, considered to be immersed in their own culture as well as that of the dominant North American population, were being forced to choose between the two), I argue instead that it was a question of *two* vaguely articulated but distinct sets of conflicted ideals which emerged from these 1897 essays, each erected upon a different foundation of the German idealist philosophical tradition. The first, invoking the phenomenology of Georg Wilhelm Friedrich Hegel and subsequent-ly incorporated into *The Souls of Black Folk*, described attempts to satisfy (narrow-ly defined) American and Negro existential ideals at the same time, with a negat-ed black self-consciousness—or "double consciousness," as Du Bois would have it—resulting from the failure to do so. In "Conservation of the Races," on the other hand, a more conventionally *implied* but unstated "double consciousness" on the part of blacks was linked to a supposed clash between (essentially undefined) Negro ideals and corresponding (but similarly undefined) American ones. The sub-stantive, underlying premise, however, was that African Americans were torn by a desire to become full citizens within U.S. society, yet retain their distinctiveness as a group. In this instance the framework within and against which Du Bois strug-gled derived from Johann Gottfried Herder's philosophy of history, having to do with the supposed impossibility of two or more national ideals to coexist beneath the sway of a single governing apparatus. In both instances, the clash of incompat-ibilities, according to Du Bois, took the form of a tortuous conundrum experi-enced by blacks. This dilemma, in the first formulation at least, was taken as a *gen-uine* one, to be resolved through long-term education; but the second manifesta-tion Du Bois considered to be merely *imaginary*, one whose solution was to be found in rethinking the entire issue from a fresh perspective.

Both problematics invoked issues of conflicting social identity: "being a Negro and an American at the same time." In *The Souls of Black Folk* opposing ideals were ascribed to blacks in general, but the examples of discord drew primarily upon the experiences of the educated black middle class. The dilemma expressed in "Conservation," however, acquired a vaguer attribution: the "Negro who has given earnest thought to the situation of his people in America…" (Presumably this, too, was a reference to the "thinking Negro" of the educated black petite bourgeoisie.)

While both of Du Bois' notions tended to evoke a vague sense of "culture" in one way or another, in neither case was the agony which he depicted the result of a broad-based "cultural conflict" of the sort referred to above. Sheathed in the language of large-scale cultural difference, the first antagonism actually sprang from a narrow range of ideals. But the second one also manifested itself within an unstated context: the political implications posed by the existence of autonomous black social and cultural institutions. In either case, rather than *celebrating* an authentic "dual consciousness" as a tool for achieving enriched cultural or political syntheses, or as a platform for generating multiple levels of understanding—in other words, as a potential solution in whole or in part—Du Bois treated the question of "twoness" chiefly as a (real or imaginary) problem, even as he affirmed the desirability of preserving certain of its (unspecified) forms.[3] Elsewhere (Allen 1990–2) I have elaborated in some detail upon how the subject of "twoness" was handled in *The Souls of Black Folk*. Here, for the most part, however, our concern will involve a close reading of "Conservation of the Races" framed against the backdrop of Du Bois' companion work.

SAVING SOULS: "DOUBLE CONSCIOUSNESS" AS NEGATION

In *The Souls of Black Folk* "double consciousness" was defined as a "sense of always looking at one's self through the eyes of others, of measuring one's soul by the tape of a world that looks on in amused contempt and pity" (Dubois [1969]: 45). This is not how the term was generally understood by prominent 19th-century Western writers, however, even as they imparted their own specific meanings to it. Ralph Waldo Emerson, for example, employed "double consciousness" in a multitude of ways: to signify a felt tensions between the individual and society as well as between the oppositional pulls of fate and liberty (or necessity and freedom), and in a more elevated sense, to signify the division between the mortal and immortal selves of the individual. More descriptively, he also spoke of the "double consciousness" of dreams (Emerson [1966]: 161), as well as instances when "the man and the poet show like a double consciousness" (Emerson [1972]: 155).[4]

In the case of the individual versus society, Emerson believed that society's very functioning required the squandering of individual creativity, the subordination of one's activities to dreary routinization; on the other side, the true flowering of individual creativity necessitated one's withdrawal from societal structures—a course which, if followed by all of its members, would soon lead to a collapse. Thus condemned, spirit forever found itself at odds with understanding. "The worst feature of this double consciousness," wrote Emerson,

> is that the two lives, of the understanding and the soul, which we lead, show very little relation to each other; never meet and measure each other: one prevails now, all buzz and din; and the other prevails then, all infinitude and par-

adise; and, with the progress of life, the two discover no greater disposition to reconcile themselves. (Emerson [1903]: 353–4)

As for the contradiction between freedom and necessity, the path to salvation was not the evasion of "double consciousness," but rather its embrace: "A man must ride alternately on the horses of his private and public nature…" (Emerson [1904]: 47). And, finally, in one of his many sermons Emerson also pointed out "the distinction of the outer and inner self" as yet another manifestation of self-reflective doubling: "that is, there are two selves, one which does or approves that which the other does not and approves not; or within this erring passionate mortal self, sits a supreme calm immortal mind, whose powers I do not know, but it is stronger than I am…" (Emerson [1938]: 200).

For his part, Arnold Rampersad notes that in 1893 the psychologist Oswald Kupe wrote of "the phenomenon of double consciousness of the divided self…characterized by the existence of a more or less complete separation of two aggregates of conscious process…oftentimes of entirely opposite character" (Rampersad: 74). Without specifically alluding to the term, other 19th-century Western thinkers expanded upon the concept as well. For example, William James (as Rampersad also observed) spoke of the existence of "*simultaneously* existing consciousness," a state James considered to be beyond the pale of the normal "brain-condition"—a malady (James: 399). And, finally, how was it possible to ignore the immortal lament of Johann Wolfgang von Goethe's Faust that "Two souls, alas! reside within my breast, and each is eager for a separation"?

One readily perceives that Du Bois' own use of the term, "double consciousness," could not easily avoid the battery of connotations commonly associated with it, notwithstanding the fact that his specific definition was of an altogether different nature. For what Du Bois strictly meant by the phrase was the *absence* of true self-consciousness on the part of black Americans, the inability to recognize one's black self other than through the mediated veil of the unacknowledging white gaze. In this instance, Du Bois' frame of reference can be traced ultimately to Hegel's phenomenology, where true self-consciousness—supposedly lacking in the Negro—was dependent upon the mutual recognition of human beings by one another (see Adell). This *negation* of self-consciousness Du Bois ascribed to the twinned collapse of specified "double ideals ," of which he offered four examples: the "double-aimed struggle of the black artisan" to "escape white contempt" on the one hand, and on the other "to plough and nail and dig for a poverty-stricken horde"; secondly, the dilemma of the "Negro minister or doctor…tempted toward quackery and demagogy" on the one side, and on the other (due to having internalized the criticism of whites) by "ideals that made him ashamed of his lowly tasks"; thirdly, the dilemma of the "would-be black *savant*…confronted by the paradox" that although whites possessed the knowledge needed by his people, the knowledge capable of teaching whites (presumably regarding the practice of

ALLEN

human values) was an unknown quantity to him; and finally the black artist who, altogether incapable of expressing a sense of beauty other than the one revealed through the "soul-beauty" of his own race, a race which his larger potential audience despised (Du Bois [1969]: 46–7).

In addition to the dubiousness of attributing such values to African Americans in general, Du Bois' "warring ideals" were inconsistently framed. While all four examples spoke either to the necessity or difficulty of coming to terms with "white ideals" in order to leverage approving recognition from the white community, the nature of the counter-ideals is not always clear. Several of the diametric couples, for example, offered little more than the *appearance* of the polar oppositions which Du Bois believed he was depicted.[5] It seems to me that only two pairs of the corresponding couples depicted above can be deemed "authentic." The first consists of obligation and desire—"the *felt obligation* of 'upper-class' blacks to serve the needs of their corresponding 'lowest classes'; and a *desire for positive recognition* from whites regarding the value of this sacrifice" (Allen [1992]: 268)—the best portrayal of which can be found in the dilemma of Du Bois' black artisan. A second dialectic revolved around the question of aesthetic values: the impossibility of devising cultural criteria universally applicable—or palatable—to both white and black America. Seeking the largest audience possible, Du Bois' African-American artist was placed in the dilemma of projecting "the soul-beauty of a race" which most of that audience despised, yet "he could not articulate the message of another people" (Du Bois [1969]: 47). The stress surrounding the lack of respect accorded African-American accomplishments led ultimately to an internalizing on the part of blacks of stereotypical Negroid images commonly held by whites. The result, in Du Bois' estimation, was an eclipse of black self-consciousness. The solution he proposed was education: for the black common folk, in order to lift them out of their state of general ignorance; and for white folk generally, that they might come to a fuller realization of African-American humanity.

As noted earlier, a problem with both Du Boisian "double ideals" and "double consciousness" was that they were too narrowly defined. In the case of the first, a dilemma purportedly faced by the "Talented Tenth"—but probably more attributable to Du Bois himself—was transformed into "universal" paradigm of African-American double aims, with negated self-consciousness the infelicitous outcome. However, the refusal on the part of whites to recognize the value of self-sacrifice on the part of educated blacks belonged to a much larger tendency of white Americans to deny black humanity *tout court*.[6] This refusal posed difficulties for most African Americans not just in everyday interpersonal relations with whites, but also in the former's being subjected to social structures of domination and inequity for which the myth of black sub-humanity served as legitimation. In this larger context, hesitancy and self-doubt were problems which tended to afflict all black folk to one degree or another, of whatever class derivation.

Nonetheless, another way out of the purported dilemma was already prefigured by Du Bois' mentor, William James. One possesses, according to James, "as many social selves as there are individuals" to grant one the favor of recognition, and it is one's image in the eyes of one's own "set" which "exalts or condemns" as she or he "conforms or not to certain requirements that may not be made of one in another walk of life" (James: 294–5). Stated otherwise (and quite apart from the material implications attending the issue), it was not necessary to the healthy psychological edification of the black individual that African-American self-recognition be tied absolutely to recognition by whites; for there was also always the *mutual recognition* which black folk bestowed upon one another, an acknowledgement which, under prevailing conditions, served as a bulwark against the possibility of absolute black self-deprecation. Hence the dilemma which Du Bois considered to be authentic, "universal," and resolvable primarily through longterm education is shown to be narrowly based and subject to multiple solutions.

CONSERVING RACES: IMPLIED "DOUBLE CONSCIOUSNESS"

In contrast to Du Bois' equating of "double consciousness" as negated self-consciousness in *Souls of Black Folk*, in "Conservation of Races" he portrays, *but without identifying as such*, a notion more in keeping with that of his intellectual contemporaries—an erupting of fractious interplay between competing social identities within a given individual:

54

> Here, then, is the dilemma, and it is a puzzling one, I admit. No Negro who has given earnest thought to the situation of his people in American has failed, at some time in life, to find himself at these cross-roads; has failed to ask himself at some time: What, after all, am I? Am I an American or am I a Negro? Can I be both? Or is it my duty to cease to be a Negro as soon as possible and be an American? If I strive as a Negro, am I not perpetuating that very cleft that threatens and separates Black and White American? Is not my only possible practical aim the subduction of all that is Negro in me to the American? Does my black mood place upon me any more obligation to assert my nationality than German, or Irish, or Italian blood would? (Du Bois [1970a]: 256–7).

ALLEN

In this, the first of Du Bois' 1897 formulations made public, the source of African-American emotional (and consequent political) turmoil was attributed to a paralyzing hesitancy surrounding the riddle: "Am I an American or am I a Negro?"—an apparent conflict of social identity. "If I strive as a Negro," asked Du Bois, "am I not perpetuating that very cleft that threatens and separates Black and White America?" Unfortunately, however, Du Bois was never sufficiently explicit regarding what it actually meant to "strive as Negro." As in the case of his semiarticulated "ideals" in *The Souls of Black Folk,* his failure to do so has led numerous readers to erroneously equate his unarticulated, national-racial ones in

"Conservation of the Races" with notions of "cultural conflict." But the most visible, late 19th-century manifestation of "striving as a Negro" could only have been found in the existence and continued growth of black voluntary organizations—including the American Negro Academy before which Du Bois first presented his "Conservation of the Races" paper in March 1897. It was the seemingly contradictory attempt to preserve black institutions (and, by extension, African-American nationality) while at the same time pressing for full inclusion as American citizens that lies at the heart of the "incessant self-questioning" and "hesitation" which Du Bois described in "Conservation of Races."

Revealing an altogether different context than that expressed in *The Souls of Black Folk*, Du Bois opened his "Conservation" argument with the assertion that "if the Negro is ever to be a factor in the world's history," this goal must be accomplished by black hands, black heads, black hearts. From this it follows that the destiny of blacks "is *not* absorption by the white Americans[,]...is not a servile imitation of Anglo-Saxon culture, but a stalwart originality which shall unswervingly follow Negro ideals" (Du Bois [1970a]: 256).[7] In order to accomplish these ends, Du Bois averred,

> we need race organizations: Negro colleges, Negro newspapers, Negro business organizations, a Negro school of literature and art, and an intellectual clearing house, for all these products of the Negro mind, which we may call a Negro Academy. Not only is all this necessary for positive advance, it is absolutely imperative for negative defense (Du Bois [1970a]: 258).

And here began the complications. For a number of Du Bois' colleagues, apparently, the national-identity implications of autonomous, African-American institutions invoked an inordinate sense of dread—a fear, first of all, that the strengthening or expansion of any such bodies would *imply* something other than a demand for full citizenship rights for blacks. Even worse, this autonomy might provide yet another rationale, if one were actually needed, for an additional stripping away of these rights. Or worse still, that such behaviors might afford just one more excuse for the physical expulsion of African Americans from the North American continent, or their annihilation if they remained.

This, of course, was neither the first nor last time that such an issue would arise in the lives of black Americans—and that of Dr. Du Bois as well. During the 1830s, for example, a handful of Northern free blacks led the charge against the continuance of all-black, or what they termed "complexional," organizations in order to undercut the efforts of white colonizationists who denied African-American citizenship claims. Taken to logically rigid extremes, this "commonsense" schema posed antithetical, mutually-exclusive possibilities for Afro-Americans: *either* the assimilation of blacks into the so-called mainstream of American life with full citizenship rights and a consequent dismantling of all-black organizations; *or* an

African-American separation from U.S. society, that is to say, a realization of black political self-determination, with an implied merging of autonomous black institutions with an equally autonomous African-American national/civil identity.

But what were these institutions, after all, and how could organizations which had contributed so much to the material and spiritual well-being of the black community now be considered a threat to its existence? Towering above them all, of course, was the black Christian church, to which Du Bois later referred in *The Souls of Black Folk* as bearing the character of a *government* (Du Bois [1969]: 215). Such independent organizations—which also included sickness and burial societies, distinctly middle-class women's clubs operating under the aegis of the National Association of Colored Women, lodges run by Prince Hall Freemasons, Elks, Odd Fellows, Knights of Pythias, and other semiclandestine male associations (along with their respective female auxiliaries such as, for example, the Order of the Eastern Star), fledgling business groups, and, shortly to come, Greek-letter college sororities and fraternities—were largely the result, at least at the onset, of black exclusion from similar institutions among the dominant population. Moreover, the exclusion of salutary news stories about blacks in the dominant press had led to the formation of hundreds of black-owned, black-oriented newspapers. (Negro colleges constituted a special case: nominally run by blacks, they remained under the financial suzerainty of the Rockefeller and Peabody funds, for the most part.) Because many such groups fulfilled vital social and economic needs within black communities, it is likely that those who depended upon their services would have expressed the least ambivalence towards their existence. What should be remembered as well is that the existence of black institutions had *not* posed any particular dilemma for hard-shelled assimilationists such as Frederick Douglass, who though willing to support them as a temporary expedient, generally denied the need for their existence. Nor was it a conundrum experienced by the more economically nationalist-oriented such as Booker T. Washington, who, in the belief that the rights of citizenship for blacks would eventually flow from their economic indispensability, elaborated a long-term strategy which, in part, was predicated on the existence and support of independent, black economic institutions. However, the situation did create an untenable paradox for a handful of educated African Americans committed to achieving full American civil identity, but who also, by the century's end, had come to a double revelation: that for reasons of sheer survival the existence of autonomous, mass-based black institutions would likely prove of *long-term* necessity; and that there was actually something in black culture worth preserving—an admission that bucked against the assimilationist proclivities of most college-bred blacks of the era.

HERDERIAN CONCEPTS OF NATIONALISM AND CULTURE

Du Bois, of course, owed a number of his earliest formulations to German thinkers of his own as well as preceding epochs: in the realm of historical economics, older

56

ALLEN

contemporaries such as Adolph Wagner and Gustav von Schmoller, with both of whom he studied at the University of Berlin; in philosophy, it was both Hegel and Herder who exerted their respective influences, Hegel with regard to the phenomenology of consciousness and the philosophy of history, and Herder with respect to cultural critique intertwined with the philosophy of history.[8] While Du Bois had many a source to draw upon in his elaboration of "twoness," a number of his basic concepts of culture—of national ideals, of cultural "gift," of cultural relativity, and of folk culture—most certainly were derived either directly or indirectly from Herder. In the case of the latter, it was likely that black intellectuals such as Edward Blyden and Alexander Crummell played an influential middle role (see Lynch: 60-1; Moses: 108).

Herder, Jefferson, and the Multi-National State

The sense of ominous, impending conflict underlying "Conservation of the Races" actually flowed from some of the earliest ideals of European nationalism where nationality was considered a category of Nature and the assembling of multiple nationalities beneath the folds of a single state apparatus deemed "unnatural" and subject to disastrous consequences. The sentiment was first expressed by Herder, one of the most influential proponents of romantic nationalism, in the late 18th-century (Herder [1969]: 324). Although Herder emphasized nationality and even used the term *race* in his thought, Herder was firmly opposed to the notion that innate, racial differences existed within humanity. For him, national distinctions were purely a matter of culture, and especially of language (Herder [1969]: 284). Elsewhere Herder darkly affirmed that "Where nature has separated nationalities by language, customs and character one must not attempt to change them into one unit by artifact and chemical operations" (in Ergang: 97). Ominous results awaited those who defied the natural order of things: "forced unions"—empires comprised of diverse peoples thrown together as the result of the actions of imperialist rulers—were but "lifeless monstrosities" formed of clay, "and, like all clay, they will dissolve or crumble to pieces" (Herder [1969]: 324).

Such thoughts carried over into the dominant ideals of the newly formed United States. For whites, the African-American presence commanded a two-fold fear of unnatural consequences. First of all, the acceptance of citizenship for blacks—implying a necessary *somatic* broadening of the definition of American national character—was unthinkable; Nature might tolerate the black presence only if Africa's descendants were held to the most ruthless forms of suppression. On the other hand, the prospect of miscegenation—with its attendant implications regarding the eventual disappearance of white (and, consequently, black) "biological identity" as such—posed equally horrendous a prospect. The consequence: European Americans and African Americans might inhabit the same country only under two possible conditions. Either one "race" would brutally dominate the other (which, though "tolerable" when blacks were the victims, nonetheless went

57

ALLEN

against the grain of Enlightenment ideals of individual freedom), or an unchecked and barbarous state of miscegenation would occur (which ran contrary to dominant American moral and aesthetic ideals). Thus, in his *Notes on the State of Virginia,* Thomas Jefferson warned of deep perils in freeing the slaves without providing for their expulsion from the North American continent:

> Deep rooted prejudices entertained by the whites; ten thousand recollections, by the blacks, of the injuries they have sustained; new provocations; the real distinctions which nature had made; and many other circumstances, will divide us into parties, and produce convulsions which will probably never end but in the extermination of the one or the other race. (Jefferson: 186)

To these political objections, wrote Jefferson, "may be added others, which are physical and moral." These latter factors had not only to do with the color and hair texture of blacks which, in his estimation, debased prevailing standards of beauty. There were suppositions as well that Africa's descendants required less sleep than whites, experienced only transient griefs, were more sensual than reflective, inferior in reason and imagination, that males of the race possessed greater sexual drive, and that blacks in general were incapable of creating poetry—Phillis Wheatley's heroic efforts notwithstanding.

> Among the Romans emancipation required but one effort. The slave, when made free, might mix with, without staining the blood of his master. But with us a second is necessary, unknown to history. When freed, he is to be removed beyond the reach of mixture. (Jefferson: 193)

58

It was logic such as Jefferson's, of course, which tied certain strains of abolitionism to plans for the colonization of American blacks outside North America in the era prior to 1865. Given this broader contextual overlay, the choice for many whites had become one of either the complete subjugation of blacks or their expulsion from the North American continent; for blacks the historical choice was often seen as existing between cultural and/or biological assimilation, on the one side, emigration on the other. This compelling *either/or* logic was so pervasive, having been repeated on faith for so long, that it continued to shape the outlook of black spokespersons well into the late 19th century (see, e.g., Turner [1971]: 74).

With abject failure of attempts at colonization or emigration arrived, in the aftermath of Reconstruction, the most judicious compromise to which American democracy was capable of rising: the imposition of a racially determined, spatial segregation upon white and black communities.[9] But with unabated talk of black repatriation in Congress and other quarters from the late 19th through the early 20th centuries, the threat of African-American expulsion from the U.S. appeared genuine enough. Du Bois for his part, however, had calculated by 1897 that "any

ALLEN

general migration of American Negroes to Africa is neither possible nor desirable; it is not possible, for the Negroes as a body do not wish to go, and the forcible expulsion of a nation of eight million would be simply impossible without civil war and an expenditure of not less than two and one-half billions of francs" (Du Bois [1985]: 47–48).[10] By the late 1930s, however, he had reevaluated his position: "We may be expelled from the United States as the Jew is being expelled from Germany" (Du Bois [1968]: 306; see also Du Bois [1985]: 155).

Borrowing a number of concepts traceable to Herder, Du Bois sought to demonstrate that an apparent conundrum—the supposed impossibility of white and black citizens peacefully pursuing their separate but intertwined racial ideals— was a false one. With an adjustment of the economic and political conditions of African Americans there was no reason why the pursuit of differing aims might not be successfully explored. But it was, after all, Herder's ideas on nationality which had given shape to the dilemma from which Du Bois was now attempting to extricate himself; and through the selective embrace and rejection of a number of Herder's precepts, Du Bois would offer a unique resolution. Du Bois had embraced the notion of cultural "gift"—an idea derived from Herder's writings on folk culture—as the foundation of "national character"; the latter theme itself was translated within the Du Boisian lexicon as "racial ideals." But he had also accomplished his aims by substituting racial formulations for Herder's own nationality paradigm—a solution which Herder, of course, would have rejected out of hand.

To be an "American" (in the way that inhabitants of the southern half of the North American continent have onesidedly appropriated the term all to themselves) signifies a double meaning: a *national identity* born of the imprint of socialization within "American" society; and a *civil identity*—natural citizen or denizen— based upon a specific relation to the "American" state. Rephrasing Herder's prohibition against the assignment of more than one nationality to a given state in these latter terms, one might say that for American civil identity as a whole there could exist but a single American nationality, a single national identity. Du Bois, however, parted company with this Herderian formulation on at least three counts: first, that American civil identity itself might properly accommodate the ideals of more than one (national) group; second, that the concept of nationality was to be reconfigured as that of *race*; and third, whereas both Herderian *national character* and Du Boisian *racial ideals* pointed towards the overall "way of life" of a people, Du Bois himself placed far more emphasis on the selective ideals of aesthetic, or "high" culture, as well as on the guiding role of an educated elite in their development.

Folk Culture Versus Artistic Culture

As Gene Bluestein has observed, Western tradition has carried within itself a fundamental opposition "between folk and formal art, the first conceived to be 'childlike,' primitive, and unaware of its techniques; the second defined as mature, civilized, and conscious of this craftsmanship" (Bluestein: intro). Whereas folk art was

ALLEN

the domain of the peasantry, formal art remained that of the talented, select few of the upper classes. It was Herder, of course, who discovered a way to reconcile these antithetical concepts: folk culture, or the "way of life" of the agrarian common people, was reconceived as the *foundation* of national character, elements of which an intellectual elite might develop further through more formal artistic expression. Still, the distinction between folk and formal culture, between collective crafts-manship and individual artistry, were never fully obliterated. "God acts upon Earth only by means of superior, chosen men" wrote Herder, a notion that coincided with Du Bois' own concept of a "Talented Tenth" for blacks (Herder [1966]: 230). Herder, on the other hand, was quick to maintain that art was a *national* treasure, not the private inheritance of a handful of individuals (Ergang: 209). And Du Bois, too, when dwelling upon the Negro spirituals, marvelled at the intrinsic beauty of a music which had required neither composers, arrangers, nor performers of pro-fessional stature for its execution. But although Du Bois had engaged the overall contours of Herder's bridging concept, he himself opted for a preeminence in the role assigned to the "Talented Tenth" of African Americans in the production of salutary "racial values," even as he acknowledged that the fluorescence of Afro-American folk culture owed nothing to black elites. For Herder "national charac-ter" was synonymous with *Lebensweise*, or "way of life" of a people. However, at the turn of the 19th century the employment of the English version of the concept was still in its infancy, and Du Bois, although surely aware of its use by 18th and 19th-century German writers, managed to avoid it as well—perhaps out of a con-cern for its Herderian links to "national identity," as well as a disdain for African-American popular culture other than that expressed, for the most part, in Negro spirituals and folktales.[11]

National Character Versus Racial Character

Some of the most prominent writers of the Enlightenment subscribed to the uni-versality of ancient Greek and Roman as well as contemporary French ideals (Ergang: 83). For Herder and other Romantics, however, universality resided in the contention that every nationality possessed its own unique national culture and language which contributed to world civilization (Ergang: 88). The underpinnings of national culture, moreover, were seen to be constituted by the "folk"—that is, the numerically predominant *peasantry* of a given country. "For every nation is one people," insisted Herder, "having its own national form, as well as its own language: the climate, it is true, stamps on each its mark, or spreads it over a slight veil, but not sufficient to destroy the original national character" (Herder [1968]: 7; [1966]: 166). In Herder's lexicon, *national character* was virtually synonymous with the "way of life" of the common folk: "thus every one bears the characters of his country and way of life on the most distant shores" (Herder [1968]: 10; 169). However, it is also true that Herder's descriptive renderings of *Lebensweise*—for non-European peoples, in any case—brushed all too near at times against the specter of the "noble savage": the Native American of California, wrote Herder, "on the verge of the earth, in his barren country, and amid the vicissitudes of his climate, complains not of heat and cold, eludes the force of hunger, though with utmost difficulty, and enjoys happiness in his native land" (Herder [1968]: 9). Rough depictions aside, however, national character in Herderian terms was fundamentally "inexpressible," yet unique to each national group (Ergang: 87).

Herder, moreover, had advanced the claim that every national group was the repository of a singular character which furthered the development of humanity as a whole—or to employ Du Boisian terms, each nationality had a unique cultural "gift" to offer the world. This "gift," after coming into bloom, would rise to its highest possible summit, then, lapsing into senility, would wither and die, thereby making room for the contributions of other nationalities. No national culture was to be accorded greater significance than any other, and each had to be judged, not at the bar of any so-called "universal" standard, but from criteria extracted from the very culture in question. Maintaining a consistent pluralism in the face of a pre-vailing Eurocentric view of culture, Herder proclaimed to "Men of all the quarters of the globe, who have perished over the ages, you have not lived solely to manure the earth with your ashes, so that at the end of time your posterity should be made happy by European culture. The very thought of a superior European culture is a blatant insult to the majesty of Nature" (Herder, cited in R. Williams [1976]: 79; the trans. is somewhat different from that found in Herder [1966]: 224).

Herder's remarks bring to mind yet another way in which the initial chapter of *Souls* differs from "Conservation of the Races"—by way of the differing philoso-phies of history which inform them. Invoking the "Egyptian and Indian, the Greek and Roman, the Teuton and Mongolian" in *The Souls of Black Folk*, Du Bois reit-erated the "six world-historical peoples through whose histories the world-spirit achieves realization" according to Hegel's philosophy of history (Gooding-Williams [1991–2]: 525; Williamson: 404). Bypassing Hegel's contemptuous dis-missal of peoples of African descent, but retaining his ideas bearing upon the unfolding of universal Spirit, Du Bois proclaimed the arrival of the Negro as the prophetic "seventh son," destined to bring forth a special contribution to world culture. In "Conservation of the Races," however, following the unpredictable but nonexclusive pattern of succession of national cultures envisioned by Herder, Du Bois treated the Negro merely as one "national" group among many whose turn upon the world stage had finally arrived.

Echoing Herder's cosmopolitan-nationalist sentiments, but swapping the con-cept of nation for the equally vague one of "race," even as he particularized the notion of cultural "gift," Du Bois avowed that black Americans, as a *race*, had a gift-message to offer to the world, a message no less distinguished than that of any other racial grouping. Yet all race groups were striving, "each in its own way, to develop for civilization its particular message, its particular ideal, which shall help to guide the world nearer and nearer that perfection of human life for which we all long, that one far off Divine event" (Du Bois [1970a]: 255). Extending yet another of Crummell's arguments, Du Bois proclaimed that the "history of the world is the history, not of individuals, but of groups, not of nations, but of races, and he who ignores or seeks to override the race idea in human history ignores and overrides the central thought of all history" (Du Bois [1970a]: 252).[12] The irony, of course, was that *à propos* the question of race, Du Bois had taken a step backward with respect to Herder, who had denied the very existence of such (see Herder [1969]: 284; [1968]: 7).

"Turning to real history," wrote Du Bois, "there can be no doubt, first, as to the widespread, nay universal, prevalence of the race ideal, and to its efficiency as the vastest and most ingenious invention for human progress" (Du Bois [1970a]: 253). Du Bois' sidestepping of Herder's views on race, however, enabled him to shift the debate from one bearing upon the impossibility of several *national* cultures coexisting beneath the same governing apparatus, to one asserting the possibilities of a harmonious interplay of differing *racial* cultures under the aforementioned political conditions. To have raised the issue of a distinct African-American nationality, as opposed to "race," would have been to breath life into the specter of black political separatism—the very issue Du Bois was attempting to neutralize in the first place. Second, had Du Bois chosen to apply the concept of "nationality" to black Americans, it would have been a terribly difficult task to surmount the prevailing sentiment that it was language, of all the traits, which embodied its outstanding characteristics: "Has a nationality anything more precious than the language of its fathers?," Herder had inquired. (Ergang: 105, 285). Following such logic, to have proposed, at the turn of the century, the existence of a black American national identity separate from that of white Americans would have required the claim that the language of the former was critically different from that of the latter—and contrary to the language-oriented national liberation struggles of the late 19th-century, one can be certain that neither Du Bois nor any other African-American intellectual of this epoch was quite prepared to embrace a concept of "Black English."

Unraveling the Riddle

Indirectly responding to each of the objections of Herder and Jefferson outlined above, Du Bois affirmed, without elaboration and without evidence that, "while it may have been true in the past that closed race groups made history, that here in conglomerate America *nous avons [changé] tout cela*—we have changed all that, and have no need of this ancient instrument of progress" (Du Bois [1970a]: 253).[13] For Du Bois, the destiny of African Americans was neither absorption by, nor the Africanization of, white Americans, a pledge by which he also sought to disarm white fears of miscegenation on the one side, and of "Negro domination" on the other ([1969]: 45). (He did confess, however, that the incorporation by the dominant culture of African-American "gifts"—the unique message which blacks had to give to the world—would result in an eventual "softening" of the Teutonic

62

ALLEN

whiteness of North American society.) Hence, there was no logical reason why whites and blacks alike, pursuing diverse but nonetheless intertwined ideals, could not co-exist peacefully beneath the same governing machinery.

What Du Bois wrought to make clear, above all, was that the dilemma of "being a Negro and an American at the same time"—by which he meant the institutional fortification of Afro-American "racial ideals" ("national ideals" by any other name) and the institutional fulfillment of U.S. citizenship pursued concurrently—was a false one: African-American "twoness" might be fully preserved, without incurring liability on either side. "Here, it seems to me," wrote Du Bois, "is reading of the riddle that puzzles so many of us. We are Americans, not only by birth and by citizenship, but by our political ideals, our language, our religion. Farther than that, our Americanism does not go" ([1970a]: 257–8).

The key to this novel exposition of "diversity without conflict" (of cultural pluralism, actually) was the notion of "gift," which Du Bois seems to have appropriated from Alexander Crummell: "I know no people coming to this land which can offer the rights the Negro has to offer to save this nation," noted the venerable reverend-scholar in the late 1880s (Crummell [1992a]: 242).

Anthropologists have long understood that "gifts," bearing magical qualities, "simultaneously acknowledge and create social relations," relations which may eventually be forged into bonds of equality. Demanding recognition of the giver and return from the receiver, "gifts," as Robert Paynter has noted, "are the media of politics among equals" (Paynter: 286). The "gifts" of culture proposed by Du Bois thus served a two-fold purpose: to elevate the status of blacks in the eyes of the world and at the same time serve as an offering to those who feared the clash of irreconcilable ideals inherent in the "gift" itself. American and African-American in the same creative breath, and if openly acknowledged and received as such, the presents of blacks held out the promise of linking two, seemingly irreconcilable worlds.

But just as Herder's concept of national character bore an elusive stamp, so too did Du Bois' elaboration of African-American racial ideals tend to remain in an inchoate state. Altogether absent from "Conservation of the Races," they do make a brief appearance in *The Souls of Black Folk*: "Will America be poorer if she replace her brutal dyspeptic blundering with light-hearted but determined Negro humility? or her coarse and cruel wit with loving jovial good humor? or her vulgar music with the soul of the Sorrow Songs?" inquired Du Bois in his opening chapter (Du Bois [1969]: 52). But it was not until the final pages of the book that he revealed the most important of the gifts which he had in mind: the Negro spiritual, uniquely American as well as African American, to be recognized and accepted by whites as an offering to American culture. Black folktales, though playing a secondary role, were acknowledged as well. Several decades later Du Bois elaborated upon the specifically African-American *joie de vivre* which he had previously acknowledged: "a certain spiritual joyousness; a sensuous, tropical love of life…;

ALLEN

slow and dreamful conception of the universe, a drawling and slurring of speech, an intense sensitiveness to spiritual values…" More significantly, he was further prepared to extend the notion of a black cultural "gift" into other areas: to the economic independence of women (a development which, he points out, black women not only prefigured, but exerted a direct influence upon); to the (conflicted) role of the slave woman as "the medium through which the two great races were united in America"; the efforts of black women such as Harriet Tubman and Mammy Pleasants towards the extension of American democracy to blacks; and finally, to the rhythmic punctuations of black oratory, especially that of the ministry (Du Bois [1975]: 262, 268, 270–2, 308, 320).

THE PATH NOT TAKEN

It was W.E.B. Du Bois who, at the turn of the last century, first articulated the existence of a counter-pull of double aims experienced by a narrow strata of Afro-Americans, a dilemma which he attributed to blacks of all social classes. But this twist of consciousness was really not so much the worry of African-American proletarians, artisans, or agrarian workers, or of black men and women engaged in domestic service. Not even among black professionals was this supposedly "universal" dilemma the particular concern of assimilationists of biological or cultural persuasion, of political emigrationists seeking self-determination on other shores, or of entrepreneurial Negroes who, with one eye fixed on the balance sheet, accepted segregation out of sheer expedience. Rather, it was the concern of late 19th-century educated blacks who, first of all, possessed reflective capacity as well as the time to reflect; who refused to view the world through imposed categorical blinders; and who, constrained by the absence of possibilities for direct political struggle, yet repulsed by the brutishness of economic competition during the so-called Gilded Age, chose as their principal battleground the domain of culture. (Here one discovers rough parallels underlying the muted politics of both Du Bois and Herder, where societal problems were to be addressed through a cultural optic.)[14]

Du Bois' blueprint for cultural coexistence between whites and blacks was essentially of the same spirit as Booker T. Washington's program for economic coexistence—an indirect political response to the collapse of Reconstruction. While coming close to transferring to the *cultural* realm Washington's notion of "separate as the fingers, yet one as the hand in all things essential to mutual progress," Du Bois, nonetheless, was unprepared to relinquish the terrain of political and civil rights.[15] For if, in Washington's eyes, the legitimation of African-American civil and political rights derived from a demonstration of their economic indispensability, W.E.B. Du Bois was not disposed to advance the claim that those same rights should derive from a demonstration of African-American cultural prowess. Rather, it was a question of blacks' affirming their American citizenship

64

ALLEN

and receiving all benefits to be derived therefrom, while at the same time main-taining an institutionalized African-American distinctiveness.

Contrary to present-day misreadings of Du Bois, this last, perceived dilemma was the underlying source of purported African-American agony described in his "Conservation of Races" essay. The issues of "brutal blundering versus determined humility," of "cruel wit versus good humor," or "vulgar versus sublime music" were hardly the stuff of which "two warring souls" were made. Moreover, even where Du Bois speaks of a refusal on the part of the Negro either to "Africanize America" or to "bleach his soul," this was not the same as defining a problematical "twoness" in which African Americans found themselves torn between the cultural practices of surviving Africanisms, on one hand, and those of Euro-Americanisms on the other.[16] The latter is an argument which, under the heavy influence of African writers of the postcolonial period, did not and could not emerge within an African-American context until the heady, late-1960's era of black cultural nation-alism and the simultaneous and unprecedented entry of upwardly mobile blacks into bureaucratic corporate structures.[17]

In a somewhat different form, the debate surrounding the simultaneous pursuit of full civil equality and African-American institutional distinctiveness was to con-front Du Bois once again in 1934; in the wake of a controversy surrounding his editorial support of autonomous economic institutions, a position which the NAACP hierarchy feared would contaminate the struggle against imposed segre-gation and for the securing of unconditional rights for blacks, Du Bois was led to resign the editorship of the *Crisis* magazine (see Du Bois [1968a]: 303–15; and [1985]: 143–57). The legacy of Du Bois' dilemma—the choice between liberty and community—bears heavily upon us today. By the mid-1960s, it is true, the narrow, legal pursuit of civil rights led to the securing of formal political and civil liberties for African Americans. But in the context of a continued denial of economic democracy to Americans as a whole, this victory also contributed, however inad-vertently, to the subsequent collapse of autonomous institutions essential to the well-being of African-American communities. That issue, of course, remains unre-solved to this day.

NOTES

1 For a cogent discussion of differences existing between Du Bois' early published essays and their subsequent revision into chapters constituting *The Souls of Black Folk*, see Stepto: 52–91.

2 The dualist terminology employed by Du Bois in the latter work can be divided into three essential categories: "double consciousness," "double ideals" (and corresponding surrogate terms such as "double aims," "double strivings," "two souls," and the like), and "second sight." The topics of "double consciousness" and "double ideals" are addressed in the text above. "Second sight," on the other hand, referred to a magic practice first attrib-uted to early 17th-century inhabitants of the Scottish Highland: "the ability literally to 'see' the future, through visual images of future events" (Stevenson [1988]: 126). That Du Bois intended the term to be taken at face value can be discounted, leaving one with the

task of deciphering an elusive trope. Previously I have suggested that Du Bois may have implied by the term "an expanded consciousness allowing one the ability to navigate two disparate cultures fluently…or from the perspective of one's own culture, the skill to perceive in another that which is opaque to its practitioners." The latter meaning is implicit in a remark made by Du Bois in 1926: while life "behind the veil" supposedly revealed no true self-consciousness for blacks, it also permitted them, in his words, to "see America in a way that white America cannot" (Du Bois [1970b]: 279). See also Allen (1990–2): 55–69, esp. 56.

3 As a counter-example, Estes-Hicks has pointed out that unlike Du Bois and others "who regarded their twoness as a painful burden," Jean Toomer "saw the heightening of consciousness cause by racial/social diversity as an exhilarating experience—the fortunate fate of modern man" (Estes-Hicks: 26).

4 For a discussion of Emerson's penchant for dualisms, see also Nicoloff: 44, 50–53, 59, 134.

5 What is one to do, for example, with ideals upholding "quackery and demagogy" which should have induced shame in their practitioners, pitted against counter-ideals which made one ashamed of one's "lowly tasks"? And under circumstances described by Du Bois, how might one be torn between two apparently different bodies of knowledge?

6 The issue finds a close parallel in our own time relative to "affirmative action" in employment practices, a policy now under extreme attack by right-wing ideologies aided by confused or malevolent Negroes. Steven A. Carter's puerile lamentations to the contrary, white opposition to "affirmative action," so-called, is but a special case of white opposition to blacks in general: prior to the existence of "affirmative-action" guidelines, it would seem that African Americans who managed to obtain employment through an occasional outbreak of fair employment practices tended to face at least as many difficulties from white coworkers as those who later entered through the "affirmative action" door.

7 African-American art historian Judith Wilson observes that "To this day, many commentators on the work of African-American artists remain tangled in the inherent contradictions of this nationalist-oriented program, struggling to separate some fixed set of 'Negro ideals' from an 'Anglo Saxon culture' they have conceptualized in equally ahistoric, essentialist terms and expecting a 'stalwart originality' to result from a pursuit of such Sisyphusian efforts" (Wilson: 32).

8 Although (as Adell has shown) the very first chapter of Souls is largely framed by Hegel's phenomenology and (as Williamson and Gooding-Williams have also demonstrated) by his philosophy of history as well, Du Bois' eclecticism would seem to preclude our assigning him to a single philosophical tradition, whether Emersonian, Jamesian, Hegelian, Herderian, or any other. For treatments of Du Bois' philosophical leanings and/or Germanic influences, see Broderick: 367–71; B.W. Bell: 16–24; Adell: chap. 13; Gooding-Williams (1987): 99–114 and (1991–2): 517–42; and R.C. Williams (1983): 11–19. Zamir (1995) arrived too late to include in this discussion.

9 In the case of segregation, of course, there is no question that an ideal such as this could not have been so readily and globally imposed had it not coincided with the need of Southern landowners and merchants for a firm control over black agrarian labor.

10 The cultural invention of the "sterile mulatto" and self-delusion concerning the "inability of blacks to survive outside the institution of slavery," indirectly expressed the fears of white Americans concerning the impossibility of peaceful African–European coexistence.

ALLEN

11 Culture as a "way of life" was first formulated in the English language by anthropologist Edward Tylor in 1871: "Culture or civilization, taken in its wide, ethnographic sense, is that complex whole which includes knowledge, belief, art, morals, law, custom, and any other capabilities and habits acquired by man as a member of society." See also R. Williams (1976): 76–82.

12 See also Crummell ([1992a]: 203; and [July]: 108). If, in their efforts to erect an oppositional worldview to 19th-century white racial dominance, a Du Bois, a Crummell, or a Blyden were guilty of "racism"—and it is necessary to be perfectly clear on this issue in the face of recent effusions from a handful of writers of African descent—then it was, in the more meaningful terminology of Sartre (1949), an "antiracist racism" with which they should be charged. To argue otherwise, to de-historicize and decontextualize the issue is, in effect, to place the counter-racialism of African Americans on the same plane as that of white institutionalized racism wielded at the former's expense. Appiah's (1992) categorization of 19th-century African-American thinkers as "extrinsic" or "intrinsic racists"—a dubious distinction, in any case—only further muddles the water. Although he is absolutely correct in challenging the scientific validity of "race," alas, neither Appiah's negative preachings to blacks on the subject nor his erudite, scientific denials of the existence of "race" exert much practical effect upon its existence as institutionalized social reality. To my mind, a greater emphasis on the elimination of racism rather than "race" would come closer to achieving the "raceless" world that many utopians have envisioned (cf. Gordon [1995a] and [1995e]).

13 Du Bois went on to state that the counter-assertion, "of which the Negro people are especially found, can not be established by a careful consideration of history." Significantly, while agreeing with Du Bois' general direction, Alexander Crummell's reading of the past supported neither conclusion: "...singular as it may seem, there is no fixed law of history by which to determine the probabilities of the race problem in the United States. We can find nowhere such invariability of result as to set a principle or determine what may be called an historical axiom" (Crummell [1992b]: 181).

67

14 Ergang has noted that in the late 18th century, "the political condition of Germany, as a whole and also in many of the states, was so wretched that the better minds turned with disgust from the consideration of political matters to literature, aesthetics, and philosophy, and the people in general, after experiencing the futility of inveighing against the political conditions of the time, settled down to contemptuous indifference to public affairs" (Ergang: 241).

15 Du Bois, e.g., posed the question: "What should be the attitude of Negroes toward the educational qualification for voters? What should be out attitude toward separate schools? How should we meet discrimination on railways and hotels? Such questions need not so much specific answer for each part as a general expression of policy, and nobody should be better fitted to announce such a policy than a representative honest Negro Academy" (Du Bois [1970a]: 260).

16 Rather, this position represented a tactical maneuver on Du Bois' part, where he reassured his white readers that rather than miscegenate, African Americans sought to preserve their distinctive (cultural and, presumably, biological) traits; on the other hand, such racial conversation would not lead to the "Africanization" of American society. In other words, two nationalities and two national idealism might comfortably function beneath the umbrella of a unitary state apparatus (see Du Bois [1969]: 45).

17 Mercifully, from the early 19th century to the present this peculiar manifestation of cultural schizophrenia among educated African Americans has tended to diminish, for three reasons: the gradual decline in threats of forced expulsion of blacks from the U.S. on the part of whites; successive stages of incorporation of black American popular culture into the "mainstream," so-called, as well as the progressive acculturation of masses of black Americans to the dominant culture, thus rendering the choice between cultural identities progressively less draconian; and the developing sophistication of the African-American intelligentsia in their recognizing that, in order to eliminate categorical difference, it is sometimes necessary to foment a heightened sense of creative difference for the purpose of demonstrating a sense of qualitative sameness.

EXISTENTIAL DYNAMICS OF THEORIZING BLACK INVISIBILITY

Lewis R. Gordon

*His shadow, so to speak, has been more real to him
than his personality.*

— Alain Locke

chapter 4

AT LEAST four Africana theorists, W.E.B. Du Bois, Alain Locke, Ralph Ellison,
and Frantz Fanon have theorized dimensions of antiblack racism in a way that
is so clearly indicative of an existential phenomenological turn that their work
bears a great deal of affinity with the work of Jean-Paul Sartre, particularly his
discussions of overdetermination and sado-masochism. According to Du Bois,
the African American is forced by limited options into a doubled reality—a
single body split into two souls with two correlated worlds. The consequence,
argues Du Bois, is that problems faced by African Americans sink into the
shadows of a skewed conception of African Americans as the problems themselves. Alain Locke takes a similar position in "The New Negro," his famous
manifesto for black intellectuals, when he points out that the black intellectual is induced to see himself through "the distorted perspective of a social
problem." In *Shadow and Act*, Ralph Ellison refers to this phenomenon as

human evasion ([1972]: 24–44). And Fanon, through the course of four classic volumes, has demonstrated not only the human-evading dimensions of antiblack racism, but also its peculiarly *phobogenic* and *Manichaean* dimensions, dimensions that enmesh black reality outside of the dimension of the symbolic into the seriousness of the *real* (see esp. Fanon [1952/1967a]).[1] In his philosophical corpus, Jean-Paul Sartre explicates a critical philosophical anthropology that provides a framework for understanding how such evasion is possible. His answer rests in the subject of philosophical anthropology itself and its resistance to the modern conception of the human being as embodying a determined "nature."

The convergence of Du Bois, Locke, Ellison, Fanon, and Sartre suggests at least a general sense of purpose, although the "situations" of their struggles are markedly different. What these figures have in common are a passion to understand human beings and a passion to articulate a liberation project that does not lead to the estrangement of humanity from itself. They each resist the forces of institutional invisibility and the seduction of constructing theoretical maps that lead nowhere. In what follows, I would like to focus on some dynamics of black invisibility that emerge from the theoretical resources of these five thinkers, with special emphasis on the work of two—Fanon and Sartre.[2]

I

Any theory that fails to address the existential phenomenological dimension of racism suffers from a failure to address the situational dimension, what Fanon called *l'expérience vécue* ("lived experience"), of race. On the one hand, there are familiar instances of skewed racial visibility:

"Hey, a Negro!"

Or perhaps, as exploited symbols of gastronomic delight in the form of a black face on hot cereal boxes and pancake mixes and all the array of Jungle innuendos, "Sho' good banana!" (Fanon [1952/1967a]).

Antiblack racism calls for causal explanations and typifications that come to their conclusion, figuratively and literally, in the lynch mob trailing behind bloodhounds in pursuit of a black body. The pursuit is Manichaean in purpose; it is an effort to weed out the pollution of blackness from the purity of whiteness. It is also, in its essence, theodicean. For in such a world, blackness functions as an aberration that has to be explained without blaming the system in which it emerges. The system of antiblack racism is lived as a self-justified god in its institutions and its inhabitant's flesh. Emersed in itself, it can only see its faults as "contaminations" of the system. As a consequence, the bloodhound pursuit of a black body takes on a logic premised upon an identity relation between fact and value. The system is fact; it is "what is." It is absolute. Whatever "is" is what ought to be and hence ought to have been. The inferior Other becomes a fundamental project for the establishment of the Superior Self, whose superiority is a function of what it *is*.

But consciousness of the inferior Other takes broader significance than visual perception. One can, it is true, see a black before an African American or Afro-Caribbean. Thus the morphological feature of color distortion—transforming brown into black—offers an accessible locus of disdain beyond the various nationalities of blackness that may stand before us. Since blackness transcends Africanness, the aetiological significance of blackness unfolds in the drama of purgation. The morphologically white man standing next to us may be "polluted" by an aetiology of blackness. He may have, for instance, "a drop of black blood" (a dreaded element of an antiblack world). Such "knowledge" has an impact on who or what he is perceived to be in his totality. His flesh becomes "black flesh"; his thoughts, "black thoughts"; his "presence" a form of absence—white absence.

This presence-absence dichotomy is constituted by a particular way of existing. The phenomenological tradition, both existential and transcendental, considers the locus of this dichotomy to be in the unsurpassability of the material standpoint of inquiry itself—the body. In existential phenomenological literature, it has been argued that the body is every possibility from perspective to freedom to meaning. These are not, however, mutually exclusive possibilities. Perspectivity, value, freedom, and meaning can be, as Alain Locke ([1989]: 34–50, 111–126) and Maurice Merleau-Ponty (1962 and 1968) have observed, coextensive features of the lived-experience of embodied consciousness.

The body is our perspective in the world. This perspective has at least three dimensions—the dimension of seeing, the dimension of being seen, and the dimension of being conscious of being seen by others. These three matrices are from Sartre ([1956]: Part III, chaps. 2 and 3). Among their obvious correlates are meaning, meaning-as-seen, and meaning-as-meant; or valuing, value-as-seen, valuing-as-meant. We shall call *sadism* and *masochism* the attempt to deny the coextensivity of these three dimensions. It should be borne in mind that the kind of sadism and masochism to be discussed here are ideal types premised upon what will be regarded as existential *seriousness*—the treatment of our values as material features of the world. This form of sadism and masochism is not the form we find in sexual "play," where there are sadism and masochism with agreed-upon "rules," so to speak. The sadism and masochism that will be the focus here are lived by a leitmotif of earnestness, by a hidden flavor of serious "reality."

Our sadist is a figure with an attitude toward consciousness in the flesh. He wants to believe he is the first dimension without the other two, in the hope of evading the framework of being constituted in the first place. He thus seeks to evade even his own perspectivity. Flesh nauseates him with its propensity to make him aware of his embodiment. He seeks fortification from a world that constitutes who he is. So he retreats into the denial of such a world. He denies the situatedness of existence and opts for the magic of disembodiment. He wipes away the framework from which to be understood as a human being. His path leads to solipsism, the position in which one literally becomes the world, which in principle cannot raise the question of perspectivity since there are no relations from which to establish being-related in the first place. Free, he thinks, from the judgment of others, judgment that limits the options available to him to believe what he wants to believe, the world becomes the comfort of his ideas. The anguish of ought is believed eradicated, and he is able to saturate himself with sheer seriousness of Will. For our sadist, then, visibility extends out "there," but never "here." He takes advantage of the invisible dimension of himself as seer, speaker, feeler, to deny the fact of his being seen, heard, and felt. He lives himself as though he were disembodied.

Our masochist, on the other hand, denies he can see himself being seen. He throws himself into the sight of others while denying their otherness. He becomes an ossified substance—limp, passive flesh straddled under the look of him who stands as the source of responsibility. No longer regarding himself as responsible for who he is, he constitutes himself as helpless and controlled. His body is not regarded as an active participant in the constitution of a meaningful world that we may call his "life." It is given up. It is on the table. It is a thing. It is corporeal.

We shall regard both sadism and masochism in our sense as forms of misanthropy since both involve forms of evading human being in the flesh. From the standpoint of bad faith, this type of sadist regards himself on the level of "subject" before whom all others are "objects." The masochist regards himself as an object before a subject. Both are, however, objectification of human reality into forms of being-in-itself. For the sadist's effort to make others objects fixes his self-identity into a subject-in-itself, which is not only a form of object, but also tantamount to being a god. Similarly, the masochist's effort to fix the look of the subject-Other calls for the Other as subject-in-itself, which is a form of object, a god. The failure of both sadism and masochism is a function of their being rooted in the evasion of human beings qua consciousness in the flesh.

No human being is a subject alone, nor an object alone. It is even incorrect to say that a human being is "both." A human being is neither a subject nor an object but instead, in the language of Simone de Beauvoir and Merleau-Ponty, "ambiguous." This ambiguity is an expression of the human being as a meaningful, multifaceted way of being that may involve contradictory interpretations, or at least equivocal ones. Such ambiguity stands not as a dilemma to be resolved, as in the case of an equivocal sentence, but as a way of living to be described. The phenomenological task at hand is thus to draw out a hermeneutic of this ambiguity.

In the Africana experience this calls for description of the ways in which human ambiguity is manifested or evaded. As is well known, the procedure usually taken when it comes to studying blacks is that of evasion.[3]

II

A stark evasion manifests itself in the face of the black body. The black body lives in an antiblack world as a form of absence of human presence. Sartre and Frantz

72

GORDON

Fanon have identified this phenomenon as "overdetermination." In *Black Skin*, Fanon declares,

> I am overdetermined from outside. I am not the slave of the "idea" that others have of me but of my appearance. I move slowly in the world, accustomed to aspiring no longer to appear. I proceed by crawling. Already the white looks, the only true looks [*les seuls vrais*], are dissecting me. I am *fixed*. Having prepared their microtome, they slice away objectively pieces of my reality. I am disclosed. I feel, I see in those white looks that it is not a new man who enters, but a new type of man, a new genus. Why, a Negro! (Fanon [1952]: 93/[1967a]: 116)

Overdetermination transforms consciousness in the flesh into a thing, a form of being-in-itself. An ossified reality emerges. But this ossified reality is not on the level of ordinary sadism, where one's own invisibility is the project through an Other's visibility. To take such a route would entail a failure to appreciate the existential dimension of the black perspective on this phenomenon. In order to see the black as a thing requires the invisibility of a black's perspective. The situation is familiar, as we can see in Ralph Ellison's *Invisible Man*:

> I am an invisible man. No, I am not a spook like those who haunted Edgar Allan Poe; nor am I one of your Hollywood-movie ectoplasm. I am a man of substance, of flesh and bone, fiber and liquids—and I might even be said to possess a mind. I am invisible, understand, simply because people refuse to see me....That invisibility to which I refer occurs because of a peculiar disposition of the eyes of those with whom I come in contact. A matter of the construction of their inner eyes, those eyes with which they look through their physical eyes upon reality...(3)

73

The black body is confronted by the situation of its absence. A binary world is imposed upon it which functions as a constant source of evasion. Like Dostoyevsky's Underground Man, who exists in spite of logic, the black body finds itself existing in spite of Reason. "As the other said it, when I was there, it [Reason] was not; when it was there, I was no longer" (Fanon [1952]: 96/[1967a]: 119–120).

That black presence is absence and white presence is presence leads to a skewed logic. Rules that apply to white bodies, by virtue of a bad faith, substantiated identity of being-what-it-is, change when applied to black bodies in an antiblack world. Observe:

> An unusual clumsiness came upon me. The real world contested my place. In the white world the man of color encounters difficulties in the assimilation of his bodily schema. Consciousness of the body is a uniquely negating activity.

GORDON

> It is a third-person consciousness...Then the bodily schema, attacked from several points, collapses and gives way to a racial epidermal schema. In the train, it is no longer a matter of knowledge of my body in the third person, but in a triple person. In the train, instead of one, I am left with two, three places...(Fanon [1952]:89–90/[1967a]: 110–112).

The black body in situation faces more than DuBois' observation of a double soul. Fanon identifies three. And in *Women, Race, and Class*, Angela Y. Davis has identified at least four. The black body stands humanoid, colored, engendered, institutionalized. Deleuze and Guattari's body without organs is the black's nightmare of sealed exteriority epidermalized; there is *only* an outside. The fallacy is set in motion.

"How does it feel to be a problem?"

Whereas the white body lives a slippery spirit, by virtue of its institutional posture of sadism, the black body is sticky and easily caught. Antiblack racism problematizes blackness so as to evade black problems. For black problems are difficult problems for everybody. Four hundred-plus years of super exploitation are difficult to erase over night. So denial emerges on levels that are almost magical. *Presto!* Blacks disappear and so does responsibility for blackness. Consider Ralph Ellison's observation from *Shadow and Act* that

> Color prejudice springs not...from misinformation alone, but from an inner need to believe...Hence whatever else the Negro stereotype might be as a social instrumentality, it is also a key figure in a magic rite by which the white American seeks to resolve the dilemma arising between his democratic beliefs and certain antidemocratic practices, between his acceptance of the sacred democratic belief that all men are created equal and his treatment of every tenth man as though he were not. (28)

Let us consider two additional forms of invisibility that emerge from such inner need to believe. Black bodies take on peculiar forms of anonymity. Alfred Schutz speaks of anonymity as the mundane ability to stand for another in the realm of understanding.[4] Anonymity both wipes away and preserves the very notion of a private language and epistemological privilege. In this regard, anonymity is restricted to a form of universality of human presence, where the rules *qua* rules are expected to apply to all human beings. Implicit in anonymity, then, is its own limitation. There is a dialectic of a private life in virtue of a public life that is so mundane that it ceases to function as a general concern of any one else. When concern emerges, it is in terms of recognizing an individual's uniqueness, that although one can stand in another's place as a human being, one cannot stand in the place of another's life.

The logic of anonymity is, however, perverted in an antiblack world. If a black is overdetermined, then to see that black is to see every black. The black's individual life ceases to function as an object of epistemological, aesthetic, or moral concern. For although an empathetic dimension of anonymity disappears, a racially relative form of anonymity emerges. The black becomes an opportune, economic entity. One is led to believe, for instance, that one can "have blacks" by virtue of having that black, that anonymous black. The black representative emerges. One seeks out black leaders. Black novelists emerge as more than symbols of blackness; they become blackness on our shelves, our curricula, our mythology. We can stand as a society without responsibility for the blackness we exclude by way of the blackness we include, which we identify as blackness *in toto*. This is because a little bit of blackness is always too much blackness from the disease of overdetermination. Blackness in an antiblack world is always superfluous.

In addition to overdetermination, Fanon has described this superfluous dimension of antiblack "perception" of blackness as *phobogenic*. What this means is that the black body does not live on the symbolic level in an antiblack world. It is locked in the serious, material values of the real. Thus, whereas the white body can live a symbolic alienation rich with neurotic content and thereby serving as a foundation for psychoanalysis, the black body, whether in dream content or awake intentions, always stands for "what it is"—*the black*. The black therefore does not symbolize crime and licentious sexuality in an antiblack world. The black *is* crime and licentious sexuality, bestiality, in an antiblack world. That is why "Africa" means jungle and wild animals, in spite of rain forests and animal preserves comprising only a small portion of its ecology, and why Egypt and other supposedly "civilized" regions were severed from their African links.[5]

What psychoanalysis could not achieve, then, was an explanation of blacks in the world of dreams and even Jungian archetypical fantasy, for everywhere in the case of the former, the black has been structured as the material manifestation of evil, and everywhere in the case of the latter, the black has been negatively impacted by the growth of Europe. Psychoanalysis cannot therefore understand the black woman and the black man because both stand below the symbolic in the racist context of perverse anonymity: their alienation is not neurotic. It is the historical reality of a phobogenic complex. For psychoanalysis to be able to understand the black woman and the black man, the rapists in her dreams and the object of desire in his dreams must be psychosexual displacements of historical reality with an ultimate reference in family life—their father and mother. But racism and colonialism have left the matrices locked on a near historical-ontological schema. The black and the white in such a world are "real," and no amount of neurotic catharsis will in itself change the historical reality of their "place." The black woman and black man are therefore invisible beyond perverse anonymous subjects, Fanon argues, in psychoanalysis, whether Freudian, Jungian, Lacanian, and we may add today—Irigarayan.[6]

75

GORDON

The second form of invisibility turns inward and can be regarded as what we may call "a black *thang.*" We return to Fanon for our example. He declares, "We knew [a] black girl who had a list of Parisian dance-halls 'where-there-is-no-risk-of-encountering-niggers'" (Fanon [1952]: 40/[1967a]: 50). Among blacks the phenomenon is familiar. Imagine this black woman going to a cocktail party in which she is the only black person. She looks around and is comforted by the sight of whiteness. Let us say that these white people continue to behave in a seemingly mundane manner. The situation is seductive. Seduction is an effort to get what we want by permitting another to be responsible for it. The seducer assures us of the world we claim to want while giving us the world we desire. This assurance is a mirrored unreality. Jean Baudrillard agrees when he writes that

> "*I'll be your mirror*" does not signify "I'll be your reflection" but "I'll be your deception."…*To seduce is to die as reality and reconstitute oneself as illusion…* Narcissus too loses himself in his own illusory image; that is why he turns from his truth, and by his example turns others from their truth… (Baudrillard: 69).

We return to the cocktail party. What truth is this black turned from when she looks around her? In Schutzean language, let us synchronize ourselves with this meaning-context.

The whites: "There is nothing abnormal here. This is how we behave when there are only whites at a party."

The black: "Gee, they are acting as though there is nothing abnormal about my being here. They don't notice me. They must be behaving the way they do when there are only whites in the room. They are not rejecting me as one of them. I must *be* one of them. I am white."

Liberated, she thinks, from the burden of blackness, our black lives her (false) whiteness. She tells jokes, she speaks of other white friends, there is laughter, the white masks encircle her, and in their face she sees her own white skin; the pink flesh clasps glasses, tugs at the shoulder to meet other guests, the others become symmetrical, in an intoxicating dance of I-thou—until the door opens and a black stranger looks around for a moment and *locates* our black. The black stranger smiles, waves, or takes that black look of *acknowledgment.*

Translation?

The whites (to our black): "We'll be your mirror."

The other black (to our black): "I *am* your mirror."

On two levels, then, the dialectic is set in motion against the black body. Problematized, it faces what Fanon calls de-negrification. Its task is to disappear. It is difficult to maintain the illusion of seeing-without-seeing. No greater evasion of the flesh promises more certainty than its extermination. But in the meantime, this extermination is role-played, and it is psychically and socio-politically structured with oblique sight. Born of evasion, it evades every effort at identification.

We have learned many ways of evading race. For instance, Cornel West says that race matters in the midst of his discussion of contemporary race matters. The contemporary antiblack racist self-righteously responds,

"Is it more so than gender? Isn't class division the real problem?"

Blacks are oppressed by the weight of overdetermination.

"But I didn't personally victimize any black people."

Blacks are racially discriminated against in the work force.

"But unqualified people shouldn't be hired over qualified ones."

Blacks with excellent credentials are passed over in the work force.

"But whites with excellent credentials are passed over too in favor of blacks."

There is hostility to black presence in the United States and the United Kingdom.

"But there are blacks who don't like white people, as well as other colored people. Look at that black racist who injured and killed all those people on the Long Island Railroad."

Blacks are marked by inferiority everywhere.

"Now, now, that is generalizing a U.S. disease. We treat our blacks very differently. In fact, we downright valorize them. That's why U.S. blacks are usually happier here—in Europe—or here, in Latin America."

Fanon is nauseated. "From all sides tens and hundreds of pages assail me and impose themselves on me," he writes. "Still," he continues, "a single line would be enough. Supply a single answer and the black problem will lose its seriousness. What do human beings want? What do blacks want?"[7]

Fanon's initial response was to dream of walking into a sea of mundanity, anonymously situated as whites are among whites, but the existential dimension of his response, the formulation of humanity in terms of desire, suggests another possibility. To want at all, to desire at all, is to be a human being. To desire in bad faith is to want to be a free substance—God—which in an antiblack world amounts to being white.

But to desire in critical good faith is to reach out to humanity, to resist closure, to fight against sado-masochistic substantiation. But the query of desire is a trap, is it not? For who is ever really satisfied with getting what she or he wants?

Does the antiblack racist really want to know what blacks want?

"What do blacks want?"

Decoded, it is a variation of,

"What can I do to make them shut up?"

What does the black want?

Ask a black woman.

Ask a black man.

Ask a black child.

Ask a thousand, a million, a billion blacks, and perhaps at some point along the way the error will be realized.

GORDON

III

There is a great deal of work to be done on the problem of understanding race and racism.[8] In the black context, which is in fact many cultural contexts, it should be clear that there is no chance of coming to any level of understanding without realizing the factors at work in their invisibility as subjects of human study. It is political reality that black people are not the primary players in their ossification as objects of a sadistic political gaze, so it would be problematic to construct them as masochistic, even though there certainly are masochistic antiblack situations in which masochism emerges, as we have seen in our cocktail party example. The question that remains is the degree to which those of us who seek to understand black people also bear in mind that black people are human beings. This was certainly W.E.B. Du Bois' realization while conducting his *Philadelphia Negro* and his criterion of studying the problems faced by people of African descent instead of studying them as the problems themselves. But for a hermeneutic of Africana reality, as well as the more broad *black* reality, the problem as problematization needs interpretation. In this regard, the existential phenomenological rejection of a nature and insistence on human reality's ability to live on the level of a false, binary reality of sadistic subject and masochistic object are helpful. Their implications are only hinted at here. But it should be clear that their development warrants further study.

NOTES

1 All of the translations of Fanon's work are mine. Citations refer to page numbers in the French and English editions, separated by a slash.

2 The focus on Fanon and Sartre is primarily due to my having written full-length treatments of their work. See Gordon (1995a) and (1995b). A list that emphasizes the existential more than the phenomenological dimensions can, however, be broadened to include obvious figures like Richard Wright and, in the 19th century, Anna Julia Cooper, as I have demonstrated in the introduction to this anthology.

3 Today this evasion is particularly acute in the desire to "decenter" blacks in race discourse; see Omi and Winant and my criticism of the "racial formation" turn (Gordon [1995e]), where I argue that Omi and Winant confuse social constructivity (which is an ontological claim about reference) with racial meaning (which pertains to the concept of race and a claim about sense).

4 See all of the Schutz references in the bibliography and Natanson (1986) and Gordon (1995b): chap. 3.

5 For a full-scale discussion of the African question, see Shaw, et al, and for the "Western Civilization" question, see the controversial Bernal. A great deal of the controversy over the latter stemmed from obvious phobogenic dimensions of Classical Scholarship. Bernal was demonstrating, as Fanon would say, something like Rodin's *The Thinker*—with an erection.

6 For discussion of Luce Irigaray and race, see Patricia Huntington (this volume, below).

GORDON

7 I have translated this passage from Fanon's Introduction to *Black Skin* in the plural because of the generality of the definite article in the French and the problem of its specificity in English. Here is the original French:

Que veut l'homme?

Que veut l'hommme noir?

The last two questions can also be translated, "What does man want? What does black man want?" Fanon is clearly here speaking of the Manichaeanism of separating human kind into separate *species* of a new genus—"Man."

8 For those who are in doubt, see Rose and Ross: 1–52.

THE "SITUATION"

part II

RETURN FROM THE UNITED STATES

Jean-Paul Sartre
translated with comparative notes on the problem in 1995[1]
by T. Denean Sharpley-Whiting

SOMEONE TOLD me: "If you are not a United States citizen, do not broach the subject of the black problem: you risk wounding your listeners with reflections that you will judge the most innocent; besides, even if you prove tactful, you will give the impression that you are meddling, without being invited, in a family quarrel."

I have spoken of it, however, and I write of it today. First and foremost, this issue, which one was perhaps able to avoid twenty years ago, has become, for America, a national problem whose continued struggle increases its urgency. Second, I have encountered here a new nationalism; when I am bothered by the fate of blacks, nearly all Americans change the conversation, they hasten to provide me with information, they go out of their way to put me in contact with specialists on black problems with blacks.[2]

In this country, deservedly proud of its democratic institutions, one man out of ten is deprived of his political rights; in this land of equality and liberty live 13 million untouchables.[3] This is fact. These untouchables, you cross them in the streets at all hours of the day, but you do not return their stares. Or if by chance their eyes meet yours, it seems to you that they do not see you and it is better for them and you that you pretend not to have noticed them. They serve you at the table, they shine your shoes, they operate your elevators, they carry your suitcases, but they are not your business, and nor or you theirs; their business is with the elevators, suitcases, shoes; they attend their tasks like machines, and you pay no more attention to them than as if they were machines. Not one of their words, not one of their gestures, not one of their smiles are destined for you; it is dangerous for you to go out in the evenings in quarters that are reserved for them; if you were to stop in passing, if you were to bear them some interests, you would unpleasantly stun them and you would risk displeasing all the other (white) Americans. These thirteen million men, who slip by your sides like shadows, are no longer slaves. More than a half century ago, the United States freed their grandparents. They are not all necessarily from the laboring class, yet the majority of them live in horrible misery; some are lawyers, doctors, professors, some manage major newspapers, but their recent fortune does not confer upon them any rights; they count as much as the elevator boy in the eyes of whites. They refer to themselves as "third-class citizens." They are the blacks. Do not call them "niggers": you will insult them. They prefer the expression "man of color" which is from official use or that of "brown American," which flatters them, or, if need be, "Negro." Besides, it isn't necessary for them to present themselves as our great Negro athletes from the Sudan or from the Congo: they form a particular race. Some slave traders brought them here during the course of centuries passed from all the regions of West Africa; unions were made during the course of the slave trade, and this produced an enormous mix of African races. There was also frequent mixing with Native Americans and even Chinese. And it was of such common practice for plantation owners to take black slaves as mistresses that hardly a quarter of American Negroes are of pure African descent. The colored man is thus a specifically American product (and he is conscious of such).[4] It is only in Brazil that one would find analogous mixings.

Some have claimed to find among these Negroes common characteristics: it is possible; but at first glance, they offer extreme diversity. Some are big, some small, some white or nearly—whose origin uniquely manifest itself through the white marks which appear under their nails[5]—some are yellow, some brown, and even black. Some are athletic with round faces and flat noses and some others are frail with horse-like faces and long sinewy noses. The one characteristic that they have in common is the treatment to which they are subjected. Again it is appropriate to make a fundamental distinction. At the end of the last century, blacks were dispersed within eight Southern states; the Northeast was unknown to them. But during the war of 1914–18, migration towards the North began. It has since continued and the present war has accelerated it. Today, 77 percent of blacks still live in the South and 21.7 percent in the North. There are 460,000 blacks in New York; 300,000 in Chicago; 250,000 in Philadelphia; 190,000 in Washington, DC; 150,000 in Detroit, etc.[6] And their circumstances are especially different depending upon whether they live within the regions of the South or within the industrial agglomerations of the North.

In the South, they make up essentially a rural proletariat. Sixty-four percent of the total black population of the United States is employed in agricultural or domestic spheres.[7] Ninety percent of blacks from the South have an insufficient income of $1,000 while the annual minimum is around $2,000.[8] Indebted, contracted to the land through virtual force by the farmers, who are their creditors, they have not gained much in freedom.[9] Everywhere in the South they practice "segregation": there is not one public place where one sees blacks and whites mixing together. The access to theaters, restaurants, cinemas, libraries, swimming pools, etc. frequented by whites are forbidden to blacks. On the railroads and the tramways, they have separate places; they have their churches and their schools, poorer and fewer than white schools; even in the factories, they often work in separate locations. These pariahs are entirely deprived of political rights. Undoubtedly the 15th amendment of the Constitution foresees that "the right of citizens of the United States to vote will not be deprived, nor refused by the United States or by one of the States because of race, of color, or past servile conditions." But there are thousands of ways to twist it. First, there is the "poll tax." In several Southern states, voters must present a receipt indicating that they have paid electoral tax. Showing it is the minimum: one dollar or two; in any case one cannot consider it as a qualification for the vote. Its sole function is in fact to qualify the voter because it is cumulative, that is, it is due retroactively for past elections. At once, it is raised quickly for blacks to 15 or 20 dollars, a sum that they never have. There are other measures: in order to have access to the voting booths in Louisiana, it is necessary to prove sufficient knowledge of the Constitution; naturally the proceeding examination is conducted in such a manner as to eliminate Negroes. On the other hand, the Democratic Party does not accept blacks among its members; this is a strict right and the Federal government cannot intervene. Besides this party is virtually the only one in the Southern states; the important vote does not take place on the day officially fixed, but several months before in the "primaries," the first assembly meetings where the members of the party designate their candidate. As blacks are excluded, this amounts practically to denying them the right to vote. In 1942, at the occasion of the legislative elections, one could appreciate the results of this politic. If one compares the vote from eight Southern states with those of eight Northern states of equal population, one recognizes that in the North for one population of 23,941,368 persons, 8 million voters elected 79 deputies. In the South, at the same moment, and for a population of 23,997,909, seventy-nine deputies were elected by 829,000 voters. When ten men vote in the North, one alone votes

85

in the South. In the North, the condition of blacks is better. They vote; segregation is less strict and less visible. They have access to all the seats on the railroad, to all the compartments on the subway, to certain theaters and restaurants which the whites frequent; there are mixed schools. They are less-skilled workers, semiskilled and sometimes even skilled workers. In many of the large industries—but not all—blacks and whites receive the same salary for the same job. Only 40 percent of blacks from the North have an inferior annual income of $1,000.[10] But again it is rare that they rise very high: two out of five whites and two out of thirty blacks are among those that one calls here "white-collar workers."[11] Moreover, segregation, if it is less seen, has some effects one hundred times more disagreeable, for it is exercised in the domain of housing.[12] Originally, when a Negro succeeds in moving into a building, whites desert the entire block.[13] As well, in many Northern cities, local associations of landlords are formed whose members pledge never to accept black tenants. In Chicago, for example, 60 to 80 percent of landlords join this association. Those who are not members own dilapidated buildings in the quarters that whites have abandoned: they rent their slums at incredibly elevated prices and blacks must crowd themselves here in deplorable hygienic conditions. I have seen the famous black quarter of Chicago where 300,000 blacks are forced to live when this area can barely accommodate half of them. Within these deteriorating buildings, which preserve from the outside under the filth, a vague air of pretentious elegance, live two, three, and up to six families per floor. Further up on the side streets, in wooden shanties surrounded by piles of refuse, without windows, sometimes without roofs, 20 to 30 people live. Here, a black family lives underground, in a basement deprived of water, air and light. Elsewhere the steps are collapsed. The tenants access their floors by an exterior fire escape. These wretched people pay as much for these miserable living quarters as a white worker pays for clean and ventilated housing with electricity, running water, and bathrooms. The merchants—black and white—who set up their businesses in these reserved quarters sell their foodstuffs and basic necessities at higher prices than elsewhere. The housekeeper of a well-to-do American woman in Chicago does her shopping in the rich quarters at the same time she does her patron's because the prices are significantly less for those same products sold in the Negro quarter. Thus, even at an equal salary, the money does not have the same value for blacks and whites. All of this takes place as if blacks receive dollars which are devalued. In these conditions, it goes without saying that they are the prey of illnesses. Promiscuity in these overpopulated regions has had as a result a frightening increase in the proportions of cases of syphilis;[14] tuberculosis exacts its toll.[15] Moreover, the black region of Chicago is infested with rats which are, as one knows, the vehicles of epidemics. Also, the infant mortality rate is 73 out of 1,000 for blacks versus 40 out 1,000 for whites; on average a black dies 10 years earlier than a white.[16] And since one includes in these averages Southern blacks who live in the country in clearly better hygienic conditions, one can imagine the black mortality rate in Chicago or

Detroit. It has gotten so out of hand that many Southern black leaders try to check the exodus of their brothers to the North; what does it matter that they are better treated there, better paid, that their children receive a superior education, if the very vitality of the race must suffer? To an emancipation too rapid which puts the very existence of black people in danger, they prefer still the semislavery of the South.

Such is the situation today of the black population of the United States. It is tragic. But it would be all in fact unjust to predict the future in the development of America according to the current state of affairs. Without a doubt, there still exists here some considerable forces that militate against the improvement of the fate of Negroes. And above all, there is an almost inextricable state of affairs resulting from the suppression of slavery and the economic structure of the country. And it is that which one must examine first. But as of late, the black problem, partly because of the growth of the black population, partly because of the war, has assumed such an urgency and acuteness that it is no longer possible to ignore it: it has become a national problem, the unity of the American nation is at stake.

It is easy enough to understand the causes of the ills, much easier than to remedy them. In Baltimore, someone told me, "The black problem is solely one of feelings. It is that which renders it unresolvable." And this is the impression that I have received from my first contacts in the South with the white population. I spoke leisurely with a doctor from Louisiana. A big, pale courteous man, very competent in all that pertains to his trade. On the subject of international politics, on the relations of France and America, on American literature, he responded to me with much intelligence and broad-mindedness. When we entered upon the subject of the black problem, all changed. A little time before, the Red Cross asked for blood donors. The walls everywhere are still covered with posters of a considerable and admirable effort, urging civilians to give blood for the soldiers. In order to meet the most pressing needs, they had first envisioned accepting blood from black donors in the same way as the others. Immediately, the negrophobic press launched a furious campaign expressing their objection.

"You, who are a doctor," said I to my interlocutor, "you do not believe, however, that the blood of blacks has some specific qualities?"

He shrugged his shoulders: "There are three blood types," he responded to me, "which one finds nearly equally in blacks and whites."

"Well?"

"It is not safe for black blood to circulate in our veins."

87

NOTE

1 Sartre's discussion here was originally entitled, "*Retour des Etats Unis: Ce qui j'ai appris du problème noir.*" It appeared in *Le Figaro* (16 June 1945), on page 2. Sartre arrived in the United States for the first time on the January 12, 1945, in New York City. He stayed approximately four months. The article, thick with sarcasm and criticisms of U.S. antiblack racism, is also interspersed with the Sartrean concept of *bad faith*. For a systematic discussion of that concept and its relation to antiblack racism, see Gordon (1995b). All notes are comments by the translator.

2 While the problems of U.S. blacks are an American problem, Sartre emphasizes the fact that white Americans regard the problems of blacks as other blacks; thus, blacks themselves are regarded as the problem.

3 In 1995, the U.S. black population was 33,118,000. By the year 2000, the projected population will be 35,475,000 and in 2010, the population is expected to increase to 40,227,000 (*U.S. Bureau of the Census, Current Population Reports*). These figures include only those who are designated blacks by the Census or who designate themselves as such, and not necessarily all peoples of African descent, nor those who may be "passing."

4 Although this article was written for a general audience, and some readers might consider Sartre to be "dabbling" or "meddling" in the affairs of U.S. blacks without a thorough understanding of the U.S. institution of slavery and black Americans, such readers are encouraged to consult the seventeen-page analysis of the oppression of U.S. blacks in Appendix II of Sartre (1982). See also bibliography for Sartre's discussions of blacks.

5 These white marks often appear where the nail meets the bed. Here Sartre is ridiculing the physical racial stereotyping by white Americans.

6 Sartre's assertion is true for the most part. There were nonetheless a small percentage of blacks in the Northeast. As of 1990, 21 percent of blacks lived in the Northeast; 26 percent in the Midwest, 32.8 percent in the South, and 20 percent in the West. Indeed, the black population is still heavily concentrated in the Southern regions of the U.S. (U.S. Bureau of the Census, *1990 Census Population, General Population Characteristics, United States*).

7 Due to gains in education and affirmative action, blacks now make up 9.5 percent of the agricultural labor market, 7.0 percent are employed as farmers. However, 17.3 percent of the black population are employed in the service occupations (such as janitors, domestics, etc). Of this number, 17.1 percent work in private households as domestics and 21.6 percent work as servants or cleaners (*Statistical Abstract of the United States 1994*).

8 As of 1993, 33.1 percent of black families lived below the poverty line compared with 9.9 percent of white families. Eleven percent of white individuals lived below the poverty line compared to 33.3 percent of black individuals.

9 Here Sartre is talking about sharecropping.

10 In 1993, the median income for black families was $21,161, while white families earned $38,909. Black families median income was 54.8 percent of white families (U.S. Bureau of the Census).

11 Ten and two-tenths percent of blacks are in managerial or professional occupations.

12 According to the *Federal Financial Institutions Council*, in 1993, thirty-four percent of mortgage applications filed by blacks were denied versus 15 percent for whites.

13 This phenomenon has been dubbed "white flight." According to William Julius Wilson (1987), there was also a black middle-class flight from the inner cities to the suburbs between 1979 and 1980, which exacerbated the depressed conditions of the inner city.

14 Sartre was visiting the U.S. during the infamous 40-year Tuskegee Syphilis Study (1932–72). His information was provided by U.S. public health officials and medical practitioners whose theories and studies of blacks were conducted and constructed in such a way as to represent blacks as a syphilis-soaked race whose promiscuity leads to disease. For more on this, see Jones (1981).

15 The ravages of tuberculosis have since declined. AIDS (Acquired Immune Deficiency Syndrome) as of 1992 disproportionately affects blacks at a rate of 34.9 percent (U.S. Center for Disease Control and Prevention, Atlanta, GA). Blacks are equally disproportionately the victims of violent crimes with a homicide rate of 72 percent for black men versus 9.3 percent for white men and 14.2 percent for black women versus 3 percent for white women as of 1991 (U.S. National Center for Health Statistics, *Vital Statistics of the United States*).

16 Mortality rate for black infants is 17.6 percent versus 7.3 percent for white infants. The mortality rate for blacks has improved. On average, blacks die 6.7 years earlier than whites. Life expectancy for blacks is 70.3 versus 77 for whites. Out of all races and genders, black men have a life expectancy of 65.8 versus 73.8 for white men, 80.3 for white women and 74.8 for black women.

89

WHITE NORMATIVITY AND THE RACIAL RHETORIC OF EQUAL PROTECTION

Robert Westley

That Jewish community which is based neither on nation, land, religion—at least not in contemporary France—nor material interest, but only on an identity of situation, might indeed be a true spiritual bond of affection, of culture, and of mutual aid. But the Jew's enemies will immediately say that this bond is ethnic, and he himself, at a loss how to designate it, will perhaps use the word race. Then at one stroke he has justified the anti-Semite: "You see very well that there is a Jewish race; they recognize it themselves, and besides they crowd together everywhere." And, in fact, if the Jews want to draw a legitimate pride from this community, they must indeed end up by exalting racial qualities, since they cannot take pride in any collective work that is specifically Jewish, or in a civilization properly Jewish, or in a common mysticism.

—JEAN-PAUL SARTRE

chapter 6

IN THE above quoted passage from *Anti-Semite and Jew*, Sartre reminds us that the Jewish experience of racism in Europe is not far different from the black experience of racism in the U.S. Especially with respect to self-understanding and social perceptions, blacks are a "race" and hence *racialized*. The racialization of Jews in Europe permitted those not subject to a racial social perception—in this case, the French—to constitute themselves as a norm, as "true" Frenchmen. *Anti-Semite and Jew* reminds us of the normativity at center of racial ideology. To the extent that the dominant group escapes racial or ethnic identification, it is free to act as a value-free norm for the rest of society. The black community is a racial community in the sense that Jews are considered to be "ethnic" or a "race" by the anti-Semite. Or, as Omi and Winant might say, the black "situation" is the current "articulation" of racial ideology in America.

My understanding of "race" adopts the perspective first formulated by Omi and Winant as the theory of racial formation. In *Racial Formation in the United States*, Omi and Winant show that the "social-constructedness" of "race" may be grasped by examination of the various paradigms through which "race" has historically traveled, forming at each phase the "racial" common sense in policy determinations about "race" relations.

In their view, there are three paradigms, ethnicity, class, and nation, that have served in the 20th century as major theoretical constructs for situated communities attempting to understand and (re)articulate the significance of "race." By examining the process through which commonsense understandings of race are rearticulated concurrently with social transformation, Omi and Winant reveal the way in which racial meanings and racial identities are not static, but are *transformed* over time.

The argument of this paper is that current hegemonic interpretations of equal protection have led to the racialization of white Americans in a historically unprecedented way. In other words, the equal protection rhetoric that places affirmative action in jeopardy and questions its constitutionality, concurrently displaces whiteness from a position of normativity by racializing it. In order to sustain the thesis of so-called "reverse (racial) discrimination," white Americans must be seen as constituting a racial community in an analogous sense as, but the polar opposite of, the black community. White people are a "race" in contradistinction to the black "race," in particular, and other "races" generally. But whiteness has always been seen as a norm constitutive of full humanity and thus permits a degree of individualism that substantive racial identification negates.

The transformation of whiteness from a position of normativity to the racial margin, however, is merely doctrinal. White normativity persists, rearticulated as a social ideal of colorblindness and equality of opportunity. Moreover, because of the persistence of even racialized white normativity, state racial policy, under the banner of colorblindness and equality of opportunity, can now be formulated without appearing to be *racial* at all.

Omi and Winant identify three paradigms of race that at various points during the twentieth century have claimed a counter-hegemonic function in relation to prior conceptualizations of race. According to the theory of racial formation, class-based theory, nation-based theory, and ethnicity-based theory represent the three most general and distinct attempts to distill American "common sense" about race in a manner consistent with the formal post-bellum requirement of equal black citizenship and personhood. These paradigms of race were responsive to yet an earlier paradigm of race—"biologism"—which originally served as justification for racial ideology.

THE BIOLOGISITIC PARADIGM

The roots of racial thinking in natural science is a phenomenon seldom examined. However, the importance of understanding the early career of "race" as a biological concept consists in the fact that racial paradigms do not simply disappear once a new paradigm is introduced. Although "race" has come to be regarded in academic circles as a "preeminently *sociohistorical* concept" (Omi and Winant: 60, n2), race is still commonly "seen" as a *natural* category.[1] In American society, "race" is perceived just as often phenotypically, as it is determined and understood "culturally" or by descent.

In his monumental work, *White Over Black*, Winthrop Jordan characterizes the early "scientific" conception of "race" as an allegory about the nature of man that also functioned "as a means of expressing the social distance between the Negro and the white man" (239). Eighteenth-century scientific theorists, under the not inconsiderable influence of Christian doctrine, hypothesized that all men descended from a common ancestor (Adam and Eve, as Genesis taught), and that "species" were fixed in number and kind (also in line with the Genesis creation myth). This scientific framework tended to negate the association of Africans with beasts that had already been popularized in travel literature generated by explorations overseas begun in the fifteenth century (Jordan: 216).

The idea of the Great Chain of Being, typically associated with Linnaean descriptive classification,[2] introduced the notion that all things, from the inanimate objects, to the lowliest forms of life, to more intelligent animals, to man, to the myriad heavenly creatures, to God, formed a synthetic unity. It also introduced the notion of natural hierarchy and natural order. Crucial to the future fate of social as well as scientific perceptions of the African, Linneaus classified man on the same order as simians (Linneaus: 218).

While Linneaus did not intentionally impose hierarchy on his classifications of the varieties of men, his intellectual scion, Johann Blumenbach, considered white men to be the primeval type of man, and many other natural philosophers used their classifying schemes to advance the belief that "Caucasians" were "superior to the other kinds of men." As Jordan notes, "It is clear that when Europeans set about to rank the varieties of men, their decision that the Negro was at the bottom and the white man at the top was not dictated solely by the facts of human biology" (Jordan: 226).

Hierarchy itself requires some normative standard in order to discriminate high from low, base from superior. The idea of the Great Chain of Being, as a universalized principle of hierarchy, operated within the developing "natural" sciences programmatically as a *will to distinguish and rank difference*. What is not obvious is why color, physiognomy, or anatomy should have been chosen as signs of developmental distinction.

Moreover, it is unclear why European intellectuals would have concluded that white skin was normal and healthy, while black skin was abnormal and diseased; or

93

WESTLEY

that large human skulls and pointed noses were a sign of advanced development, while smaller skulls and flat noses were primitive; or that small sexual organs were more "human" than large ones.

Perhaps no interpretation beyond the unself-conscious parochialism of the age is required. But it must be recalled, such "scientific" determinations were propounded during what historians have called the Age of Reason and Enlightenment. And, it should also be recalled that the scaling of bodies took place in discourses that gave these determinations the stamp of scientific authority, and the imprimatur of a universal natural order of things.[3]

The concept of "race" was formed in the crucible of scientific speculation in an age marked by encroaching secularism, advancing nationalism, and a seemingly obsessive interest in imposing rational order on the chaos of new discoveries (see Anderson; Arendt [1963]). European man was anxious about his place in the natural order of things, and his cultural heritage had disposed him to find order in patriarchical structures. Unfortunately for the African, blackness was seen as being the extreme opposite of whiteness on a spectrum of humanity that was not horizontal but vertical. Racial ideology, under the biologistic paradigm, pronounced black men closer to beasts and *naturally* inferior to white men, just as "man" in the Great Chain of Being was subordinate to God (see Gordon [1995a] and [1995e]).

Questions therefore persisted among intellectuals about whether the African had derived from a union with apes, the animal seen to be highest on the chain below man (Gilman: 231). Would not such a union explain the prognathism of West Africans, their frightful color, their low culture and stunted intellectual development, their libidinous practices and shocking lack of modesty by European standards, their primitivism, their savagery? Was not Africa a "dark continent" filled with strange monsters and unnatural acts? (JanMohamed; Freud: Vol. 20, 212; and Jefferson [1784–85]).

While such questions posed working problems for natural scientists and philosophers, they were not posed in critical isolation from other discursive fields of inquiry or practice. Natural science itself, in the process of problematization of the body, was only beginning to discover its own disciplinary divisions. The lines between *natural* science and *social* science, far from being sharply drawn, were quite indistinct. Men of opinion, which included natural scientists themselves, had views about the cultural development and political rights of the African that seemed to be authorized by the biological degradation of the Negro. Cultural critique went hand in hand with the pseudoscience that made blacks the natural inferiors of whites. As JanMohamed argues, "a profound symbiotic relationship [exists] between the discursive and the material practices of imperialism," to which, of course, Africa was increasingly subjected (JanMohamed: 83).

Throughout much of western history, cultural critique and analysis proceeded from the assumption that culture is a closed system of meanings and practices for discrete groups. In *Reason in History*, Hegel expresses a view of culture as based on a hierarchy in which the European experience was dominant. He thus introduces into the field of ethnological theory the notion of "high" and "low" culture. He asserts, "Such peoples of weak culture lose themselves more and more in contact with peoples of higher culture and more intensive cultural training" (Hegel [1955]: 200–201). Hegel's views on culture were neither original nor idiosyncratic. They were generally shared among the privileged classes of Europe, imperial administrators, colonial bureaucrats and merchants, and informed the writings of other influential philosophers. In this way, the discourse of natural science and philosophy provided a rationalized text for the support of ethnocentrism and racism. The transition of thought by which the body came under the scrutiny of science, accompanied by two interrelated phenomena of nationalism and imperialism, made racism an ordinary feature of social institutions (see Harwood and Banton: 1; Fanon [1967b]; Gordon [1995b]). As Sander Gilman explains, if their sexual parts could be shown to be inherently different, this would be a sufficient sign that the blacks were a separate (and, needless to say, lower) race, as different from the European as the proverbial orangutan (Gilman: 235, n15).

Racism thus begins as a "naturalized" social science of the body, which is, at the same time, an allegory about the nature of man. The scientific assertion that populations may usefully be categorized according to the race concept has always been accompanied by the prejudice of white superiority and black inferiority. This is called the "natural (biological) inequality of the races." This notion has been politically discredited.[4] But the assumptions about "race" which underlie the allegory continue to operate alongside of more current articulations of race as ethnicity, class or nation.

95

EQUALITY RHETORIC

One purpose behind the periodizing paradigms is to help explain historical developments that have been crucial to the (in)ability of blacks to articulate an emancipatory rhetoric. Under the various formulations of the truth about race since the demise of biologism, race has typically been denied theoretical primacy. It is subsumed under purportedly more fundamental categories and then assimilated to putatively more basic social dynamics.

After women, blacks, as a social and cultural group, are most closely associated with their bodies. In a society that is generally marked by its adherence to a mind/body dualism in which the mind is privileged and the body devalued, association with one's body is of particular concern. As Young points out, "The experience of racial oppression entails in part existing as a group defined as having ugly bodies, and being feared, avoided or hated on that account" (123). The association of blacks with their bodies, in my view, is an inescapable dynamic (see also Fanon [1967a] and Gordon [1995a]).

The governing trope of black (and minority) identity is race. Whether that trope is articulated as ethnicity, class, or nation, race is the socially constructed truth about

WESTLEY

who black people are. Black people are race people. In the racial rhetoric of equal protection, race is the metanarrative of blackness. White identity, on the other hand, is only racial by contrast to social perceptions of black and minority people, on a scale of humanity that is vertical, not horizontal. This is the reason, for instance, that white political engagement is regarded as (normal) politics, and black political engagement is considered "racial politics."

Antidiscrimination law accepts the view that populations can usefully be organized under the race concept. The role of law in a society divided according to race is to prohibit the state use of the category of race in assignment of benefits and burdens. This is the distributive side of justice. Justice for so-called "racial" minorities becomes a question of fair distribution of benefits and burdens under the law *regardless of race*.

Since race is a hierarchically ordered metanarrative of black identity, the antidiscrimination approach functions as a rotation of the axis of race relations, from vertical to horizontal. A central problem with this approach is that it assumes the truth of a false premise: No one is "discriminated against" or oppressed *because of race*. Race, simply, does not exist as a biological fact. From a scientific point of view, there is no defense for the coherency of the race concept (Appiah [1985] and [1992]), and certainly no justification for the belief that the so-called "white race" is superior to the so-called "black race." The antidiscrimination principle, therefore, under which black people must seek protection from oppression of their embodiment, depends on a racist vision of humanity that can find no sanction in modern biological science.

If, on the other hand, one wishes to uphold the use of "race" as a social fact,[5] a social construct that facilitates the discussion of differences between peoples in language, moral affections, aesthetic attitudes, morphology, melanin content, political ideology, national and ethnic origin, and so forth—those differences which, in Professor Appiah's words, "most deeply affect us in our dealings with each other" (Appiah [1985]: 22, n28)—then the antidiscrimination approach faces a different set of problems.

Detached from its bioligistic moorings, "race" has become, from a scientific standpoint, a floating signifier, gathering meaning and momentum over time in ways that are difficult to predict, impossible to tether, resistant to rationalization. "Race," in such usage, functions as a mere metonym of "group that has some importance for some community of persons." It would then be fair to speak of "the Democratic race," or "the Republican race," just as we once spoke (and some still do) of "the German race" or "the French race." In some more progressive environments, it may become acceptable usage to speak of "the disabled race," or "the elderly race," or "the homeless race," etc.

From the standpoint of antidiscrimination law, this is a problem—not because the homeless, the elderly, or the disabled do not need or deserve protection against discrimination. One may legitimately entertain doubts about the Democrats and

Republicans. It is a problem because the type of protection needed may not indeed be "race" protection.

Rather, I suggest that the protection that all oppressed people need and deserve is assistance in the struggle against institutional conditions which inhibit or prevent them from participating in determining their actions or the conditions of their actions (Young [1990]). Recognizing, as I do, the unique experience of black people with racial oppression, on balance, I believe that my analysis of the problem applies *a fortiori*. "Race" is not oppressed in American society. Black people are oppressed. Native Americans are oppressed. Chicanos are oppressed. People of color are oppressed.

And yet, the equal protection rhetoric that places affirmative action in jeopardy and questions its constitutionality, concurrently displaces whiteness from a position of normativity by racializing it. The doctrine of suspect categories, upon which the application of "strict scrutiny" (equal protection) review is based, is a racial rhetoric. "Race" is a suspect classification. This gives standing to white Americans, as racial subjects, to challenge affirmative action, or any other remedy, that favors blacks and other oppressed minority groups, as a form of racial discrimination. Racial ideology, as articulated in the Supreme Court's most recent state affirmative action decision, (*Richmond* v. *Croson* [1989]),[6] requires that the white subject be considered racial in an analogous sense as, but the polar opposite of, the black subject. Such a characterization is certainly unprecedented. White normativity, that is to say dominance, has always been presumed in racializing discourse.

White racial identity, prior to the shift in consciousness that current equal protection appears to effect, has been more *contrastive* than *substantive*. White people are a "race" in contradistinction to the black "race," in particular, and other "races" generally. But whiteness is presumed to be a norm constitutive of full humanity, and thus permits a degree of individualism that substantive racial identification negates. Moreover, whiteness remains a privileged status in America.

Displacement of the white subject from a position of normativity to the racial margin is merely doctrinal. It authorizes the treatment of race as a species of the more egalitarian concept of ethnicity by negating genuinely racial aspects of the social order. In doing so, the racial rhetoric of equal protection symbolizes racial reform. White supremacy is repudiated as a matter of state policy, and white Americans are encouraged to adopt a consciousness appropriate to an egalitarian racial stance. But crucially, racial identification itself, under the doctrine of suspect categories, escapes criticism. Race is the truth of black/white, minority/majority relations, although for all practical purposes, it is only the minority, only black people, who are subject to social perceptions and self-understandings that are racial.

Rotation of the axis of race relations, thus, operates as both an affirmation of black and white civil equality, and a denial (indeed, annihilation) of black humanity. Inasmuch as the hierarchical racial social order mirrors accumulated material and power inequalities, refusing to acknowledge the normativity of whiteness as a

97

WESTLEY

matter of policy, is a refusal of black social justice claims as an oppressed people. When the law says "regardless of race," it seems to promote an ideal of individual freedom and human dignity. It does. But it also says that there are races. It also says that races are equal, and should be treated equally. These articulations already fail to escape the discourse of domination inherent in racial ideology.

But if the law should further insist that the races are treated equally by treating them as if they are the same, that is, by negating the normativity of whiteness, dominance is reconstituted. The malingering inequities of a hierarchical racial social order, rendered invisible by a facile egalitarianism, remain disturbingly unchallenged and unrecognized.

NOTES

1 As recently as 1962, anthropologist Carleton Coon published *The Origin of the Races* which proposed that blacks were the youngest subspecies of homo sapiens, and therefore the least advanced intellectually and socially. See also, R. Horseman (in bibliography), which traces the development and mass dissemination of scientific proof of white superiority.

2 As Jordan reports, Linneaus' categories were not hierarchical; they were merely confusing. Jordan finds it of the "greatest significance" that Linneaus himself "seems never to have expounded the metaphysics of the Chain of Being and that he was able to employ the traditional phrase 'one chain of universal being' in a manner which completely robbed it of its traditional meaning." See Linneaus' *Systema Naturae* (221).

3 See, e.g., Gilman (232–5) where the medical inquiry into the "origins" of blacks was chronicled through dissections of black female bodies, and for a detailed discussion of the primary instance that Gilman cites, see T. Denean Sharpley-Whiting (1996) and *Black Venus* (1997b).

4 But interestingly, it has not been discredited for a long time, nor in the political context that one might suppose. See Gates (1985); Stephan; and cf. Dickens:Vol. 18; and Carlyle.

5 The only case that my research has uncovered in which the Supreme Court speaks directly to the question of what it means by "race" is not an equal protection case. See *Saint Francis College* v. *Al-Khazraji* (1987). In *Saint Francis College*, an Iraqi-born U.S. citizen brought a discrimination suit against the college under §1981 for denial of tenure based on race. Section 1981 does not use the word "race," but the Court construed the section to forbid all "racial" discrimination in the making of private as well as public contracts. The Court's conclusion was that "Such discrimination is racial discrimination that Congress intended §1981 to forbid, *whether or not it would be classified as racial in terms of modern scientific theory*" (2028, my italics). It is, however, unclear where the Court stands with respect to the meaning of "race" for purposes of equal protection, suspect category doctrine. In footnote four of its opinion, however, the Court clearly demonstrated that it was aware of the ill-repute in which the race concept is currently held in the scientific community, where it is regarded as sociopolitical, rather than biological in nature, although the Court was at pains to point out that "not all" scientists accept this.

6 See also *Adarand Constructors, Inc.* v. *Pena* (1995), which holds federal affirmative action programs to the same strict scrutiny standard.

RACE, LIFE, DEATH, IDENTITY, TRAGEDY, AND GOOD FAITH

Naomi Zack

In spite of so many stubborn lies, at every moment,
at every opportunity, the truth comes to light, the
truth of life and death, of my solitude and my bond
with the world, of my freedom and my servitude…
—Simone de Beauvoir

THE CONCEPT of race as ordinarily used in racialized and racist cultures is based on pseudoscience and ill will. Even though race is commonly taken to be biological, not all people of a racialized group have the same heritable biological traits. No genes or chromosomal markers for any of the designated racial groups have been identified.[1] There are also no verified correlations between so-called racial biological traits and any cultural traits.[2] Empirically, the assumed biological foundation of race turns out to be nothing more than a changing range of biological traits—no different from other biological traits by anything biologically "racial" about them—that have been selected as racial.

The modern concept of race emerged in the 18th and 19th centuries as a rationalization for actions of enslavement and other forms of colonial exploitation that contradicted political theories premised upon universal human rights. Without the concept of race, the enslavement of kidnapped Africans and the colonial exploitation of Native populations in the Americas, which included genocide, would have been recognized as the crimes they were.[3]

A response to the conceptual problems with racial categories that arise from the absence of empirical racial essences and the presence of rules of hypodescent for persons of mixed race is to say that *race* is the result of complex myths and social fictions that form a powerful cultural reality, and to resist dislodgement of the concept on that basis. A more urgent response is to reread race as the result of a web of lies told about oppressed people by their oppressors, to justify the oppression. It is important, however, to realize that oppression would not necessarily end with the historical end of the concept of race. The African Slave Trade was well established and supported by major Western European, African and Arabic nations by the end of the seventeenth century, without modern concepts of race (Zack [1996]: chap. 12). Without a concept of race, immoral and illegal acts of oppression against racialized peoples would probably continue, although the mediating lies about those people would have to change. That shift in cultural construction could provide opportunity for new emancipatory offenses, at least on the side of theory.

Suppose one were tried and convicted for a crime one had not committed, and this conviction was based on lies told by accusers for their own financial and social benefit. As a result, one would be imprisoned among others who were also unjustly convicted. Suppose further that all in this situation were given life sentences in perpetuity, so that their descendants could inherit the unjust convictions. This would entail an attachment of guilt to inheritable biological traits that in themselves had no relation to crime. There might be an experience of solidarity among colleagues in prison, based on this shared "heritage" and other contingencies of culture that accompanied it. Those who had the time to talk, write, and think about their identities as prisoners might approach the subject in either of two ways: an inmate identity could be constructed based on the situation in prison, an identity that did not address the injustice of past convictions and sentencings; or, one could construct an identity that took into account the lies told by accusers. I favor the second alternative. To accept the lies because of their evident force and wider social acceptance would be deliberate participation in a delusion. So if racial designations are based on "fictions and myths," it is wrong to accept them as part of one's identity. What does it mean to be a racially designated person who does not accept her racial designation as part of her identity? What does it really mean, from the "inside out" (so to speak)?

RACE, LIFE, AND DEATH

The existential question raised by the powerful cultural reality of race is this: How relevant is race to a life that in each case is some human being's *my life*? I conceptualize my life as the period of time and the events therein experienced by me from my birth until my death. My life in this sense will look different to me depending on where I am in it. But I can't know where I am in my life; no one ever knows where she is in her life because death is possible at any time. I can always die tomorrow or in the next moment and should that happen, my present will be rearranged as my end, from someone else's surviving perspective that will necessarily fail to coincide with my perspective on my life.

Although no one knows where she is in her life at any given moment, different stages can be marked. By way of example, this is what I know about my life so far: When I was a child I passively accepted the people and events that surrounded me. I had dreams but no power to shape my life. As a young adult I wanted to be happy. As a middle-aged adult I am preoccupied with survival—for myself, for my children, and for my work. I know that the survival of my children and my work are largely out of my hands. I also know that I myself am not going to survive and that the survival of what I value is not only largely out of my hands, but in the long run, completely out of my sight. Death appears to be increasingly inevitable the older I get. Now, what has the web of lies of race got to do with that?

Although my stage of life is not shared by all, the foregoing account and question has been offered in a spirit of accessibility to everyone. Nonetheless, some racialized readers might be uncomfortable at this point, even if some such outline of a particular life is shared. A racialized reader may feel that such an abstract sketch of a life leaves out the richness of shared racialized life. This reader may think that racialized life, as a concrete particular experience, from situations within racialized families and communities, is the meat on the bones of the mere sketch, and she may believe that a fully human existentialism requires that some attention be paid to one's specific racial experience, especially if one is nonwhite.

However, just as all intellectuals are situated human beings, so are all racialized intellectuals, in a word—"intellectuals." From the standpoint of intellectual identity—and here the ground admittedly shifts—an appreciation of the inevitability of my own individual death leaches out any of the relevance to life lies may have, no matter how powerful those lies are in cultural reality. When I *think* about the inevitable catastrophe of my death, it simply does not matter to me that my too-short life will have been racialized.

The racialized reader may wryly observe here that (to use my language) the catastrophe of death occurs more frequently for racialized people because demographically their lives are shorter and they are more likely to be murdered than nonracialized people. So race is relevant to death. Yes. But everyone dies. If I understand my own life better than anyone else does or can, and this personal, that is, subjective and direct, understanding is a universal human structure, along with death, how can I know that my life would have been "better" had it not been racialized? I do know it would not, could not, have been made so good by the absence of those lies of race that death would be (or would have been from my falsely imagined perspective after my death) less catastrophic. Surely it would be just as inevitable, even given greater statistical longevity.

RACE, LIFE, DEATH, AND IDENTITY

Death comes to us all, regardless of race. As intellectuals constructing identity on the ground of that fact, it is important to begin with some idea of what is involved in having an identity. First of all, identity is not the same thing as identification, although the two are often conflated. Identification refers to how others categorize me. It does not necessarily encompass my view of myself that is connected to my decisions, choices, will, and action. This view of myself may include how I am identified, or not, but it importantly must include some sense of my agency. Rocks, trees, can openers, and cars are all objects of identification. So are black, Asian, Native-American, and Hispanic people objects of identification. When these racial identifications are accepted as foundations for identity, care should be taken to make sure that identity in the sense that includes agency can be based on them. To the extent that American blackness or African-American identification has live roots in Negro, and chattle-slave identification (the last of which was not initially founded on a concept of race), then that identification is the identification of a victim of oppression by his or her oppressors. Oppression limits agency, subjectively, which is not surprising because oppression always limits agency objectively—it always curtails the liberties of those oppressed.[4] Therefore, nonwhite racial identifications cannot be accepted as foundations for identity if one chooses freedom.

It is now possible to connect the foregoing considerations about race, life, death and identity in order to answer the question of what my race has to do with my life. It was noted that part of the structure of my life is an unavoidable and existentially catastrophic death. When life is considered in that way by the human being whose life it is, something very different from simple biology is the subject. Biological death is not a catastrophe but merely part of the natural order of things. But given human agency that encompasses decision, choice, will and action, in the space of consciousness of a situation, any *my* death is a drastic and irrevocable cessation of that unnatural, or "metanatural," human order. The conscious awareness of causation illuminates how death will eliminate the continuation of agency. And quite simply, any *I* would rather have its agency continue without conclusion by death. Existentially, the awareness of the inevitability of death makes all agency something of a return-to-agency. Awareness of death, in rupturing the virginity of life, creates what existentialists have called existence.

The return to *my own life*—in the sense that applies to everyone's own life—as an agent, and as the only agent in it from the only possible existential point of view on it, namely my own, after the acceptance of my inevitable death, which could happen at any time, may catapult me into the here and now. Existential literature, Zen Buddhism, and the wisdom of popular culture tell us that the realization of the evanescence of life can make the experience of being alive more intense. It is not always clear whether such a heightened sense of living occurs spontaneously after the encounter of consciousness with death, or whether such intensity is a special psychological state that has to be cultivated, that is, an artificial state or a pose. Also, the loss of innocence about life that awareness of death brings, may result in less intense experiences of being alive.

At any rate, there is an existential return to the here and now after the realization of death's inevitability and readiness, which, assuming that one does nothing except wait for death, would seem to entail a fresh commitment to own's life, or a realignment of one's fundamental attitude toward one's life. The new upsurge (be it spontaneous or artificial) or the deliberate change in attitude, means that one either has more energy as an agent or feels less impelled to act. In either case, there is very likely more freedom as an agent, and a higher value placed on freedom so that limitations on agency become less tolerable.

I submit that to experience oneself as a member of an oppressed race in the existential return-to-life after awareness of death constitutes an intolerable constraint on freedom after the return. Oppression experienced from the inside is psychologically dragging, in a word, de-pressing, when what is required by the existential return to one's life, after the acceptance of death, is either an irrepressible upsurge of some kind, or a lightening up of engagement. Such freer agency can only be assumed by a racialized being if she casts off all racial oppression in her own first person identity. In doing that she casts off racial identification, and race insofar as it pertains to her. The perpetual moment of freedom is therefore race-less. Race has nothing to do with *my life* in the existential sense of identity.

RACE, LIFE, DEATH, IDENTITY, AND TRAGEDY

The acceptance of life after the realization of inevitable death does not mitigate the catastrophic nature of death. However, it does avert the pity for oneself and terror of one's fate in the face of death, because once death has been accepted, as the natural cessation of *one's own* unnatural agency, one is no longer a spectator of one's own mortal fate. This means that my death cannot be a tragedy to me.

But why shouldn't my death be a tragedy to me? Might I not be entitled to that much, at least, as a racialized American? In the Aristotelian meaning of "tragedy" as a spectacle, there is a protagonist who is a good person but not so good as to preclude the viewers' ability to identify with him. Surely, that could always be some *me*, about myself.

However, the question of who gets to be a tragic hero can be blown out of proportion so that the glory of the role obscures its structure for consciousness. The content of the role of tragic actor is a downfall based on a chain of events caused by a serious character flaw in an otherwise good (virtuous) human being. The glory of the role is a reaction to the greatness of the tragic actor, which is expressed when the tragic actor's character is not diminished by self-caused external misfortune. But the structure of the tragic role contains both actor and audience, only the latter of which, as spectator, experiences pity and terror.[5] This pity and terror on the part of spectator is what glorifies the tragic actor. Without the spectator, the grief of the tragic actor would be, not glorious, but merely a very hard experience, like grief in ordinary life for those who suffer alone.

The acceptance of racial identification as part of one's identity, assuming some heroic personal stature, has the capacity to transform one's death from a catastrophe into a tragedy, because racial identification is third-person description, with built-in distance from a self. Seeing oneself as the member of a group that has been described, and even constituted as that group, by its oppressors, can thereby furnish the distance necessary to experience pity and terror as a spectator at one's own life. Racial identification itself often requires the development of at least minor heroic personal stature in order to survive in contemporary (American) society. Racial identification thus assumed into one's first person identity has the capacity to racialize one's inevitable death. Racialized death, as an object of pity and terror, is tragic death. But the tragedy one thus imagines for oneself is false, because one is not a spectator at one's life, or death. (Of course, someone else may experience a genuine tragedy, as a spectator at the racialized death of another that was based on the actor's error of judgement in incorporating racial identification into self-identity. The tragedy would then lie in the witnessing of the suffering of an actor who is aware of the racial dimension of her own death.)

The racialization of one's death to oneself obscures the inevitability of death for all human mortals. The way one dies may be an effect of the evil of others but death itself is not the effect of evil. For biological life, death is part of the natural order of things and for the life of an unnatural human agent it is a catastrophic end to the unnatural order of agency.

Whether one dies peacefully of a disease in advanced old age, or from AIDS, hypertension, or violence by others, the racialization of one's own death is an error. Death comes to us all regardless of race and it can happen to anyone at any moment, regardless of race. This is not to say that any form of death should not be forestalled or that it doesn't matter how one dies, whether it is senseless or meaningful. It is to say that once one apprehends the existential catastrophe of death, which in its nonbiological sense comes only to a being with agency, race looses its sting—even in a life focussed on resisting racism. A racialized person cannot effectively resist racism from within a racialized identity. This is perhaps a great irony about racialized existence: one accepts that others have said one is *this*; one sees that one is not *this*; one's resistance in action requires some affirmation of oneself as the *this* one is not.

Heroism, even the heroism of basing one's life on a struggle against racism, will not save one from death any more than avoidance of such struggle. Achilles put it very well when he decided to return to battle: "Fate is the same for the man who holds back, the same if he fights hard. We are all held in a single honor, the brave with the weaklings. A man dies still if he has done nothing, as one who has done much" (Homer: IX, 318–20). Achilles' point was that even if one does nothing, one dies. The relevant point, here, is that one dies if he or she has done *much*. Achilles

104

ZACK

finally returned to battle within the full knowledge of the inevitability of his death, determined to destroy the Trojans. The violence of Homeric glory makes it an ill-advised choice for most intellectuals. But Achilles' insight about the inevitability of death is an example of acceptance of the universal and pure fact of death which frees an agent to choose what to do, without fear or pity for the consequences to oneself. Achilles' return into action left no space for a tragic view on his own life.

RACE, LIFE, DEATH, IDENTITY, TRAGEDY, AND GOOD FAITH

If a racialized person acknowledges her racial identification and her unracialized death and, on that basis, struggles against racism, which may include a struggle against racial identification, she may nor may not succeed. But when she dies her unracialized death, it will not be a tragedy for her, but a simple catastrophe. Catastrophe has less poetic spectacle than tragedy but it is in better faith. To view one's life as a tragedy is in bad faith because it requires pretending that one is a spectator who identifies with one's self and thereby experiences pity and terror for oneself. To view one's life as a tragedy requires an imagined distance from that life, and from one's self, which is a form of self-deception. In imagining oneself at that distance, the real self that can still act is deprived of its power to act because it has been imagined into the role of a spectator.

In the smaller actions of life that are not directly concerned with death, the refusal to include racial identification in one's identity as an agent is all round in better faith than complying with such identification. Not only is racial identification itself a web of lies constructed to rationalize oppression—and endorsing a web of lies is an epitome of bad faith—but the nature of the lies one endorses as the racialized person who is their object will impede one's freedom as an agent. People who are racially identified are thereby identified as agents lesser in intelligence, moral virtue, and social competence, all of which are necessary for optimally free agency. This suggests that racialized persons have to perform a special process of self-purification before they can decide, choose, will, and act. They have to remove from themselves external identifications about their biology and culture which would, if incorporated into their identities, be impediments to their agency.

If a racialized person constructs a nonracialized identity in the United States, colleagues are likely to accuse her of wanting to be white, because whiteness is defined as the absence of black or other nonwhite identification (Zack [1993]: chap. 1). That is, since there are no positive definitions of whiteness, almost any position of agency that repudiates nonwhite racial designation elicits this shameful charge. It is shameful because of the guilt that is attached to racial identification, in the first place. To be racially identified is to be *wrong* in contrast to those who are not thus identified. Many who are racially identified accept the identification and among themselves repudiate the fact that they are thereby *wrong*. But, they have no confidence that the wrongness can be repudiated if the identification is not accepted.

105

ZACK

Returning for a moment to the analogy of unjust criminal conviction, it does not do, morally, to become a fugitive because honor requires clearing one's name as well as escaping the punishment. To want to change one's race, which is what a repudiation of racial identification may look like, is to take on a fugitive status, in the eyes of one's racial colleagues. One is called upon to acquit oneself, and by extension, one's racial colleagues, of the wrongness associated with the racial identification. In order to do that, one is required to keep the identification, because the wrongness has been tightly attached to the identification, through its association with heredity. Without the identification, the accusers would not be shown that they were wrong in their punishment.

However, the charge that a racialized person who rejects racial identification in identity wants to be white, is somewhat vague as it stands. In one sense, whiteness means simply not being racialized. And in that sense alone, wanting to be white is not morally base because if everyone were white in that sense, there would be no problem with race and probably no concept of race. But in a second sense, from the standpoint of some racialized people, whiteness has positive biological, ethnic and morally wrongful (because whites have been the oppressors of nonwhites) characteristics of its own. It is in this second sense, which is also viewed as the source of the first non-racialized sense of whiteness, that wanting to be white appears shameful. But, the biological characteristics of whiteness are insufficient to empirically ground a concept of race. Wanting to be white in that biological sense would constitute a delusion, in principle, for whites as well as nonwhites.

106

The morally wrong aspect of white ethnicity, as an opportunity for oppression, is another matter, unrelated to biological foundations of race in physical reality, although strongly related in human thought. For a racialized person to want to be white in the sense that would permit her to oppress other nonwhites is morally blameworthy, because it is a desire to be unjust. Becoming ethnically white through acts of revenge against former white oppressors also requires close moral scrutiny.[6]

Good faith and bad faith forms of the denial of racial identification can be distinguished. Lewis Gordon has characterized critical good faith as a structure of action and identity that does not evade freedom or responsibility through the bad faith of *substantiation* or *disembodiment* ([1995a] and [1995f]). Racial identification falsely purports to have one's biological body as its subject. Thus, a person who has been racially identified would not, in critical good faith, make more of her racialized existence than its real biology allows (substantiation), or pretend that she does not have a body that has been racialized (disembodiment). To shed one's racial identification, as a locus for identity, in such good faith, would be to regard one's physical characteristics as what they are without adding false racial qualities to them. For example, brown skin, in any of its particular hues, is exactly what it is visually perceived to be in the normal course of human visual perception and its racialization is a false addition. One may, in good faith, look in the mirror and see a person with the shade of brown skin one has. To think one sees a "black person"

ZACK

or a "brown person"—or a black or brown man or woman, as gender is relevant— is in bad faith. That is, the racialization of one's skin color is part of the cultural mendacity of the construction of race. Assuming that the word "brown" as a description of a person's skin is not in itself a racial term, the brownness of a person's skin does not have the biological force to operate as an attribute of the entire person, for example, her internal organs, bones and nerves, not to mention her emotions, thoughts, and action.

Race is oppressively attached to human biology but race is not itself biological. To battle false stereotypes of race by changing the parts of one's body that may be stereotypically racially identifiable is a kind of bad faith of substantiation, whether one tries to minimize, erase, create or exaggerate these physical characteristics. This would suggest that physical racial pride, as well as physical racial shame, is in bad faith because it unreflectively, when reflection is possible, accepts the racist grounds for the shame in order to "rehabilitate" or revalue them, into grounds for pride. If the shame is in bad faith, then so is the pride.[7]

Race is not "in the body" but "in the minds" of those who perform racial identifications. However, if one is the object of one of these identifications that have been attached to one's biological body, one cannot in good faith deny that social reality by pretending that people who have identified one racially are not aware of one's physical "racial" difference from them in ways that place one at a disadvantage. If after having been identified racially, which often seems to be instantaneous, one is aware of revulsion, fascination, fear, lust or any other fantastic effect of the identification on the identifier, one can get away, pretend indifference, project scorn or anger or choose some other course of action (for a multiplicity of reasons).

107

More complex and ambiguous forms of racial disembodiment and substantiation can be read into rejections of racial identification that relate to the cultural goods or positive ethnicity of whites and nonwhites. Denial of racial identification in this domain seems to be most vulnerable to the charge of "wanting to be white" (which supports nonbiological analyses of race). Despite widespread consensus that culture is not genetically heritable—although one may inherit it from one's genealogical family in ways similar to the inheritance of material objects—there is even more widespread association of culture with old, biologically false ideas of race.

ZACK

In principle, all forms of human culture, in its full global and historical diversity, are accessible to the identity of every human being on the planet. Although racially designated nonwhites have traditionally been excluded from the "high" culture of Western Europe (which includes for example, classical music, university education, professional training, academic canons and botanical gardens), that exclusion is presently no more than *de facto*. If one chooses Mozart, Flaubert, orchids or the medieval architecture of elite college campuses, nonwhite racial identification is not in itself sufficient to characterize such preferences as an expression of bad faith. This is especially so in the United States where Native-American property and African-American work have contributed much to white wealth without just compensation, and where the contributions of nonwhites to nonmaterial cultural products have also been ignored. Furthermore, the reality of mixed nonwhite and white genealogy among racially designated groups calls for a reinterpretation of preferences for what was previously prohibited, as nothing more than "taking back the white."

Of course, some may prefer the traditional or popular cultures associated with the racialized group with which they have been identified. But such preferences are choices and ought not to be simply assumed as natural, normal or morally good in oneself or others. By the same token, to deny one's traditional culture for no other reason than a desire to avoid false racial biological foundationalism that one does not recognize to be false, would be a choice based on bad faith.

Whether the good faith–bad faith dichotomy goes by that name or not, Americans dynamically play it out in terms of style. We make quick moral judgments on that seemingly superficial basis, often with great accuracy. However, when it comes to ourselves or those close to us, we are more easily fooled: We unduly blame ourselves when we have done no more than exercise an existential freedom or, under the gun of convention and habit, dispense praise for self-imprisonment.

NOTES

1   For discussion and further sources for the lack of empirical foundation for the ordinary concept of race, see Zack (1994): 14–21 and (1993): esp. chaps. 1–3. For a summary and further sources of the rejection of the concept of race by anthropologists and biological scientists, see Wheeler: A–8–9, and 15.

2   See Lévi-Strauss for a definitive article on the independence of concepts of race as genetically hereditary, from concepts of culture as hereditary.

3   On the independence of the 17th-century African slave trade from racialization, see Zack (1996): chap. 12, "Slavery without Race."

4   For a recent analysis of the importance of positive beliefs about the self and free agency see Benson: 650–68.

5   Since Aristotle analyzes tragedy within the context of theater, the presence of the audience (spectator) is taken for granted. See his *Poetics* (Gk: 1253a13).

6 See Lewis Gordon's discussion of Fanon's views on postcolonialist black violence against former oppressors (1995b): 67–83, and revenge (1995a): 117–23.

7 For further discussion of this notion of immanence and racial identity insofar as it pertains to Sartre's discussion of the French anti-Semite, and new racial identities for persons of mixed race, see Zack (1993): 151–164.

TONI MORRISON AT THE MOVIES
Theorizing Race Through *Imitation of Life*
(For Barbara Siegel)

Gary Schwartz

THE MAIN feature of this viewing is the initial film version of *Imitation of Life*, released in 1934, and its imbedded presence in, and interactivity with, the text of Toni Morrison's *The Bluest Eye*. Film is itself the essence of the imitation of life, achieved primarily by the creation of images through the capture and recording of light and shadow. After nearly seventy years of soundtracked film, one tends to forget the preceding more than thirty years of silent film, in which the image was all. A recent documentary, *Visions of Light*, about the role of directors of photography in film making, emphatically establishes the primacy of illumination over the aural. The entire thrust of visual art, up to the successful development of photosensitive paper, was the imitation of life, and the more detail and precision the artist-produced image contained, the better the art of the artist. The black and white *Imitation of Life* is itself an imitation of the life of imitation offered by whites to black people. The narrative of *The Bluest Eye* explores the profundity of the desperation of a life lived in imitation.[1]

Imitation, commonly considered a "woman's movie," is a complex narrative about aspects of the life of women in America along with the differential axis of black and white. Two young women, husbandless and desperate for employment, one black (Delilah Johnson), and one white (Bea Pullman), and their daughters Peola and Jessie, make a fortune running a pancake restaurant. The restaurant thrives through Bea's shrewd business sense, Delilah's nonpareil pancake mix, and the strenuous labor of both women. Aunt Delilah is Aunt Jemima, but her relationship with Peola will take us into the substructures of the stereotype to the bitterness deep underneath the slatherings of butter and maple syrup of the box illustration.

The two women live and raise their daughters together. All goes well except that Peola nurses a strong desire to "pass" for white or become white. Peola is very light; Delilah is very dark. Peola publicly denies that Delilah is her mother. Peola apologizes for rejecting Delilah but cannot restrain herself from rejecting her mother once more. Delilah falls ill—this is certainly illness as a metaphor—and dies. Peola returns for the funeral and in remorse, shame, and guilt admits that she killed her mother.

Imitation delineates the dilemma of the need to attain whiteness to "be." Peola is an heiress but renouncing her mother and, thereby, her earnings establishes the primacy of whiteness in the hierarchy of Peola's values. Peola was raised with Jessie and the life she wanted was the life, the full unimpeded life of her white counterpart. The hell of Peola's life is her deprivation of the world of full rights and privileges and the self-deprivation and rejection of her mother, her own blackness, and her very self.

What is imitation of life? Imitation of life is the state, condition, process, result, or concatenation of phenomena in which one cannot lead one's life as one is naturally endowed. Color, ethnicity, gender, and age, among other visible realities, are designated as inferior, worthy of no rights or privileges, and excludable with impunity for the excluders from the franchise of free society. Those in power—of the right color, ethnicity, gender, and so on—issue both a pronouncement upon, and an imperative to, those who are depredated of their right to live as entities born human. The pronouncement is: "You are different and thereby inferior. You are neither real nor authentic and in effect not fully alive. This because you do not look like us." The imperative is: "You will always be this way, and you will live an imitation of life in exclusion, half-dead, enslaved to our needs and your own inferiority. You must thereby always assure us that our life is real and that we are substance and you are shadow. Do not deviate from these commands. Do not invite your own destruction."

Imitation of life, then, as an operant principle whose infliction upon people is the predominant focus of this inquiry, is a prevalent and powerful imposition of bad faith. Although I have presented imitation of life as a compound of pronouncement and imperative, i.e., an articulated interpretation which is not seen or is shrouded by the hood of cultural/self/economic blindness by the people who enforce it and would deny it if presented to them, they would hold that "these people" have done "this" (their state of life) to themselves.

For example, housing for the poor is usually much more inexpensively built, smaller inside and out, and without air conditioning. The message is that if you are poor and of color, you can sweat your summers out; those who can be "cool" are those who have a real life; they are not distracted and defeated by physical pain, three-dimensional inconvenience, and paralysis. The "cool" advance further and further beyond physical impediment with each successive step.

Pain, however, celebrated by apologists as an ethical growth stimulant, in reality invests itself at a negative interest rate, invites self-destruction, courts suicide. The ultimate enforcement institution for imitation has been segregation, both legal and virulently tacit. "Separate but equal" is another way of phrasing imitation of life. One is always a copy, a phoney, a factory reject, not genuine and not able to become, a limbo at best. While those in power want to annihilate those whom they have condemned to live their lives in imitation, they cannot destroy the host of their hatred, their sustenance, their reason to live. Even if this were to take place, exhibition of the now "former" subject people would be a necessity. This is what the Australians did with the "last queen of the Tasmanians." More authoritative and detailed were Hitler's plans for a Jewish Museum to house the physical and cultural anthropological remains and artifacts of the extirpated race. There is a "love" which resides in the hatred of one group, a "love" which too often "dares to speak its name," which generates a need, perversely, to tend the hated group. Fascination is clearly the other side of repulsion.

Ultimately the imitation of life phenomenon demands from its victims the praxis of "passing." Passing is the grand metaphor for authenticity/inauthenticity in life. We try to get by in any circumstance: faking it, flying by the seat of our pants, looking like someone or something we are not. Elected officials, chief executive officers, and others pass as paragons of honesty. In the U.S., however, the idiomatic use of "passing" is in its relationship to color. Color, or the lack of it, has been the most requisite item for the white individual's practice of natural liberties and the most impenetrable barrier for those who have color. How one *looks* is the ultimate test. One cannot obtain the physical property of white skin. Meanwhile a majority of white people spend at least one-third of the year attempting to "bronze" themselves. A base, frivolous caprice of perception determines who lives and who imitates. This is the barrier of denial which demarcates the genuine full life from an imitation. *Imitation* and *Bluest* atomize the structure of the problem and its consequences.

There are also two Australian narratives, David Malouf's *Remembering Babylon* and Thomas Keneally's *Chant of Jimmy Blacksmith*, both enmeshed with the perplex of the imitation of life, which are important because they expand the horizon of the problem's ubiquity beyond America and are essentially precinematic in their dramatic/historical dates. Their highly visual focus will allow the reader some foresight into *Bluest*.

Let us consider the following observation: "The very habit and faculty that makes apprehensible to us what is known and expected dulls our sensitivity to other forms, even the most obvious" (Malouf: 9). These words are from down under, from the botanical notebook of a Protestant clergyman, Mr. Frazer, who collects specimens, draws them, and describes them. His companion, Gemmy, is a white British male, age twenty-nine, who had worked the streets of London for an older criminal. At 13 he stowed away on a sailing ship, was washed ashore on the Queensland coast and adopted by Aboriginals. After 16 years with "his" tribe, Gemmy bursts into a white settlement shouting, "Do not shoot....I am a B-b-british object!" (Malouf: 3) Gemmy is not seeking asylum; he is, however, driven by a dominant, almost primordial, force to people of "his own" color:

> [W]hen news drifted up from the south of spirits, white-faced, covered from head to food in bark [clothing] and riding four-footed beasts that were taller than a man, he was disturbed, and the desire to see these creatures, to discover who they were, plucked at him till he could not rest.

Although Gemmy was accepted by the tribe, it was "guardedly, in the droll half-apprehensive way that was proper to an in-between creature" (Malouf: 28).

Twinness and twixity are often deeply rooted in the outsider contemplating another who is outside of one's own skin. Twinness implies separation and invites comparison; in fact, the numeral adjective for second in Greek—*deúteros*—has a comparative suffix. Twixity is a somewhat different situation which isolates and detaches both the subject and the object. The externality is not only from the perception of a single active subject acting visually on the perceived object as we react to skin color in European culture as object which is generated by what is integument only, but the external defined as object is itself a subject acting on the object which objectifies it. What the beholder cannot comprehend (in fact, denies and rejects comprehension) is that the object has an existence of its own person independent of the objectifier; this subject, however, is not engaged in a process of reification, but of being, which does not necessarily involve transitivity. Intransivity, the engagement of the choice not to objectify, gives potential objects self-generated internally-defined choice of expression and action.

The problem of other is doubled in the person of Gemmy Fairley because he is perceived as being a compound neither: neither white nor black. Gemmy's initial announcement is a brilliant condensed grammar of color and colonialism. His reversal of subject and object is perfect—he can be done unto and is not to be feared. Being a British subject would give him rights and certain powers. The situation is more threatening to a white requiring objectification for reassurance and stability since the conjunctive combination presents what is most to be feared: contact and a collapse of boundaries. The thoughts of the settlement community attempting to access him and put him in "his place" are despairing of understanding and solution:

> He was a parody of a white man. If you gave him a word for a thing, he could after a good deal of huffing and blowing, repeat it, but the next time round you had to teach it to him all over again. He was imitation gone wrong, and the mere sight of it put you wrong too, made the whole business somehow foolish and open to doubt…He had started out white. No question. When he fell in with the blacks—at thirteen, was it?—he had been like any other child, one of their own for instance. (That was hard to swallow.) But had he remained white?…For the fact was, when you looked at him sometimes he was not white. His skin might be but not his features. The whole cast of his face gave him the look of one of Them. (Malouf: 39–40)

On this crude anthropological quest, the liberal and sensitive Mr. Frazer reasons:

> …but also the effort he must have made, in those sixteen years, to blend in and make himself one of them, to find facial expressions, picked up by imitation or reflection and all quite different from white man's…In taking on, by second nature as it were, this new language of looks and facial gestures, he had lost his white man's appearance, especially for white men who could no longer see what his looks intended, and become in their eyes black. (Malouf: 40)

115

Gemmy has an acceptable integument, but by contact with Aboriginals he has become more deeply and indelibly black; the blackness of the Aboriginal is in Gemmy's bones, inside of him, the shape of his face forever altered, foreign, unable to be deciphered. Gemmy's Aboriginal discoverers did not require him to be one thing or another; he was regarded in "…[a] half apprehensive way that was proper to an in-between creature" (Malouf: 28). This accommodative perspective admits the existence of an other; moreover, whatever the deficit of skin color might be, the credit of the substance of the person behind the outside is understood to be human and therefore equal. The white Australian men cannot acknowledge even this "in-between creature." The twain and twixt, in fact, present more of an obstacle to the dominant culture, for contact leads to contamination, which yields dilution and disintegration. Latent always in the fearful thinking of white males, a nausea, arising from an ineffable realization that they cannot successfully "compete" with black men, grips the souls of white men. Gemmy's bothness was intolerable to the farming settlement, and ultimately as the narrative of *Remembering Babylon* progresses this white black Aboriginal does the will of the white men—he

SCHWARTZ

becomes invisible without a whisper as to where and how. He simply disappears, as unexpectedly as he had appeared, almost as if into the dream time. The inevitability of contact is confronted by denial.

Australian literature and history are filled with illumination for American readers. The disease of racism has run rampant in both nations. Thomas Keneally's narrative, *The Chant of Jimmy Blacksmith*, based on an historical ax-murder spree of revenge and frustration of a "half" Aboriginal at the turn of the century, is an example of who looks how to whom in a world where one can be only white if one is to be considered human. Effort, good faith, dignity, hope—all these goods turned to humiliation and disappointment resulting in a violence comparable to Nat Turner's Rebellion but on a smaller scale.

That promise of becoming "genuine," embarking on a progressive regimen of albescence, an exercise in magic or alchemy, a "white magic" which offers metamorphosis, ending in a heroic attainment, indeed, an apotheosis, demands Jimmy live, not his life, but an imitation of life. The white man is God, and because black people can only imitate, there will be no attainment of the promised land because the path is perpetual. This denial of attainment surpasses the claustrophobic mythological hells of Sisyphus and Tantalus; they, at least, are punished for their transgressions and not simply for their being. In the text of *The Chant of Jimmy Blacksmith*, to be white is to have a valid claim of being. Jimmy Blacksmith is "half-white." His father is white. Gemmy Fairley was a street waif in London for most of his life until he torched his own boss and headed outward-bound for the docks. He operates primarily as a survivor wherever on the time-space curve he happens to be; he is a creature of impulse, condemned to live horizontally. Whatever finally happened to him, and this is the panalgic question left to hang over the reader, is never revealed; it is the great mystery of Australian life because it remains to be solved because it remains to be seen.

Jimmy Blacksmith, however, took himself on the path of whiteness, following on the advice of his employer, the reverend Neville, and his wife. After Jimmy's capture, Mr. Neville, writes an unsubmitted letter of repentant explication to the editor of the *Methodist Church Times*:

> I believe that I carry some responsibility for the recent sad history of the atrocities committed by the half-caste aborigine, Jimmy Blacksmith. It was I who, lacking any definite instructions on how to proceed in the management of a mission station, encouraged particular ambitions in Jimmy Blacksmith—the ambition to work and complete work, the ambition of owning property, the ambition of marrying a white woman. (Keneally: 175)

> So that one wonders if society is yet ready to accept the ambitious aborigine. And the question arises, what, should we, as pastors, do in regard to our black and brindled flocks? Should we raise our own kind of hopes and ambitions in

them, ambitions of industry and honorable labor, of increase and ownership of property, connecting these hopes and ambitions to the message of Christ? I certainly thought so once, but wonder now. (Keneally: 176)

Jimmy is a blacksmith and a black Smith: his name contextualizes him; he is primary, primal. He is non-Aboriginal because Aboriginals did not work metal (they were paleolithic), but he is a smith of sorts, and certainly he is black enough to be a "blacksmith." Conjunction and change of shape are tasks of blacksmiths; Jimmy as "Blacksmith" conjoins with a white woman in marriage an attempt to turn a base metal into gold.

All smiths are vulcanized, illuminated by their forgefires and blackened by the soot of metallurgy; some smiths who keep the forge are lame, as is Hephaestus. Black-smithing is annihilatory work. Consider one of the most valuable perceptions of fifth-century Athens: physical work is to be avoided if at all possible. How many stones did Socrates actually cut? Compare his chiseling of words. In *The Chant of Jimmy Blacksmith*, the terrible engagement of whites with blacks is excruciatingly detailed. Even the invitation to imitation is a denial. If one were to be identified as white—to "look" white—there is no ultimate disappearance. Jimmy discusses the child (which is not his) with one of his employers, Mr. Newby:

"How yer goin' to raise yer pickaninny, Jimmie?"
"He be no pickaninny boss, he be three-quarters white."
"Yair. And his kid'll be an eighth black and his a sixteenth. But it doesn't matter how many times yer descendant bed down, they'll never get anything that doesn't have the tarbrush in it. And it'll always spoil 'em, that little bit of something else."

How can one alter the thinking of those who will always see and think "something else"? There is no invisibility for the Aboriginal even though it is this visibility which makes him otherwise invisible.

Bluest locates the generative organ of the nosology of color. The eye is physically one of the hardest of the body's organs, one which antibiotics, particularly those which are applied topically, have difficulty penetrating. Physiologically, the eye has difficulty with getting medication into itself. This is due to an increased pressure inside the eye caused by the axillary temperature of the body which inhibits cellular osmosis. Therapy for metaphoric vision encounters an even more resistant disease in which the chief symptom is hallucinatory and manifests itself in an inability on the part of the afflicted to perceive others in terms other than themselves. Everything else is an imitation, an aberration and inferior. Morrison focuses the entirety of her first novel on the complexities of seeing and being seen, but the innermost loaded spring of the phenomena is revealed in her anatomy of the mechanism of imitation. The pursuit of personal authenticity is shunted into the

SCHWARTZ

117

confines of imitation which results in a life of shadow, a life of burial, a life of low visibility at best. While the idea of imitation of life is not abstruse, i.e., people understand its existence and effect on themselves, it has received titular enshrinement in a novel and two films. In part, the idea meets its destiny and its most excruciating articulation in *Bluest*.

There is a strange destiny which leads one work of art into another medium and back again. Novels are commonly the matrices for film scripts. There are cycles within the same genre which are closed many centuries apart such as the one beginning with Ovid's (or pseudo-Ovid's) epistle of *Sappho to Phaon* (Heroides, xv) and closed by John Donne's *Sappho to Philaenis*, incidentally the first surviving example of lesbian literature in English (Allen [1964]: 188-91). In Toni Morrison's *Bluest Eye* we see a contemporary cycle closed. In 1933, Fanny Hurst, a highly popular and perennially prodigious producer of novels, published her *Imitation of Life*, which, almost immediately, became the axis of John M. Stahl's film, *Imitation of Life*, itself a very close rendering of the best-seller. In 1959, Douglas Sirk's remake of *Imitation of Life*, a great commercial success, offered a more contemporary treatment, altering certain details from Hurst's novel and the original screen play, but mostly maintaining the essential power of the very clear social and feminist elements of the novel and the 1934 film adaptation.

The cycle closed with the 1970 publication of Toni Morrison's first novel, *The Bluest Eye*, in which Morrison makes direct use of Stahl's version of *Imitation of Life*, qua film, as an emblematic and determinant force in her text and thereby lays the idea of passing deep into the foundation of the book's structure, for this is what *Bluest* is about: seeming to be seen as acceptable to an external viewer. This is where the victim of visual violence attempts to take the very weapon which paralyzes one into one's own control, install it into one's own head and turn it against the assailant while disguising oneself as a white person, because this is what they signify. The black person with the bluest eyes becomes instead the whitest person because of her/his superlative eyes which in turn allow that individual to see the world in black and white from the white standpoint. If the eyes have the power to make distinctions, perhaps one's own skin color is of no consequence; if one can look at the world as a white person, that individual has no need to look at oneself. One then turns away from the problem and pain and does not consider oneself as black because as a white seeing a black the latter is seen as of no consequence. To see as a white person is to be as a white person. In Pecola Breedlove, Toni Morrison has constructed a character of mythological momentum; Pecola hurtles forward towards her driven end; she needs the eyes to have any purchase on life. One recalls the American standard popular song "I Only Have Eyes For You," recorded and performed by many, but most memorably by Billie Holiday.

The mythological compass and *auctoritas* of Morrison's characters are unique and awesome outside of ancient mythologies. By means of insinuating an epic heft of character into her narratives, she relates the universal with the individual, the epic hero with the picaro. This characterology animates all of her novels. Pecola is not simply a forlorn little girl. She has a life and death mission, she quests for the grail, she has a wound, and she must steal the golden fleece. She is, however, doomed to the disappointment of mythological existence; even if she could obtain the bluest eyes, they would not do what she desired. In Greek myth, there is Teiresias, a prophet who has been both a male and a female, and who has been blinded by Hera because of his specifically sexual experience, his analysis of which (that the female enjoyed the sexual act nine times more than the male) infuriated her. This is a clear example of the conservative equilibration of most myth: for every gain there is a loss and for every loss there is a gain, but one cannot acquire capabilities or attributes without divesting or being divested of others. For Teiresias' loss of physical sight at the will of Hera, Zeus compensates him with mantic insight.

Oedipus, whose hallmark is clear sight and great acumen in practical matters, gains real insight only after his self-inflicted blindness. One of mythology's most signal functions is that it sets boundaries for the quotidian while illuminating the extreme perimeter of the most wildly conceivable possibilities; that is, what if you kill your father, marry your mother, and have children with her? What if you tell, as did Teiresias, the supreme female divinity in the pantheon that, on the basis of your expert experience, the perceived truth is that in an androcentric universe women have more pleasure from sex in a nine-fold return? There is an aspect of mythology which is theoretical, observational, almost laboratorially detached; it is the world of "What If?" The scope of mythology has encompassed all possibilities and has been the vessel of all contemplation and all wish and desire. Pecola Breedlove performs as a form of culture hero within *Bluest*, and she finds vile disappointment. Deluded by the insane character Soaphead Church, Pecola finds her own insanity propelled by the force of her father's rape of herself: there is no mechanism, charm, or organ through which to negotiate the value of blackness: the solution lies inside.

In the latter half of the 20th century, however, all the thaumaturgy of mythology has been realized or, at least, approximated to the point of being at the ready to become enfixed in the matrix of daily intercourse. We are entering into a period during which we will see the death of mythology through the nonritualistic tangible enactment. Technology, predominantly in long distance travel and communication and medicine and surgery, has subsumed mythological accomplishments; we can go anywhere, see everything, change sexes, transplant organs, and in some cases nearly raise the dead. It is as if the Aboriginal dreamtime has all returned to Earth and operated in real time. Into the legacy of the literary and cinematic versions of *Imitation*, Morrison adds her own device of the "bluest eye," the focal point of the book and filter through which the action and passion of *Bluest* are perceived, and the exquisite instrument inwoven into the more palpable texture of the beast of the life of passing. Morrison moves the reader from the broad sweep of the dra-

119

matic expanse of "life," or "a life" to the specificity of physical phenomenon, which is a sainthood, and, of course, Pecola is searching for a purity which she cannot find in herself. Her very name is resonant of sin, or at least off the mark or mistaken by her mother from "Peola" the name of the young black woman in the film.

Pecola Breedlove enters the text early (*Bluest*: 19) in the novel, after we are settled in the household of Frieda and Claudia, two schoolgirls, and their stolid, assertive mother. Frieda introduces her:

> Cholly Breedlove, then, a renting black, having put his family outdoors, had catapulted himself beyond the reaches of human consideration. He had joined the animals; was, indeed, an old dog, a snake, a ratty nigger. Mrs. Breedlove was staying with the woman she worked for; the boy, Sammy, was with some other family; Pecola was to stay with us. Cholly was in jail (*Bluest*: 18–19).

The presence of Stahl's *Imitation* begins to seep into Morrison's narrative with the entrance of "a new girl in school named Maureen Peal":

> A high-yellow dream child with long brown hair braided into two lynch ropes that hung down her back...There was a hint of spring in her sloe green eyes, something summery in her complexion, and a rich autumn ripeness in her walk.
>
> She enchanted the entire school. When the teachers called on her, they smiled encouragingly. Black boys didn't trip her in the halls; white boys didn't stone her; white girls didn't suck their teeth when she was assigned to be their work partners; black girls stepped aside when she wanted to use the sink in the girls' toilet, and their eyes genuflected under sliding lids.

Maureen is a superwoman among girls; she comes in a perfect envelope which ensures the good news of its contents. Maureen has two-way skin making her acceptable to all, accessible and having access to all, and in this novel the "dream-child" is also the dream conduit and weaver of dreams. The Anglo-Celtic "Peal" comes quickly and crisply off the tongue; Pecola's last name—Breedlove—is about family in its most hopeful and positive aspect, but the rhythm section behind the name propels it with a thud and funk and drive of internal activity in reproduction for survival. Maureen "Peal" is aural and visual. The aural is something to be heard of, transmission and reception medium over which Maureen's fame is heralded, and our chief idioms using "peal" make this evident. Morrison uses the name homerically, a paronomasia or pun; this is not at all infrequent in her nomenclature as, for example, in *Song of Solomon* where Milkman and Pilate's names speak for themselves. In *Bluest*, Maureen is skin and surface. She is a peel; she is covering and externality. Maureen is the dream child because she is not real; she seems to bring black and white together, to acknowledge the myth—the non-dominant myth—

that a blend of color is possible. Maureen is charismatic and pacificatory, but Claudia and Freida search for flaws:

> Freida and I were bemused, irritated, and fascinated by her. We looked hard for flaws to restore our equilibrium, but we had to be content at first with ugly-ing her name, changing Maureen Peal to Meringue Pie. Later a minor epiphany was ours when we discovered that she had a dogtooth—a charming one to be sure—but a dog tooth nonetheless. And when we found out that she had been born with six fingers on each hand, and there was a little bump where each one had been removed, we smiled. They were small triumphs, but we took what we could get—snickering behind her back and calling her Six-finger-dogtooth-meringue-pie. But we had to do it alone, for none of the other girls would cooperate with our hostility. They adored her. (*Bluest*: 53)

Special or marked by several characteristics, Maureen extends beyond her boundaries both digitally and dentally. Whether the edible part of her is lemon of the traditional meringue, she is, at least, unmistakably the browned beaten fluffy sugar-fortified white of eggs, a kind of icing, a layer. She is dessert, and almost everyone wants dessert. Claudia and Frieda omit "lemon" in their noun epithet dis-riff, but the implication is unavoidable. Because of her own lusciousness, Maureen will be hoisted by her own braids. The beast—the base beast which does not admit of metamorphosis—will hang the beauty.

Knowledge of the 1934 *Imitation* is conveyed to us by Maureen; she is a medi-um who brings a message of another world, the Hollywood film world. Maureen is a go-between (compare the 1971 British film, *The Go-Between*, directed by Joseph Losey). She links up Hollywood mythology with the real pain of the small town in which *Bluest* plays its own run. Maureen passes between, and this suggests Hermes who is an exemplar of all that has to do with going between: speed, prof-it, potency, fertility, luck, theft, exchange. She is, after all, a goddess in her landscape and everyone else's vision except for the narrating sisters. Maureen reports infor-mation to Pecola about Pecola's name, but Pecola is beyond the reach of benefit. The narrative reveals a flesh and blood causality of literature and celluloid. "As we emerged from the school with Maureen…A group of boys were circling and hold-ing at bay a victim. Pecola Breedlove" (*Bluest*: 54).

Pecola's physical and syntactic objective isolation is striking here. The boys chant at Pecola: "Black e mo. Black e mo. Yadaddsleepnakked. Black e mo black e mo ya dadd sleeps nekked. Black e mo…" (*Bluest*: 55). The narrative comments and informs the reader:

> It was contempt for their own blackness that gave the first insult its teeth. They seem to have taken all of their smoothly cultivated ignorance, their exquisite-ly learned self-hatred, their elaborately designed hopelessness and sucked it all

up into a fiery cone of scorn that had burned for ages in the hollows of their minds—cooled—and spilled over lips of outrage, consuming whatever was in its path. They danced a macabre ballet around the victim, whom, for their own sake, they were prepared to sacrifice to the flaming pit. (*Bluest*: 55)

Pecola, surrounded by the pickets of male cruelty and racist resonance, drops her notebook and covers her eyes, not her face, with her hands. Frieda attacks one of the boys. Her physical and verbal force enable Pecola's release. Maureen, who has been peripheral, "suddenly animated, put her velvet-sleeved arm through Pecola's and began to behave as though they were the closest of friends:

"I just moved here. My name's Maureen Peal. What's yours?"
"Pecola."
"Pecola? Wasn't that the name of the girl in *Imitation of Life*?"
"I don't know. What is that?"
"The picture show, you know. Where this mulatto girl hates her mother 'cause she is black and ugly but then cries at the funeral. It was real sad. Everybody cries in it. Even Claudette Colbert."
"Oh." Pecola's voice was no more than a sigh.
"Anyway, her name was Pecola too. She was so pretty. When it comes back I'm going to see it again. My mother has seen it four times."

122

The ritual of the fiery pit and the circumvallated victim yields to exorcism by film. Does this mulatto girl speak her own life and destiny or Pecola's? Claudette Colbert is a towering image of whiteness in the film. She appears in a dazzling white, contour-enhancing gown—a reiterative second skin—at one point in *Imitation*, and generates a dominant iconography for what is white and crystalline. R.D. Laing reported that a female patient whom he had been treating for schizophrenia arrived one day "amazingly transformed…Obviously something very decisive had happened" (Laing [1978]: 154-5). She had seen Fellini's *La Strada* every day for a week and was moving towards curing herself. Whatever "curing" means, something aligned with caring for oneself is involved. We have all tried similar forms of visual narrative therapy through multiple viewings of the same film. We do not know what Maureen's mother looks like, or what her father looks like. Is one parent darker than the other? Are they both fair skinned? Is one of the two white? The permutations are without end. Even Claudette Colbert cries.

Maureen's awareness and rendering of the film's essentials (which she has not seen) play against the experience of Pauline, Pecola's mother, but the actual name of the girl in *Imitation* is Peola. The source of the mutation is either Maureen's mother, Maureen herself, or the intensity of the moment in which Maureen needs to identify with Pecola and move her from the commonplace into the rare by tying her to the stars or a nonearthbound lineage. The conflated name is interesting;

Pecola is either what Pauline "misheard" or "mispronounced" and it is certainly what Maureen misidentifies. While various mistaken identities are there, the identities are inescapable. Pecola is Peola—dead on. Pauline puts her own creative imprimatur on this child with a predestined name. The name with the "c" has some suggestion of Latin *peccatum* (mistake, fault, error) while Peola sounds floral.

Maureen presents informed hearsay, but Pauline has logged the real movie time. Pregnant with her first child, Sammy:

> She went to the movies instead [of staying home doing chores]. There in the dark her memory was refreshed and she succumbed to her earlier dreams. Along with the idea of romantic love, she was introduced to another—physical beauty. Probably the most destructive thoughts in the history of human thought. She was never able, after her education in the movies, to look at a face and not assign it to some category in the scale of absolute beauty, and the scale was one she absorbed in full from the silver screen...There the black and white images came together, making a magnificent whole—all projected through the ray of light from above and behind. "I 'member one time I went to see Clark Gable and Jean Harlow. I fixed my hair up like I'd seen hers on a magazine. A part on the side, with one little curl on my forehead. It looked just like her. Well, almost just like."

When Pecola was born, Pauline thought:

> She looked like a black ball of hair...A right smart baby she was. I used to like to watch her...You know they makes them greedy sounds. Eyes all soft and wet. A cross between a puppy and a dying man. But I knowed she was ugly. Head full of pretty hair, but Lord she was ugly. (*Bluest*: 98, 99–100)

Pauline, by her visual education through the movies, is both reeled up and reeled in; she is loaded up, cast out and searching for a catch. Activity and passivity are difficult to differentiate in this predicament. The unwinding and rewinding of the motion picture projector may be active or passive—depending on how one construes forward or backward motion—nevertheless, it is the motor of the machine which moves the film in one direction or the other. The tether is not infinite, no matter how many reels a film may fill, what is printed on them is exactly what is there on them. The show stops with the last developed frame. There is ultimate containment of the material and contents. The content of *High Noon*, for example, will never change, regardless of the number of viewings. Pauline, as the viewer and learner, has absorbed the visions of light and darkness and becomes the engine of their reproduction—a projector, as she projects *Imitation* onto the screen of her own black vs. white life experience. Wittingly or otherwise, Pauline not only becomes the *Imitation* but, in turn, imitates it. She is an imitation of an imitation.

The narrative of Ray Bradbury's *Fahrenheit 451* deals similarly, but much more sanguinely, with a person becoming a container/housing for a work of art. In the dystopic environment of *Fahrenheit 451* people drop out of society to join a countercultural movement and become, by memorization, the very books which are being torched into extinction by the "firemen" whose expertise is to ignite rather than extinguish.

The narrative is never explicit about whether Pauline herself saw *Imitation*, but we know that she named her daughter Pecola and saw many films at least during her first pregnancy. Maureen lets us know it coincidentally by her recognition of the significant name. Pauline, wefted into the warp of the film's loom, generates her own pattern for herself and her child's life by the naming process. The "c" intruded into the movie character's name is Pauline's private stock blend, but her daughter's destiny is a mirror of Peola in *Imitation*: denial of herself and her mother, repudiation of life, a life of disorder and sorrow. What made Pauline want to feed her daughter into the equation of the film's desperation? Pecola is infected, tormented with her blackness. Her only escape or hope is through her eyes, a way out from her head. As Pauline took film in through her eyes, made it her reality, and projected the world, Pecola, through her bluest eyes sees through an idealized camera whose basic power is to see as the white camera of Hollywood.

Another effective cinematic element involves Cholly Breedlove, husband and father. Although he is not a moviegoer, he is early in his young manhood forced to perform and engage in motion under the lights. At his aunt's funeral banquet, Cholly and Darlene slip off into the pine woods. As they are about to make love:

> There stood two white men. One with a spiritlamp, the other with a flashlight. There was no mistake about their being white; he could smell it. Cholly jumped, trying to kneel, stand, and get his pants up all in one motion. [One of the men] raced the flashlight all over Cholly and Darlene. (*Bluest*: 117)

Cholly and Darlene are now subject to a command performance: "I said, get on wid it. An' make it good, nigger, make it good. He could do no more than make-believe. The flashlight made a moon on his behind...The flashlight wormed its way into his guts." The two hunters hear their dogs barking in the vicinity and interest in human prey dissipates: "'Wait,' said the spiritlamp, 'the coon ain't comed yet.' 'Well, he have to come on his own time. Good luck, coon baby'" (*Bluest*: 117).

These are pornographic circumstances from a multiplicity of components and constitute a pornographic film scene. We watch Cholly and Darlene from the black on black species of the porno genre, not only as readers but with another set of observers who are also integral cast members and direct the entirety of the action, cut to the heartbeat of their absolute whim and enabled by their insensitivity. Flashlight and Spiritlamp, two sources of white light, looking at what looks most fascinating to them: what is not white. What is not white is obscene, and here in the act of intercourse orgasmically obscene because this is the act by which black people make new/other black people. Reproductivity is in itself a practice which implies imitation, an outcome of intercourse regardless of the cause or impulse of the act. Thus, the act is an imitation of life, but it goes farther here. Under the guns of the two hunters Cholly cannot perform the act:

> Cholly began to simulate what had gone on before. He could do no more than make-believe. Cholly, moving faster looked at Darlene. He hated her. Afterwards, he cultivated his hatred of Darlene. Never did he consider directing his hatred toward the hunter. (*Bluest*: 117–08)

Pornographic films involving males have to demonstrate the actual ejaculation of each male participant. The passing of this muster attests to the incontrovertible potency of each male character, but in *Cholly and Darlene Meet the White Hunters* this traditional element is absent. Cholly's "impotence" as the text has it, refuses the "imitation of life." The denial is an assertion of strength. The real thing will not happen with the hunters watching. The hunters do not want to see it, even though Cholly cannot manifest himself.

There are dire consequences from this disastrous experience, and they emerge unpalliated when Cholly rapes his daughter Pecola. On a Saturday afternoon, perfect for a matinee, he comes home staggering drunk:

> She was washing dishes…He wanted to break her neck—but tenderly…Guilt and impotence rose in bilious duct. What could a burned-out black man ever say to the hunched back of his eleven-year-old daughter?…What could his heavy big arms and befuddled brain accomplish that would earn him his own respect, that would in turn allow him to accept her love? A bolt of desire ran down his genitals, giving it length, and softening the lips of his anus…He wanted to fuck her—tenderly. But the tenderness would not hold. (*Bluest*: 127–8)

The text in this section of *Bluest* requires far more attention than it can receive here, but the parallel of the hunter/black-black "film" with the father-predator/daughter-prey incest species of film pornography is tight. As a young man Cholly is watched, and as a man he watches his daughter with a hunter's heart. Pecola is the showing, her father is the audience. The film is rolling but this time it is not an imitation of life recapitulating life. Pecola becomes both Cholly and Darlene. By raping his daughter, Cholly imitates the process by which she was created. He annihilates her by not allowing a normal future to take place, for she carries the future within her, but, for it to unfold—for it to have independence, however fragile, from the past, the seminal source cannot be the seed of the past generation but the present. People object strenuously to talking about intercourse because this is the one experience they want to think about least, even though they pursue it. Intercourse is the primal experience, the ground zero of perpetuation of the genus. The problem with the act is consciousness of it. Talking about intercourse raises it, for many people, into the realm of consciousness and out of the realm of the senses, the unseen, the undefined, the undifferentiated. Consciousness brings responsibility with it. Cholly is a working-class black man. Cholly, pursued by the events of his own life and history, roots Pecola, confines her to his old well-known script of life. He is the director and the outcome of his direction will remain the same. He is Pecola's producer as well as her director. The narrative is fixed just as it is in *Imitation*.

Pecola's final destination is flight into her own head. Crazy is the place that when you have to go there you have to let yourself in. R. D. Laing, in *Sanity, Madness, and the Family*, suggests that individuals beset by circumstances which do not allow solutions create a place of refuge in their minds to which they repair. A state of *insanity*—that is, of *unhealthiness*—promotes the development of a tolerable environment which offers the hope of a sane existence. The movies are a place to go when one needs to go somewhere, and once inside a dark comfortable theater what is projected on to a screen is recorded onto the "film" in the viewer's head. Pecola goes away from the self-salting wound of a black life lived within the confines of a white-dictated dominant culture and its chromatic aesthetic. She "splits" the scene which is already "split," "unbearable, and unattainable." Her intense dialogue with herself (disguised lightly as a friend) in the narrative's final pages (*Bluest*: 150–8) remind us that the price of bluest eyes is eternal vigilance; how blue is blue, and how do you know if you have the bluest of blue eyes? These blues are the worst of all blues. The song line "Am I blue…?" as Pecola's blues, means "Am I white?" Pecola cannot escape the schizoid nature of her existence. To escape her father and all the life around her she becomes schizophrenic. The "choice" of an alternative space is particularly appropriate because a racist society forces people of color into social schizophrenia. Pecola's dual-self interlocution, which Plato would liked to have written, tried to write but couldn't, brings us into the turmoil of escape:

How many times are you going to look inside that old thing?
I didn't look in a long time.
You did too…
So what? I can look if I want to.
I didn't say you couldn't. I just don't know why you have to look every minute. They aren't going anywhere.
I know that. I just want to look.
You scared they might go away?
Of course not. How can they go away?
The others went away.

They didn't go away. They changed.
Go away. Change. What's the difference?
A lot. Mr Soaphead said they would last forever.
Forever and ever Amen? (*Bluest*: 150)

These lines are just the lips of Pecola's dialogue. She discovers a locus to provide herself asylum, but her obsession asphyxiates her.

Mr. Soaphead Church, who makes himself available as the instrument which delivers the coup de grace to Pecola's sanity, is one of a number of males in the text who prey on women and young girls. In fact, the male presence in the text is lecherous, surly, distempered, violent, and rapinous. Mr. Soaphead is, moreover, a *primus inter pares*. His appearance as the narrative begins to close, gives us a man of pain; he radiates the agony of his own, not only racially but sexually, repressed life. He has been a practitioner of the imitation of life. His light complexion, his white roots, his attempts to do the same type of thing Pecola wants, makes them an ironic match. No one in town is clear on who and what Soaphead is, and Soaphead is not clear about his own life. He seems to run a chronic skirmish against the inroads of the truth of blackness. The confusion—the impediment to vision—is in his head. He is unable to wash himself out; the soap remains on his head and his head cannot come clean. He can, Pecola thinks, fulfill her "phantasy," even though his step places her in the vestibule of hell. Pecola is the neophyte child star whose new star eyes the will be divine blue orbs which will shine down from heaven. Soaphead "Church" has the power to communicate with natural forces; he can perform miracles and place her in the heaven of the gods. He is Pecola's director, as was Cholly Breedlove, but on a much higher plane because he appears to be legitimate theater, although he is even more acutely pornographic, much like the impotent Wizard of Oz who is an obscene faker. We move back into the cinematic matrix of the narrative even more because Soaphead becomes the make-up person when he "applies" the blue eye "treatment" to Pecola. Dorothy makes it back to reality, Pecola does not.

Claudia and Frieda, Pecola's contemporaries, advance much of the narrative of *Bluest*. They also exert a force for insight and integrity over against the assumption of the garments of imitation. For a brief time, a boarder, Mr. Henry, comes to stay with their family as Pecola did. When he meets the sisters, he flatters them with filmstar references: "'Hello there. You must be Greta Garbo, and you must be Ginger Rogers.' We giggled. Even my father was startled into a smile" (*Bluest*: 17). Mr. Henry will, however, violate propriety with the girls and be summarily banished, but the sisters make it clear that they loved him and their memory of him was without bitterness. The bestowal of star names upon the girls wishes them whiteness in extremis. Their father, who is elsewhere imperturbable, is caught off guard, and that smile reflects just how much he might buy into the swindle. After all, these are the most serene complements from the very dapper and wonderfully

127

SCHWARTZ

fragranced Mr. Henry. Claudia, the younger sister, strikes a blow for reality, establishing a path for sanity:

> Frieda brought her [Pecola] four graham crackers on a saucer and some milk in a blue and white Shirley Temple cup. She was a long time with the milk, and gazed fondly at the silhouette of Shirley Temple's face…I hated Shirley. Not because she was cute, but because she danced with Bojangles, who was my friend, my uncle, my daddy, and who ought to have been soft-shoeing it and chuckling with me. Instead he was enjoying, sharing, giving a lovely dance thing with one of those little white girls whose socks never slid down under their heels. (*Bluest*: 19)

Consonant with her anti-Shirley Templeism, Claudia fights a guerilla war with white baby dolls:

> I destroyed white baby dolls.
> But the dismembering of dolls was not the true horror. The truly horrifying thing was the transference of the same impulse to little white girls. The indifference with which I could have axed them was shaken only by my desire to do so. To discover what eluded me; the secret of the magic they weaved on others.
> If I pinched them, their eyes—unlike the crazy glint of the baby doll's eyes—would fold in pain and their cry would not be the sound of an icebox door, but a fascinating cry of pain. The best hiding place was love. Thus the conversion from pristine sadism to fabricated hatred, to fraudulent love. It was a small step to Shirley Temple. I learned much later to worship her, just as I learned to worship cleanliness, knowing even as I learned that the change was adjustment without improvement. (*Bluest*: 22)

128

Claudia navigates her way around, through and past Hollywood's bombardment of images, cultural icons, poison gas and nonwhite ethnic defoliants. In *Imitation*, Peola rejects her blackness on the screen. In *Bluest*, Pecola's mother has force imparted on her life and even more intensely on her daughter's life by the film. Although there is a message in the film for the white Hollywood audiences, it states very little about cause or resolution of the problem and its magnitude. Claudia's disquisition about media and toys reveals the impact of Hollywood on black audiences who want to fight back and claim their right to American filmic consciousness, conscience, and representation.

SCHWARTZ

NOTE

1 *Imitation of Life* is cited throughout as "*Imitation*" and *The Bluest Eye* will be cited as "*Bluest*."

OF PROPERTY

On "Captive" "Bodies," Hidden "Flesh," and Colonization

G.M. James Gonzalez[1]

chapter 9

*El pensamiento es mas malo que la brujeria...No
hay dos cosas mas malas que la lengua y el pensamiento.*
                                    —Catalina Serrano

*American domination—the only domination from
which one never recovers. I mean from which one
never recovers unscarred.*
                                    —Aimé Césaire

*Every man has a property in his own person...The
labor of his body and the work of his hands, we may
say, are properly his. Whatsoever then he removes
out of the state that nature has provided and left it
in, he has mixed his labor with, and joined to it
something that is his own, and thereby makes it his
property.*
                                    —John Locke

IN A recent conversation with my aunt Catalina (Tita) Serrano, she declared
that thought and tongue were among the most damaging tools a person can
employ against another. As I think about the subject at hand, Tita's very clear,
perceptive, and incisive statement summarizes and captivates my point of
departure. Tongue (language, voice, rhetoric) and thought (ideology) have
been among the deadliest instruments of colonialism. Their deeds unleashed
muster, brew, and stir roots whose effects still engender our general malaise
called colonization. Tongue and thought are, therefore, infectious and untrust-
worthy within the colonizer and the colonized; for the colonized has also
been infected.

This is where we begin, weaving with the threads of this pronged snare.
Tongue and thought move on different levels as they infect their victims in
multilayers and textures. The images and their meanings, hieroglyphic in their

motif, are violent and corrupt; the nature of their forcefulness produces, as Aimé Césaire suggests, scars from which one never recovers. In this context, tongue, thought, and scars become important in understanding the dynamics of the creation and maintenance of "human" entity (objectified entity) as property. The notion of property here invoked is Lockean in nature where property is originally acquired when an agent mixes his labor with a preowned object. (Though Hegel and Marx provide very interesting approaches to understanding labor, this essay is only concerned with Locke's.) In this context, the slave, the colonized, is that being transformed with the tools of tongue, thought, physical scaring and carnal molding. It is important to understand that the transformation of human beings into property is not part of what some might consider a brief and dated historical event (slavery) but a continuing colonial infectious disease that weaves into our lives unsolicited ways of becoming and understanding who we are.

In "Mama's Baby, Papa's Maybe: An American Grammar Book," Hortense J. Spillers describes her existence as part of a larger system of identification—what she has called "a locus of confounded identities, a meeting ground of investments, and privations in the national treasury of rhetorical wealth" (65). She links herself, an entity of historical and national significations, to current discussions of black womanhood and, especially to the myth of black matriarchy propounded by *The Moynihan Report*. Spillers creates a critical methodological conception which is useful in the discussion of the transformation of being (human) into property. This methodological conception is the distinction between "body" and "flesh."

Spillers argues that "body" represents the corporeal object which not only labors but is disciplined and tortured. "Flesh," on the other hand, can be understood as ethnicity, that which holds channels and conducts cultural meanings and inscriptions. In this paradigm, Spillers has identified the "body" as that which is "captive" and the "flesh" as that which is "liberated." Reading this methodological distinction into the question of property, then, one can deduce that in the process of becoming propriety we are physically and symbolically transformed from "flesh" into "body." This transformation of an objectified entity from "flesh" into "body" is akin to the conversion of a tree into lumber, and eventually into furniture, a carved sculpture, a building structure, or the leaf of a page.

In the process of converting a tree into useful property the tree undergoes a series of transformations. First, loggers must choose and chop the tree. Once severed it is stripped of its bark and further reduced to various sizes and cut into differing shapes to suit a purpose. Through this process the tree becomes "simple" property, that is, an object fit for special use. The wood once prepared is bought by a builder who finalizes the transformation by laboring on this wood to construct the item of utility, that is, the chair, the factory building, or sculpture. By means of this process the wood moves through a second tier of change, that is, a modification invoked by "labor-mixing." Objectified "human" entity experiences a similar process of transformation. The captive being once identified is severed and removed from its roots, its habitat. This objectified entity journeys in a state of non-identity, packed inhumanely and in transport to a place where it is further stripped of its "outer" appearance—slightly molded into something identifiable, useful and valuable to the property owner. However, the lumber is of no use until it is converted by the property owner. Hence, beyond the moment of capture, a period of transfer (the middle passage), the period of preparation (bathing, clothing, and oiling of the skin) and the point of sale, there exists an additional more fundamental laboring process employed by the property owner who like the builder transforms the "raw" material. In this process, where branding, naming, labor training, language acquisition, Christianization, racialization, and so forth occur, the human entity is fully transformed into a slave, an object of utility. It is precisely at this juncture that the objectified entity changes from "flesh" into "body." Most importantly, just as it is the craftsman's skill and purpose to turn wood into certain kinds of items of utility, with equal measure the property owner of objectified entities must excercise his role in turning "flesh" into "body."

From Spillers' point of view, the "flesh" never totally disappears. Instead, it remains hidden or unseen in lieu of the process of transformation just described. Now, though the tree (of mahogany, oak, maple) is turned into "raw" usable wood the distinct character of this tree, that is, its "mahoganyness," "oakness," "mapleness" never disappears and constrains the set of uses to which it can be put. In a similar fashion, the "flesh" of the objectified entity never vanishes. The point is that just as the wood is resistant to certain modes of transformation so does the "flesh" of the "body," unseen, cause resistance to modes of treatment and change. Thus, "body" as appropriated mechanized substance is in performance or on display. But the wood constructed does not remain "raw" in its appearance. Furniture, for example, may be carved, polished and stained. In this way, one can understand the aesthetic function/signification of the wood. What we place on the raw wood furniture to "finish" the treatment is as essential a part of the propertied process as purchasing the wood and making the furniture. Likewise, the slave is given a second "flesh," a masking of its identity filled with new cultural significations. This imparting of the second "flesh" is the completion of the propertied process.

"Africans" experienced a process of transformation into slaves which was simultaneously phenomenological and Foucaultian. As the being is transformed into an object of utility, that is, converted from "flesh" into "body" a rift occurs whereby individually situated vision and existence is obscured and reproduced in a new fashion by a mode of new world being. This new world being is not simply objectified; objectification of the slave takes on a different dimension. The mode of objectification described here is one where ideology creates not only a lingual figure (riddled with meaning as to its relationality to this social situation) but also a carnal figure one that is physically transformed to act in accordance with this new relation. Utility as applied to the slave means creation of an appropriated mechanized substance that has been shaped and conditioned to act in concord with racist and capitalist structures of domination.

"Body" as appropriated mechanized substance becomes a catalyst for incurring a different mode of understanding selfhood in the slave. That is, the slave is transformed in virtue of this carnal mode of being seen, and temporally related, that is, renamed and recognized only as an instrument of utility and coerced into performing this role. Thus, "body" as appropriated mechanized substance lends itself to existing as performance. "Captive" takes on a new meaning. It means not simply enslaved but a special kind of invisibility, that is, at the same time seen and unseen.

It is important to point to varying levels and movements that influence the shift in this mode of new world being. Existing in relation to and to some measure in formation by the property owner, as appropriated and mechanized the preexisting ethnic and cultural being, and as slave, this entity is unseen (hidden) through the process of conversion into property. Therefore, the foremost presence (mode of being) "seen"/recognized in this social situation is that which the legitimacy of the second "flesh" engenders. The subject in question is in performance within the ideological bounds given to his converted character. However, just as the first "flesh" never disappears, a differing point of vision which it can manifest (the mode of behavior, naming, and recognizing the world) is always possible for the appropriated entity. Thus, the second "flesh" is a shell, and the estranged colonized entity, now known as slave, is not always forced to be solely in relation to the property owner; for there always exists the potential to exist in relation to another reality outside this relation. Thus, colonization can also be understood as a movement to which one is and is not simultaneously a part of the colonizer where the present social situation for the slave suspends, as if it were, the first "flesh." This first "flesh" is recognized while at the same time a mode of operation has been created where "flesh" appears unseen.

Lynching, raping, whipping, maiming, callousing hands and feet, as well as other physical markings, bodily demeanor, and language, create a figure who is but unqualifiably owned by an agent with power to create transformations. "Flesh" does not disappear but creates a movement towards itself-a replenishing of its own. The colonial condition is precisely this. We are not "new" trees but wood from the same trees taken apart, processed, transformed, and recycled attempting to put ourselves back together. Contemporary Afro-Diasporic-American women writers, such as Marlene N. Philip and Toni Morrison, address this motion of the self toward itself as a kind of entity (bodily) that seeks to recollect, revive, and return:

> the smallest cell
>
> remembers
>
> a sound
>
> (sliding two semitones to return home) (Philip: 63)

132

GONZALEZ

The body as an instrument, fossiled and rhythmic sounding tones, chords and measures calls absent parts of itself to appear at the stroke of memory. In the essay "The Site of Memory," Toni Morrison addresses the movement of the self back to itself in a similar fashion. She writes:

> All water has a perfect memory and is forever trying to get back to where it was. Writers are like that: remembering where we were, what valley we ran through, what the banks were like, the light that was there and the route back to our original place. Its emotional memory-what the nerves and the skin remember as well as how it appeared. (305)

But, where is home? In a fragmented state, home is a mythic place to which there is no return.

Colonization today can be understood as containing different features—movements of new world being inherited from occupation of the America's. To put it simply, not only is there a movement where "body" (disciplined and mechanized) calls upon attributes and motions of ownership, that is, I am not simply metaphor but even more, I am manually manipulated, disciplined, if you will, into this transformation informed by racist ideology. This discipline is the result of ideological ways of being which perpetuate structures of domination.

Each hieroglyphic mark on my body, each way of understanding those scars that is not my own and from which the world comes to understand who I am, each physical event that shapes my physical experience with respect to an other which constructs for me a second existence are *las huejas, los tracos* (evidence), of the presence of tongue and thought which informs and infiltrates my daily existence in unrecognizable ways. *Las huejas, los tracos,* still appear in our present. They point to the presence of several movements (phenomenological and Foucauldian) which perpetuate "captive" bodies and hidden "flesh." So we are caught, as if were, in a five hundred year storm, ensnared by its winded tentacles.

As we ended our conversation my aunt declared, "*Así que you nunca me duermo en las pajas. No te me duermas en las pajas!*" (That is why I never fall asleep in the bushes. Don't you fall asleep in the bushes!)

GONZALEZ

133

NOTE

1 Special thanks to the following individuals whose encouragement, conversations, and reading of draft versions informed the writing of this final product: Jeffner Allen, Tom Broccleman, Lewis Gordon, Charlse Peterson, Paul Taylor, and Greg Thomas.

TOTING TECHNOLOGY

Taking it to the Streets

Bobby R. Dixon

HOW HAS technology transformed the souls of black folks and their communities? What technological images infiltrate and dominate black existence? How do these images function in black communities? Do they serve to liberate or to corrupt black existence?

Rethinking and applying some of Marcuse's hypotheses to black existence, I argue that technology has become a new form of enslavement for black communities (Marcuse [1964]). Marcuse criticized technological society (East and West) for its totalitarian features: (1) its promotion of its ideology through its products, (2) its reduction of the individual to an "external person," (3) its logic of domination or "operationalism," (4) its suppression of Historical Reason, and (5) its total mobilization and total administration of society. "Totalitarian" here does not mean merely the terroristic. The takeover of the Information Superhighway by the consolidation of MCI, Bell Atlantic, Turner

Broadcasting, and others aims toward a new total administration over the individual. This "megamedia shakeout" is bound eventually to occur with unforseen consequences. Technology is capable of abolishing "labor time" so that the masses can enjoy "free time" and become self-determined producers who meet their real needs, but instead consigns its citizens to the status of "sublimated slaves" who are driven by false needs.

Operationalism validates what "is" and manages to contain all challenge or opposition to this "truth." Here the concept is equivalent to its corresponding set of operations. This totally empirical treatment of concepts (which invaded philosophy via the analytic school) proclaims that thinking is doing. The concept is wedded to some fact or thing, and the thing is identified with its function or operations. Operationalism militates against abstract concepts. Metaphysical concepts are particularly disturbing to operationalism because of their powers of transcendence, and hence must be eliminated. Any transcending powers of Reason are devalued by this logic. Thus, the lost dimension of one-dimensional society is the dimension of Negative thinking, the ability to see or imagine what ought to be beyond what is. The "ought" is the lost potential of the masses. The "is" is the superficial policy of containment, absorption of all difference into the whole where it is neutralized and made impotent. The logic of Positive thinking, the logic of domination, characterizes the "rationality" of this society. This logic is grounded in the ritualistic, abridged language of the one-dimensional society. The "conquest of transcendence" is secured. The "conquest of thought" is accomplished.

Technology has also found the proper techniques to immerse us as individuals in the present moment while suppressing the past (or Historical Reason) and making impossible a genuine future (with real possibilities). Concepts and social categories have lost their critical capacities within this system, and a remembrance of past critical categories is shut down by hypnotic formulas and the link between concepts and facts.

Existing within the flux of technological paraphernalia and "progress," Americans have been brought up close with the futile and absurd side of their existence. The camcorder becomes the new sight, making the consumer a virtual eyewitness, while simultaneously losing sight of the real. The car phone (and the plane phone) allows instant communication with those far away as one travels, while simultaneously allowing one to avoid communication with the immediate other. The beeper makes an individual as accessible as a 911 call without the urgency of an emergency. In short, the feeling of closeness, of presence, of being there without being there, is created. The resulting feelings of autonomy, control, and access, are illusory. It is this false sense of freedom and control that is absurd and objectionable.

This absurdity is magnified even further in "the black world." While the image of the young brother toting a boom box on his shoulders is fast becoming extinct like the dodo; it is being replaced by new images of blacks who "tote" technology in various ways in and through the streets of various black communities. Armed with everything from camcorders to car phones, these electronic figures emerge everywhere, appearing to possess the power of a single, consolidated black Atlas in the contemporary world, bearing the bulk of the weight of technology, lifting its latest hardware (and ideology) onto their shoulders as they strike a pose, whether in their automobiles or walking casually down the streets.

Yet there are ways of resisting the sweeping immediacy of technological society and its political absurdity. By restructuring rather than eliminating the technological base of society, as Marcuse recommended, we can reclaim our souls and our powers of self-determination. We can implement a political reversal by the reinstitution of a self-sacrificing black intelligentsia as opposed to an avaricious black business class, as W.E.B. Du Bois proposed. Finally, we can accelerate this reversal by constructively recounting our experiences as victims of technological society (see Ramirez). I will use Wallace Terry's *Bloods* as an example of the victimized voices that have become enabling voices.

DRIVING ON THE HIGHWAY

Driving on the highway, I am struck by the numerous "technological images of coolness" that have infiltrated and corrupted black communities. I observe my brothers and sisters assume a supreme coolness in their sleek, brand-new (and not-so-brand-new) automobiles while chatting on their cellular phones. I see and hear boom boxes installed in the back of jeeps that are filled with cool teenagers who seem determined to "pump up the volume." I see pedestrians stroll by with beepers. A "cool black man" must have his beeper. It is a sign of being wanted or being in high demand, which is cool in itself. I see private citizens operating camcorders with the finesse of professional newsmen. I see intoxicating signs and billboards that add to and encourage the very technological takeover of our communities that I am observing. Exiting into the suburbs, I see homeowners cutting lawns, even minuscule ones, with the ease of riding lawn mowers. I observe the cool pose of police officers who openly tote guns on their hips. Everything and everyone are totally cool. I think of the Gwendolyn Brooks poem, "We Real Cool." Could this absurdity be the result of ads, billboards, and other signs of ethnic coolness that have inundated black communities, such as the ads that suggest that blacks who smoke Kools look cool, walk cool, and talk cool?

There is one sign outside an automobile dealership that I find especially intriguing: WE TOTE THE NOTE. Immediately my mind flashes back to images of slavery, aided by the popular song "Old Man River." Tote that bar! Lift that bell! The word "tote" rings with ambiguity as it is co-opted for capitalistic purposes. WE TOTE THE NOTE carries the irony of Nietzsche's creditor paying the debtor's debt. Who is meant by "we"? Creditor or debtor? In a totalitarian universe, creditor and debtor have seemingly coalesced into one. Are we being liberated or enslaved by the "kind deliverance" of our creditors? Their right to tote the note

137

DIXON

means our right to tote technology home. I fancy images of blacks toting those automobiles home like members of a chain gang. Chained to merchandise and to debt, black consumers are burdened not only with technological junk, but often also with repair bills, insurance costs, gas bills, and of course, the note.

Technological society is able to control us because its "ideology is in the production process itself." In other words, "The products indoctrinate and manipulate" (Marcuse [1964]: 11, 12). Beyond the "white products," certain products are packaged as "black products," promising instant assimilation into white culture. Black hair products promise to manage "unruly," or "unmanageable" (kinky) black hair, leaving it " bouncy" and "silky smooth." In a totally administered society, it follows that everyone and everything must obey, including one's hair. The message is out, or rather the messages are out: "Obey Your Thirst [Sprite]," "Just Do It [Nike]," "Don't Leave Home Without It [American Express]." With all these messages, how can one resist the temptation to buy, "to be like Mike" or like all the other kids who wear Jordan sneakers? The public is like an infant being spoonfed the "infant formulae" of commercialism, ultimately regurgitating what they have swallowed. Self-control is an improbable virtue when America promises "We'll be right back after these messages." All messages can be read as "Just Do It" without any restrictions or consequences whatsoever. Hundreds of direct commands to the public dictate daily, hourly even, the conception of *eudaemonia,* of the good life. The good life is the life of goods: "The people recognize themselves in their commodities; they find their soul in their automobile, hi-fi set, split-level home, kitchen equipment. The very mechanism which ties the individual to his society has changed, and social control is anchored in the new needs which it has produced" (Marcuse [1964]: 9). "Calvin Klein" is not only stamped upon my jeans, but also upon my consciousness.

The American automobile is the prototype of technological coolness, allowing Americans to be "king (or queen) of the road," to experience temporarily the feeling of mastery. The Cadillac has represented the quintessence of technological coolness; it has represented, in many black communities, the cool, soulful stride of the race. As a consequence of being locked out of the possibility of homeownership through such racist practices as "redlining," blacks settled for the next best symbol of American success, the American automobile. This misguided "investment" has contributed to the arrested development of black communities, which have often failed to save and invest in future black existence or in black economy.

The boom-box, in making its recent appearance, contested public spaces. Disrupting avenues and parks with their powerful vibrations, young people were essentially asserting their new-found power vis-à-vis the status quo. This power can be best described by MC Hammer's compelling, chartbusting refrain "Can't Touch This!" It was an "argument" for liberty, independence, free speech, and much more (Baker: 43). The boom box generation could also feel like rulers or "master-blasters." They could identify with power and prestige expressed in the names of

138

DIXON

artists such as: Prince, Queen Latifah, the King of Pop (Michael Jackson), the Godfather of Soul (James Brown), Dr. Dre, and others.

As an extended organ, the boom box is a different way of hearing. It is a drum, beating secret messages to a community of young listeners, hypnotized by the messages, unaware of their "bleeding" ears. The boom box or rap music is the black ear cut off and taken as souvenir by white capitalists for distribution, sales and consumption—a primitive act of violence, not unlike lynching.

Rap music is just one of the latest areas of social conquest in which producer and consumer are brought together in a process of identification and unification with the whole society through the goods sold to the consumer by the producer. White sonic capitalists and black rap artists have become countercultural brothers and sisters for the sake of huge profits. A handful of large, monopolistic record label companies are able to shout along with their artists: "I Got the Power" (Snap), "Control" (Janet Jackson), or "It's My Prerogative" (Bobby Brown). And as the consuming public buys the lyrical ideology, everybody participating in the sonic technological revolution can scream in unison like James Brown: "I feel good! I knew that I would!" The sonic psychedelic, pseudoradicalism of rap artists incorporates and dilutes the real radicalism of the sixties and seventies. Rap music has tempered violence with coolness, and created a whole industry out of coolness: Ice-T, Ice Cube, L.L. Cool J., Kool Moe Dee, Coolio, Vanilla Ice (a white rapper). Ethnic coolness has been successfully marketed as "liberation" from the "heat" of oppression.

Driving on the highway, I begin to realize too how much of a consumer I am. I begin to understand my relationship to my people. I can read the ATM expressions on their faces, the Visa look in their eyes, their American Express–ready lips, already dreaming of their next cool purchases as they command others with cool indifference to "charge it." I begin to understand why blacks are consumers par excellence. Bob Johnson, CEO of Black Entertainment Television, mentions the importance of the black consumer to the cable industry alone: "The black consumer on cable is more likely to buy cable service than the general population on almost a two-to-one basis. Blacks, for example, constitute about 25% or 26% of HBO's subscriber base" (*Broadcasting Cable* [3 July 1995]). Collectively blacks have 428 billion dollars (after taxes) to spend annually, more than a number of third-world nations. However, more than ninety-five percent of our dollars are spent outside our communities. As a result, we are committing community suicide. Despite (and because of) our sickness, we feel good. The euphoria of the Happy Consciousness is expressed in slogans from "Oh what a feeling! Toyota!" to "I love what you do for me!" These are the exclamations of both producer and consumer. Technological images serve to validate that everyone is happy and that all is well. Therefore, I feel good! I knew that I would!

Let us look at some of the controlling features of one-dimensional society. Institutions have become larger and larger technological instruments for the

139

DIXON

express purpose of carving up the individual into dysfunctional parts for maximum exploitation. Marcuse argued that technology has whittled down the individual to the point where the individual has lost his or her soul or has been reduced to the external person. In this way, institutions have promoted themselves at the expense of the individuals that they claim to serve. Even the medical profession has become an industry. Churches, built like sports arenas, demand their share of the profits. Multinational corporations dominate the globe, giving capitalism, as Marx noted, a cosmopolitan character. As a result of this self-promotion, institutions have become oversized, abstract bodies, boards, and corporations (legalized persons) that shield human administrators within from moral accountability, while fashioning everyone in their image. Thus, they can become and often do become reckless, unwieldy forces in our lives. Rap slogans like "Fight the Power" really "Can't Touch This" technological organization. These are the "great public bodies" that Descartes too left untouched as he carved up the individual's body and dispensed with it entirely.

A change in our "habits of thought" is promoted by key players in politics and mass communication: "Their universe of discourse is populated by self-validating hypotheses which, incessantly and monopolistically repeated, become hypnotic definitions or dictations" (Marcuse [1964]: 14). For example, the repetition of the mere word "free" or "freedom" conjures up cherished notions so that the Powers who utter them can rely upon them as a means of instant identification with the people they rule. These include "the free world," "the free press," "free enterprise," and "freedom fighters." The system considers itself free and labels everything outside of it as "unfree."

Another controlling feature of technological society is its militaristic, defensive posture, mobilized putatively to protect "the free world." Ironically it is through the strategies of peace and civility that it is able to dominate. Terrorism or torture is turned inward or sent back to the individual who inflicts torture upon himself or herself and takes pleasure in doing so ("frying" one's hair, getting a nose job, bleaching one's skin—in fact, all of consumerism belongs here; see Graham). The pacification for the struggle for existence is turned into a crude joke, for peace is defined as the brink of war. We are expected to accept this contradictory logic which allows for the total mobilization and total administration of society.

The perceived enemy (the Soviet Union) is built into the system, Marcuse claimed. However, since the dismantling of the Soviet Union, the notion of "an evil empire" has no force whatsoever. But "the enemy" remains built into the system. The enemy or scapegoat for America's ill is once again being assigned primarily to blacks (and the homeless). This is clear in the language of the system when it declares a war on crime (and thus builds more prisons), welfare, and affirmative action. The system falsely assumes that blacks are criminal, and are the primary beneficiaries of welfare and affirmative action. The system creates, welcomes, and feeds off of "enemies" like Minister Louis Farrakhan, Khalid Muhammad, and

Rev. Al Sharpton. The enemy in the '60s and '70s was Vietnam, and blacks were deliberately trained to perceive the Vietnamese as animals. "Right away they told us not to call them Vietnamese. Call everybody gooks, dinks…They told us they're not to be treated with any type of mercy or apprehension. That's what they engraved into you. That killer instinct" (Wallace: 90). Yet we also find a more subtle approach to victory that buttresses Marcuse's theory:

> Sometimes I think we would have done a lot better by getting [the Vietnamese] hooked on our life-style than by trying to do it with guns. Give them credit cards. Make them dependent on television and sugar. Blue jeans works better than bombs. You can take blue jeans and rock 'n' roll records and win over more countries than you can with soldiers. (Wallace: 10)

Many black soldiers ultimately realized that the United States was the enemy and that they had acted, regrettably, in complicity with its terroristic mission (Wallace: 248). America tried to do to Vietnam what four policemen did to Rodney King. Yet when a tiny, nontechnological country such as Vietnam can defend itself against the technological power of the United States, then there is much hope for humanity. Perhaps there is a "technology" of the human spirit, of human will, of human resistance.

At home, "the intellectual and emotional refusal 'to go along' appears neurotic and impotent" (Marcuse [1964]: 9). Black radicalism (The Black Panther Party, Stockley Carmichael, Angela Davis, et al.), which sought to transcend the values of the establishment, was made to appear neurotic. Anyone who uttered terms like "genocide" or "government conspiracy" was routinely accused of being paranoid.

A fitting metaphor for the control that technological society has over the individual is remote control. From a distance, some groups are magically controlling our lives as though with some physical instrument, switching our aspirations, feelings, and interests from one moment to the next. They are wiping out countless jobs and allocating a few new ones that depend less and less upon physical abilities. They are "channeling" our inner selves and thereby controlling our outer selves, while taking opinion polls to make us feel like our voices are being heard. Nintendo's slogan accurately assesses the false sense of power held by the masses: "Now you're playing with power." If we could "rewind" or "play back" our history, we would see that we have been watched and "programmed" by the very media we watch. In the end, "the medium is the message" (McLuhan). Until black communities establish and control their own media, the message is not likely to represent their interests.

DRIVING ON THE I-WAY

In 1983 *Time* Magazine's "Man of the Year" actually went to a machine, the personal computer. The accolade "Machine of the Year" or, better still, "Machine of the Century," may have been more accurate. The invention of computer microchips and the personal computer is representative of the "miniaturization of the age." A new "territory," a new New World, is being discovered on the desktop. Will blacks be brought to this new New World like slaves, serving in inferior positions, or will blacks find a way to participate freely in "cyberspace" with equal and fair access to electronic information?

Driving on the I-Way (the Information-Highway), I discover another form of technological coolness. I observe a world within a world, a mirror image of reality being created, a replica of this world with a major difference—accessibility of global information with incredible speed. I enter the datasphere. A virtual neighborhood exists on my screen. I can send and receive e-mail, join a newsgroup, purchase airline tickets, buy a "store" in a "shopping mall" for a fee and conduct business. I can connect virtually with anyone from anywhere on the planet as long as that individual is "hooked up to" (many are "hooked on") the Internet. Situated in pantheistic mediaspace, I am involved in "nets" and "webs" and "threads" and "looms" and "hyperlinks." I feel good; I knew that I would (the moment I purchased my Macintosh).

Yet this virtual neighborhood is a strange one for me, inhabited primarily by "white" bulletin boards and services. I am also just as likely to encounter racism and bigotry here as I am in the real world. But I have faith in my Internet community and remain online. I become aware of the Black Data Processing Association, the largest group pushing African-American "bulletin boards" on the Internet. I discover African-American bulletin boards, such as MetroLink and Afrinet. These on-line services provide users with e-mail, discussion groups, listings of black-owned and black-targeted businesses, and more. I begin a search for my cool brothers and sisters.

Currently computers are cool, but apparently black households are not yet hip to computers. *Crisis* reports: "According to the U.S. Census, only 8.4 percent of African Americans 18 and older use computers at home. That compares to 18.3 percent of the white population" (Putt and Valdes-Dapena [April 1995]: 7). Thus, more than twice as many whites use home computers than blacks.

The Internet, a global network of computers with no central hub, is the center of the Information Superhighway. The militaristic origins of the Internet in Arpanet disturb me (see Ellis and Rushkoff). The often quoted statistic of 30 million users having access to the Internet is, nevertheless, misleading. Stoll writes: "Quarterman estimated around two and a half million users making minimal use of the Internet, and somewhere around five million people who have access to the network" (17). This is part of the media's goal of glamorizing going online. I vacillate. My ambivalence grows. I learn that an essential part of the Internet is the World Wide Web, which has taken off recently.[1] The widespread media coverage of the Internet includes coverage by the black press that is constantly gauging what impact the Internet will have on black communities.[2] Besides the question of equal

142

DIXON

and fair access to the Information Superhighway, other issues include "electronic redlining" and black participation in the construction of the Information Superhighway. While we should all keep abreast of the changes in information technology, we should not expect it to be a panacea for our social and economic problems.

Are black communities, which play such a small role in information technology, being managed and controlled by white media conglomerates? Here we may learn from past issues of technological control in communications between "first-world" and "third-world" countries, if I may digress for a moment. Multinational corporations tend to argue for the free flow of information, which sounds prima facie rational, given the operative word "free," which has been discussed above. Closer examination will reveal that the expression "free-flow of information" is a deceptive license to exploit underdeveloped nations. This doctrine advocates that no restrictions should be placed on the massive exports of Western media to the third world, along with a flood of manufactured products. The free flow doctrine is part of the developmentalist perspective that claims that such freely flowing media will lead to urbanization, increased political development, and eventually modernization (see Mosco). In a recent interview, Douglas Rushkoff uses a useful metaphor to support his belief in the free flow of information on the Internet: "At the end of the day, you can't really control the flow of the Internet any more than you can control the flow of the ocean. It's like water—it's going to spread where it wants to, and even if they build a little dike here and there, it's gonna eventually bust through" (*The Net* [June 1995]: 61).

The same is true of the free flow of highway traffic, but we still justifiably have restrictions on such traffic. Rushkoff uses another metaphor, a biological one of "viruses," to describe the mediaspace, except for him it is not just a metaphor (1994). Media viruses are real. Media events are infectious. Like plants, media viruses consist of "self-similar" patterns that replicate, and as they grow they overlap to form complex networks that are difficult to uproot. Roots and leaves function this way. Uprooting a plant may involve a whole web or tangle of roots.

Media viruses are protected by shells that act like "Trojan horses." Once they are allowed to enter the mediaspace as a result of their deceptively friendly appearance, they set out to attack the mediaspace, their host. They do this through "memes" inside the shell. Memes, as opposed to genes, are the "genetic" ideological codes that change the codes of the host. Rushkoff claims that this change is a beneficial, evolutionary "mutation" of the system rather than a change that would destroy or harm the system. Rushkoff's analogy is fine up to this point. I contend that media viruses tend to harm the mediaspace. A case in point is with the free flow of information from the West to third-world countries. Without any restrictions a Western media virus would overwhelm a third-world host, leaving the host weak and underdeveloped, a condition that is profitable to the Western media virus, allowing

143

DIXON

it to thrive indefinitely. Criticism of the developmentalist view, in fact, blames the failure of modernization upon such free flow.

The world system perspective makes this more clear (Mosco: 143). This perspective assesses the effects of the global information order: (1) core (capitalist) countries, (2) periphery (third-world) countries, and (3) semiperiphery countries (such as China and Singapore). The latter act as a buffer between the core and periphery countries, as core countries extract profits from the periphery (and semi-periphery). In the process, a plethora of human abuses are committed (Mosco: 152).

Returning to the United States and its relation to the black world, we can see a "self-similar" information order. White media conglomerates are the core using black artists and entertainers as semiperiphery agents or buffers in their exploitation of the periphery, the black masses. By stealing, albeit usually legally, black culture and selling it back to blacks via black artists, they are protected from any perception of transgression. The free flow of white media into black communities is overwhelming us as hosts. WE TOTE THE NOTE for this "freedom." Black artists are paid for their services after capitalists reap profits from them. This is the time and place for black artists to "Just Say No." However, such refusal to go along would make them appear as neurotic as the radicals of the '60s and '70s. Thus, they give in to sonic psychedelic, pseudoradicalism. They parade as "Cop Killer," "Public Enemy," and "Sister Souljah," fighting quixotic, revolutionary battles for their people. The black world once represented the oppositional force to the white world. Since the end of the Black Power movement, it has been contained as a moment of the larger, white society. Nevertheless, the contradictions are always there, threatening to explode the whole. Such a feeling of explosion emerged after the Rodney King verdict. But once again, the contradictions have been canceled and held in abeyance by the whole.

The developmentalist view was often argued in the Rodney King case (and the Anita Hill case). The Rodney King virus spread rapidly because it had an extremely high media iteration. Iteration and feedback are related concepts. Feedback is like a thermostat interacting with its environment. Iteration is the magnification of feedback, similar to a microphone that feedbacks sound into itself millions of times per second. Rushkoff claims that such an iteration leads to social reform, in this case, reform of the social justice system. Police cars would be armed with camcorders, many people thought, and that would be the solution to criminal justice for the black man. On the contrary, one could argue that the King virus did more harm than good. One could argue that its iteration served to anesthetize the public to the brutality of the beating (hence the first jury decision), that it neutralized initial disgust, and even helped to further criminalize the black male. The media accentuated King's fleeing from the police, drug allegations, his prior criminal record, and his "monstrous" physical size. The black media, overwhelmed by the free flow of the white media, could do little to alter such perceptions, just as it can

144

DIXON

do little to alter present perceptions of welfare and affirmative action. Psychologically the iteration was the black man's nightmare and the white man's daydream. The repetitious blows were also blows to the black psyche.

In order to effect social justice today that will be meaningful to black existence, traditional forms of protest and resistance may no longer be sufficient. Can protesting and organizing be revolutionized by networking through the Internet? The Internet presently represents an alternative form of communication to the traditional media. The images of blacks that have been fabricated by Hollywood and the media may be undermined by the Internet, only if we seize the opportunity to develop networks of communication. The "talented tenth" that Du Bois envisioned exists, but the media would never divulge this to the public. Too many of the talented tenth have been alienated from each other as well as from their people. Once the talented tenth connect with each other, hopefully they will develop plans for improving the conditions of black existence.[3] This can be achieved without the whole race going online. With all the talk about coalition-building among blacks and other groups, this may be the best moment for capitalizing upon this approach, especially given the recent crisis of the NAACP (see Lerner and West [1995]; and Curry).

If we believe the simple premise that information is power, we should immediately realize the endless possibilities that information technology can provide for black existence. If the media have been among black America's worst enemies, could the Internet represent a possible political reversal? While I do not see a revolution here, I do see unusual opportunities for the race. We could supplement traditional forms of organization and protest with organization and protest on the net. Since the church is still probably the greatest asset of black communities, the church should not feel that it is beneath its spiritual dignity to make available these technological resources for its congregation. Black college campuses must certainly become centers of information technology.

But most of all, blacks will have to make tremendous sacrifices. That means foregoing luxuries, and investing instead. This would be part of the "great refusal," of not going along with the absurd interests of technological society. In the past we have lost our land, our patent rights to inventions, and much more. Investing in items of information technology would be one of the best investments for the race. During the '60s and '70s, radical blacks talked about making such sacrifices by living simply and frugally in the hills, preparing for guerilla warfare. The new "guerilla warfare" may be sacrificing our luxuries in order to afford information technology from which we can map out our strategies for not only future survival, but also future self-sufficiency or well-being, a future *eudaemonia in black*. Anna Julia Cooper developed an interesting theory of value that understood the nature of black consumerism and sought to combat it. We would do well to take heed of her words. Cooper's theory categorizes the worth of individuals according to how much they produce or consume. One who consumes as much as he or she produces is nil, a mere statistic to be taken in the census. One who consumes more than he or she produces is a parasite, a thief. One who produces more than he or she consumes is a treasure to the world, giving back more than what was taken. In a sense, blacks seem to be natural-born consumers by their extravagant lifestyles. Yet Cooper also realizes the unremunerated labor that blacks have given to the world, and imagines with a sense of irony how a black individual would respond to the question of whether he or she is more of a producer or a consumer, more of one who has taken or one who has given back to the world: "Yea, Lord; I give back *all*. I am even now living on the prospects of next year's income. I give my labor at accommodation rates, and forthwith reconvert my wages into the general circulation. Funds, somehow, don't seem to stick to me. I have no talents, or smaller coins either, hid in a napkin." She adds: "It will be well for him to learn, however, that it is not what we make but what we save that constitutes wealth" (Cooper: 272). We must, however, be willing to think big and act boldly like the late Reginald Lewis, who was the wealthiest person of African descent in the history of the USA, and ask: "Why should white guys have all the fun?"

Until we have a full understanding of our history, especially our economic history, there will be no significant progress of the race. We need to understand everything from the Freedman's Savings and Trust Company debacle to the prosperity of the black community of Durham, North Carolina (see Quarles: 270; Du Bois [1995]: 253-8.) We need to understand that much of the attack on Garvey was not the result of his political power, but a consequence of his economic enterprises, even though he may have been financially inept at times. We need to understand why black businessmen especially were lynched in this country (see Wells-Barnett [1970]). We need to understand that the Black Panther Party was attacked by the government for its sound economic (socialist and capitalist) impact on black communities—its free-shoe program, its breakfast program for kids, and its impact in making black capitalists give back to the black communities from which they profited. We need to understand the reasons for the downfall of our everyday economic adventures, including the stories of rags-to-riches-and-back-to-rags of black artists. Economics or wealth is the key to results. But we must also be mindful of Du Bois' adjustment to his theory of the talented tenth, and balance economic good sense with moral values. Du Bois recognized one of the false assumptions of his theory of the talented tenth, namely that the talented tenth would be disciplined, self-sacrificing men of goodwill, strongly interested in the promotion of their race: "Negro businessmen exploited Negro labor directly in their enterprises, and the rest of the Negro Middle Class became links in the white exploitation of all labor. Meantime the Negro money-makers began to displace the black intelligentsia of the race" (Du Bois [1995]: 356). Hopefully we can say once again like E. Franklin Frazier before he discovered the shame of the black middle class: "No longer can men say that the Negro is lazy and shiftless and a consumer. He has gone to work. He is a producer. He is respectable. He has a middle class" (333). If we must be

146

DIXON

consumers, let us be first and foremost intelligent consumers of information. Let us take information technology to the streets and to the people.

NOTES

1 See *Business Week* (April 1995).

2 See, e.g., *Ebony* (January 1995; April 1995); *Crisis* (April 1995); *Ebony* (January 1995) *Broadcasting Cable* (July 1995); *Black Enterprise* (February 1995): 176–184.

3 We await the significance of the "day of absence" for black consumers: 16 October 1995.

147

DIXON

SOCIAL DISAPPOINTMENT AND THE BLACK SENSE OF SELF

Bill E. Lawson[1]

The hard-hearted individual never sees people as people, but rather as mere objects or impersonal cogs in an ever-turning wheel. In the vast wheel of industry, he sees men as hands.

—M.L.K., Jr.

chapter 11

MOST PEOPLE have experienced disappointment in their lives. Disappointment occurs generally when someone fails to satisfy the hopes, desires, or expectations of someone. Disappointment also occurs when someone frustrates or thwarts the hopes, desires, or expectations of someone. Disappointments can come from many quarters. We can be disappointed with our own failings, the failings of others, and when events do not turn out the way we expected. What is interesting is how we deal with the experiences of disappointments. We can think of disappointment as a function D that ranges over various entities. Thus there is an x such that $D(x)$. What are the possible values of x, that is, what can be disappointed? A person, of course, but not only persons: stockholders, a board of directors, the Senate and so on. Of course, not all disappointments are equal. Disappointment presupposes some expectations. For example, if I fail to win a lottery that I didn't expect to win, I cannot sensibly be said to be disappointed.

Some disappointments are minor, while others can be life changing. Our responses to experiences of disappointment will vary according to the social context in which the person finds himself or herself and to the level of expectation of outcome. The social understanding that one brings to the events can also impact on the response to the experience of disappointment.

In a discussion with my nine-year-old son William during a train ride from London to Oxford in the summer of 1995, he cited what for him would be two different experiences of disappointment and the ways in which these experiences would impact on him. In the first example, I fail to bring home a particular computer game that he wants to play. William is disappointed only if he expected me to bring the game. The mere fact that he wanted the game does not establish that he experienced disappointment. William admitted that he would be dissatisfied but not disappointed.

On the other hand, if I had failed to take him with me on my trip to England, his disappointment would be greater and that experience of disappointment would be more profound. This, of course, presupposes that he expected to be taken to England. If I told William that I was going to take him and then failed to do so, he would be greatly disappointed. The trip had taken on greater significance because his expectations were high. I knew that going to England was a trip he really wanted to make. His reactions to the different experiences of disappointment are connected to the social context and his level of expectations.

We can nevertheless think of a social context where my failure to bring home the games caused greater disappointment than my failure to take him to England. For example, I had made promises to him before and failed to keep them, and so William views my bringing the game home as a final test of my willingness to keep my word to him. I do not bring the game home and William is crushed. On the other hand, if I had made many promises and failed to keep them, my not keeping this promise might not generate a deep feeling of disappointment. A person's reaction to experiences of disappointments is connected to his or her expectations. Our expectations are in turn shaped by our own social circumstances. Social circumstances and expectations may impact on our response to the experience of disappointment.

We have many examples of disappointments in our personal lives. However, I want to consider the experience of disappointment in the more specific context of the lives of blacks in the U.S. I am concerned not with the day-to-day experiences of disappointments, but with the experience of disappointment that comes from the failure of the government to satisfy the expectations of the majority of blacks. I call this type of disappointment "social disappointment." I take social disappointment to be the failure of the government to do it duty to protect the rights of a group and the experience of disappointment that follows.

A classic example of social disappointment is Frederick Douglass' admonition of the Emancipation as a fraud. Douglass had hoped that the U.S. government would live up to the tenets of the Declaration of Independence and the Constitution after emancipation. After a trip to the South in 1888, he wrote that former slaves were in fact worse off, in many respects, than they had been as slaves (Douglass [1972]: 526).

Douglass was disappointed that the federal government and former slave holders had not lived up to his expectations about the treatment of former slaves. One might find fault with Douglass for putting his faith in former slaveholders to do right by their former slaves. Nevertheless, Douglass was clear about his disappointment with the government for not working to make the lot of former slaves better. That is, the government had failed to ensure that these citizens were protected from violations of their basic constitutional rights to the elected franchise or the right to basic physical protection. Not only was Douglass disappointed, but a review of the literature by blacks during this period in history shows that many blacks were disappointed with the failure of the government to protect blacks.

In this regard, a critical factor of expectation is that one expects the government to behave in a positive fashion towards blacks. Most African Americans would claim that in general life in the U.S. as citizens has been a series of disappointments. The experience of disappointment has come from a failure of the government to live up to their expectation about their treatment as citizens. The greater the expectation, the greater the experience of disappointment when the expectations are not met. (My comments at this juncture only refer to those blacks who still have such expectations.)

What is the effect of social disappointment on the black sense of self? We find many different answers to this question. Some writers have claimed that the experience of disappointment causes a sense of nihilism (see West [1991]). Others have claimed that it produces a sense of resentment (see Grier; Cose; and Hayes). While others have claimed that the experience of disappointment has crushed the spirit of blacks (see Griffith and Bell: 2265–70). It is my contention that given the social realities of the black experience, any definitive claims about the impact of the experience of social disappointment on the black collective view of self should be viewed as suspect.

A HISTORY OF SOCIAL DISAPPOINTMENT

Most blacks would claim that overall life in the U.S. as citizens has been replete with experiences of social disappointment. The experience of disappointment has come from a failure of the government to live up to their expectation about their treatment as citizens.

While the treatment of blacks during slavery caused much disappointment, the disappointments that came after the Civil War will concern us herein. It is bad enough when the government does not protect members from physical intimidation by other members of the state, but it is worse when the government itself is involved in the intimidation. We can acknowledge that blacks have long complained about the treatment they have received at the hands of law enforcement officials and the criminal justice system. The instances of police brutality are common, as in the cases of Arthur McDuffie and Rodney King. Police officers are rarely convicted for offenses against blacks. As the case of Rodney King illustrates to many blacks, even if there is ample evidence of police brutality, blacks will not prevail in the justice system. The acquittal of the police officers in the beating of Rodney King did not aid the perception that the criminal justice system protects blacks (see Gooding-Williams [1993]). The criminal justice system has been a source of disappointment. When blacks go to court, many think that they will not be able to get a fair trial. The belief that the legal system is stacked against blacks is common in most black communities. Blacks have the experience of disappointment because of the lack of protection by the criminal justice system. There are those blacks who still expect the government to protect the lives and property of blacks. The greater the expectations the greater the experience of disappointment when the expectations are not met.

Yet, as important as physical protection is to citizenship, citizenship is not having just one important right, for example, protection. Citizenship includes a cluster of rights of which protection is an essential one. There is, however, no definitive connection between the denial of certain rights and one's political status. It is not as if the denial of protection releases one from one obligation to the political order (see Lawson [1989]: 49–63). In this regard, the reactions or responses to the denial of a right will be factored through the diverse life experiences of each black. Still, we must understand these life experiences as blacks experience them in a racially stratified country (see McGary [1992]: 57–70).

152

STRATIFICATION AND SOCIAL DISAPPOINTMENT

Many different actions have produced the social stratification that most blacks have to confront daily. These acts have caused a racially stratified society. Most blacks would agree that they have collectively been the subjects of political oppression. When we claim that a group is oppressed, it means that certain discriminatory actions have already stratified a society. That is, a social gap exists in that society between identifiable groups. It is important to note, however, that oppression as a product does not end in the following sense. It is not the case that the oppressor psychologically indoctrinates and stops—that is, his conversion of the oppressed is logically completed. Nor is it the case that the oppressor, say, racially discriminates and then stops doing so. Rather, it is the continuous nature of these actions by the oppressor that warrants us in claiming a group is oppressed. Oppression, as a product, is like a cultivated garden in that the requisite cultivation is a continuous process. Thus, psychological indoctrination, racial discrimination, housing discrimination and the like are the tools of the oppressive gardener. They are not oppres-

LAWSON

sion in and of themselves, but when used effectively they produce an oppressed product, a socially stratified society. Oppression, as a product, is the outcome of disparate clusters of actions. When we examine the causes of the oppression of blacks in America, we fine housing discrimination, gerrymandering, poll taxes, selective literacy testing, residential segregation, school segregation, occupational discrimination and discrimination in the military and many other discriminatory acts. We also know that both the federal and state governments supported these practices.

Thus, the oppression of blacks was not just the lack of material well-being or being psychologically indoctrinated or racially discriminated; it was a combination of discriminatory and socially stratifying actions supported by the government. When we view oppression in this manner, we can see it why the cessation of one act in question—for instance, residential discrimination—would not by that end oppression.

In this light, one can also understand the difficulty of any piecemeal solution to the problem of oppression and the subtle ways in which oppression can arise, indeed slowly step by step. Oppression, quite simply, is a cluster of discriminatory actions. Philosophers and social scientists often fail to distinguish between the discriminatory practices that can result in an oppressive state and the description of the oppressive state itself. It is the interaction of these discriminatory actions that causes a society to be socially stratified and a group to be oppressed. The social cooperation of disparate groups in a society will be required to maintain the sort of social and political environment needed to keep a group oppressed. Of necessity, this sort of cooperation will take place through the politics of a state. The behavior of the government has helped keep this society racially and socially stratified. The "experience of disappointment" of most blacks has to be understood by reference to the actions of both state and federal governmental actions.

What will be the response of "black people" to the experience of disappointment of life in the United States? I contend that because of the way American society has been socially and racially stratified, blacks will have many different responses to the experience of social disappointment. There is no "black peoples'" perspective that can be used to view what life in the United States means for all "black people." The problem of collective identity and personal agency is indeed a concern of black social activists. Possibly, no person grappled with this issue more than Frantz Fanon. Lewis Gordon, in his engagement with the thought of Frantz Fanon (Gordon [1995b]), addresses the issue of collective identity and the problem of agency and cites the following passage in which Fanon concludes:

> The object of lumping all Negroes together under the designation of "Negro
> People" is to deprive them of any possibility of individual expression. What is
> thus attempted is to put them under the obligation of matching the idea one
> has of them. Is it not obvious that there can only be a white race? What would
> the "white people" correspond to? (Gordon [1967b]: 17)

LAWSON

153

Gordon adds: "whatever 'Negro people' are, living, breathing, flesh-and-blood black folks have to go on with their lives and day-to-day problems within culturally different contexts" ([1995b]: 46–7).

The lives of blacks in the U.S. consist of a wide variety of individual social contexts. These social contexts will give rise to a variety of social and political realities. Thus, the political awareness of blacks will vary greatly and so will the individual responses to experience of disappointment. What to some will be a crushing blow, will to others be the impetus for continuing the struggle. What makes the political and social situation of blacks unique is that their political struggles have been so multifaceted.

DISAPPOINTMENT AND THE BLACK SENSE OF SELF

After the Civil War, many blacks expected the U.S. government to protect their rights as citizens. Of course, the experience of disappointment can force persons to alter their goals. Those things that one once thought where possible can come to be seen as out of reach or too dangerous to attempt. When it became clear that the government was not going to protect them as citizens, many blacks were drawn to schemes that promoted immigration from the U.S. The popularity of the Garvey movement attests to the power of experience of disappointment to force persons to alter their beliefs about their life chances and their expectations about the United States government's behavior towards blacks.

While it is true that we can see the behavior of the government in protecting the rights of blacks as a cause of social disappointment, it does not follow that all blacks will have the same response to the experience of disappointment. Not all blacks saw immigration to Africa as the correct response to the experience of disappointment.

The lives of Frederick Douglass and W.E.B. Du Bois present an interesting contrast in the possible responses to the experience of social disappointment. Both Douglass and Du Bois worked endlessly for the full inclusion of blacks into the social fabric of the U.S. Douglass died, in Washington, DC, disappointed with the turn of events in the latter half of the 19th century but still committed to making the system work. Du Bois died in Ghana, disappointed and disgusted with life in the U.S. Douglass and Du Bois both had expectations about how blacks would fare in the U.S. and when those expectations were not met reacted differently.

In this regard, how any given black will respond to governmental actions will vary according to a myriad of factors. In fact, there are far too many social factors to give any adequate assessment of some collective feeling of disappointment. The social history of blacks contains many overlapping experiences pertaining to being black in the U.S. On the other side, there are many different approaches to understanding even these common overlapping experiences.

Some social and political activists may find my position unsettling. The social realties of racism are truly disappointing. The "experience of disappointment," according to these writers, should lead to the same response in all blacks. In this line of reasoning, blacks should have the same psychological reaction to any given racial experience. Accordingly, it must be believed that racism and racist experiences impact on each black in the same manner, no matter what his or her life experiences have been. It is unclear, however, what is meant when it is claimed that the experience of racism has been the same for all blacks. To make that claim, one has to ignore the multiple lifestyles available to blacks and how these different lifestyle shape the experience of racism.

It may seem strange that someone would believe that there would be the same reaction to the experiences of disappointment in all blacks despite their life experiences. One can sensibly believe this only if one believes that racism touches or impacts on the conscious of all blacks in the same fashion. Clearly, this is not true.

DISAPPOINTMENT AND COLLECTIVE ACTION

Let me be clear: I am not claiming that there cannot be a collective response by blacks. There is nothing I have said that implies that blacks cannot rally to protest police brutality, job discrimination, and other socially stratifying actions by the state. It is not, however, as if there can only be a collective response, if blacks have the same psychological reaction to the experience of disappointment. I think that the experience of disappointment can be an impetus for collective action. Indeed, the history of collective action by blacks shows that in spite of different understandings of what it means to be black in the United States, blacks can still put together a united front. However, my position also explains why there is often heated debate by blacks about what is the best course of action for blacks collectively.

DISAPPOINTMENT AND DISSATISFACTION

Let me close with a brief discussion of those blacks who no longer have any expectations of any positive behavior of whites towards blacks. Thus, they cease to be disappointed when they hear of or experience racism. Even if it is true that some blacks have given up expecting the U.S. government to behave morally towards blacks, these blacks are still dissatisfied with the treatment of blacks in the U.S. The majority of blacks is clearly unsatisfied by the present state of things; presumably most black Americans are dissatisfied with the actions of state and federal governments.

The response to the verdict in the Rodney King trial is an excellent example of the wide range of black responses. Some blacks thought that the video tape would be "proof" that blacks were truly victims of the criminal justice system. This group was truly disappointed by the verdict. There were other blacks, as Jerry G. Watts notes in his discussion of the Rodney King verdict, who claimed not to be surprised or hurt by anything that white Americans do to black people. Such individuals will claim that they knew that the racist LA cops would be acquitted. While

155

some blacks have acquired a rather matter-of-fact, stoic grasp of the viciousness of racism in American politics, most of us have not (see Watt: 242). Thus, the majority of blacks who are disappointed or dissatisfied must face each day with what Martin Luther King, Jr., called "divine dissatisfaction."

Let us be dissatisfied until America will no longer have a high blood pressure of creeds and an anemia of deeds. Let us be dissatisfied until the tragic walls that separate the outer city of wealth and comfort and the inner city of poverty and despair shall be crushed by the battering rams of the forces of justice. Let us be dissatisfied until those that live on the outskirts of hope are brought into the metropolis of daily security. Let us be dissatisfied until slum are cast into the junk heaps of history, and every family is living in a decent sanitary home. Let us be dissatisfied until the dark yesterdays of segregated schools will be transformed into bright tomorrows of quality, integrated education. Let us be dissatisfied until integration is not seen as a problem but an opportunity to participate in the beauty of diversity. Let us be dissatisfied until men and women, however black they may be, will be judge on the basis of the content of their character and not the on the basis of the color of their skin. Let us be dissatisfied (King: 251).

While one can agree with King that "divine dissatisfaction" sets the tone for the social struggle in the United States, I think that King's list represents the kind of dissatisfaction that most blacks face in America every day. Still each black will bring his or her own understanding of the social realties of that disappointment or dissatisfaction to the struggle for social justice.

156

NOTE

1 I thank my son, William Lance Lawson, Margo Perry, Ron and Marilyn Whittington, and Paul Ziff for their helpful comments on this paper.

RASTAFARIANISM AND THE REALITY OF DREAD[1]

Paget Henry

AMONG THE various groups that make up the Jamaican religious landscape, the Rastafarians have devoted the most theological space to the delegitimating of imperial domination. To understand this particular characteristic of Rastafarianism, we must recognize the peculiar state of "non-being" that its symbolic productions attempt to analyze, interpret, and overcome. The word most often used by Rastafarians to describe both their subjective and objective condition is "dread." A dread experience is one that confronts or challenges the subjectivity of the Rastafarian. He/she becomes "a dread" through the repelling of this challenge. Thus it is the experience and conquest of a certain kind of terror that defines the Rastafarian concept of dread. At its most profound levels, it embodies "the awesome, fearful confrontation of a people with a primordial but historically denied racial self-hood" (Owens: 3). Because of its institutional power, this denial interrupts normal ego genesis and forces the Rastafarian into anguished struggles against persistent threats of ego collapse. This wrestling with the subjective impact of socio-historical denial constitutes the deepest meaning of Rastafarian dread.

Although closely related, this is not the dread of Kierkegaard. Kierkegaard's concept of dread concerns the anxiety that paralyzes the human self as it senses its aloneness in the face of the cosmic dance of life. This dance has its own moments of nonbeing through which it takes the human self. In these moments of nonbeing, the self experiences negativities such as an absence of intentionality, the loss of ego capability or a paralysis of the will. These negativities interrupt and unmask the falsely deterministic moves made in "normal" processes of ego genesis. They also threaten the ego with failure and keep it suspended over the possibility of collapse.

The anxiety that accompanies this interrogating of our projects of selfhood by cosmic non-being is the key to Kierkegaard's concept of dread. For Kierkegaard, this anxiety "consumes all finite ends and discovers all their deceptiveness." Further, "no Grand Inquisitor has such dreadful torments in readiness as anxiety has,…and no discerning judge understands how to interrogate and examine the accused as does anxiety, which never lets the accused escape, neither through amusement , nor by noise, nor during work neither by day nor by night" (Kierkegaard [1980]: 55–6). This anxious unraveling of the necessary inadequacies and deceptions of our attempts at self-projection is the essence of Kierkegaardian dread. It relentlessly threaten the individual with ego collapse. For Kierkegaard, relief from all of these woes comes only when the God-self relation replaces in the right measure the ego-self relation. The former Kierkegaard viewed as an ontological structure of the self. The dread of the Rastafarians does not derive immediately from such an anxious relation of the self to God or to nature's continuous movement. That is, it is not immediately existential in its source. Rather, this dread springs from the dance of social life; from the unjust and impersonal conventions of Jamaican society that threaten the identity of many of its members with insignificance. Yet the power of the Rastafarian concept of dread springs in part from its ability to echo many of the above existential themes. Hence Bob Marley's portrayal of the Rastafarian as both a conqueror of duppies (evil or troublesome spirits) and a shooter of sherrifs.

Rastafarianism is the creation of the Jamaican working and lower classes. In slightly varying degrees the members of these classes experience themselves as being marginal and expendable in relation to rules and activities. Historically, this marginalization has been the result of the processes of class and racial domination that accompanied the introduction of African labor and the capitalist mode of production to the region. These processes of domination were not simply physical or external in nature; they also had their subjective aspects. These included the stereotypical redefinition of Africans as "Negroes" and the devaluation and disruption of their traditional cultural practices. As a result, Afro-Jamaicans were unable to project and legitimate their accustomed identities. Positive self-images were routinely contested by the stereotypical images and patterns of racist interaction. The major threat to the identity of many Jamaicans, thus, came from the grinding of the social machine, not from the natural dangers and chances of life. This, I believe, is a critical source of the extensive linking of political and religious symbols we find among the Rastafarians.

The existence of this peculiar pattern of symbol formation among colonized people has already been pointed out by Fanon. He suggested that "There is, in the *Weltanschauung* of a colonized people, an impurity, a defect that forbids any ontological explanation." He continues, "Ontology, when it is admitted once and for all that it leaves existence by the wayside, does not permit us to understand the being of the black. For the black no longer has to be black, but to be it in front of the white" (Fanon [1967a]: 109–10: trans. revised—ed.). In other words, in colonial societies, anxiety in relation to rhythm of social life replaces, or eclipses, the anxiety experienced in relation to the rhythm of cosmic life. Hence the shift in the pattern of symbol formation that sustains the construction of world views. This it seems to me, is the key to the particular characteristics of Rastafarianism.

Rastafarian theology of existence is based upon a dialectical projection of a symbolically mediated presence that negates the specific subjective absences generated by the processes of marginalization and stereotypical redefinition. The salvific project of Rastafarian theology is not founded on a "courage to be" that maintains the self in spite of such natural phenomena as sickness, death, the hiddenness of god, and other obscure and paradoxical aspects of life. Rastafarians assimilate these matters quite readily as nature and spirit are for them very positive and friendly forces. Rather, the soteriological program of Rastafarian theology is oriented towards a courage that reconstitutes the self in spite of such social phenomena as class/race domination and stereotypical redefinition. That Rastafarian theology is based on such a dialectical projection can be shown from an analysis of some of its central symbols.

More than any other set of symbols, the interpretations that have developed around the symbolic use of Ethiopia gives us important clues to the slavific project of the Rastafarians. The Rastafarians were not the first to create a complex mythology around Ethiopia. This has been a persistent theme in the thought of Africans in the Western world. Along with Egypt, Ethiopia is one of the oldest and better-known African nations, and it serves as a symbol for all Africa. References to Ethiopia appear in the Bible. Also, the symbolic importance of Ethiopia increased in the early decades of the twentieth century as it was the only nation in Africa that was not colonized. It continued to crown its own kings and to govern itself. In short, it was doing everything that the racist definition of Africans claimed that they were incapable of doing. This phenomenon of Ethiopianism has received its most detailed elaboration among the Rastafarians.

Sparked by the crowning of Haile Selassie as Emperor of Ethiopia in 1930, the Rastafarian religion started in Jamaica in the ashes of Garvey's movement. Garvey's many references to the crowning of African kings and to African redeemers were seen by many as prophecies that had been fulfilled by this event. Leonard Howell, Archibald Dunkley, and Robert Hinds, among others, were convinced that Haile Selassie's coronation was a fulfillment of prophecy. Quite separately at first, they elevated Haile Selassie to divine status, proclaiming him the long awaited redeemer from Africa, and gave him the additional titles of Jah and *Ras Tafari* (King Tafari). Armed with this new message, these early Rastafarian leaders set out to preach the good news.

This attempt to spread the news of the arrival of a redeemer soon brought these leaders into conflict with the colonial authorities. In January of 1934, Howell and Hinds were arrested and sent to prison on charges of sedition. The guilty verdict rested largely upon a public speech in which Howell advocated the following: (1) the hatred of the white race; (2) the superiority of the black race; (3) revenge on whites; (4) the rejection and humiliation of the colonial government in Jamaica; (5) preparation for the return to Africa and; (6) the recognition of Haile Selassie as the Supreme Being, and sole ruler of African people (Barrett: 85). This account of Howell's address is one of the earliest formulations that we have of Rastafarian doctrine. Very visible are its delegitimating stands on colonial domination that are inseparable from their religious framework.

After his release from prison, Howell formed a commune in the hills where he continued to develop and institutionalize the Rastafarian alternative. His community was attacked by the police in 1941 and again in 1953. These attacks came as Howell, among other things, advocated the paying of taxes to Haile Selassie and not to the Jamaican government. Thus, the period from 1934 to about 1960 was a violent one for the Rastafarians. It was in the latter phases of this period that members of the group began growing and wearing their hair in "dreadlocks," first calling themselves "Ethiopian warriors" and later, "locksmen." It was also the period in which the term "Babylon" became the primary symbol for the interpretation and assessment of the colonial establishment. The delegitimating power of this symbol clearly allowed the Rastafarians to extend to contemporary Jamaica the Biblical destruction of ancient Babylon.

This violent phase ended and was followed by one in which faith was placed in the divine fulfillment of the prophesied destruction of European imperialism and the global redemption of Africans. This shift was accompanied by the more careful study of the Bible and its reinterpretation. This was a very fruitful period for the growth of Rastafarian doctrine. In examining these beliefs our focus will be on the delegitimating aspects. However, it is important to stress that these are systematically linked to a larger whole that includes a doctrine of man, a well-developed mysticism, rituals for living, a doctrine of divine judgment, and a view of the future of the world.

The foundation of Rastafarian theology is the mystical knowledge of the divinity of Haile Selassie. This mystical knowledge grounds the importance that

Rastafarians attach to direct participatory spiritual experiences as opposed to belief. This is a difference with Christianity that is often expressed. The directness and originality of this mystical knowledge is captured in the I-language of the Rastafarians. Among Jamaicans, Rastafarians are unique in their use of the pronoun "I." It is substituted for the "me" and "my" which represents the old self before awakening to the divinity of Haile Selassie. "I" represents the new identity that emerges from participation in the divinity of Haile Selassie. Thus, all things and persons that have acquired this new identity through mystical participation, have "I" attached to them in some form. Thus Selassie himself becomes Haile Selassie-I. The Rastafarian individual becomes an "I." He becomes "I-man" or she becomes "I-woman." A plurality of Rastafarians produces not a "we" or a "you and I," but, "I and I." "My children" becomes "I children." One often hears sentences like: Haile Selassie-I I-rated (created) this universe, and his truths I-dure (endure) forever. Or, I and I have been made strong by the almighty GOD-JAH-I. These unusual uses of "I" all signify a participation in the divinity of Haile Selassie.

Membership in this I-worded spiritual community has been the basis for the primordial self that Rastafarians have been able to affirm in spite of social contempt, police violence, and other forms of socio-historical denial. This grounding of identity in the self-God relation strongly supports Kierkegaard's claim that this relation is an ontological structure of the self. The historical reality of Rastafarian dread comes clearly into view through its persistence in spite of this active cultivating of the relation that removes Kierkegaardian dread and brings existential peace.

Although this peace has not been able to extend its calm to the social life of the Rastafarian, the affirmation of the self-God relation is the foundation of his/her identity. It is more important to self-affirmation than any specific Judeo-Christian belief. Because of it, the Rastafarian feels endowed with religious knowledge that is hidden from the socially powerful—particularly the divinity of Haile Selassie. Intuitive knowledge of this fact is the basic experience that defines the Rastafarians and is the source of their prolific interpretive activities. In one sense the development of Rastafarian theology is the result of simultaneously rejecting and reinterpreting their Christian heritage in the light of the intuitive knowledge of the divinity of Haile Selassie. This hermeneutic undertaking reveals both the extent to which Rastafarian thought has remained within and moved beyond the categorical framework of Christian thought.

The Rastafarians are very bold in their approach to the Bible: They do not take it literally. They see it as a fallible and internally contradictory text that has been flawed by the white man's translation. Hence it is viewed as a text that must be interpreted and one that will yield additional insights about their condition and fate. In this spirit the Rastafarians begin by making themselves the heroes of the biblical drama. They see themselves as the descendants of the ancient Israelites. Thus, it is through the Rastafarian experience that the biblical odyssey continues in the present period. Parallels and continuities are established between the suffering and enslavement of Africans in the Western world, and the suffering and enslavement of the Israelites by groups such as the Babylonians. In both cases the enslavement is seen as divine punishment for sins committed.

In this reading of African enslavement, spiritual and socio-historical negation are conflated in rather problematic ways. Is it the punishment of Jah or the greed of the Europeans that explains African enslavement in Jamaica and other parts of the Western world? For the Rastafarian, their oppressed condition is primarily due to the latter. However, because of the sin of their forefathers who ignored Jah, they must go through this period of painful expiation. From it, the Rastafarians should recover the knowledge of who they really are. Thus the greed of the Europeans and the spiritual purposes of Jah coincide in the suffering of the Rastafarians. When the spiritual purposes of Jah are fulfilled, there will be an uncoupling of this "alliance." The period of captivity will be ended, and the evil of European greed exposed.

In the context of Jamaican society, the interpretation of the concepts of good and evil goes beyond personal disobedience of divine laws. They are reinterpreted to include the socio-historical forces that "downpress" the Rastafarians and threaten them with personal and social insignificance. The "downpressors" are, of course, Babylonians, and Rastafarians often refer to themselves as "being in captivity in Babylon," with Babylon referring to the central countries of the West. However, this reference also includes their local supporters and representatives, particularly within the police, the state leadership, and the church. In this biblical representation of the imperial West, Rastafarian theology reserves very specific places for Britain and the United States. The former is responsible for the relocation and enslavement of Africans in the Western Hemisphere. However, the coronation of Haile Selassie was the sign that marked the end of the British hegemony and the decline of Babylon. But, during this period of decline, a new power, the United States, known to the prophets as Rahab, has attempted to set itself up in Britain's place. The Untied States, according to Rastafarian theology, "is the Northern country of which the prophets Jeremiah and Isaiah spoke. The brutal invader which seeks to blot out the life of God's chosen ones" (Owens: 80). But in the Rastafarian reading of Isaiah, this imperial project of the United States is also doomed to failure.

Although both of these imperial projects are expected to collapse in the future, at present the British and the Americans along with their local supporters are the "downpressors." They are the evil ones that are keeping Rastafarians oppressed in Jamaica and away from the Africa. In this context Jamaica (and all of the geographical regions in which the subjugated black diaspora live) becomes identified with hell and Ethiopia with heaven. Haile Selassie becomes not only the Supreme Being, but also the returned Christ who is expected to judge the world and set it right. This setting right of the world should bring about the liberation of Africans and their return to the homeland (heaven).

HENRY

What is truly remarkable about this salvific project is its use of Judeo categories and symbols (e.g., the central role of Mount Zion in Rastafarian theology) mixed with Christian escathology to make coherent a set of contents that are anti-Christian and largely this-wordly. In other words it uses the cosmic framework of the Judeo-Christian drama of human creation, fall, and salvation to make coherent the socio-historical fall and future salvation of Africans. In the resulting politico-religious discourse the concept of dread is only partly determined by Kierkegaard's "disrelationship" between God and self. It is so determined to the extent that its stings derive from punishments that Rastafarians are receiving for the disobedience of their forefathers. It is not to the extent that understanding its socio-political dimensions requires the "disrelationship" between the bullets, words and interests of Babylon on the one hand, and the resurgent images of black humanity that spring so persistently in the hearts of Rastafarians. This shift in the pattern of symbol formation is suggestive of the particular type of non-being in spite of which the Rastafarians have been attempting to maintain a positive identity and a sense of significance.

The repeated projecting of images of black humanity points to a Rastafarian dialectic of self assertion that bears comparison with Fanon's. In Fanon's dialectic, the attempts at self projection were not restricted to self-assertion "as a BLACK MAN" (Fanon [1967a]: 115). While Fanon made several black projections, he also attempted ones that were rooted in the physiological, the universal, or the irrational that were not particularly black. Fanon's net was more widely cast in the effort to maintain self in spite of socio-historical denial. Hence the greater variety in his dialectical projections of selfhood.

In contrast, the unique power of Rastafarian ego genesis is its ability to repeatedly conquer the dread of socio-historical denial by reasserting the Rastafarian as a black dread. In other words, the dialectic of its response to the domination of the other never abandons its black framework. This suggests that the Rastafarians have been able to get more counter-punching power out of the black and African symbols they have created than Fanon got out of his. In Fanon's language, they were able to get more "ontological resistance" (Fanon [1967a]: 110) out of their Ethiopian and other black symbols. There may be an important lesson about the power of counter symbols to be learned from the differences in these two dialectics of self assertion.

This brief account of Rastafarian theology should give an idea of the forces that are motivating the reinterpretation of a transcendent drama into such an explicitly socio-historical one. Sociologically speaking, the significance of the Rastafarian movement is its theology, which strongly delegitimates a secular system of external authority that undermines both individual and collective identity. This tendency is an important factor in the shift from more metaphysical modes of thought to more socio-historical ones that have been characteristic of peripheral countries in the postcolonial period.

163

HENRY

The importance of Rastafarianism is not in the size of its following; indeed, the number of members is small. Rather, the world-view and value system expounded has permeated not only Jamaica, but also a good bit of the Caribbean as well. Rastafarianism is an unlikely candidate to become a major religion in the region; however, by delegitimizing old cultural and economic arrangements, it serves as a transition to something new.

NOTE

1   This is an expanded version of the Rastafarian section of an earlier paper, "Indigenous Religions and the Transformation of Peripheral Societies," which was published in Hadden and Shupe.

QUESTIONING THE POSTMODERN, QUESTIONING BLACK EXISTENCE

part III

NIETZSCHE ON BLACKS[1]

William A. Preston

WHY SHOULD not a black existentialist who is also a leftist turn to Nietzsche? After all, Nietzsche's name—along with Heidegger's—emblazons the banners held high by those who march in the literature and philosophy regiments of postmodernism. And postmodernism boldly advertises the hope of a rupture with modernity and all its ills, with bad things such as hypocritical bourgeois declarations about "equality," "human rights," and "progress." A black existentialist philosophy would of course examine black suffering, and Nietzsche did examine suffering. Nietzsche's philosophy is renowned for its genealogy of morals, its analyses of *ressentiment*, guilt, bad conscience, and the like. It is commonly assumed that Nietzsche diagnosed the spiritual ailments of modernity with a subtlety and nuance *in psychologicis* totally absent from the scientific socialism of Marx and Engels. Marxism is, I submit, the most advanced form of bourgeois consciousness. Precisely because of its bourgeois, thoroughly modern character, though, Marxism is popularly seen by the well educated to be doltishly oblivious to the dimensions of human suffering plumbed by Nietzsche. The raging, mysterious abysses in the depths of the human soul are matters about which Marxism must not have the slightest idea.

Given this presumed blindness of Marxism, it is hardly surprising that, after the end of socialism—that dying breath of Christian faith—men and women of the Left feel strongly tempted to turn to Nietzsche. Can Nietzsche in fact save not only radical-Right and apolitical thinkers but also those who crave a new Left dispensation? Can Nietzsche help black existentialists find answers to *their own* questions? Nietzsche's advocates on the Left might well wish to think so.

To be sure, Nietzsche is no hypocrite in the sense that Marxists and liberals so often are—but he is no hypocrite, it must be noted, because his theory aims to be as evil as his practice. Nietzsche strove to be as *inegalitarian, illiberal,* and *anti*-progressive as possible. Nietzsche addressed black suffering—of that there should be no doubt—but his intent, it appears from his writings, was *to make blacks suffer more.*

Given the fact that Nietzsche has so displaced Marx among contemporary academic leftists, one could almost be forgiven for regarding the famous critique of the subject as some sort of "grammatological" revolt of the masses against the dominion of reason. A rebellion against reason it very much is. But a rebellion against dominion of man over man? I think not. The subject of grammar, morally accountable for decisions to harm or not harm, must, Nietzsche argues, be overcome in favor of the morally unaccountable ego of the aggressor. The "critique of the subject" as Nietzsche enacts it in the *Genealogy of Morals* aims to demolish moralities that would try to restrict the license of successful aggressors to lord it over the weak. Nietzsche's critique of the subject would find its consummation in the formation of a new aristocracy from the ranks of the bourgeoisie. It is typical of the "Nietzscheans" of the Left to miss the essential connection between the critique of the subject and the anti-socialist urge to create a new ruling caste. But then, to be a Left Nietzschean is, in the first place, to subscribe to a *contradictio in adiecto.* What those who subscribe to this particular contradiction in terms thereby evade are the global power-stakes involved in Nietzsche's critique of the subject and his assault on the idea of moral accountability.

The problem is as follows. The concept of the subject especially plagues the "Indo-Germanic" peoples, among whom Nietzsche numbers the Aryans of the Orient and the Occident, the Nordics as well as the Brahmanic caste, plus the ancient Greeks (*BGE* #20: 217–8).[2] This "concept of the subject," originating on Nietzsche's account in the grammar of the Aryan hordes who once roamed Eurasia, is now with democracy and even more so with socialism being exploited to postulate the moral worth and political accountability of every person on earth. The descendants of the Aryan originators of the subject (i.e., the spiritually higher men) are expected to be politically accountable to the conquered race in the

West (i.e., the European workers) and to the nonphilosophic peoples of the South (e.g., the Africans).

Nietzsche's writings, unlike, say, John Rawls', do not address themselves to an anonymous aggregate about whom practically nothing is presumed. Nietzsche excludes many people, and this exclusion is at the core of his philosophy. It is not a mistake or a mere "bias" somehow separable from that which is of enduring value in his writings.[3] It cannot be historicized away as inessential to Nietzsche's serious philosophy, as if Nietzsche's racism is the unfortunate intrusion into his philosophy of an alien element. Nietzsche's writings address themselves only to people from certain cultures: Brahman India, Aryan Persia, Jewry, Semitic Islam, Russia, Scandinavia, and Europe with England as its westernmost outpost. What Nietzsche calls the "poles of philosophical endowment" run from India to England (*GM*: 106). Japan he admires for its noble men of prey, China he despises for the allegedly proto-socialist essence of its culture (*GM*: 41; *GS*: 99, 338; *EH*: 330). America has its exceptions, like the Yankee Emerson, but remains on the whole peripheral to the creation of new values. Africa, philosophically speaking, is not even on the map. Black people, he affirms in a casual aside, are not even fully human:[4]

> [L]et me declare expressly that in the days when mankind was not yet ashamed of its cruelty, life on earth was more cheerful than it is now that pessimists exist....Perhaps in those days—the delicate may be comforted by this thought—pain did not hurt as much as it does now; at least that is the conclusion a doctor may arrive at who has treated Negroes (taken as representatives of prehistoric man) for severe internal inflammations that would drive even the best constituted European to distraction—in the case of Negroes they do *not* do so. (The curve of human susceptibility to pain seems in fact to take an extraordinary and almost sudden drop as soon as one has passed the upper ten thousand or ten million of the top stratum of culture; and for my own part, I have no doubt that the combined suffering of all the animals ever subjected to the knife for scientific ends is utterly negligible compared with *one* painful night of a single hysterical bluestocking.) (*GM*: 67–68)

169

Nietzsche is a cruel racist. This should be directly acknowledged, and his cruelty and racism in no way played down. Upon what basis would Nietzsche consign even "prehistoric men" to the category of laboratory animals? And how really does Nietzsche know that "pain does not hurt as much" to the Negro and to the prehistoric man and to the animal and to all those others who do not have the good fortune to share the top stratum with the hysterical bluestocking? Something other than a logical argument is at work here.

If blacks, as *On the Genealogy of Morals* quite clearly suggests, are more akin to animals fit for laboratory experimentation than to people of "the top stratum of culture," then what is to be gained by feeling superior to them? Nietzsche, to be sure, does not mention blacks that much. When he does, of course, they are described as inferior.[5] All in all, blacks simply do not figure that much in Nietzsche's writings, and with good reason: the feeling of distinction derived from a sense of superiority towards blacks is not worth much. A man of distinction, on Nietzsche's account, could not feel ecstasy in his pathos of distance from blacks. In Nietzsche's scheme of things, the value to life of black people is so negligible it is absurd to try to acquire a rise by oppressing them. Heightened, and infinitely more refined, feelings of power, though, are obtainable through cruelty towards people who are more racially equal, for instance, European working-class people. Oppressing lower-class whites is so much more enjoyable and fulfilling precisely because upper-class whites recognize in the rage of the white proles the envy of a relatively racially superior being. That such a being envies them makes them even more superior.

The new world, according to Nietzsche, is an antiblack world. So was the old world. But it was not antiblack enough. In the old world, European imperialisms dispatched missionaries to conquer the Africans for Christ. That would now be passé, but not because it is imperialist. Rather, such proselytizing among black people would be passé because Christianity affirms—however much it honors in the breach—that the souls of black people are equally precious to God. All that changes when God dies. Black equality, on Christian grounds, is argued for in terms of the equality of all souls before God. Democracy only secularizes this religious claim in the normative order of the state. Socialism, that most dreadful regime, would put the poor, including the poor blacks, in charge of the world. But if God is dead, then there is no longer a watchful spirit in whose eyes the poor and the black are the equals of the rich and the white. And a whole new world, wondrously abundant with possibilities for a novel kind of domination, opens up. There is disclosure, after the debris left by Christians and democrats has been lit up in the clearing, of authentic possibilities for a world rather shocking. In the future as Nietzsche would, cruelly but actually, envision it, black people would exist only—and explicitly—to be dominated, experimented on, or just simply killed.[6]

In the most profound sense, Nietzsche's whole philosophy—and not just his view of blacks—is racist. Blacks to Nietzsche are at a lower stage of evolution than whites, and as such are generally of marginal consideration. But the European bourgeoisie is racially inferior, too. The crucial difference, though, is that Nietzsche cherishes hopes for the European bourgeoisie he does not in the slightest feel for blacks. The centrality of race to Nietzsche's deepest concerns becomes apparent in his discussion of bourgeois racial inferiority. Equating class with race, Nietzsche attacks the individual members of the bourgeoisie for failing to embody the nobility of blood they must somehow incorporate if they are ever to purge themselves of their slave instincts. Nietzsche's wish to ennoble the bourgeoisie is also a wish to elevate the bourgeoisie racially. A higher race-quality must be incorporated there. Two kinds of racist commitment are manifest in Nietzsche's thought: one, affirming the need to heighten the race-quality of the European bourgeoisie, the other, denying the full humanity of black people. The democratic movement Nietzsche detests would realize black political equality and sap the will to power of the European bourgeoisie, thereby effecting a blood-poisoning of its instincts by way of a dissemination of lies about equality in general. Nietzsche's racist commitment aims to counter these different but ultimately related forms of the egalitarian peril.

Not a New Left but a New Right is the genuine political expression of Nietzsche's philosophy. By "Right," I mean any party opposed to the progressive legacies of both the French and the Russian revolutions. By "New" I mean a Right that is really worthy, unlike twentieth-century European pretenders, of being called new.

The common confusion that Nietzsche is neither Right nor Left was expressed even through Georges Bataille (1897-1962), perhaps because, rather than in spite of, the fact that Bataille was the foremost Nietzschean anti-Nazi of his generation. Nietzsche was neither Right nor Left because, Bataille informs us, the subordination of thinking to a political cause appalled Nietzsche (Bataille: xxii). Bataille is correct about what appalls Nietzsche. But Bataille also misconstrues what it means to be a man of the Right. He projects his own left-wing concept of the political cause onto the rightist thinker, as if Right and Left thinkers can be easily equated in terms of their respective relations to "a cause." Bataille ignores that what makes Nietzsche a rightist is not only his hatred of leftist goals but also his violent objection, as a superior human being, to the voluntary discipline and dutiful commitment that characterize Left commitment. Joseph de Maistre phrased it rather well when he indicated, in regard to his own royalist intentions, that wise monarchists did not want a *counter*revolution but rather the *opposite* of revolution (de Maistre: 105). Nietzsche is no restorationist. But like de Maistre before him he would rather not join a cause, even an antirevolutionary cause. He would rather there had not been a revolution in the first place. As the revolution exists, though, Nietzsche must oppose it—but without mimicking its militant conformism.

Nietzsche is a man of the Right. But his philosophy charts a course toward a Right remade as atheist, forward-looking, and trans-European. Nietzsche counsels conservatives to lose their hopes for a return to the feudal-medieval epoch, and he despises the nationalistic thoughtlessness. An authentically New Right would found a New Order beyond—and above—"modern ideas," a new Order that would legalize arson against the individual freedom and social justice to which the wretched of the earth feel entitled as a result of Western reason, religion, and politics. Prometheus, Marx's favorite god, is to be replaced by man-become-god who gives new meaning to the sacrilegious calling: "bring the fire to the people." Even the fascists, presuming as they do the *national* superiority of one people over another, could never be right-wing enough for this politics. For their politics are still of "the people."

171

PRESTON

NOTES

1 This article is dedicated to the memory of Ruth Weiss Ulansey. "Nietzsche on Blacks" is here excerpted from a larger manuscript, *Nietzsche as Anti-Socialist: Prophet of Bourgeois Ennoblement* (forthcoming).

2 References to Nietzsche are lettered as follows: *Daybreak* (*D*); *The Gay Science* (*GS*); *Beyond Good and Evil* (*BGE*); *On the Genealogy of Morals* (*GM*); *Ecce Homo* (*EH*).

3 In *Nietzsche and Political Thought* (1988), Mark Warren blatantly disregards Nietzsche's politics after this fashion, conceding, for example, that "Nietzsche's view of biological determination...underwrites his politics" but concluding that "reconstructing his metaphysics of domination according to what his politics demands is a waste of time: the result would be of little interest for questions of postmodern transitions." Whatever his "postmodern transitions" ultimately portend, Warren clearly believes that their theorization is compatible with "the integrity of [Nietzsche's] philosophy as a whole" (241, 228).

4 In an otherwise commendable article, Yirmiyahu Yovel states that Nietzsche "rejects *value* differences linked to biology alone;" that he "rejects *racism* as a normative doctrine and ideology" (1994: 226). Richard Schacht likewise avers that it is unfair to call Nietzsche a racist (1983: 335). But on the issue of the humanity of black people, there is no equivocation in Nietzsche.

5 See also aphorism #241 of *Daybreak*, where Nietzsche suggests, scientifically, that black skin color might be "the ultimate effect of frequent attacks of rage" among the less "*intelligent*" races." He furthermore draws the conclusion that the ape-like ancestors of both blacks and whites might very well have been of a "brownish grey" color. The implication is that in the case of blacks there has actually been a regressive evolution, in contrast to the evolutionary progress towards whiteness (*D*: 141)

172

6 Historically, the antiblack dimension of Nietzsche reception has been less visible than the antiproletarian. That was understandable given the needs of the antidemocratic struggle in Europe until well after the Second World War. Nevertheless, note should be made of one book, published in 1935, and authored by an anti-Nazi exile named Alfred Rosenthal, *Nietzsche's "European Race-Problem": "The Struggle for World Domination*," which interpreted Nietzsche's call for race breeding in terms of the need to forge a new ruling caste whose overarching purpose would be to intensify the oppression of Europe's non-white colonial populations. See also Aschheim: 284–5, where Aschheim cites and briefly discusses Rosenthal's book.

THE CONCEPT OF DOUBLE VISION IN RICHARD WRIGHT'S *THE OUTSIDER*
FRAGMENTED BLACKNESS IN THE AGE OF NIHILISM

Floyd W. Hayes III

AT THE dawning of the 21st century, the issue of black identity and its representations still capture the attention of thinkers, scholars, and writers. Black people's desperate struggle to understand the meaning of blackness in an antiblack American world is in large part an ambiguous and absurd adventure (see Gordon [1995a]). This is the case because the challenge faced in the constituting of black subjectivity is a function of the social relations of power between black and white Americans. In the dynamics of this interaction black identity necessarily is rendered problematic and contradictory; it is an invisible presence; it is a powerful indictment of a racialized culture.

Focusing on Richard Wright's novel, *The Outsider*, this essay examines the character of black subjective alienation in a society experiencing change and challenge. Much of the critical discussion of *The Outsider* has centered largely on the existential condition of Kierkegaardian dread as the central organizing concept in the novel (see Lawson [1971]; and Tate). Although attentive to this perspective, the present essay slightly shifts emphasis and investigates Wright's use of the concept of double vision—assuredly appropriated from W. E. B. Du Bois' earlier concept of double consciousness—as an interpretive strategy for understanding the disjointed character of black subjectivity. The novel can be considered a classic text that deals with the problems and possibilities of black (male) identity, and in its figuration of the difficulties of the marginalized subject, it suggests the extent to which black identity generally will become problematized and even fragmented in the postmodern era.

The major problem with which this essay is concerned is the construction of black identity in what for the black subject is an absurd, despairing, and antiblack world. As Linda Hutcheon points out: "The study of representation becomes…an exploration of the way in which narratives and images structure how we see ourselves and how we construct our notions of self…" (Hutcheon: 7). Hence, this paper focuses on the internal dialectic of the black existential situation. In order to understand this phenomenon, this paper aims to examine the manner in which Richard Wright represents black subjectivity in America's racialized culture. By presenting a narrative motif, Wright's *Outsider* provides a context in which we can consider the effects of social and historical factors on this self-constitutive process as it operates for black people. It will be argued that Wright's complex and fragmented construction of black subjectivity positions him within the historical transition between modernity and postmodernity. Wright hints at a conceptualization of the multiple, fragmented black self in the postmodern age of nihilism—modern Western culture in ruins.

174

DREAD, POWER, AND THE COMPLEXITY OF DOUBLE VISION

Richard Wright's early life experiences with extreme poverty and antiblack racism in the American South shaped his proletarian outlook. Born in peasant conditions near Natchez, Mississippi, in 1908, Wright searched to discover whether *black men* could live with dignity and without fear in a world dominated by *white male* power. Wright's own complex consciousness, while strongly influenced by modern rationalism, also made him fascinated by the irrational aspects of life. He wanted to find out if black men could be or become psychologically free of their white oppressors. Accordingly, Wright felt a strong responsibility to contest the white man's conception of existence and, in the process, to assert the validity and complexity of the black experience (see Gayle; Walker [1988]; and Webb). In his 1937 essay "Blueprint for Negro Writing," Wright stated:

> The Negro writer who seeks to function within his race as a purposeful agent has a serious responsibility. In order to do justice to his subject matter, in order to depict Negro life in all its manifold and intricate relationships, a deep, informed, and complex consciousness is necessary; a consciousness which

HAYES

draws for its strength upon the fluid lore of a great people, and molds this lore with the concepts that move and direct the forces of history today. (In Gayle [1972]: 320-1)

In his 1953 novel, *The Outsider*, Richard Wright ostensibly deals with the problems of self-identity and the search for meaning in a Godless world. Drawing largely upon the existential nihilist conceptual apparatus of such thinkers as Kierkegaard, Husserl, Heidegger, Nietzsche, Camus, and Sartre, Wright constructs an image of black subjectivity that is complex, knowledgeable, and powerful. Wright also portrays the black self caught in the grips of meaninglessness and alienation; it is a self riddled with disappointment, frustration, and pain. In the words of philosopher Donald Crosby:

> The existential nihilist judges human existence to be pointless and absurd. It leads nowhere and adds to nothing. It is entirely gratuitous, in the sense that there is no justification for life, but also no reason not to live. Those who claim to find meaning in their lives are either dishonest or deluded. In either case, they fail to face up to the harsh reality of the human situation (Crosby: 30)

The novel portrays Wright's hero, Cross Damon, who, overwhelmed by a sense of dread, seeks meaning and values in a world where he assumes there is no God and where "man is nothing in particular" (135).[1] Entitled "Dread," the first section of the novel contains the epigram: "Dread is an alien power which lays hold of an individual, and yet one cannot tear oneself away, nor has a will to do so, for one fears what one desires" (1). This quotation appears in translator Walter Lowrie's introduction to Søren Kierkegaard's text, *The Concept of Dread* (Kierkegaard: xii). Kierkegaard expresses the same idea in slightly different form in the body of the book, and the context surrounding it there helps us to understand the dialectical manner in which Cross Damon must be viewed and lays the foundation for the novel's ending. Damon eventually dies, having found neither meaning nor values— or so it would appear. His apparent predicament is complicated when, after he has committed four murders and has been directly responsible for two other deaths, he whispers in his dying moment, "In my heart...I'm...I felt...I'm innocent...That's what made the horror" (440). Again, the significance of Damon's dying statement is contextualized by Kierkegaard's observation: "The qualitative leap is outside of ambiguity, but he who through dread becomes guilty is innocent, for it was not he himself but dread, an alien power, which laid hold of him, a power he did not love but dreaded—and yet he is guilty, for he sank in the dread which he loved even while he feared it" (Kierkegaard [1957]: 39).

Cross Damon has found no absolute standard by which to appraise his actions. Though Damon enters the novel with a conviction that life means nothing in particular, he undertakes a search for self-identity, supposedly in regard to a more pos-

175

HAYES

itive philosophy than his existential nihilism. Meaninglessness apparently is insufficient; it is too negative to realize the identity he desires. Wright emphasizes the theme of identity by placing Damon in situations where it is necessary for him to take on different identities. At one point or another Damon is Brown, Charles Webb, Addison Jordan, John Clark, or Lionel Lane. His own name also suggests the theme of ambiguous identity, for "Cross" implies, as one critic has written, "the hero's god-like desire to be the autonomous and self-enclosed martyr," whereas "Damon" signifies his demoniacal attributes (Lehan: 193–4).

The Outsider is about a black man in urban America who in many respects transcends the assumed limitations of his blackness. In this way, Wright fashions a concept of blackness as a complex system of meanings. Wright demonstrates this observation when District Attorney Ely Houston, who is white but also an outsider states: "I am profoundly interested in the psychological condition of the Negro in this country…Only a few people see and understand the complexity of this problem" (128). As the novel opens, Damon experiences a great amount of alienation and self-loathing. He works in the post office where he has developed a friendship with several fellows; yet his reading, intellectual autonomy, and search for the meaning of things separate him from them. Damon drinks heavily; he does not like himself. Similarly, his relationships with black women are alienating and discomforting; Wright does not construct a positive view of black women. Having bequeathed to him a contradictory name (god-like but demoniacal) that seems to have rendered him always guilty of something and engulfed by a sense of dread from birth, Damon's mother constantly berates him for this sorry performance as husband and father. His wife appears antagonistic and conniving; Damon suggests that she entrapped him into the marriage. Finally, he is entangled with a minor whom he impregnates. She and her friends are out to get Damon; they intend to take legal action against him. In essence, Damon's blackness is significant because it constitutes the cultural matrix for understanding his predicament; it embodies the moroseness of existential dread.

Yet, as a result of a freak subway accident, Damon is enabled to escape his situation and to (re)create himself in familiar existential terms. Thinking he is dead, his relatives and friends hold a funeral for him, as Damon watches in God-like fashion. Following this event, Damon leaves Chicago for New York City. On the way, he tries to master his dread and control his guilty thoughts and feelings. It is during this journey that Wright complicates even more his representation of black existential life. He chooses this occasion to demonstrate how the ordinary experience of black people in the United States enables them to see with a special clarity of vision—dreadful objectivity—the same constellation of problems which existentialist thinkers had identified in more lofty and abstract arrangements.

In this way, Wright creates an almost superhuman (clearly Nietzschean) black hero whose alienation and dread place him both outside of and yet very much inside modern American, that is to say Western, civilization. In contrast to (but recalling) Du Bois' representation of double consciousness as a horrifying burden in *The Souls of Black Folk,* Wright's complex image of blackness as double vision is a source of strategic power, freedom, and knowledge. Wright speaks through District Attorney Ely Houston, who, because of his physical deformity, also is an outsider:

> "I mean this," Houston hastened to explain. "Negroes, as they enter our culture, are going to inherit the problems we have, but with a difference. They are outsiders and they are going to know that they have these problems. They are going to be self-conscious; they are going to be gifted with double vision, for, being Negroes, they are going to be both *inside* and *outside* of our culture at the same time. Every emotional and cultural convulsion that ever shook the heart and soul of Western man will shake them. Negroes will develop unique and specially defined psychological types. They will become psychological men, like the Jews…They will not only be Americans or Negroes; they will be centers of *knowing,* so to speak…The political, social, and psychological consequences of this will be enormous." (129)

Wright's representation of the complex psycho–political condition of outsiderness is grounded in the everyday life-world of modern black America and yet in some ways is suspended above it. Although Damon must deal with antiblack racism and negative stereotyping, he uses these situations to his advantage. For example, Cross Damon takes advantage of white people's stereotyped image of the ignorant and grinning black man in order to obtain a duplicate of a dead man's birth certificate in Newark, New Jersey, for the purpose of creating one of his identities. In an act of bad faith to match theirs, Damon allows the Communist Party to employ him in New York to draw public attention to the larger racial, social, and economic issues behind the problems and conflicts. Skillfully, Wright represents both communists and fascists as enemies of the black masses in whose interests he writes. In one of the most powerful scenes in the novel, Damon has moved into the apartment of the local communist leader and his wife. The landlord clearly is an antiblack fascist. Damon happens upon these two men engaged in deadly fight and he kills both of them. In this way, Damon transcends the assumed victimhood of conventional representations of black existential life in racist America.

Nevertheless, Damon is haunted by philosophical and psychological turmoils that constantly plague him, as they plague Western culture. Although Damon rebels philosophically against God, his gesture also contains a psychological dimension: his "unbridled hunger for the sensual" (18). He is unable to resist the guilt feeling apparently prevalent in Western culture and identified by Nietzsche's man of power and intuition. Familiar with the literature of the irrational—Nietzsche, Heidegger, Dostoyevsky, and Kierkegaard—Damon holds the view that all men are free to create their own futures. Consequently, Damon is his own God. Theoretically, he can do whatever pleases him, and he can privately evaluate his own actions. However, before he can apply his "lonely will" in designing his new life, Damon must find the answer to an "awful question": "What's a man?" (91).

What is compelling about the psycho-political situation of the outsider is its rebellious character and its ability to pierce through the veil of received ideals and illusions. Moreover Damon both desires and dreads the need to communicate with other rebellious outsiders. At one point, Damon thinks to himself:

> His heart went out to these rejected men whose rebel laughter banished self-murder from his thoughts. If only he could lose himself in that kind of living! Weren't there somewhere in this world rebels with whom he could feel at home, men who were outsiders not because they had been born black and poor, but because they had thought their way through the many veils of illusion? But where were they? How could one find them? (28)

Damon does find other rebellious outsiders—the district attorney and members of the Communist Party—and he engages them in analyses of the absurd and decadent character of the human situation in modern Western culture. The district attorney is conflicted by his requirement to uphold the law and by his great sympathy for rebels "who feel that they have a right to break the law" (134). In a cynical critique of law in Western culture, Wright constructs the district attorney as one who is sworn to uphold a system of law in which he does not believe. For him, life is a pretense.

What is clearly significant about the outsider's double vision is his Nietzschean will to power and knowledge, according to Wright's construction. In his narrative, Wright employs a dialogue between Damon and the district attorney in order to deal with the human predicament in modern Western culture. Wright identifies the growth of urban life with the process of industrial capitalist development which he describes as a kind of war against all humankind. He notes that great industrial cities created a cultural environment which nurtured a whole class of Nietzschean supermen like himself. In the following exchange, the district attorney Ely Houston and Cross Damon discuss the emergence of the pagan urban industrial man. Wright's existential nihilism is evident in this long exchange:

> "Could there be a man in whose mind and consciousness all the hopes and inhibitions of the last two thousand years have died? A man whose consciousness has not been conditioned by our culture: A man speaking our language, dressing and behaving as we do, and yet living on a completely different plane? A man who would be the return of ancient man, pre-Christian man? Do you know what I mean?"

Cross felt his body grow hot. His judgment told him to keep quiet, to pretend ignorance; but his emotions clamored to enter this discussion, to tell what he knew. He drew his breath, pushed his personal feelings aside, and when he spoke he was discussing himself in terms that were displaced and projected: "He's a man living in our modern industrial cities, but he is devoid of all the moral influences of Christianity. He has all the unique advantages of being privy to our knowledge, but he has either rejected it or has somehow escaped its influence. That he's an atheist goes without saying, but he'd be something more than an atheist. He'd be something like a pagan, but a pagan who feels no need to worship…And, by the nature of things, such a man sooner or later is bound to appear. Modern man sleeps in the myths of the Greeks and the Jews. Those myths are now dying in his head and in his heart. They can no longer serve him. When they are really gone, those myths, man returns. Ancient man…And what's there to guide him? Nothing at all but his own desires, which would be his only values." (316)

In one of the most intriguing episodes in the novel, Damon encounters and overwhelms members of the Communist Party. He is the murderer of two of their leaders, and he is intellectually authoritative. Since the party cannot discover Damon's true identity, they are frightened of him. As one party member says:

I mean this—Your appearance in our midst coincides with death and violence…Lane, what the hell ghastly joke is this you're pulling? Who the goddamn hell do you think you *are*? What are you doing here? When we try to check on you, we run into a maze that leads nowhere. That's no *accident*. Are you a spy? Frankly, we doubt it; we thought so at first, but you haven't been close enough to us to get hold of any information. If we were, you wouldn't be breathing now…But we want to know… (350–1)

Damon's knowledgeable double vision also puts him in possession of the double lies of the Communist Party nihilists' will to power. Employing a Marxian analysis of capitalist industrialization, he mocks the Communists' quest for power, suggesting that they are similar to the Western imperialists:

"Now, during the past thirty-five years, under the ideological banner of dialectical materialism, a small group of ruthless men in Russia seized political power and the entire state apparatus and established a dictatorship. Rationalizing human life to the last degree, they launched a vast, well-disciplined program of industrialization which now rivals that the United States of America in pretentiousness and power…Again I say that what happened in Russia, just as with what happened in America, could have happened under a dozen different ideological banners…If you lived in Russia and made such a statement,

179

HAYES

they'd shoot you; and if you lived in America and made such a statement, they'd blacklist you and starve you to death…Modern man still believes in magic; he lives in a rational world but insists on interpreting the events of the world in terms of mystical forces." (354)

Clearly, Damon's double vision gives him the intellectual power to see through and challenge the ideological duplicity of his Communist adversaries. Damon declares powerfully:

I'm propaganda-proof. Communism has two truths, two faces. The face you're talking about now is for the workers, for the public, not for me. I look at facts, processes…You did what you did because you had to! Anybody who launches himself on the road to naked power is caught in a trap…You use idealistic words as your smoke screen, but behind that screen you *rule*…It's a question of *power*. (354–5)

The outsider Damon is the product of Wright's own urgent obligation to attempt to speak on behalf of the black masses deprived of public speech, "to witness to their living." The words which Damon hurls at the Communist Party nihilist about the horror of modern life, his critique of European ideology and culture in its religious and critical communist forms, constitute a critique that emerges from black people's special history in the modern world. That critique developed during chattel slavery and positioned itself at the core of a field where industrialization, capitalism, and the institutions of democratic government intersected disproportionately (see Gilroy). Like double vision, Damon's critique represents the product of black people's turbulent voyage from racial slavery to racial segregation, from the rural south to the urban north. Through Damon, Wright expressed their predicament, as well as their hopes and aspirations.

Therefore, in rebelling against the conventional view of blackness, Wright constructs an image of double vision that is complex, powerful, and knowledgeable. As a nihilistic existentialist, Damon does not deal in illusions; he understands Western civilization's will to cynical power. He is aware of his own limitations, but his one hope is to awaken the masses from their slumberous belief in Western culture's mythological and ideological hegemony:

"Knowing and seeing what is happening in the world today, I don't think that there is much of anything that one can do about it. But there is one little thing, it seems to me, that a man owes to himself. He can look bravely at this horrible totalitarian reptile and, while doing so, discipline his dread, his fear, and study it coolly, observe every slither and convolution of its sensuous movements and note down with calmness the pertinent facts. In the face of the totalitarian danger, these facts can help a man to save himself; and he may then

be able to call the attention of others around him to the presence and meaning of this reptile and its multitudinous writhings." (367)

At the novel's end, Wright seems to suggest that a nihilistic-existential approach
bears its own chaotic and suicidal logical illogic, which, tragically, is the ultimate
irony of a philosophy dependent upon ambiguities. Wright seems to be saying that
the path of the complex, powerful, knowledgeable, yet cynical outsider ends in
destruction. In what appears to be Wright's rejection of existential nihilism, Damon
cannot walk outside of history and society and survive. The human cannot be concerned only with the self, its fears, and desires. Wright seems really to be suggesting that people must be responsible for others as well as for themselves. Shot by the
Communists and dying, Damon's existential quest has been necessary but not sufficient:

> "I wish I had some way to give the meaning of my life to others…To make a
> bridge from man to man…Starting from scratch every time is…is no good,
> Tell them not to come down this road…Men hate themselves and it makes
> them hate others…Man is all we've got…I wish I could ask men to meet
> themselves…We're different from what we seem…Maybe worse, maybe bet-
> ter…But certainly different…We're strangers to ourselves." He was silent for a
> moment, then he continued, whispering: "Don't think I'm so odd and
> strange…I'm not…I'm legion…I've lived alone, but I'm everywhere…Man is
> returning to the earth…For a long time he has been sleeping, wrapped in a
> dream…He is awakening now, awakening from his dream and finding himself
> in a waking nightmare…The myth men are going…The real mean, the last
> men are coming…Somebody must prepare the way for them…Tell the world
> what they are like…We are here already, it others but had the courage to see
> us." (439–40)

181

Wright's Kierkegaardian anguish and Nietzschean protest on behalf of the black
masses are profound. He created jarring portraits of compelling power and fragmented identities. Yet, beneath all of this, Wright seems to have hoped that in the
future human beings would operate in a more noble fashion. Wright undoubtedly understood that navigating through the maze of human consciousness and battles against historical and societal tyranny would be risky, but they might ultimately be worthwhile. He passionately hoped that he would not be a lone cry in the
wilderness. Instead, he earnestly wished that his writing would educate and liberate people, motivating them to apply themselves to building a better world.

BEYOND MODERNIST DUALISM: THE POLITICS OF CULTURAL DESPAIR

Significantly, Wright wrote within the context of the modern Western world.
Although criticizing the racist and imperialist character of Western cultural domi-

HAYES

nation, Wright's divided conception of blackness as double vision indeed was influenced by the modernist dualistic view of social reality. However, it could be argued that Wright's existential-nihilist perspective—which sustained his nuanced and complex representation of double vision and buttressed his severe critique of modern Western culture—situated him within the historical transition between modernity and postmodernity.

The modern historical moment represents Western Europe's rise to world dominance—the Renaissance, the Protestant Reformation, the Enlightenment, the European "discovery" of America, imperialism, colonialism, annihilating wars, segregation, and racism. The emerging significance of the postmodern moment witnesses the end of Western European cultural domination; the ascendancy of the United States of America as a political, economic, and cultural power; and the continuing process of decolonization in African and Asia (see West [1989]).

The modern world, which began in the West, is now coming to an end. The absolutist sensibility of the European Enlightenment is in question—its belief in the supremacy of rationalism; its search for certain truth; its faith in the power of science, the scientific method, and technology; its worship of a dualistic, hierarchical, and oppositional conception of social reality; and its belief in the superiority of Western culture and civilization and the inferiority of all others. Even Western culture's belief in humanism proved self-destructive—the European slave trade and slavery as well as Europe's and Anglo-America's attempt to annihilate people defined as undesirable—for the triumph of Europe required the death of their conception of God. But, since God had been the natural genesis of European values and the origin of all of their meaningfulness, the death of the conception of God only hastened the expansion of a smoldering culture of nihilism, an anxiety of the soul, a contamination of despair (see Gilroy; and Levin).

Drawing on the insights of Nietzsche, whose prescient vision placed him almost a century ahead of his time, the discourse of postmodernity reflects the exhaustion and deepening crisis of modern consciousness. It is the most severe case of the unhappy consciousness, a nihilism which Nietzsche perceived, in signs and symptoms, that is now obvious, too pervasive to be overlooked or explained away. It is this consciousness of this impending doom of Western culture that denotes the rupture with modernity; but postmodern discourse is not only a discourse which takes as its problem the experience of Western culture and civilization in crisis. It is also a discourse which is itself in crisis: a discourse without foundations, without a subject, without an origin, without any absolute center, and without reason. This consciousness of crisis, and of being hopelessly dislodged, as a result of this crisis, from the important questions and answers that have energized the West in the past, personifies the thinking of all those who have been influenced by the work of Nietzsche (see Levin; and Weinstein).

Influenced by Nietzsche, Richard Wright saw that it was more and more difficult for black people to live in the light of the modern—that is to say, the con-

182

HAYES

ventional—paradigm of knowledge, truth, and reality. As a writer also ahead of this time, Wright sought to examine the changing character of blackness within the context of a rapidly changing and crisis-ridden Western culture and civilization. In some ways, even Wright went beyond the modernist concept of oppositional duality, especially in portraying Cross Damon with multiple, changing identities to accommodate his changing circumstances. It is here that Wright hints at a post-modernist sensibility of fractured and multiple subjectivity (see Gergen; and Glass)—of fragmented blackness in an emerging age of nihilism when modernist culture is in ruins.

NOTE

1 All references are to Wright's *The Outsider* unless otherwise noted.

183

FRAGMENTATION, RACE, AND GENDER

Building Solidarity in the Postmodern Era

Patricia Huntington

The problem of the twentieth century is the problem of the color-line.

—Du Bois

Sexual difference is one of the important questions of our age, if not in fact the burning issue...Sexual difference is probably that issue in our own age which could be our salvation on an intellectual level.

—Irigaray

IN THE late 1970s and early 1980s, W.E.B. Du Bois' forthright challenge, that "the problem of the twentieth century is the problem of the color-line," came home to roost within U.S. feminist theory. "Women of color" challenged "white" feminists to recognize and to contend with the exclusionary racial bias that their theories and practices often exhibited in spite of an express commitment, on the part of some white feminists, to combat racism. One of several responses to this challenge entailed a perhaps ambivalently motivated importation of French poststructuralist theories. As Kelly Oliver hypothesizes, this political importation offered U.S. feminists a way to deflect criticism onto the French feminists by contrasting U.S. theories with the "essentialism and elitism" inherent in the works of Luce Irigaray, Hélène Cixous, and Julia Kristeva ([1993]: 168).

Although it would be remiss to imply that the pervasive interest in French theory was entirely a species of white defensiveness, Luce Irigaray's own dictum—that sexual difference is *the* "burning issue" of our age—seems to forbode a monism doomed to conflict with a Du Boisian centering of race as *the* problem for U.S. feminist theory. Indeed, the potential danger of making gender alone "our salvation" is the subject that I want to address (Irigaray [1987]: 165; cf. [1993]). That Irigaray has not explicitly theorized the intersection of race and gender could be chalked up to her particular concern to challenge the limited conception of gender oppression held by liberal feminists within France. In spite of her own oversight, however, many U.S. feminists do *not* regard her methodology as a priori unsuited for redressing the racial exclusion that has most recently faced the second wave of feminism since the early 1980s. Some theorists look to the works of Irigaray, Derrida, Foucault, Kristeva, and others as pivotal resources for dismantling the white, middle-class bias historically exhibited by much Anglo-feminist theorizing.

What makes poststructuralist theories attractive to many U.S. feminists—feminist theorists of various racial, ethnic, national, class, and sexual backgrounds—includes but cannot be reduced to the recognition that multiple epistemic perspectives exist. Poststructuralist theories share the view that there are no purely impartial and context-independent criteria for justifying knowledge claims with many other schools of feminist thought.[1] Like other feminist epistemologies, the poststructuralist commitment to perspectivalism accommodates the fact that women of diverse racial, sexual, and other backgrounds may well have different localized experiences of the very same social and historical reality that issues in gender-based oppression(s). The peculiar attractiveness of poststructuralist theories is not first or solely epistemological, but rather methodological. Poststructuralist theories promise a powerful *methodological* vehicle for demonstrating how dominant cultural practices erect one group's point of view as normative, thereby exposing the very machinations of false universalizing as well as the correlation of such false universalizing to relations of domination and subordination.

Accordingly, the quasi-transcendental methodologies of poststructuralism tend to be interventionist in orientation. Instead of reconstructing a univocal conception of "Woman's" oppression or a normative ideal of "Woman's" liberated agency, much poststructuralist theorizing focuses on exposing the ways that a culture's discursive practices constrain women's possibilities for identity and autonomy. These interventionist methodologies are understood, first, to be eminently suited for unmasking the multiple, yet specific (localized) forms of women's oppression while avoiding false universalism. Second, such interventions are understood to be rooted in and to encourage ethical humility. That ethical impulse consists in adhering to as well as raising the theorist's critical awareness of the limits of her own perspective. By relinquishing the presumed authority that one's situation is representative of that of all women, this methodological approach implicitly strives to support a solidarity-based theoretical attitude among women of very different situations.

In this essay, I will examine Drucilla Cornell's illuminating reading of Irigaray, since Cornell offers a serious and promising attempt to adapt French theory to the problem of racial exclusion. Nonetheless, I will highlight how an Irigarayan approach to the symbolic sources of gender-based oppression poses at least one danger for U.S. feminist theory. That danger manifests itself as the tendency to confuse the minimal recognition that multiple epistemic authorities exist with having accomplished the critical task of addressing the interests of diverse marginalized groups. The minimal recognition that I cannot universalize my own perspective does not automatically decenter my perspective. Nor does it bring me to engage critically with and to develop a theory and praxis that is inclusive of other voices.

I find that Irigaray's particular intervention into Western discursive practices can neither fully counter exclusionary thinking nor foster the type of critical social consciousness, or the "ethical" humility, requisite to ground solidarity across the often conflicting concerns of women. The nominalist underpinnings of Irigaray's thought embroil her in a methodology that, in ignoring the material differences among women, minimally fails to arrive at an awareness of the biases built into her own theory. By nominalism I mean two things: first, the critical ontological view that only individuals and not real essences exist, and, second, the epistemological claim that universals exist only as we name them in language and not as substantive essences. Irigaray's poststructuralism evinces certain nominalist undertones in that she (1) views subjectivity primarily as a discursive construct and (2) treats social reality as primarily textual or symbolic in a quasi-foundational sense. These nominalist tendencies lead her to reinstate the very "white authorial presence" that some U.S. feminists believe French psychoanalytic feminism can help them to avoid.[2] As I hope to show, this epistemological myopia comfortably disavows responsibility to local sites of liberation struggle other than one's own, thereby normalizing the status quo of U.S. racial segregation.

THE PROBLEM OF WHITE AUTHORIAL PRESENCE

The productive promise that U.S. feminists have found in poststructuralist philosophies has been twofold. First, by treating personal identity as a discursive social construct and not a pre-given essence, poststructuralist theories have often advanced feminist efforts to uproot fixed assumptions about the alleged nature of "Woman." Second, the nominalist view that only local narratives—or context-specific justificatory standards—exist has allowed poststructuralists to break away from the demand for coherence within feminist theory. Not only does this view avoid the essentialism inherent in theoretical efforts to pinpoint a universal conception of patriarchy that "subjugates all women everywhere" (Fuss: 2).[3] It also uproots the correlative assumption that women need to adopt a single strategy for liberation.

bell hooks acknowledges that postmodernist theorizing can help to counteract essentialist conceptions of racial oppression. In her essay "Postmodern Blackness," she states:

> We have too long had imposed upon us both from the outside and the inside a narrow, constricting notion of blackness...

> Employing a critique of essentialism allows African-Americans to acknowledge the way in which class mobility has altered collective black experience so that racism does not necessarily have the same impact on our lives. Such a critique allows us to affirm multiple black identities, varied black experience. It also challenges imperialist paradigms of black identity which represent blackness one-dimensionally in ways that reinforce and sustain white supremacy. (hooks [1990]: 28)

Here, hooks elicits the aid of postmodernist theory to "rearticulate the basis for collective bonding" or black solidarity that neither presupposes an ideal of the "authentic" black identity nor leads one to internalize white hegemonic conceptions of "black authenticity" (29).

Even so, it would be premature to *infer* that any given poststructuralist strategy for exposing hegemonic conceptions of identity—understood as the keystone underpinning a politics of difference and an ethics devoted to recognition of "Otherness"—necessarily proves inclusive of the socio-political interests of the racially oppressed. In the same essay, hooks explicitly qualifies her positive comments with the charge that the "postmodern critique of identity" is often used in ways that undercut the struggles of racially oppressed groups:

> Without adequate knowledge of and contact with the non-white "Other," white theorists may move in discursive theoretical directions that are threatening and potentially disruptive of that critical practice which would support radical liberation struggle...Given a pervasive politic of white supremacy which seeks to prevent the formation of radical black subjectivity, we cannot cavalierly dismiss a concern with identity politics. (hooks [1990]: 26)

The potential usefulness as well as the terrible dangers of postmodernist theories for advancing the situation of the racially oppressed is debated within black scholarship. Jon Michael Spencer identifies what he calls "*the postmodern conspiracy to explode racial identity*" ([1993]: 2). In response to Spencer, a general debate over postmodern theorizing appears in a double issue of *The Black Scholar*.[4] To give additional examples from the latter volume, Patricia Hill Collins echoes hooks' positive interpretation of postmodern theory as useful for dismantling "Blackness as a master status" (Collins [1993]: 53), whereas Molefi Kete Asante, by contrast,

HUNTINGTON

sees postmodern theory as harboring a "conservative agenda to construct a post-modernist web of a multiplicity of identities in order to befuddle the real issue," namely, "giving agency to African people…which might mean solidarity and African self-determination" (Asante [1993]: 50). hooks' sympathy to antiessential-ist arguments about identity, not all of which assume a postmodernist form, must be read against her arguably greater antipathy to postmodernist theorizing as use-ful for grounding political struggle. hooks' antipathy centers on how the postmod-ern embrace of heterogeneity, when posed in abstraction from material conditions of racial oppression and economic exploitation, glosses over, if not wholly obfus-cates, these very real social concerns of "the non-white 'Other'."

There are, however, exceptions. For example, Shane Phelan's recent work exem-plifies one way to avoid this problem. Reinterpreting the meaning of "coming out," Phelan rejects essentialist conceptions of lesbian identity. She replaces the essentialist view of "coming out" as a "process of discovery" with an anti-essential-ist view of "coming out" as "self-creation." Whereas the former regards coming out as overcoming the denial that one's hidden and authentic sexuality is lesbian; the latter reinterprets coming out as choosing to become woman-identified and to express that self-creation in the adoption of a lesbian lifestyle (Phelan: 773–7). Acknowledging that identities have only "provisional stability," Phelan is able to recover an open-ended basis for undertaking, rather than undercutting, local iden-tity politics. Hence, her work neither falls prey to essentialism nor prevents deriv-ing a basis for political action grounded on coalitional alliances (See Phelan: 778–86).

189

Yet hooks' criticism raises a central point. Of utmost significance for hooks is that, in spite of its potential to break with homogeneous concepts of personal and group identity, the feminist turn to French postmodern theory has functioned to recenter and to perpetuate "white authorial presence." For this turn entailed an appropriation of the efforts by women of color to dispel static conceptions of "Woman," but an appropriation *without acknowledgement* (hooks [1990]: 21). The very transmutation of these womanist critiques into postmodern form can further marginalize the voices of women of color.[5] Abstract discussions of difference allow white feminists to overlook crucial articulations of the "simultaneity" or interlock-ing character of systems of oppression that work by women of color contributes to feminist political theory. Instead of expanding feminist "discursive theoretical" strategies to become more inclusive, white feminists can, unwittingly, use the recognition that multiple voices exist to disavow ethical and social responsibility to "incorporate the voices of displaced, marginalized, exploited, and oppressed black people" (hooks [1990]: 25). The recentering of "white authorial presence" is indicative of a broad problem identified by black theorists, namely that white the-orists often use African-American culture solely as the basis for these projects: (1) finding innovative directions to move in theory; or (2) undertaking self-reflection; or (3) contributing to discussions of race. But none of these projects recognizes the work of people of color as fertile soil for the production of theory proper (see hooks [1981]: 6; for a summary of the unique contributions of black feminist theory, see Smith [1983]: xix–lvi).

This type of failure to grapple systematically (in theory and praxis) with one's own racialized and material location as a theorist belies an epistemological myopia. That is, it falsely assumes that discursive accounts of difference or group specificity have a built-in protection mechanism against white solipsism within feminist theory. It is as though the nominalist view that only local narratives exist is taken to protect the theorist herself from the threat of falsely universalizing or misassessing the bias of her standpoint. Yet hooks' critique suffices to suggest that no such built-in protection mechanism exists.

To the contrary, what different groups find attractive and what they find threatening about a given theoretical or political strategy presupposes that, even when they issue a critique of the same thing—such as the grand narratives of European Enlightenment—they still bring different concerns with them. And these differences matter because they reflect positions of relative power within a pre-given set of social and political institutions. For this reason, Nancy Hartsock has cautioned that French postmodernist theories, far from articulating the circumstances of the disenfranchised, represent "the destabilized voice of the powerful being forced to come to terms with the voices of the disenfranchised" (see Hartsock [1996]: 257; and [1987]: 196). Similarly, Leonard Harris notes,

...the conditions taken to be important (such as authoritarian uses of enlightenment metanarratives and valorizations of historical subjects) allow postmodernists to take the verities of a particular cultural strata and array them as features of the nature of knowledge and reason...(1993: 35).

Finally, Kumkum Sangari argues that two distinct motives are reflected in "First World" and "Third World" critiques of false universalism. Whereas the "First World's crisis of meaning," Sangari says, stems from "the felt absence of the will or the ability to change things," the "Third World" encounters difficulties realizing its will (Sangari [1987]: 161). The latter occurs because the hegemonic ideologies of neocolonialism so distort social reality that the disenfranchised have trouble finding a point of leverage from which to jump-start liberation struggles.

Even as the postmodern world raises the prospect of new hope for overcoming racial, economic and other forms of apartheid, it simultaneously threatens to relegate certain groups to their predetermined positions in already established systems of apartheid. The postmodern world we inhabit is enveloped by a social climate of retrenchment to local forms of life that do not, in actual fact, adhere to any broader moral obligation or humanistic vision that transcends a local set of interests. As Fanon reminds us, the colonial world remains "a world divided into compartments" (Fanon [1963]: 37). Because such localized positions reflect relations of domination and subordination relative to one another, feminist theory can hardly afford to embrace the heterogeneity of women's forms of oppression and the fragmented character of women's diverse struggles as if stretching across these struggles there opens out a perfectly leveled vista. That assumption is myopic in that the theorist is already implicated in a preexisting set of hierarchies in material and political conditions among women. We must be cautious not to assume that a commitment to difference automatically yields critical awareness of the negative ramifications of one's position relative to that of other women and, thus, necessarily supports alliances of solidarity.[6]

IMAGINATIVE UNIVERSALISM

Since one of the explicit objectives of postmodern feminist theorizing has been to bring the theorist to an awareness of the biases and relative power inherent in her position, Drucilla Cornell's insightful appropriation of Irigaray merits examination. The U.S. reception of Irigaray's work emphasizes that her primary aim is not to lay out a full-fledged political theory or program for social action. Rather, Irigaray explicitly limits her work to intervening in the psycho-sexual imaginary of Western culture as transmitted in key texts of Western tradition. The modest objective of these interventions is to cultivate the "psychic resistance" necessary to overcome the disabling effects of gender-based domination and to recover fuller agency (Irigaray [1985b]: 166). For this reason, Cornell and others do not see her methodology as tied to any specific set of material conditions, whatever complex matrix of racial, economic, and other factors those conditions might exhibit.

191

In both *Speculum of the Other Woman* (1985a) and *This Sex Which Is Not One* (1985b), Irigaray demonstrates that the Western philosophical corpus is organized around a phallocentric libidinal economy. By this she means that Western rationality "promulgates" a patriarchal value system that selectively valorizes the imagery of solids over that of liquids, an optics of sight over one of touch, visibility over mucosity, "property, production, order, form, unity and...erection" over the "continuous, compressible, dilatable, viscous, conductible, diffusible" ([1985b]: 86, 111). Moreover, Irigaray identifies how this phallocentric symbolism is rooted in a logic that projects "Woman" or the "feminine" as what lies outside impartial reason. This is to locate "Woman" as "Other" to the very formation of the rational, autonomous subject. "Woman" then is not a subject, but rather the social imaginary that grounds subjectivity. "Woman" cannot speak herself, because she is the "womb of man's language" or his "unconscious." "Woman" can have no self-derived sexual fantasy, since she must play the role of being the fantasized object of the male imaginary, both the *Archê* and telos of his unfulfilled desire (77, 94–5).

Irigaray clearly does not equate women—their specific and diverse identities—with how "Woman" is represented within Western tradition. Rather, she demonstrates that the symbolism inherent in the Western philosophical corpus, from Plato to Hegel, denies women any symbolic association by which to identify as specifically female *and* as subject. The patriarchal symbolic system thus curtails women's ability to image themselves as self-determining and in this way inhibits experimentation with their autonomous self-expression. Accordingly, Irigaray's writings focus on recovering what she calls a "female imaginary," that is, a way for women to symbolize their own desires. Irigaray attributes a central role to imagination in recovering personal autonomy, yet her concept of imagination is distinctively social in that it pertains to the norms projected by our society. For this reason, Cornell interprets Irigaray's work as a form of critical utopian fantasizing or mythologizing, aimed at counteracting the "depletion of the feminine imaginary in the name of the [patriarchal] symbolic" (Cornell [1991]: 178).

Diana Fuss ([1989]: 55–72) and Margaret Whitford ([1991]: 84–97, 177ff) argue persuasively that Irigaray does not seek to replace the preexisting Western phallic symbolic system with a new, static and dominant matriarchal symbolic system revolving around the vaginal image of women's "two lips" as opposed to the phallus. Even so, Cornell argues that Whitford neglects the utopian dimension in Irigaray's work and that the only way to prevent a "symbolization of the female imaginary" from solidifying into a substitutive, but static symbolic system is to understand Irigaray's thought as a variety of critical fantasy or critical mythology (Cornell [1991]: 77).

Cornell's reading is instructive in, minimally, two ways. First, Cornell carefully argues that Irigaray's strategy of imaginative universalizing does not reinstate a single normative model for what female sexual identity has been or should look like. "This use of the feminine as imaginative universal does not, and should not, pretend to simply tell the 'truth' of Woman as she was, or is. This is why our mythology is self-consciously an artificial mythology…" (Cornell [1991]: 178). According to Cornell, Irigaray is not committed to a transhistorical view of women's oppression, since she does not describe the way women "are" or have been. As Cornell puts it, the "origin that is lost is resurrected as fantasy, not as an actual account of the origin" (78). Nor does Irigaray erect a static ideal of who women ought to become.

Hence, the primary function of critical fantasizing is to release women's imagination from the claws of patriarchal symbolism. This goal can be accomplished, Cornell claims, by effectuating metaphoric slippage in our preestablished interpretive frameworks: "What matters is that the retelling of the feminine as imaginative universal gives body to the 'elsewhere' which makes this one appear as 'fallen,' and gives us the hope and the dream that we may one day be beyond it" (Cornell [1991]: 186). Even as our preexisting myths about "Woman" constrain women's self-reflection and action, they are also susceptible to more than one interpretation. Critical appropriations of preexisting mythologies about "Woman" provide a medium through which to release the utopian desire requisite to guide women's liberation struggles toward personal and social transformation, that is toward a truly novel future.

Secondly, this utopian reading leads Cornell to claim that Irigaray's work can be adapted to opening up racial, national, and ethnic differences among women in a way that fosters mutual understanding. Because "Woman" as such does not exist but rather women "are" only as they exist within the manifold texts that determine their situations, Cornell argues that there can be no inherent contradiction between analyzing *the* masculine symbolic structure of western tradition and fleshing out the "specificity" of women's various historical circumstances. Cornell's argument is that symbolic constructions of "Woman" do not exist a priori as free-floating universals, but only a posteriori in their localized manifestations.

This theoretical position relies upon the nominalist intuition that no substantive or real universals exist for which we find only particular instantiations in material reality. Rather, the universal-particular dichotomy gives way to exploring women's "specificities" or how, in fact, tradition has imposed linguistic and symbolic groupings onto people (Cornell [1991]: 181ff).

So recognizing that "Woman" is only an allegory or myth, Cornell rejects the twin charges that postmodern methodologies privilege white women's experiences, thereby forcing non-white women into the additive problem of tagging race or ethnicity onto "white woman's" account of femaleness. Rather, concrete critical mythologies treat women's different forms of oppression holistically. Cornell claims that imaginative universalism is "reiterative universalism" because the so-called universal, in this case "Woman," "is only as it is told, in its difference." Using Toni Morrison's *Beloved* as an example, Cornell states:

193

> Far from homogenizing the situation of Woman, the allegory of *Beloved* relies on myth to dramatize the very difference of the Afro-American mother's situation. In this sense, the "universals" expressed in myth are not and cannot be just the mere repetition of the same. Indeed, the "universal," the symbol of the "killing mother," cannot be known except as it is in context. (Cornell [1991]: 194–6)

Cornell, following Irigaray, holds that retelling and reinterpreting myths can raise social awareness of how racial difference intersects with gender and in such a way that African-American women are not isolated as absolutely different from or not human like Euro-American women. Fleshing out specificity does not reduce black women to a sub-set of "white woman" taken to represent humanity on a more universal plane. Susan Babbitt comments, "[Cornell's] point about *Beloved*…is that we see what is wrong with a basic social myth—a presumption about how women's experience in general is characterized—when we apply it to the experience of an African-American woman and it fails to make sense" (Babbitt: 3). Cornell casts *Beloved* against the Medea myth in order to reveal the concrete material and social difference of the African-American mother's reality in slavery. Such a retelling of Medea through *Beloved* reveals that killing one's children under slavery cannot exemplify, as with Medea, the mother who protects her children from patriarchy, because under slavery the mother cannot even "guarantee [the children]...an autonomous life in even the most minimal sense." Cornell argues that *Beloved* not only transforms the significance of the Medea myth but "challenges" the "idealization of mothering as the basis for a unique feminine 'reality'" (Cornell [1991]: 194, 195). In this fashion, Babbit suggests, Cornell shows how *Beloved* encourages our awareness of the ways in which Sethe, precisely as human like me, is treated differently: "If we were to think of Sethe in terms of the then dominant conceptual framework, the difference between Sethe and a white woman is that Sethe is *less* than fully human, not just that she is unjustly treated *as* human" (Babbitt: 4).

THE LITTLE DISTANCE THAT STILL FRAGMENTS?

Cornell's extension of Irigaray's method to incorporate the question of racial, ethnic, and national diversity is impressive and raises important questions about the role that critical mythologizing can contribute to fostering critical awareness of the differences among women. Indeed, Cornell makes such a contribution. Yet I remain unconvinced that adopting Irigaray's dyadic conception of the patriarchal symbolic order successfully avoids the "white authorial presence" that arrays the perspective of white, middle-class women as normative or universal. Cornell finds no difficulty in steering between a formal concept of the Western symbolic order as a dyadic or bipolar configuration and examining the concrete social and material differences in women's situations (see Cornell [1991]: 195). In spite of Cornell's defense, Irigaray's nominalist assumption that identity formation is *primarily* a linguistic construct entangles her work in an a priori, idealist reification of reality as symbolic. That reification, I hope to show, commits Irigaray to an appeal to a hermeneutical monism of meaning that threatens to reinstate the ghettoization of nonwhite women to their predefined "racial" or other groupings.

Deborah King has defined *monism* as the claim that social relations can be distilled down to *one* dimension that underpins all other forms of oppression (King [1988]: 51). Irigaray assumes that the symbolic dimension of social reality is the foundational keystone in unlocking personal and group identity. This methodological prioritizing of language leads Irigaray to sever her analysis of the discursive sources of women's oppression from the institutions and the political economy that sustain the very psycho-sexual ideologies that support women's oppression. Having severed the symbolic from the material institutions that support it, Irigaray is free to assume that the "feminine" constitutes a privileged signifier for unlocking the nature of the symbolic sources of women's oppression and for liberating women from all other dimensions of their oppression. These twin poles of Irigaray's monism betray the biased standpoint that all women experience their oppression, albeit only at the symbolical level, in terms of a simple *dyadic* mascu-

194

HUNTINGTON

line-feminine hierarchy. Here I identify several interrelated aspects of that normative bias inherent in Irigaray's monism.

First, Irigaray's psychoanalytic approach to the "masculine symbolic" is *reductionistic* and for that reason it obscures the complexity of women's relations to one another. Irigaray rightly holds that women's various forms of oppression are not substantively the same in content. Yet Irigaray's methodology not only recognizes that oppressed women are formally the "same" in that they are marginalized as women, but also treats this formal equivalence as foundational. By assuming a priori that the "feminine" can be isolated as the linchpin or transcendental signifier bolstering patriarchal symbolic practices, this approach trivializes in advance key differences in women's kinds of oppression, thereby reducing those differences to only secondary manifestations of a primary, shared condition. The issue here is not one of laundry-listing forms of oppression, as if it is possible or desirable to add oppression onto oppression so as to rank these from "best" to "worst" forms. Rather, the assumption that the "feminine" plays a special role over other terms, such as "black" or "exploited," as the discursive basis of women's oppression is not only unwarranted but may reflect social advantage.

Cornell's contribution to "specifying" unique differences in women's historical, cultural, economic, and political situations is significant. What concerns me is that Irigaray's quasitranscendental approach to symbolic structures, *pace* Cornell, tacitly fragments traditions or subtraditions into *discrete* manifestations of a univocal, in this case, dyadic symbolic structure. Women's "specificities," then, are identified not simply as unique in some regards, but rather as pristine wholes untainted and untouched by one another, at least at the most fundamental level. For these specificities are not examined as overlapping, interrelated, yet often *competing* and *incommensurable* views of and responses to a shared global set of economic and social conditions that situate groups in diverse relations not only to those conditions but also to one another. Such an abstract approach to patriarchal symbolic practices thus allows the white postmodern feminist—in specifying her experience of the "feminine"—to ignore fundamental conflicts of interest between her theoretical and practical endeavors and those of women of color. Presumably since women are the "same" in that they are marginalized, they need not worry that differences in their respective material and philosophical positions may impede the advancement of some other women. Since a given woman's personal experience of gender oppression does not necessarily sensitize her to racial or class oppression, a methodology that levels differences in power among types of exclusion better serves those with material security and racial privilege than those lacking these.

Second, these comments imply that Irigaray's abstract approach to symbolic structures poses problems for achieving even the limited goal of "psychic resistance" advanced by her work. For designating the "feminine" as the keystone in the symbolic sources of women's oppression cordons off in advance any examination of those specific conflicts among women—conflicts in perspective, in eco-

195

HUNTINGTON

nomic and political relations to one another, and in strategies for social change—that permeate all the way down to the core attitudes and to the basis of the respective positions they hold. How can critical mythologizing cultivate the type of critical consciousness requisite to found solidarity among women, when it shies away from the "sticky area" wherein conflicts in women's perspective and circumstance prove incommensurable? It remains unclear how exactly imaginative universalism could work or whether, finally, it could support solidarity and alliances among women, instead of forcing "resistance" into allegedly "discrete" local sites as if we pursued local liberation struggles independent of other struggles.[7]

On the one hand, a Cornellian retelling of Medea through *Beloved* reveals important differences in relative power among white women who are viewed as "human" and women of color who are not so regarded. Cornell's critical mythologizing, thus, can be said to foster some level of empathy for and understanding of some differences among women. On the other hand, Cornell's reliance upon Irigaray's idealist view of symbolic structures yields a critical mythologizing that avoids delving into the crucial "sticky" juncture at which the relative power that some women enjoy may well contribute to the perpetuation of the oppression of other women. Although Cornell's reading of *Beloved* brings us close to seeing the relative freedom that white women have enjoyed historically over enslaved, and by extension exploited, nonwhite women, nothing in the project of imaginative universalism so undertaken necessitates that one traverse the remaining distance between seeing differences in relative power and a face-to-face encounter with how one's own racialized and socio-economic power as "white" partakes of the exploitation of others.

This final terrain remains untraversed in large part due to Irigaray's reification of patriarchal myths into a dyadic structure that posits "Woman" as "Other" to the dominant culture. Thus, even when fleshing out important material differences in how women are specifically placed as "Other" to the norm, the very activity of specifying what is unique to an oppressed group qua that group isolates and preserves a space of distantiation among groups. It is arguable that, in fact, Euro-American women and African-American women, to take only two examples, do ultimately live in one another's "texts" and "mythic" traditions because they share complex and overlapping *her*stories. But this reality does not necessitate that we find one another in our critical mythologizing since the retelling of myths tends to focus only on what is unique to a group's existence. At what point, then, will such discrete projects of critical fantasizing lead women to cultivate that social consciousness requisite to assume responsibility for whether or not their respective situations and practices perpetuate the oppression of others? In disclosing this world as fallen, when do our respective mythic analyses add up to a viable picture of larger relations of domination and subordination that oppress women as well as implicate some women in relative degrees of power?

196

HUNTINGTON

One could argue that critical mythologizing could be applied to exploring these intersections of various women's lives. In principle, yes. However, Irigaray's assumption that the symbolic sources of women's oppression can be reduced to the Oedipal triangle prevents this possibility and so must be challenged. The psycho-sexual fantasies which fuel the oppression of women in the U.S. emerge out of a variety of institutionalized practices, including minimally antiblack racialized social norms and a capitalist political economy. While I agree with Irigaray and Cornell (as well as Fanon and others) that tapping into the psycho-sexual fantasies of U.S. culture is key to unlocking sexist ideologies, nothing in Irigaray's privileging the "feminine" as the key to unlocking these ideologies encourages white feminist theorists to grapple with *their* racial locus and to overcome the fears, habits and advantages bound up with this locus. To the contrary, analyzing gender oppression strictly in terms of a bipolar hierarchy tends to abstract from an examination of the racial and class dynamics of one's own—not just the Father's—cultural fantasies.

Because Irigaray's bipolar conception of the phallocentric symbolic centers on masculine-feminine signifiers, it tends to eclipse other kinds of power relations, dis-cursive and non-discursive. Hence, it cannot help us to uncover the erotic fantasies that circulated, for example, in nineteenth-century U.S. society around the com-plex knot embedded in relations among the white slaveholder, his wife, the black female slave, and the black male slave. Are we to materialize the masculine-femi-nine dyad in discrete white-on-white, black-on-black relationships? Even if we flesh out the white male-black female or white female-black male relationship, this would not deliver us to the white female-black female relationship as it exists in a larger racialized and genderized world. Such relations are not finally bipolar. Spike Lee's *Jungle Fever* suffices to suggest that the social practices that embody the fears, erotic fantasies and aggression bound up with this multidimensional knot, though perhaps modified in form, have not left the world of U.S. race relations. And my question is, if white women and black women are left to retell the myths of their allegedly composite traditions of gender oppression and even if women can learn from retelling these differences, who will then work on this complex knot?[8]

Materializing dyadic configurations of masculine-feminine symbolism cannot be contextualized in such a way that white women and black women in the U.S. are confronted with the distrust that surrounds their relationships to one another as mediated not simply in terms of competition for the phallus—a masculine/fem-inine symbol of power—but rather as situated within a larger set of societal con-figurations. This larger circumstance constitutes a multidimensional set of symbol-izations. Acknowledging, minimally, race as a social factor in women's struggle for liberation challenges the very conception of power as purely "phallic" at base of Irigaray's work. Moreover, as a modest strategy for "psychic resistance," Irigaray's bipolar analysis of the symbolic order seems unable to encourage a socially thera-peutic investigation into the mythology of Jim Crow. But this poses the addition-al question: Can we conceive of the "fantastic" process whereby a woman recovers her autonomy as achievable from within a discrete analysis of her "specific" situation? How will an "autonomy" so achieved be complete or make the transition to solidarity if one's autonomy is not seen as fundamentally tied to the larger global relations that form the matrix delineating the oppression of others?

Finally, by isolating the "feminine" as the primary symbolic source of gender oppression, Irigaray's methodology tends to burden women of color with the task of factoring race and socio-economic status into analyses of their specific forms of gender oppression, while absolving white women of this task. In other words, hermeneutical monism threatens not only to segregate women but in this segregating tendency perpetuates racialized hierarchies within feminist theory. It does so by dumping on women of color at least a larger share of responsibility for analyzing and fighting racism. For example, Cornell looks to Morrison's writings when she wants to discuss how race and economic exploitation complicate women's oppression. In so doing, she argues that Irigaray's theory of the symbolic does not homogenize Woman. But why is it that Irigaray's own appeals to mythic presentations of the feminine never touch on the racial and class features of white women's location in the seemingly racially pure Oedipal triangle or masculine-feminine dyad? Why do analyses of white women's gender-based disadvantage not indicate the social, political, and economic power that often accompany being located as "white"? Or why are the axes of relative power known by some white women revealed *solely* against the backdrop of the black female slave? Is this not, as Michele Wallace challenges, using the segregated "black other" as "a starting point," and, I would add, litmus test for "white self-criticism" (Wallace [1979])? Another approach might entail examining "whiteness" as a systemic, institutional category, fundamental to the economic and political structures of the world (see Gordon [1995a]).

These discrepancies result from the very "white authorial presence" built into a monistic conception of the symbolic that first isolates the "feminine" as the keystone of women's oppression, thereby abstracting symbolic practices from the pre-existing racialized economic system as well as other nondiscursive sources of oppression. For this methodology assumes a priori that women suffer first from sexism and only secondarily from economic and racial oppression. It treats "sexism" first as rooted in mythologies centered purely on gender roles and only secondarily sees these gender roles as housed in other discursive and nondiscursive relations. Accordingly, it seems to foster the illusion that materially secure, racially privileged women "experience" sexism in a pure form independent of the very socio-economic and racialized features of our society they enjoy. While an important contribution to addressing differences among women, Cornell's reading of Irigaray cannot finally compensate for this normative bias in Irigaray's work.

OVERCOMING FRAGMENTATION

I have argued that Irigaray's discursive strategies do not break fully with the status quo of U.S. racial segregation and with a long history of the failure of white women to earn the trust of women of color. Playing down the non-discursive factors influencing identity formation and treating mythical traditions as hermeneutically monistic leads to a disturbing effect. What is disturbing about the nominalist underpinnings of Irigaray's view that subjectivity is first (that is, founded as) an effect of language is that it allows white theorists to disavow responsibility for the allegedly linguistically discrete, "localized" phenomenon of antiblack racism. It feeds into the traditional impulse of racism criticized by Du Bois in *The Souls of Black Folk*; that is, it makes the "black problem" a problem of blacks. As a result, Irigaray's Lacanian-influenced analysis of the patriarchal symbolic continues implicitly to associate white woman's perspective with the more universal gender perspective; and the non-white woman's, with a more particular racialized version of gender-specificity. Pawning off the task of "factoring" race into the analysis onto women of color perpetuates the status quo, it reinforces theoretical apartheid (Hartsock [1996]) in the very name of "difference."

In this light, I wish to conclude with two programmatic statements. First, any U.S. feminist methodology committed to contending with psycho-sexual cultural fantasies needs to offer a more complex, non-bipolar hermeneutical analysis of the symbolic sources of women's oppression than a Lacanian-influenced framework allows. Analyses of the symbolic sources of women's oppression must be concrete and empirical as opposed to abstract, for this abstraction admits becoming a tool of the very ideology it criticizes. Local discourses need to be examined as responses to the larger global circumstance out of which they arise. Such an alternative model can be found, for example, in Cherríe Moraga's analysis of the mythology of Malinche in Mexican history. Moraga offers an analysis of one "specific" discourse, also a mythology, that contributes to homophobic oppression of lesbians in Mexican and chicano communities. Her analysis demonstrates that Mexican conceptions of women's alleged inferiority are deeply intertwined with ethnic concerns to resist anglo-imperialism and cultural genocide. Moraga shows how the concern to resist cultural genocide has reinforced heterosexist conceptions of family unity (Moraga: 204–5). Although centered on a culturally specific myth, Moraga's materially concrete isolation of the distinctive features of the Latina's struggle opens up, rather than obscures the contours of a shared world history of colonizer and colonized, of a global economic hierarchy of rich and poor and of racial relations as embedded in these. In addition, it reveals the complexities involved in differently motivated liberation struggles within a "local" context. For example, she argues that resistance to Anglo-imperialism has lead mistakenly to fear of giving up patriarchal power within the family, since the family, historically speaking, has provided Mexican and other latino communities a key source of empowerment against cultural hegemony (Moraga: 208–10).

HUNTINGTON

As empirically and historically concrete, Moraga's analysis of the Malinche myth harbors no a priori assumptions that the "feminine" or "la Raza" must form *the* centralized axis around which the discursive sources of the Latina's oppression revolve. Precisely by avoiding such monistic assumptions, Moraga's focus on the uniqueness of the Mexican heritage can reveal the multiple axes of power and powerlessness embedded in complex relations of culture, economics, gender and race both within a nation and across lines of national interest. For this reason, her analysis has general applicability beyond its obvious concern to reveal the difficulties that the lesbian Latina faces. It calls others to accountability for whatever investment in these networks of domination and subordination they may have (Moraga: 210–1).

Secondly, if theoretical interventions into symbolic practices are to reflect ethical humility, then they cannot begin with the assumption that as women we can foster empathy for our respective plights simply by fighting against a common enemy, *viz.*, patriarchy. Preexisting relations of power among women challenge precisely the assumption that women can rely upon even the minimalist view that being oppressed as women suffices to bind women together in a collective liberation struggle. María Lugones and Elizabeth Spelman reminded white feminists some time ago that not all women "talk the same language" and that women of various ethnic backgrounds are "ill at ease" in one another's worlds, theories and languages (Lugones and Spelman: 23). Since discussions of the "Other" and professed concerns for the suffering of "others" can perpetuate paternalistic motives, white feminists cannot begin their theories assuming that they have already unlearned these motives and that they do not slip into the practice of theorizing.

For this reason, it seems to me that feminist theory cannot move beyond the modern problem of overuniversalizing a given individual, group or cultural perspective by simply lapsing into the view that all groups have a perspective while ignoring relations of power between those groups; nor can theory avoid false universalism by advocating heterogeneous anarchism as a political strategy in which each group works incrementally and discretely toward its own liberation without assessing the ramifications, especially negative, its struggle might yield for others. Although developing such an epistemology and theory of social liberation extends beyond the objective of this paper, one of the noticeable and frightening deficiencies of Irigaray's methodology is its failure to articulate a category of interaction as a necessary condition for cultivating such a critical epistemology and for conceptualizing social agency in terms of coalitional alliances if not a deeper solidarity among the oppressed.

Arguably an interactionist paradigm proves necessary even for advancing a theoretical strategy restricted to Irigaray's limited objective of "psychic resistance." Dialogue with one another is minimally an effective vehicle for giving up presumed authority, if not a necessary means by which to develop a critical relation to my circumstance. If the objective of "imaginative universalism" is, in part, to unlearn the habits and attitudes that divide women and delimit their individual and collective agency, then how can women from different walks of life attain this objective without actually engaging with one another? Unlearning racial myopia requires the cultivation of enlarged thinking; that is, the ability to grasp any social event or phenomenon in terms of its multiple dimensions and its disjunctive and conflicting impact on various groups or individuals (cf. Benhabib [1995]). A more complex hermeneutic of gender dynamics of the type undertaken by Moraga clearly contributes to this goal; however, enlarged thinking, I would argue, also requires that women come into contact with, gather information about, and allow themselves to be challenged directly by those whose circumstances differ from their own in key regards.

I recently heard a self-identified feminist claim that she does not want to know the people behind the margins of a text. She prefers to read the text first and then determine whether or not she wants to get to know the person. In a complex world such as ours, abstract examinations of symbolic systems, that isolate "Woman" as the formal transcendental signified of a text, allow the theorist to selectively edit what texts she reads, what voices she finds in the texts, and even blatantly to ignore those whose voices have been systematically denied epistemic authority. If prejudice is a "stabilized deception of perception" that selectively edits out differences threatening to one's own identity, then the epistemological concern to develop a reflective relation to my standpoint may be achievable only via social interaction (Anzaldúa: 226).[9] Theoretical contributions that encourage overcoming fragmentation and divisiveness await a richer epistemology of critical social consciousness and a thicker intersubjective theory of women's social agency than I believe we can find in Irigaray's work.

That epistemology must arguably be empirical and interdiscursive. And those possibilities for autonomy must be understood as not only social but global because we live in a world of structural and institutional interdependence, a world in which the powerful benefit from fragmentation among the less powerful and the powerless. Social agency, then, should not be understood solely as local power over one's regional or group-specific concerns. Rather these local freedoms must be understood and analyzed as decisively curtailed when other members of society or sectors of the globe are denied participation in the decisions and policies that affect their daily lives. To the extent that women's possibilities are determined by preexisting global relations of material and social conditions, recovering "local" autonomy hinges upon combatting a "global" world that produces the multiple, yet interrelated exploitative mechanisms that sustain diverse forms of oppression in the first place.

HUNTINGTON

NOTES

1 See Alcoff and Potter.

2 Throughout this essay, I rely on hooks' usage of the phrase,"white authorial presence" ([1990]: 21).

3 Fuss provides a comprehensive definition of essentialism as referring to any of the following three positions: (1) the belief in a substantive "female essence;" (2) univocal and universal notions of womanhood, femininity, or women's oppression; and (3) totalizing conceptions of symbolic practices. Essentialist conceptions of women's oppression inevitably abstract from the specific historical, social, and material conditions of women.

4 See *The Black Scholar: The Multicultural Debate* 23 nos. 3 and 4 [1993]: 48–80.

5 See Collins' ([1993]: 52) pointed comments on how postmodernist theoretical orientations have forgotten their origins, viz., that these schools of thought emerged in response to practical challenges to existing structures of colonization and supremacy posed by African-Americans and other people of color. Accordingly, academic postmodernism has tended to focus on abstract textual analyses while abandoning any concern to effect social change.

6 Some postmodern social theory weds the acceptance of diverse epistemic perspectives to a politics of heterogeneous anarchism. Carol A. Stabile defines heterogeneous anarchism as the view that politics is necessarily fragmented, that "the only similarity among [struggling] groups is their struggle—from very different positions and in isolation from one another" (Stabile [1994]: 49).

7 The recent Zapatista movement in Chiapas offers a good example of the way that local liberation and regional autonomy depend upon global resistance to neo-liberal economic and political policies.

8 I do not mean to imply that a good many authors have not worked on this topic, but only to question whether reliance upon certain uses of poststructuralism might either give the impression that such works do not already exist or simply fail to contribute to such work. For comments on sexual relations in the slaveholding system, see, e.g., hooks ([1990], 57–64 and Davis (1983): chaps. 1–4. For a critique of the ethnocentrism latent in the earlier (white) feminist theoretical analyses of race-sex dynamics in Simone de Beauvoir (1983), Kate Millet, Shulamith Firestone, and others, see Margaret Simons. Deborah King, Aída Hurtado, and Evelyn Brooks Higginbotham make excellent contributions to isolating key differences among women's forms of oppression; they also provide manifold references to key work on the issue of race and gender and the history of racial conflict within feminism.

9 This is actually Alexander Mitscherlich's definition of prejudice; however, I refer here to Anzaldúa's discussion of prejudice ([1990]: 216–31, and see 231 n. 15 for Mitscherlich reference).

BLACK EXISTENCE AND BLACK LIBERATION

part IV

EXISTENCE, IDENTITY, AND LIBERATION

Robert Birt

EVERY STRUGGLE for human liberation is invariably a struggle for a liberated identity. A fundamental transformation of society is certainly indispensable. But if the proof (as Fanon says) of the success of a struggle "lies in a whole social structure being changed from the bottom up," the ultimate goal of this arduous transformation is to "set afoot a new man" (Fanon [1963]: 35, 310). It is the formation of a new kind of person with "a new language and a new humanity," that is the central thrust of any genuine struggle for human freedom. The human being must be transformed in his consciousness and self-consciousness, in his relation to self, the world and others. This necessarily entails a radical transvaluation of values and, as Marcuse argues, a "break with the familiar, routine ways of seeing, hearing, feeling, understanding…" (Marcuse [1969]: 6).

Now the struggle for identity may well have ontological roots, in which case it would be an unsurpassable feature of *la condition humaine*. Consequently, the human need to struggle for an identity would exist in "some" form even if alienating social oppression and struggles for liberation from oppression had never existed (or ceases to exist). Human existence and identity are not simply given. "Things are given their being ready-made," Ortega y Gassett tells us (Kaufmann: 155). But to become human and develop a human identity is a process of invention (self-invention), of personal and collective action conditioned by social relations. If Sartre is right in claiming that "freedom is impossible to distinguish from the 'being' of human reality" ([1956b]: 60), that we are void of a fixed nature or predetermined essence, then we humans can invent ourselves and create autonomous identities. But we do so through actions and choices conditioned by our social existence. In the context of a social existence free of oppression, alienation and immiseration, the striving for identity could become an exuberant expression of the joy of existence in a liberated life that is an open field of possibilities.

But what if our social existence is unfree? Then existential freedom is denied in social practice. The various forms of social oppression and domination obstruct the actualization of that freedom which constitutes the being of human reality, thereby blocking the ultimate source of energy for the creative formation of identity. Thus, oppression may be seen as an existential violation, an ontological crime. Is this not what is meant when we describe oppression and exploitation as dehumanizing? But since this violation of the human being is social, the struggle to create an identity is also social.

Oppression robs people of their identity as surely as exploitation robs people of the fruits of their labor. Oppression imposes rigid, stultifying identities on its victims. Often it imposes a deformed consciousness on the oppressed which helps to reinforce the very system of oppression which deforms them. The slave who internalizes his servitude to the degree of seeing his slavery as just or inevitable; the woman who assimilates masculinist values to the point of accepting as legitimate or unavoidable her subservience to men; those black people who develop inferiority complexes and a "degenerating sense of nobodiness" as a result of being indoctrinated with white supremacist values which denigrate black humanity and valorize whiteness as the standard of all that is good or even "human," all manifest the deformed consciousness of dominated people. All oppression begets alienation, and total oppression begets total alienation. According to Angela Davis, alienation "is the absence of authentic identity."[1] Now the oppression of black people from the time of slavery to the current era has been a *total* oppression. By a total oppression we mean a form of domination which afflicts every aspect of a person's life. This point has been well illustrated by Albert Memmi:

BIRT

To sum up, if we define total oppression as a state which affects the human being in all aspects of his existence, in the "way he sees himself" and the way others see him, in his various entrees into urban society, and in his future in history, the oppression of the American Negro is undeniably a total_oppression. A product of the whole of American society, it affects the "whole of the black man's existence." If we look closer, we see that there is no one aspect of his life, no single action of his, that is not thrown off balance by this fundamental aggression. (Memmi: 23–3)

From this total oppression arises a total alienation. One of the classic descriptions of the effects oppression on the way black people see themselves can be discerned from W. E. B. Du Bois' *Souls of Black Folk*. He wrote that the black is born into an American world "which yields him no true self-consciousness, but only allows him to see himself through the revelation of the other world." Frederick Douglass remarked that the "slave was a fixture," and bemoaned the condition whereby personality "is swallowed up in the sordid idea of property" (Davis [1983b]). As a black subject of French colonialism, Frantz Fanon also discovered himself to be "an object in the midst of other objects" (Fanon [1967a]: 109). Richard Wright found the oppression of blacks so excruciating that he imagined life under feudal oppression more tolerable—not that he preferred feudalism, but because he felt "that feudalism made use of a limited part of a man" (Wright [1977]: 6). Racial domination seemed to claim an individual's entire life. Enslaved, deracinated, relegated to the subhuman, the bestial (or the category of things)—the black people have endured a total denial of their humanity and a total subversion of their human identity.

207

Of course, the world's black people are not the only oppressed people. Most of humanity is oppressed. There is class and gender oppression (of which blacks also suffer) which also beget alienation. Memmi certainly has a point when he says that all "oppressed people resemble each other," and that they "show a family likeness" (Memmi: 7). But it is with the specificities of the black situation that we are concerned here. What does it mean to say that the slave is a fixture or that a human being is an object in the midst of objects? What is the meaning of Aimé Césaire's equation "colonization = thingification"? Essentially, it is that the blacks lose altogether the status of human beings. The black person is "reduced to pure facticity, concealed in his immanence, cut off from his future, deprived of his transcendence..." (de Beauvoir [1948]: 100). But human existence is freedom, is transcendence of the given. Only things or beasts have their being ready-made. Deprived of freedom and transcendence, the human being "no longer appears anything more than a thing among things" (de Beauvoir [1948]: 100).

One could object that this is common to the experience of all oppressed people, not a peculiarity of the black experience. Marx certainly thought that the exploited European worker was alienated, reduced to being an instrument of production—reduced to thinghood. There is truth in this objection. But it is not the whole truth. Césaire argues that while the economic question is important it is not the only thing. black people, Césaire surmises, are "doubly proletarianized and alienated: in the first place as workers, but also 'as blacks,' because…we are dealing with the 'only race which is denied even the notion of humanity'" (Césaire: 78–9). Race is the distinctive feature. It is as blacks, not as workers or women, that we are denied even the notion of humanity. There is no denying other dimensions of oppression. In fact, other dimensions of oppression are compounded and intensi- fied by racism. South Africa's white workers and women were not pent up in native reserves nor forced to carry passes. Apartheid was (is?) a racial caste system imposed on blacks of both genders and all classes. But it served (and quite by design) to make African workers far more vulnerable to exploitation and African women more thoroughly subject to patriarchal tyranny. Racial discrimination makes Afro-American laborers more vulnerable to exploitation and unemploy- ment than white workers. It makes black women in America more vulnerable to sexual oppression and violence against women. To this day, the rape of black women hardly registers as violation in the public consciousness as do the same crimes against white women. Clearly, it is ontological designation by race, racial polarization, and the imposition of a rigid racially essentialist identity, that charac- terizes the peculiar oppression and alienation of black people.

To understand the claim that blacks are denied "even the notion of humanity," we must be cognizant that in a racist society humanity is defined as white. Indeed whiteness becomes the symbol of all that is good or valuable. Blackness, by con- trast, symbolizes that which is without value—or is the very negation of value. Fanon noted that European settlers tended to paint a picture of the colonized native "as a sort of quintessence of evil" (Fanon [1963]: 41). The stereotype of the black criminal and rapist, or the common perception of African-American com- munities as criminal communities, are probably American versions of the same portrait of evil. This portrait invariably affects the consciousness of the oppressed to one degree or another. And when James Baldwin writes that "Negroes…are taught really despise themselves from the moment their eyes open on the world" (Baldwin [1963]: 39–40), he is speaking (perhaps in extreme terms) precisely of the existential violation of the human personality that is the inexorable consequence of the hegemonic away of a white racialist hierarchy of values.

If humanity itself is defined (however subtly) as white, then to be black (i.e, the "opposite" of white) is not simply to be "different," but to be radically other than human. If god, beauty, goodness, power, virtue, wealth, art, ideas, and civilization itself (indeed all values) are defined as white, then blackness symbolizes inferiority and the absence or negation of all worth.[2] To the extent that blacks internalize these values, an alienating loss of identity and a pervasive self-depreciation becomes evident. "White civilization and European culture," Fanon surmises, "have forced an existential deviation on the Negro" (Fanon [1967a]: 14).

208

BIRT

When racism categorizes blacks as other than human, it implicitly relegates them to the status of animals. During slavery blacks were actually bought and sold like cattle. To this day there is a tendency to categorize blacks in biological terms. Crude American racists often refer to blacks as "niggers," "coons," "porch monkeys," "jungle bunnies," and "yard apes." During a 1987 visit to Paris, this writer noticed graffiti on the walls of the Metro which read: "*Negrès fils de singe*" ("Niggers are the sons of apes"). But the issue goes deeper than name-calling. It is a matter of biologizing the social category of race, and imputing it as an essentialist definition of the identity or "nature" of blacks.[3] Fanon noted that under colonialism (and some thinkers see the situation of African-Americans as at least resembling colonialism), what "parcels out the world is to begin with the fact of belonging or not belonging to a given race, a given species" (1963: 40). But since it is the white "species" that is defined as human, the Others (since they are obviously not plants or minerals) must be a species of animal. And this too lends some credence to Césaire's point. For the oppressed white worker or white woman is relegated to a subordinate status "within the pale of humanity." They are not usually categorized as an alien species, nor "denied even the notion of humanity."

But this is precisely what happens to the blacks. The categorizing of blacks as beasts occurs by means of a perverse ontological designation by race. Its effect is the imprisonment of an entire people in a fixed racial essence, an essence implicitly conceived as an animal nature. On the one hand, the very color of the black person is a mark of degradation. In Western culture, blackness is traditionally symbolic of evil, ugliness, filth, wretchedness, decay, and death. On the other hand, blacks are associated with bestial physical force, inclinations to violence, simian athletic prowess, and a primitive and rapacious sexuality. "Negrophobia," according to Fanon, "is to be found on an instinctual, biological level" (Fanon [1967a]: 160). Just as the anti-Semite fears the alleged acquisitiveness and craftiness of the Jew, the racist fears the allegedly primitive physical and sexual power of blacks.

Blacks are certainly not the only victims of racism who have imposed upon them a racially essentialized identity. But with blacks this essentializing and dehumanizing is carried to its furthest extreme. Manning Marable notes that "Whites as a group have historically approached blacks not in light of their blackness…but in light of what whites believed that blacks must become from the vantage point of their own whiteness" (Marable: 75). Racists invented the Negro. They transformed the African into a Negro. Following upon the physical uprooting of the African from his/her native land, this was the first radical attack on the human identity of black people—a fundamental deracination of the human spirit. Marable also notes that while white settlers in North America regarded the Native Americans as "savages" and "heathens," they nonetheless recognized them as members of nations or "tribes." Blacks alone were set apart solely on the basis of skin color. As "Negroes," blacks ceased to be Africans (Wolof, Ashanti, and so forth), became virtual nonpersons (losing even their original names and families), and were relegated to the

209

BIRT

status of subhumans as "blackness" itself became identical to the total degradation of chattel slavery.

Given the centrality of color in antiblack racism, the alleged mark of inferiority is visible and follows the black person despite differences of class, education or gender. "Wherever he goes the Negro remains a Negro" (Fanon [1967a]: 173). Whatever he or she achieves, the Negro remains a Negro. He or she is always suspect, always guilty. Sartre was quite perceptive of the American social psychology and social order when he has one of his white characters in *The Respectful Prostitute* say: "A nigger has always done something." You are guilty because you are black, and you are black because you are guilty. You are guilty by virtue of your "Negroness." Your guilt is written on your face like the curse of Cain. Hence, it should surprise no one if American police are so obtusely incapable of distinguishing ghetto drug dealers from Harvard professors when they bear upon their persons the same primeval mark of guilt.

It is due to the "physical" or biological character of ontological designation by race, that antiblack racism is so unremittingly totalitarian. In *Anti-Semite and Jew*, Sartre noted that European Jews were also subject to essentialist designation by racists who ascribed to the Jew "an essence, a substantial form" or even "metaphysical principle" that drives the Jew "to do evil under all circumstances" (39). But Fanon, who essentially agrees with Sartre here, has nonetheless the following remarks:

210

> All the same, a Jew can be unknown in his Jewishness. He is not wholly what he is. One hopes, one waits. His actions, his behavior are the final determinants. He is a "white man," and…he can sometimes go unnoticed. Granted, the Jews are harassed—what am I thinking of? They are hunted down, exterminated…But these are little family quarrels. The Jew is disliked from the moment he is tracked down. But in my case everything takes on a new guise. I am given no chance. I am overdetermined from without. I am not the slave of the idea that others have of me but of my own "appearance." …I am fixed. (Fanon [1967a]: 115–6)

Fixed. As things are fixed. But we are not things. Hence the excruciating contradictoriness of our lives. In part, the crisis of identity spoken of by Dr. Du Bois continues. Blacks are still ensconced in a world which denigrates black humanity and yields us "no true self-consciousness." But for this self-consciousness we must continue to strive. The struggle for a new consciousness is precisely "our spiritual striving." It is a struggle which says: "No to scorn of man. No to the degradation of man. No to exploitation of man. No to the butchery of what is most human in man: freedom" (222). The emancipatory struggles of black people for authentic self-consciousness, for liberation from rigid identities and enslaving restrictions, is a struggle for humanity against thingification.

But oppressed people cannot affirm their humanity except in resistance to the forces which dehumanize them. "Consciousness of alienation entails the absolute refusal to accept alienation" (Davis [1983b]). Moral, intellectual and physical resistance is absolutely indispensable. As a struggle for humanity, the struggle of black people is of universal significance. But every struggle is historically situated. Hence one must begin with the historical situation of black people. Blacks alone are reduced to being a color (and only on condition of that color being disvalued). And though they are not the only victims of racism, black alone have been set apart, degraded and ostracized exclusively on the basis of race and color. Thus the striving to create and affirm our identity and humanity in defiance of racial essentialization and domination forms the common ground of the black liberation struggle.[4] The struggle for identity entails a struggle for a liberated "black consciousness." Against the plague of racial contempt and reification we must oppose "a more just view of black subjectivity" (1949). Sartre learned this much from the black writers and poets resident in Paris during the 1940s:

> The Negro, like the white worker is a victim of the capitalistic structure of our society...But if the oppression is a common one, it is patterned after historical and geographical conditions. The black man is a victim of it, in as much as he is black, in his role as a colonized native or as a deported African. And since he is oppressed in his race and because of it, it is first of his race that it is necessary for him to take conscience. (16)

211

The authentic consciousness of the oppressed is an expanding consciousness which comprehends the necessity to abolish oppression. It must be remembered that the actual formation of consciousness, however we describe it in ontological or psychological terms, is still socially conditioned. There can be no liberation of consciousness separate from the total struggle for social liberation, just as there can be no social liberation without a liberating consciousness. There can be no radical transformation of identity without an entire struggle to radically transform the social order. And no radical transformation of the social structure is possible (nor would it have a purpose) without the transformation of identity—the self-creation of a new kind of human being. It is this self-creation and renewal that is the aim of all effort. With slight modifications, Angela Davis' description of the path before the rebel slave still lies before us. "The first phase of liberation is to reject the 'image of himself' which the slaveowner has painted, to reject the conditions which the slaveowner created, to reject his own existence, to 'reject himself as a slave'" (Davis [1983b]). We must still reject denigrating images, reification and self-depreciation.

Still, a measure of caution is in order. For it is easy to move from one reification to another, and attempt to replace a negative essentialism with a "positive" one. Emancipation requires an affirmation of blackness, but not its glorification. Not its mystification. It is a question of trying to create decolonized minds in the process

BIRT

of decolonizing our lives. We must resist the stultifying images of ourselves creat-ed by the oppressor. But we must also resist the temptation to create an essential-ized black consciousness which reifies black identity while (or by) glorifying it. Maintaining racial essentialism while only inverting the negative valuations imposed by whites may appear liberating but ultimately leads to a new reifica-tions—and a whole framework of rigid roles, rigid identities and contempt for freedom. Inverted racial essentialism (one version of which in America is "narrow nationalism") may be an understandable response to the degradation of blacks by whites, but it invariably leads to a dead end. Fanon noted that the "Manicheism of the settlers" during colonialism "produces a Manicheism of the native." To the the-ory of the "absolute evil of the native" the theory of the "absolute evil of the set-tler replies" (Fanon [1963]: 93). But Fanon's analysis shows that the progress of the struggle for a new society and a genuinely new human being requires the tran-scendence of these gross simplifications.

In America, some forms of nationalism or "Afrocentrism" seem inclined toward a "problack" essentialism. And the Nation of Islam, in reply to the white image of blacks as bestial, criminal, stupid, and so forth, insists that it is whites who are "evil" by nature and blacks who are "good" (even divine) by nature. But there is no escape as long as we accept the notion of a racial essence, or if we posit a single mono-lithic criterion for what shall count as genuine black culture, identity or experi-ence. An inverted black essentialism may be edifying, but it tends to preserve (how-ever clandestinely or in black face) all the conservative values of the white cultur-al hierarchy, and sometimes harbor a secret contempt for black people concealed behind a rhetoric of glorification.

An authentic black consciousness forged in struggle seeks to regain existential integrity, and so must resist a mystification which reifies black identity in order to validate it. "No attempt must be made to encase man, for it is his destiny to be set free" (Fanon [1967a]: 230). Loving blackness, as bell hooks once wrote, is an act of political resistance—not myth-making. It is a question of how to "struggle collec-tively to fight racism and to create a liberatory space to construct a radical black subjectivity" (hooks [1990]: 36). The struggle for identity, for an authentic human existence which is the core of "our spiritual strivings," is a radical effort to trans-form the world, to transform ourselves, and to give birth to a new humanity.

NOTES

1 See Harris (1983). The reader should be aware that the quotation is derived from the printed version of this lecture (delivered by Professor Davis in 1969) prior to its publi-cation in Harris (1983). Professor Davis revised the lecture for the anthology. And the statement I quoted from the original version may have been deleted from the revised version.

2 It is interesting to observe in the writings of Frantz Fanon and James Baldwin, through separate interrogations of their respective French and American contexts, the discern-ment of essentially the same racial hierarchy of value—and the same myths and stereo-types concerning blacks.

3 The recent popularity of *The Bell Curve* should disabuse all but the most pathetically naive of the illusion that biological racism is dead.

4 No one should take this as license to neglect the struggle against class or patriarchal oppression. Indeed, such a neglect would undermine the black liberation struggle itself. Black people as a whole are beset by racism. But as bell hooks argues, there are class and gender based differences in the experience of racism itself. Failure to recognize this suggests the temptation to a new racial essentialism.

BLACK FEMINISM

Liberation Limbos and Existence in Gray

Joy Ann James

"LIMBO" HAS multiple meanings. In its primary negative usage, it refers to: Christian theological constructs of a site neighboring hell; prison; oblivion or neglect; suspension between two states. In its secondary meaning marked by play, struggle, and pleasure, limbo refers to the black/Caribbean dance where dancers lean backwards, with knees bent to pass below an obstacle or bar that blocks their path. When I was growing up in the Southern U.S., it was a broom handle which was lowered with each procession. As children, we danced singing, "Do the limbo, limbo rock—All away around the clock!" Only the very flexible and very audacious improvisers were determined and managed to last more than several rounds.

Black feminisms (there is no monolithic black feminism) revolve around the varied meanings, both negative and positive, of "limbo." Black feminisms respectively evade and evoke the two types of limbos. Evaded is the relegation of black women's issues to marginal sites where critiques of racial-sexual oppression are distanced from the centers of social and political debate. Like unbaptized children and the non-Christian righteous, black feminisms have been relegated to an outer realm where, while not exactly punished for their sins, they are ghettoized for an alleged poor timing and inability to encounter the "larger paradigms" undergirding existence. Women from oppressed peoples routinely find themselves in liberation limbos. For instance, when Native-American women, who survive the most intense forms of state violence in the U.S., begin to organize the Indigenous Women's Network, they face criticism from some men in their communities through the International Treaty Council and the American Indian Movement, who argue that by dealing with the specificity of their oppression, indigenous women separated themselves from indigenous men and thereby weakened the collective power of Native Americans. Similar accusations have been levied or leveled by black men and women against black feminists. Suspended midway between eurocentric or postmodern feminism and afrocentric masculinism, they are institutionally relegated to the state of oblivion and neglect.

As they interpret and dissect, describe and agitate around human existence via reflections on and interventions by and for black females, African-American feminisms display an agility in paradigm-building and trashing, an imaginative power and material resistance that grant fluidity to bend lower and lower and with limber steps dance past a descending bar of political-intellectual dismissals. Their evocative agency reasserts the centrality of struggles and analyses often passed over in mainstream discourse. Still, in the wake of (feminist) antiblack racism and (black) antifeminism, black feminisms appear to progress only with considerable effort.

CRITICIZING (BLACK) FEMINISMS

Legitimate criticisms of mainstream black feminism include its (neo)liberalism, its failure to sustain economic critiques, its antiradicalism, and its neglect of state violence. Concerning its antiradicalism, some black feminisms elide the radical nature of black women's resistance to state oppression. For instance, Patricia Hill Collins' *Black Feminist Thought* omits black women's associations with the Communists Party, the Black Panther Party, and the Student Non-Violent Coordinating Committee (SNCC), as well as self-defense organizations from black feminist history and theory. The occlusion of radical praxis is normative in a culture and state where conservatism and liberalism are hegemonic. Black feminist writers' struggles for recognition, diversity, and strategies for dismantling oppression necessitate a self-critical awareness and willingness on the part of literary elites to be reflexive about economic and educational privileges. Having made important contributions to critiques of white (feminist) racism and (black) sexism, black feminisms have offered less focused analyses of class and educational elitism, liberalism, and state nationalism in the general society and among African Americans.

Other accusations leveled by some feminists against black women and black feminisms include the charges that black feminisms speak only to the particular and that black women are, more than their white counterparts, less inclined toward feminism given their allegiance to a romanticized "black community" that privileges males. The criticism that black feminisms are not "feminist" enough simplifies the existential dilemmas of black women's lives and struggles in a racist state. The liberation of black women as a group rather than as atomized individuals is inseparable from—but not identical with or reducible to—the liberation of their people or communities of origin, what some label a black or an Africana community. With historical, cultural worldviews which privilege ancestors and community, and a historical genocidal diaspora in the Americas, and centuries of antiblack racism from a motley assortment of ethnic groups, black women's associations and experiences of sexual and gender politics—from exploitation in domestic work and economic inequities to sexual abuse and reproductive rights struggles—will necessarily reflect racist barriers and racialized worldviews. This need not constitute an inherent antifeminism or counterfeminism, although those tendencies exist. Rather it can lead to a unique form of feminism. In their best forms, countering a false unity built on the exclusion of other disenfranchised groups, black feminisms offer new languages for formulating the well-being of "community" and "family,"[1] expanding and redefining liberation politics and rhetoric to address the issues of black women as an outsider group and outsiders within this grouping such as lesbians, prostitutes, bisexual, poor, incarcerated, and immigrant women.

The dismissive by some African-American males that black feminisms are hand-maidens to Euro(American)-feminisms, or that black feminisms are not "black" enough, has been widely circulated. Sometimes in their roles as correctives to white racism, some black feminisms have served as the "clean-up woman" or domestic of racial messes and seem overly preoccupied with white, privileged women. Also, in their construction as the source of exotic, emotive stories of colored pain and bizarreness for white consumers, black feminisms have at times been commodified for entertainment. Both reflect the historic functions of the colonized black as servant and entertainer. (That black feminisms are best known, and usually taught, through fiction and film that emphasizes black male/female conflicts such as Alice Walker's *The Color Purple*, Gloria Naylor's *Women of Brewster Place*, and Terry McMillan's *Waiting to Exhale* has proved a source of contention and criticism.)

These criticisms, that black feminisms divert attention from black liberation (if they are black *feminisms*) or women's liberation (if they are *black* feminisms) construct walls of isolation. Such criticisms reflect Afrocentric arguments that sexism and misogyny are European construction (imperialism's patriarchal and racial colonizing of women does not absolve African societies from gender inequities); they also mirror Eurocentric narratives that white civilization rescued black women from the sexual barbarism and gender oppression of their traditional cultures. Both

JAMES

discourses obscure the complexities of antiracist and antisexist struggles and present a false binary. Ironically, in their antiracist discourse with an interest in multi-culturalism, certain forms of black feminism are criticized for oppositional ethnic politics. The assertions that black feminism privileges antiblack racism to reify the polarized binary between "black and white," making "race" the central issue and thereby deflecting from "universal" feminism or other "ethnic" women, ignores the phenomenon of antiblack violence which cuts across both universality and ethnicity. In the modern and postmodern eras, dark-skinned or black/Indians, Latinas/Chicanas, Asians, and Arabs occupy the lowest strata and contend with an intensity of racialized abuses, economic exploitation, and state violence from which their white or light–skinned "ethnic" counterparts are often spared.

In its attempts to synthesize emancipation theories on race, gender, sexuality and class, black feminisms improvise, constructing integrative analyses in limbos toward their own constructions. Progressive intellectuals have posited that research is mediated by the lived-experience of the scholar, not positivistic scientific objectivity. Confronting or ignoring contemporary intellectual and social crises, theoretical and political advancement will be largely determined by one's ability to deliver rather than looking backwards for authority or longing for a paradise devoid of traditional high culture.

Ability to deliver will be largely determined by the political, ethical, and intellectual projects. In limbos, the incompatibility of linearity to overlapping and contradictory relations of dominance are witnessed. In this regard, illustrating the intersections of existence, oppression, and freedom with integrative analyses might be one of black feminisms' most important contributions to liberation movements. In limbos of our own progressive movements, time is not linear. One bends backwards in order to move forwards: the past, present, and future coexist and overlap. For those who are not first born into color and ethnicity, later into an economic class, next into gender socialization, and finally into sexuality, linearity is dysfunctional. Those who are born simultaneously into experiences and relationships shaped, enriched, or vampirized by cultural, economic, and nation-state policies are assaulted by our society's acquiescence to racism, classism, and (hetero)sexism. In developing a critique of these experiences and relationships, the notion of linear struggle is inadequate and illusory. Linear projections prioritize abstract "primary" over abstract "secondary" oppression. Expressing an agile ability and willingness to grasp a multidimensional world and its multiplicity and intersection of repression, black feminisms usually forgo reified evil and trickle down liberation theories. Rather than issue a critique of a succession of oppressive institutions—"patriarchy," "white supremacy," "transnational capitalism," "colonizing culture," "homophobia"—most black feminisms examine the simultaneity of oppression and the interrelatedness of gender, race, and class struggles.

218

JAMES

ACADEMIC INTERVENTIONS

Struggling for recognition from dominant intellectuals, academic black feminisms vacillate between conservative and progressive interventions. Academics have been accused of "hyperintellectualism," of reflecting upon abstractions of reality, disdaining and distancing themselves from the ground of everyday life and the specificity of political struggles around labor and racism, immigrant's and women's rights. Black feminisms seem an unlikely candidate for the label of disembodied theory, given their largely ethical and pragmatic objectives and accessible language. Although a blueprint for liberation is generally disparaged, there are both a need and demand for functional discourse with a liberating intent that reflects peoples' material and spiritual battles to survive poverty, drudgery in labor, premature births, and deaths. With women and children of African descent disproportionately in the ranks of the impoverished, malnourished, illiterate, diseased, and dying, many of those struggling to survive and resist destructive conditions are black women and children. A black existence marked by oppression and resistance has historically galvanized and directed black women's intellectual productions.

Making the contributions of "subaltern" survivors and resistors, making the "invisible" visible has been a good part of the work of black women scholars and writers. Countering the marginalization of women's voices in academic discourse, women of color have greatly expanded academic discussions and knowledge. Black feminisms' antiracism makes it quite distinct from academic, nonradical, Euro-feminism or pomofeminism trends towards the erasure of race and racism in constructions of "woman" or the "female body." Rejecting the concept of women as a "class," Angela Y. Davis observes that some influential white feminists' "theories and practice have frequently implied that the purest and most direct challenge to sexism is one exorcised of elements related to racial and economic oppression—as if there were such a phenomenon as abstract womanhood abstractly suffering sexism and fighting back in an abstract historical context" (Davis [1983a]). Likewise, when theories and practice imply that the most effective challenge to racism is one ignorant or dismissive of sexual and economic and gender oppression, other delusions are created—those of "abstract blackness" abstractly suffering racism, devoid of gender, devoid of class, devoid of history; of "abstract impoverishment," severed from racism and sexism's effects on economic exploitation, of abstract sexual beings. Abstractions create other sites of limbo in which the specificity of liberation struggles is supplanted by theorizing on the "representative" woman or black or worker—who generally tends not to reflect the lives of women of color or black women.

Despite its slippery footing in academe and seeming dependence upon the favor of Women's or African-American/Africana Studies programs, black feminist studies have provided new dimensions for the study of women and blacks' existential intersections of economic, racial, and sexual violence. One case in point is the January 1994 conference, "Black Women in the Academy: Defending Our Name

219

JAMES

1894–1994," held at the Massachusetts Institute of Technology. At the conclusion of the conference, 2,000-plus attendees (most of whom were black women) issued a conference resolution to President Bill Clinton: "86% of black women who voted, voted for the Democratic Party ticket which brought you and Hilary Rodham Clinton to the White House and a Democratic Congress to Washington in 1992…this was the largest proportion of any constituency to vote for your administration." With copies sent to the Congressional Black, Women, and Hispanic Caucuses, the petition requested the Administration to commission a "Blue Ribbon panel on race relations" building on the 1968 Kerner report, examining that original report and its 1988 review of a diverging America and make recommendations to alleviate "the continuing injuries of racism, sexism and homophobia." It also asked the Administration to promote black women's research for the well-being of African-American communities and extend the mandate of the "Glass-Ceiling Commission to explore issues of career advancement for women of color in higher education." Increased funding for community-based service organizations for poor black families was also requested: "We stress the need to extend economic empowerment and development programs, support service, health care, housing, child care, and education. Women in prison, those with AIDS, and in crisis need special attention." The petition addressed U.S. domestic and foreign policies, calling for the end of antidemocratic covert actions against Haiti and the restoration of Jean-Bertrand Aristide to the Presidency; lifting the embargo against Cuba; as well as U.S. governmental support for the democratic process in South and Southern Africa and aid for Somalia.

Those intellectual, politicized interventions by black women academics and others are essential yet cannot serve as surrogates for political organizing with working-class and impoverished women. In their work, black feminist educators continue to build upon the contributions of their historical predecessors. As historian Evelyn Brooks Higginbotham's work on black church women notes, blacks who attained higher education, the literate and literary, have since Reconstruction been feted to function as a "talented tenth"—which in the American Home Baptist Missionary Society's proselytism meant a cadre of managerial race leaders who instilled and disciplined disenfranchised blacks into the rewards of "traditional family values" and a protestant work ethic. A deified black intellectual vanguard was rejected, however, by those who realized its constraint on a transformative praxis and that nonelite blacks sustain communities and social movements. Now many feminists or nonfeminists share an older W.E.B. Du Bois' reflective rejection of an intellectual elite leadership which he had popularized:

> My faith hitherto had been in what I once denominated the talented tenth. I
> now realize that the ability within a people does not automatically work for
> its highest salvation…[N]aturally, out of the mass of the working classes, who

know life in its bitter struggle, will continually rise the real, unselfish and clear-sighted leadership. (Du Bois [1952])

The other 90 percent created considerable political space for the talented tenth in education, politics, and business. The majority of social change agents continue to be women working in triple shifts for depressed wages, unpaid childbearing and housework, and community-building voluntarism (although underrepresented in clergy and formal political leadership). In these struggles, which often go undocumented and unnoticed in literary and academic exchanges on existence, black or otherwise, African-American women hold pivotal roles.

EXISTENCE IN GRAY: HISTORICAL POLITICAL STRUGGLES

Between black and white exist curious sites of amnesia, the gray areas surrounding political agency. Amnesia partly stems from the erasure of historical archetypes (particularly those at odds with neoliberal politics) and the erasure of the ways in which black women ancestors historically fought for racial and gender justice. One of the first U.S. women to lecture publicly on political issues and the first published African-American woman political writer, Maria W. Stewart (1803–1869), called for women of African descent to develop their highest intellectual abilities.

Born a free African-American woman in Boston, widowed at an early age, impoverished by white swindlers, and childless, Stewart wrote for *The Liberator*, an abolitionist paper established by David Walker. After Walker's death, as copublisher of *The Liberator* Stewart became noted for an antislavery militancy and religiosity that incensed white racists as well as alarmed Boston's more conservative, free blacks. Her claims to religious authority through conversations with God (Stewart maintained that divine revelations shaped her speeches, writings, and grounded her hope in African liberation) estranged her from the male-dominated church's Paulist scriptures which advocated the subservience of women and their exclusion from ministry. Assuming that the martyrdom which claimed Walker awaited her, Maria Stewart wrote in 1831 that "many will suffer for pleading the cause of oppressed Africa, and I shall glory in being one of her martyrs…[God] is able to take me to himself, as he did the most noble, fearless, and undaunted David Walker" (Stewart [1987]).

Unlike Walker, Stewart was not murdered.[2] Her militant public life was, however, cut short by African-Americans: Stewart suffered continuous criticism and censorship from the Bostonian African-American community for violating values of a proper lifestyle for a woman. Proslavery voices cursed her. Bostonian blacks silenced her for violating middle-class bourgeois gender sensibilities of church and society. In "Farewell Address to her Friends in the City of Boston, Delivered September 21, 1833," Stewart castigates those who were trying to curtail her radicalism: "I find it is no use for me as an individual to try to make myself useful among my color in this city…[M]y respected friends, let us no longer talk of prej-

221

JAMES

udice, till prejudice becomes extinct at home. Let us no longer talk of opposition, till we cease to oppose our own" (Stewart [1987]: 70–1). The "Farewell Address" was her last public speech until the close of the U.S. Civil War (during which Stewart worked as Matron of the freemen's Hospital in Washington, DC, and coordinated refugee camps for African Americans).

Likewise, one might also pull from the gray areas of political memory the work of Anna Julia Cooper (1858–1935). Cooper was ousted from her principalship at the prestigious Dunbar High School in Washington, DC, because of racist and political resentment that emerged from her preparing her black students to attend prestigious white schools such as Harvard rather than follow Booker T. Washington's vocational education mandate. (She herself eventually earned a doctorate from the Sorbonne.) One of three African-American women invited to address the World Congress of Women in 1893, Cooper also addressed the 1900 Pan-African Congress Conference in London, which she helped to organize; five years later she co-founded the colored women's YWCA. In her classic text, *A Voice from the South*, Cooper gages the progress of liberation of Africans not by the elevation or achievements of black elites, particularly those by men, but by the freedom from exploitation of the masses of laborers who worked the longest hours, for the lowest wages, under the most arduous circumstances: "Only the black woman can say when and where I enter, in the quiet, undisputed dignity of my womanhood, without violence and without suing or special patronage, then and there the whole *Negro race enters with me*" (Cooper [1987]: 30–1). Cooper's calls for a mass standard to measure the efficacy and relevance of black praxis go against the tendency to focus on elites and minimize the significance of laborers, of black women who, as change-agents in local churches, schools, streets, farm fields, factories, and prisons, reveal radical and communal traditions of democratic power.

As the lives of Stewart and Cooper exemplify, historical and contemporary black feminisms are tied to African-American struggles. From the nineteenth-century abolitionist movements to the twentieth-century Civil Rights Movement, blacks and nonblacks received and shared political training, language, theory, and strategy from and with black women as movements worked to radicalize intellectual and political formations.

Those unfamiliar with black women's radicalism will likely not be well informed on contemporary liberation struggles in the U.S. influenced and shaped by the often unacknowledged contributions of antilynching militant Ida B. Wells-Barnett, civil rights revolutionary Ella Baker, and black liberation militant Assata Shakur. Confronting the marginalization of women leaders and activists in historiography, Delores Williams observes that "By uncovering as much as possible about such female liberation, the womanist begins to understand the relation of black history to the contemporary folk expression: 'If Rosa Parks had not sat down, Martin King would not have stood up'" (1991: 68). More precisely, if Miss Parks had not sat down and later organized with E.D. Nixon, Joanne Robinson, and the

222

JAMES

Women's Political Caucus, the Montgomery Improvement Association and its Bus Boycott would not have emerged.

Black women abolitionists, Reconstruction radicals, "Second Reconstruction" civil rights activists, and black movement militants fought against racial and sexual restrictions. Their courageous commitments were responses to the threats against black existence posed under a state built on black enslavement, exploitation, and white colonization.

Today, white supremacy, economic exploitation, and the disenfranchisement of women have mutated rather than disappeared. In the U.S., the black life span, already less than that of whites, continues to decline; whereas black poverty, which is greater than that of whites, is increasing. State policing and protection are as selective and as discriminatory as state punishment and execution. Social, political, economic equality are chimerical rights for black peoples, as is equal protection under the law from racial and sexual violence/exploitation. Contemporary "existence in black" occurs among nations where blackness symbolizes sexual pathology, violence, and criminality, and where racial paranoia constructs a fetish for prison and punishment. These constructions ensure that although most violent attacks tend to occur within one's own ethnic group—for example, the majority of whites are beaten, raped, and robbed by other whites—the dominant image of the batterer, rapist, and thief is "the black," ergo what needs to be disciplined, policed, and punished (including through punitive policies for the poor is, as Fanon observed, *le nègre*).

Historically, invoking "the black" as breeder and instigator of violence conveniently masked "white" and state violence. At the same time that blacks gained notoriety as the most infamous perpetrators of crime in a racialized society, they are given less recognition in anticrime crusades as the victims of violence. Black feminisms that deconstruct "the black" as primitive morally and sexually degenerate and counter the mythology that criminalizes black existence and rationalizes antiblack violence, still must contend with the tendency among African Americans to emphasize the common but sporadic racist violence of police brutality, Klan killings, or hate crimes over the more prevalent racial and sexual violence inflicted by blacks on other blacks.[3]

223

CONCLUSION: BLEACHING BODIES

As a preteen in the 1970s, visiting my first big city, L.A., I met an older play-kin who instructed me on smoking, sex, race, and politics. My study, sequestered from family trips to Disneyland, was relegated to our visit to Hollywood's drag strip, hanging out in the neighborhood, or running errands to local stores. The most memorable lesson occurred while my play-kin, with her large Afro, hooped earrings, and dark black skin, reclined one afternoon in a great-aunt's clawfoot, cast-iron tub. The visual memory survived the verbal instruction. With face and knees

JAMES

pointing to the bathroom ceilings, expounding on racial and sexual politics, my tutor soaked in hot water splashed with bleach.

Whatever we did or did not talk about had a great deal to do with bodies, beauty, color, and marketing (but not antiracist or black feminisms). Her fifteen-year-old savvy at the height of the Black Power movement recognized aesthetics as socially constructed and that altering, even mutilating, the body was an investment to play the market. The point was not to erase but to tamper with blackness, to alter existence in black in its female teen form. Too savvy to desire or believe in "whiteness" as an available option, she opted for some distance from, or at least some control over, blackness—but always with an eye on what the market demanded.

In the antiblack performance, shaping some contemporary race discourse, the play-kin of my youth reappears. The market provides steady incentives. It seems that bleaching bodies, like bleaching feminisms, produces a color of ash, a grayness. Those too sophisticated to believe that they can obliterate a seemingly unassimilable "blackness" might project it into gray areas of intellectual-political peripheries. Others might seek to manage blackness out of its "too black" state, altering its appearance to make it more of an indeterminate color palatable to market consumers. Still others, outsiders, in limbo might proceed past lowering booms—contracts on America, epidemics of sexual violence and poverty, elite intellectual discourses that posit the "irrelevance of race" or "imaginary of community"—to formulate and form black feminisms in the movements of liberation.

224

NOTES

1 Problematizing the African-American (heterosexual) family is a practice shared by black nationalism, Afrocentrism, liberal and conservative racism. As Fran White notes: "you can read anyone from Ron Karenga to Patrick Moynihan, from Haki Madhubuti to Bill Moyers, and you will find that the problem with the black community is that we have weak heterosexual bonds…[these] building blocks for a strong community don't include welfare dependent families, single-parent female-headed households, and especially they don't include gay, lesbian and bisexual family members" (36). The writings of lesbian and gay African-American social critics—Audre Lorde, James Baldwin, Essex Hemphill, Marlon Riggs, and others—confront the sexual politics mythologizing "family" and "community" among African Americans.

2 Walker has been presumed to have been poisoned by whites who were pro-slavery.

3 With the exception of incarcerated women and women on reservations, African-American women's material lives are controlled by the government more so than by male partners who more often only control levels of physical violence and sexual abuse rather than economic resources in the household.

JAMES

LIBERALISM AND THE POLITICS OF EMANCIPATION
The Black Experience

George Carew

chapter 18

I

THE BLACK presence in the U.S. commences with a struggle against the twin evils of slavery and racism. As a racialized group, blacks were not only contesting their political, economic, and social subjugation, but also their racial subjugation as well. Thus, black advocacy for freedom and justice included not only a demand for political and economic justice but also for racial justice. Mindful that these demands were to be addressed in the context of a liberal democratic society, black theorists advocated a number of strategies in pursuit of their goal. An African-American philosophy of liberation, existential or otherwise, must then come to terms with the context of its theorizing.

In this essay I propose to identify the dominant liberal influences on African-American political thought, analyze implications of this ideology, and consider reasons for considering it flawed. I shall argue that liberalism, the dominant normative doctrine in the U.S., has prestructured the racial discourse in such a way that only certain outcomes are permissible. Its conception of emancipation as the transcendence of group difference gives rise to moral and social controversies that implicate liberalism itself. I therefore argue for a shift in focus from moral and social discourse to political discourse on the adequacy of the normative framework in addressing justice in general, and racial justice in particular. At the heart of the problem is liberalism's inherent difficulty in resolving the tension between liberty and equality—between autonomy and participation. I argue that a way out of this dilemma could be found in a certain conception of discourse theory which incorporates the cherished liberal values of autonomy and social unity into communicative politics.

To explicate black strategies on freedom, I shall revisit the debate between Booker T. Washington and W.E.B. Du Bois on black freedom.[1] This debate is significant for more than one reason. It does not only reveal black thinking at the time on the emancipation question, it also highlights the complex problems generated by the intersection of race and class issues. This complication, I shall argue presently, has disturbing implications for the way liberal discourse treats the emancipation issue. As Bernard Boxill rightly observes, liberal theorists interpret the discourse on racism as a class-based discourse. However, critics of the liberal view argue that this approach obscures the racial issue and implicitly calls into question liberalism's ability to resolve the problem made worse by the intersection of racism and classism.

In characterizing the debate this way Boxill also shows how current thinking has been affected. Those who adopt the classical liberal view would adopt a class-based analysis, while those who dissent would see this approach as failing to treat the uniqueness of the racial issue (cf. John Locke's defense for a class-based society). These conflicting views or "schools of thought," as Boxill calls them, have adherents among black theorists. Starting with Booker T. Washington, the main proponent of the class school, we have contemporary black theorists such as Sowell, Loury, and W. J. Wilson. The race school is represented by Du Bois, Douglass, Martin Luther King, and the majority of black philosophers, including Boxill himself.

To spell out the issue which separates these two schools of thought, it is important to note that both groups were at least in agreement on one thing: that they were to seek freedom through *political, economic, and racial equality*. Their strategies, however, for achieving these goals vary widely. The class school argues that the main path to freedom lies in economic viability. On this view, the inequalities in society are likely to be removed or narrowed only if blacks acquired skills and were thus able to compete on the same footing with every one else for jobs. The race school for its part holds that full emancipation is possible only when racism in all its forms is eradicated.

Boxill states that a crucial assumption of the class school is that human being are overwhelmingly self-interested (see Boxill [1992]; and [1992–3]). If it would benefit a person to hire or utilize the talents of a black individual that person would need to put aside his or her racial prejudice in order to promote his or her interest. Boxill disputes the claim however, that naked self-interest would lead whites to recognize and compensate the economic viability of blacks. In the view of the race school, the appeal to the enlightened self-interest in a racist culture might in fact lead whites to exploit black economical viability. But proponents of the class school might argue that one ought not to conflate the need to eliminate racism with the desire to promote self-interest. Thus, both schools appear to be agreeing on the undesirability of racism for the promotion of individual liberty. Where they disagree is on how they should perceive the task of securing freedom. It is to that issue in liberal theory we must now turn.

We have seen that black theorists are supportive of the view of political, economic, and racial equality as necessary for the achievement of freedom. What this means in liberal terms, however, is that freedom could be achieved only through the transcendence of group difference. On the liberal view, a person's race, class, and gender are to be regarded as irrelevant to the issue of membership in the political community. Ascriptive qualities generally may be relevant for other contexts but not for citizenship in a political community. Liberal individualism's goal is twofold in this regard: it seeks to protect individual autonomy at the same time that it constructs an inclusive public. To secure both individual autonomy and social unity liberal theorists have conceptualized two discrete and separate spheres of individuality, namely, the public and private spheres.

On the one hand, the abstract universalist's definition of the public represented values that citizens presumably had in common. These values were obtained by abstracting from particular or concrete individuals. The norms and rules derived from the abstract sphere are therefore rules that all would consent to. On the other hand, the private sphere defined the realm where the different values and interests coexisted. One ideal associated with the public realm is neutrality with respect to the different values and interests that coexist in the private autonomous exercise of all values. Thus we may conclude that in both (i.e., the public and the private sphere where he is immune from outside, unwarranted interference), individual autonomy and social unity are secured.

Before embarking on how the liberal view shapes the race/class controversy, there are some important differences within liberalism that need to be laid out. There are two different accounts of what it means to transcend difference. The first version is clearly Lockean. The second version has been identified with John Rawls' reworking of the liberal view. On one view, the formal equality that characterizes social relations in the public realm is interpreted to mean that agents require equal opportunity to compete for various positions and offices. Given this, whatever position or reward an individual derives would be justly deserved. On the other view, equal moral consideration simple means that, in addition to providing equal opportunity, we must do what is best for the least well-off. These two dis-

227

tinctions can be combined to generate different versions of liberalism. Much of the controversy over the race/class issue has been concerned with exploring these variations and it seems clear that each version will lead to different results. However, both versions share a fundamental flaw. I will argue that there is something inherently unattractive about the liberal commitment to the transcendence of difference. Before I take up this point, however, I wish to show how these two opposing viewpoints on liberalism have shaped the race/class controversy.

Since the race school views black disabilities as due to the absence of skills, it adopts the strategy of encouraging blacks to acquire skills so that they could compete in the market place and thereby win social recognition. But if one of the social realities of race in society is that races enjoy various social and economic advantages because they are race, then the enjoyment of these advantages is part of the social significance of race in society. Du Bois thus was certainly right to point out that the persistence of racism would render impossible the Lockean ideal, which Booker T. Washington was trying to achieve.

The modern version of the class school claims that the removal of procedural racism ensures equality of opportunity.[2] Since race is no longer socially significant, people would be judged on the basis of their abilities and efforts alone, and the resulting inequalities would be justified on grounds that they are the result of choices made. This argument would ideally favor colorblind policies to replace racist policies because they do not allow racial differences (understood as differences of a cultural ancestry and phenotype) to function as the basis of unequal treatment.

Theorists of the race school consider this move grossly inadequate for the simple reason that the lingering effects of racism are still current. Substantive racism, as they are referred to, are the direct result of past institutional or procedural racism. Arguably, then, the question is not whether many blacks are unable to compete for jobs, but why are they unable to do so? In light of such criticism, class theorists are likely to point to the fact that our commitment to an impersonal, objective meritocracy limits us to securing only equality of opportunity. Yet it should be apparent to even the class school that the equality of opportunity presupposed in the color-blind, passive, nondiscriminatory policies does not provide answers to the question posed, nor can they formulate adequate responses to the debilitating effects of past racism.[3] To illustrate the point, let me draw attention to Sowell's unhelpful distinction between activities meant to bring about "equal opportunity" and activities meant to bring about "affirmative action." In his view both activities lead to contradictory outcomes: equality of opportunity proscribes discrimination on the basis of race while "affirmative action" confers benefits on ground of race.

But Sowell, like most class-school advocates, is guilty of confusing the issues. Affirmative Action should not be viewed as undermining activities aimed at equalizing opportunity. It was never the intention that affirmative action should serve as an alternative to color-blind policies. Properly understood, its role is to help bring about a discrimination-free society through the *equalization of circumstances for those with undeserved disadvantages* so as to ensure that they would be able to compete with everyone else on an equal footing. For example, the disabilities blacks experience as a result of racism are undeserved disadvantages. Consequently, blacks have a moral claim against society not to allow the undeserved inequalities to affect adversely the outcome of competition. Removing well entrenched inequalities between different groups is clearly a precondition for applying color-blind policies. Without the removal of undeserved inequalities color-blind policies reinforce rather than remove discrimination on the basis of race. Thus, far from undermining the goals of color-blind policies, affirmative action policies actually complement that goal.

The shift in focus from whether blacks can compete to why they have been unable to compete remains undifferentiated in the thinking of the class school. In the view of the class school, blacks cannot compete because they lack skills. And they lack skills largely because they have dysfunctional values. Thus the question whether blacks can compete is collapsed into the question why blacks *cannot* compete. The point this argument makes is as simple as it is misleading. Blacks cannot compete because of dysfunctional values; therefore, once these values are transformed through equal educational opportunities, blacks would become competitive. This argument makes no reference to how disabilities are incurred, nor how they could be removed.

One way to make this point clearer is to compare both schools on race matters. The class school strategy lies in colorblind policies. Since the concept of color blindness entails the rejection of racial categories in law and policy, the strategy is to remove race as a constraint thereby allowing the individual to compete on equal footing with everyone else. The race school charges that this strategy ignores the social reality of race in society. In the U.S., for instance, these social realities include the historical magnitude of the experience of slavery and the persistence of racial discrimination. In the view of the race school, therefore, the eradication of procedural racism is an inadequate response to the problem of racism. The strategy of the race school then is to take these social realities of race seriously in determining which policies aid equality of opportunity (see Mosley).

It would be wrong to construe this controversy as disagreement over strategies. There is more to it than that. It involves two different ways of interpreting equal consideration. The presumption underlying equality of opportunity is that people must be judged on the basis of choices they make rather than on their social circumstances. In other words, an individual's social standing or rewards must be based on choices he/she makes. This way, the individual's success of failure will depend very much on the autonomous action of the individual himself or herself rather than on social circumstances over which the individual has no control.

On the model of class theory, social differences such as race was undeserved, but natural attributes such as ability was deserved. As Locke noted, we are all endowed

229

CAREW

with rational ability, thus those who use their ability to promote their interest merit what they get. But what if abilities also are undeserved? One might then argue that if it is unfair to treat people differently because of their race, it should also be unfair to discriminate on the basis of ability because, like race, people do not deserve their abilities. The individual can no more determine his skin color than he can his IQ. The question we must pose is not so much whether there are legitimate differences as how to treat differences. In other words, can we prevent differences from creating situations that are harmful to people? This is a moral concern, given that both social and natural differences are arbitrary (Locke [1991]: 286–8).

John Rawls provides a way out of this Lockean dilemma. The question to which Rawls provides an answer is simply this: If differences, both social and natural, are not significant is it possible to have a basis for legitimate discrimination? The answer to this query is contained largely in Rawls' principle of difference. According to Rawls, even though no one deserves his or her natural abilities, it may not be unfair to allow those with socially desirable skills to pursue their individual goods if in so doing they would benefit everyone in society, including the less well-off. Rawls' difference principle in a way combines both individual utility and social utility. There are grounds to believe that the race school shares the moral intuition of Rawls. They do not, as I would show, interpret equality of opportunity as promoting only individual utility. The latter view, I believe, is held by the class school. On these two distinctions, however, rest the different outcomes in our moral and social analysis of the race/class problems.

230   The class school view of equality of opportunity is rooted in the classical liberal view of merit as ability. Merit in this sense is an objective and impersonal standard which determines desert independent of social utility. This is decidedly an individualist orientation. People are rewarded or penalized solely on the basis of the choices they made or the actions they pursue. Any distributive process which fails to countenance this fact is deemed arbitrary and unjust. This is the reason why affirmative action is considered unjust because it only treats as meritorious an arbitrary quality such as race or gender, but it also deprives deserving individuals of their rights. Class theorists have consistently made this point. Loury, for example, attempts to shift our focus from disparities among groups per se, to disparities in the rewards to the different types of activities toward which various group members incline (see Kymlicka: chap. 3). This liberal individualist orientation is designed to draw attention to the fact that benefits and rewards must be based on the kind of choices individuals make rather than on racial grounds. He drives the point home by means of an analogy which he states in the form of a question. "Why is inequality among individuals of the same group acceptable when inequality between groups is not?" (Loury: 250).

The point Loury makes is at least clear on one thing: that class or socio-economic differences among individuals must be determined by their relative standing in the meritocratic hierarchy. What I find unclear and troubling, however, is his

CAREW

attempt to assimilate the subordinate relationship of groups to the meritocratic hierarchy. Loury, I believe, wishes to argue that if individuals can be said to deserve their place in the meritocratic hierarchy, then groups similarly can be said to deserve their subjugated position in the social hierarchy. Loury no doubt assumes that race has no part to play in the subjugated role of either the individual or group. Otherwise he would not argue that they merit their respective positions.

To understand Loury's dilemma better, we must reconnect class/school theory with abstract individualism from which it derives. Since in classical liberalism the individual is committed only to the promotion of her/his self-interest, she/he cooperates with others solely for the purpose of realizing her/his interest. This could be interpreted to mean that she/he views others as economic categories whose relevance is contingent on their usefulness in promoting her/his good. Thus what matters is efficiency, not race. Social differences such as race and gender are bracketed in abstract individualism because they are irrelevant (or ought to be irrelevant) to the pursuit of individual interests. This point is underscored by Martin Delany when he observed that moral consideration was not a feature in the enslavement of Africans. Delany did not say this because he believed that Europeans were immoral, but rather that moral considerations did not enter into the calculation of enlightened self-interest (Loury: 250). Booker T. Washington and Julius Wilson make similar points in preferring the appeal to self-interest over moral suasion.

Admittedly, Boxill and the race school have failed to grasp why moral suasion does not appeal to the class school. In truth, African Americans who embrace the Lockean legacy have often been viewed with suspicion by their peers for their stance on the race/class issue. But the class school is certainly not guilty of moral blindness. It is merely constrained by its limited view of moral equality. The race school for its part envisions merit in broader terms and as socially determined. Since ability is not the only thing that is valued in society, it must be pressed to serve socially useful ends together with the other things that are valued. Thus, while both schools value ability, they differ widely on whether merit as ability should be socially determined. I have already argued that the class school views merit as based on an independent objective standard. On the race school view, however, people "deserve" their ability only if they can prove that its use would not disadvantage anyone or would at least contribute to the general welfare of the least well off. This is exemplified in the justification most African-American theorists offer for "affirmative action."

The social determination of merit is particularly attractive to the race school for the simple reason that it renders vulnerable historically determined entitlement claims by subjecting them to acid test of proven social utility. For example, no one can be said to merit a position prior to the determination of whether the occupant of that position would add significantly to the welfare of everyone in the society. At best it must increase utility, at worst it must not result in harm to anyone.

231

CAREW

This way of looking at merit provides an entirely new angle to the whole spectrum of race/class discourse. The issue of compensatory justice, remedial and preferential policies could now be treated differently and in a way is partial to the race school point of view.

The race school argument for compensatory justice is premised on the assumption that blacks as a group are owed compensation for the moral wrong inflicted on them by whites. Owen Fiss puts the case this way: "This redistribution may be rooted in a theory of compensation, blacks as a group were put in that position by others and the redistributive measures are owed as a form of compensation" (Boxill [1992–3]: 120). It is clear from this observation that the Lockean Merit Principle, with its twin commitment to objectivity and individualism, would not apply in this case. But Rawls' revised liberal view does apply. It makes room for such appeals on grounds that moral harm, even when ostensibly done for the good of the society or the majority, are impermissible. To make the point clearer, for example, notice Wilson's attempt in his book, *The Truly Disadvantaged*, to make a case for the socioeconomic rehabilitation of the black underclass. Wilson's acknowledgement that an appeal to the moral sense of the majority would be out of place was an implicit admission that the Lockean normative framework was woefully inadequate. Let me elaborate by using Dworkin's distinction of preferences. According to Dworkin, there are two kinds of preferences—"personal" and "external." Personal preferences describe the needs and resources individuals require for their everyday lives. External preferences, on the other hand, express what people feel others deserve. This distinction is particularly useful to the race school argument. As Kymlicka states it, "Someone may want blacks to have fewer resources because he thinks they are less worthy of respect…If we believe that everyone is to be treated as equals, then it offends our deepest principles to allow some people to suffer because others do not want them to be treated as equals" (Fullinwider [1992]: 360).

Let us return to Wilson's claim. Wilson believed that racist attitudes would make it impossible for the white majority to support race specific measures that would eradicate the problems facing blacks trapped in the underclass. As a result, he proposes a "hidden agenda" that would present programs for black upliftment in the guise of universal programs. Following Dworkin, one can argue that the inability of the Lockean system to preclude the external preferences of whites who do not believe that blacks are due equal respect, makes it virtually impossible to appeal for justice. If what blacks who are harmed by slavery and racism deserve is to be determined not by a theory of fair share, but by what their oppressors think they deserve, then it is unlikely that even an appeal to self-interest would ensure fair treatment for blacks. This clearly is the implication of writing in the tradition that seeks the dominance of self-interest over morality.

Since the social context which Rawls envisions does not give priority to self-interest over morality, Wilson ought to be able to make his case the way he would have like to. Racism is in large part to blame for the black underclass; thus race specific program would be warranted to correct the unjust situation. And Boxill is right to point this out. After all, it is as a group that blacks were singled out for unjust treatment, on account of their race (Fullinwider [1992]: 361). Why then must benefits be provided only for those blacks who are deemed useful to the system? If blacks are owed benefits not because they have ability the system can use, but because they deserve compensation for the moral wrongs they endured on account of their race, the focus must be not on efficiency but on justice.

Moving from reparation to "affirmative action" may require a shift away from a defense based on rights to one based on a genuine effort to transform a bad situation. Again, the Rawlsian model is better able to address this problem. Since it is Rawls' position that people do not deserve their abilities, it make perfect sense socially to determine what constitutes merit. A society that historically had been torn apart by racism and slavery might consider it a socially desirable end to improve the social, economic, and political power of those groups whose interests have been marginalized by the system. Clearly, such a society would consider the preservation of social peace of equal value with efficiency. Individual talents would be indulged only if they do not harm anyone and if they also increase social utility. Affirmative action, then, would be justified on grounds that it would bring about the desired goal in the shortest period of time. The objection might of course be raised that policies aimed at achieving such goals lead to reverse discrimination. People who are denied positions to make room for blacks who are regarded as less qualified are likely to argue that their rights have been infringed upon. One way to address this problem is to point out that there is no objective determination of merit outside of the social context in the Rawlsian view. Rawls does not offer an entitlement theory. Furthermore, the analogy breaks down when we come to consider the reasons why blacks are preferred and whites feel discriminated against. Blacks are preferred because they have been treated as an inferior and despised group. There is therefore every reason to end this kind of discrimination. Whites who are discriminated against, on the other hand, are not considered inferior to blacks and therefore cannot claim to have been robbed of their self respect in the way blacks were robbed of theirs. Furthermore, since Rawls does not countenance historically determined entitlement claims, whites cannot claim that they have been denied positions which are due them. There are no entitlement claims prior to the determination of what constitutes fair share. The so-called reverse discrimination is thus not morally equivalent to the discrimination experienced by blacks.

The opposing views on what constitutes equal consideration is not the only thing separating the race and class schools. There could be an even more fundamental disagreement between the two schools. We will see that the race school formulated rejection of the class-school view of politics constitutes an approach to politics wholly antithetical to the class-school strategy to achieve freedom.

233

CAREW

II

I have thus far argued that the race and class schools do not share the same moral intuition as evidenced in the moral and social discourse or race relations. Let us now shift to the political context of the debate which defines the normative framework for addressing racial justice.

There are two independent, and indeed conflicting, paths to the politics of emancipation: the view which asserts that emancipation would be achieved only when group differences are transcended and its opponent, the view that particularities and differences must be acknowledged if freedom is to be achieved. The former view is contained in liberal discourse, while the latter view is held by one version of discourse theory. Discourse theory, I shall argue, is a genuinely distinct form of liberalism and not simply a different way of describing the same theory. But first let me show why politics as the transcendence of group difference fail.

There is nothing indeed problematic about politics as the realm of freedom. What is problematic is the liberal interpretation of this view. On the liberal view, the politics of emancipation must lead to the transcendence of group difference. Liberals introduced this distinction to protect individuals against unwanted interferences with their autonomous actions. This explains why it was necessary to reconstruct social relations in such a way that formal equality will be secured. Securing formal equality was deemed necessary to protect against all sources of coercion, including the tyranny of group norms. As long as individuals could make autonomous choices unhindered, they would be considered free.

234   This approach to freedom is limited in many ways. It is commonly referred to as "negative liberty" because Lockean libertarians tend to oppose the idea of the redistribution of resources to ensure equality of opportunity, since this would be interfering with the historical entitlements of others. *There is no room in this view for the remedy of the undeserved disadvantages of others in the polity.* As Nozick observed, the only condition worth rectifying is that resulting either from the infringement on one's property or bodily harm inflicted by another person. Considerations involving the welfare of the community is not covered by Nozick's rectification principle. Yet the unwillingness to intervene to rectify unequal circumstances clearly undermines classical liberalism commitment to equal freedom. Thus the Lockean framework offers little scope for affirmative action. Individuals with undeserved disadvantage do not stand a chance if the majority of members of civil society are dead set against providing remedies (Rosenfeld: 52–64). The question we must then ask is how can race transcending policies work when the public realm clearly exhibits racism?

The answer to this query is simple and straightforward. Race transcending policies have no place in racist societies. The source of the problem however does not lie in the policies as such but rather in the way we have come to conceive of the public. The public has been construed not only as the ideal of collective freedom but also as the ideal of impartiality and neutrality. Feminist social theorists and postmodern critics have raised serious objections against the enlightenment conception of a universal, impartial public. Iris Young describes how the incoherence of this approach advanced instead the hegemonic interest of certain dominant groups: "The designers of the constitution specifically restricted access of the laboring class to the rational public, and of course excluded slaves and Indians from participating in the civic public as well" (Young: 110). Since members of the civic public were presumed to possess such virtues as rationality, dispassion, and social grace, the excluded were by contrast, believed to be disorderly, intemperate, and morally bankrupt.

The normative justification of the principle of impartiality rests on tenuous grounds. Since it constitutes the core of liberal belief about structuring a society based on achievement criteria, its rejection undermines achievement criteria. The presumed alternative in the view of some people (i.e., a society based on ascriptive criteria) thus becomes an attractive option. This is, however, a trap and those who had been seduced by it have been led to reject universal citizenship in favor of differentiated citizenship. But the way out of this trap, in my view, lies in a compromise worked out by Seyla Benhabib. It advocates fusing some version of the public sphere with the discourse model. The task of the next section is to elaborate and defend this view.

This public sphere as the realm which is collectively determined under conditions that are acceptable to all have been shown to be affected by the dispositions and aspirations of some members of society. Since this could be hazardous in a society in the process of transformation to a discrimination-free polity, we require a conception of collective freedom that would not endanger the freedom of individuals even as it manages change to a discrimination-free society. Following Seyla Benhabib, I shall defend a discourse model which attempts to retain the liberal democratic character with it emphasis on an equilibrium between group norms and private spaces. But, first let me spell out the particular conception of discourse model Benhabib defends.

According to Benhabib, a discourse model takes all differences into account. The procedure calls for rules that are fair and acceptable to all in the polity. More specifically, the following conditions must obtain: (1) participation should be governed by the norms of equality and symmetry; (2) there should not be a preset agenda; and (3) participants should be free to discuss not only the issues but to raise when necessary any objections they might have with respect to the rules or procedures.

Since a proceduralist model of democracy does not offer a pregiven agenda, it provides the perfect setting for articulating and resolving conflicts of interest under conditions of social cooperation mutually acceptable to all. One of the other advantages, as Benhabib points out, is that the discourse model offers opportunity for participants in the public to gain valuable information about others. Only a forum of this type allows individuals to access the perspectives of others and to enlarge their own understanding of their society. Furthermore, the principle of

235

CAREW

giving good reason for one's action is an invaluable lesson in moral tolerance and respect for the interest of others. The discourse model is essentially an educative process in that if fosters civility and solidarity in society.

To further amplify the workings of the discourse model, the following two problems of the discourse model have been raised: (1) liberal theorists view the discourse model as entailing a rejection of the public sphere; (2) discourse theorists are also suspected of preferring the participatory process of the discourse model to representative democracy.

With the collapse of the enlightenment public, some versions of discourse theory have proposed what they consider the only alternative to a unified public, that is, a collectivity of concrete others. This view entails a rejection of universal citizenship and an endorsement of differentiated citizenship. However, without universal citizenship the very idea of a nation-state will be lost and each subgroup will become a nation within a nation. I believe this is a fair criticism of the views of Frazer. I argue with Moon and Benhabib that some conception of a public is required to hold a collectivity together. A collectivity of concrete others, each with its own preferred ideal, cannot form a community of any kind unless there were common concerns which unify them. Thus, as the later Benhabib observed, some formula of the moral ideal of impartiality as a regulatory principle which should govern not only our deliberations in public but also the articulation of reasons by public institutions is absolutely central to democratic legitimacy (Benhabib: 40).

Following Oakeshott, Chantal Moufee makes a similar point:

> What we share and what makes us fellow-citizens in a liberal democratic regime is not a substantive idea of the good but a set of political principles specific to such a tradition. The principles of freedom and equality for all; to be a citizen is to recognize the authority of those principles and the rules in which they are embodied to have them informing our political judgment and our actions (231).

The unifying elements described above are not derived from an enlightenment variety but from the normative principles of equality and liberty. Our concern is with what would serve the interest of all equally.

Liberal critics were on the right path in point out the inherent dangers in a unified society living with cultural pluralism. Since it tends towards a hierarchical encapsulation, it lacks the ability to block efforts at infringing the rights and freedom of national minorities. Yet assimilationist theorists such as Glazer and Walzer ignore the possible loss of liberal freedoms for minority groupings as they become "absorbed" into the culture of the dominant group. The pragmatic justification for preserving the national ethos seems to outweigh any other consideration, in their judgment. While it is true that neither Glazer nor Walzer have been able to justify the exclusion of national minorities from the public realm, it does not follow that the solution to this problem lies in the promotion of cultural or ethnic identities? Views such as Nancy Frazer's endorse rigid ascriptive boundaries. Yet since this leads more or less to a fragmented community it cannot serve as the expected outcome. The liberal goal of an inclusive public must therefore be pursued by other means.

According to critics, there appears to be an incompatibility between representative institutions and the discourse model. On at least one approach this might be true given that the public consists of everyone and every group. In this radicalized participatory process group interests are not represented by anyone but the individuals themselves; the idea of each perspective or interest being represented by those who hold them replaces the discredited impartial representative of the objective public. However, civil society theory's approach to the discourse model finds no incompatibility between representative institutions and discourse framework. In point of fact, representative institutions are in this case formulated in the context of discourse theory (Benhabib: 42). A step by step approach would reveal how Rawls' and Benhabib's views combined and supplemented each other.

Rawls supports the idea of public dialogue and the justice of institutions. Rawls however restricts discussion of public matters to the state (Rawls [1993]: 215). Benhabib shares Rawls' concern for public dialogue and just institutions, but considers the restriction of the public sphere to the state level a serious mistake. In her view, the restriction of the public sphere to the state level would prove inadequate for resolving the issue of unifying disparate cultural entities (Benhabib: 36). In other words, she is raising the issue of whether there can be a democracy without democrats. This is because a community of self-serving egotists cannot constitute a democracy. Such a community would lack the social cohesion and fellow feeling necessary for the exercise of collective freedom. Can the fact that the public realm exists ensure that those who run the state are democrats? In other words, does the mere presence of representative institutions guarantee that those who participate in the activities of the state have acquired the civility requisite for a democratic life? Benhabib does not think so, and Kymlicka agrees. Kymlicka accuses liberals of neglecting to account for the moral transformation necessary for the creation of citizens.[4]

Benhabib views the task of the discourse model as aimed at creating conditions for civility and solidarity in society. Since the public with its "top-to-bottom" policies already exist, there is a felt need to create those conditions in civil society which would ensure a receptive audience for laws and policies of the state. For example, just laws and policies to eradicate racism would succeed only if (1) those who are charged with the responsibility of implementing policies are willing to do so, and (2) society itself is committed to a discrimination-free society. Thus, as Benhabib observes, "the discourse public" belongs in civil society where it would ensure that the conditions for civility already exist to render laws against racism enforceable. Clearly, the "bottom-to-top" policies of civil society must be consid-

237

CAREW

ered vital for the success of statist policies because they prepare the grounds for legitimate state action. Whether or not "the people" consent to a particular policy may very well be based on their attitudes and preferences. For example, policies designed to promote the general welfare of the public would be receptive in a society characterized by civility and fellow-feeling. Benhabib has shown that there is only a contingent connection between democratic institutions and the sentiments required to ensure the success of democratic practice. It is in this sense that Benhabib supplements Rawls' view of the public sphere. Rawls' reliance on the just institutions of the state and "public reason" leaves a gap which Benhabib tried to fill. She argues that the civility of anonymous publics is also required to ensure the freedom of every citizen in the society.

Since communicative politics is a formulated rejection of unified society, it tends to view society as having many publics; for example, the economic and socio-cultural publics. Thus the issue here is one of coordinating the activities of the various publics so as to achieve an equilibrium. The activities of the public at the state level must be coordinated with the various activities of the public spheres in civil society. What this entails is that the form of reasoning associated with the activities of the economic or bureaucratic spheres must be kept separate from the reasoning desired by the socio-cultural sphere. In other words, as Habermas observed, unless we distinguish the instrumental rationality appropriate to the economic and bureaucratic spheres from the communicative rationality desired by the socio-cultural spheres we run the risk of treating all spheres alike. In effect, failure to distinguish instrumental rationality from communicative rationality has led to the dominance of instrumental rationality in all spheres, creating what Habermas has defined as "the colonization of the life-world." Limiting instrumental rationality to its appropriate spheres will help prevent "the commodification of society." The main purpose of communicative politics as I see it then is to promote democratic freedoms through the development of civility and the coordination of the activities of the various publics in society.

I have argued that the race school argument in the context of the classical liberal framework is incoherent. Liberalism's theory of rights makes no provision for an interventionist principle to rectify unequal circumstances. Thus there seems to be not legitimate argument of affirmative action based on distributive justice. The race school is on the right path in the Rawlsian framework. However it is an uncompleted argument. The supplement, I have argued, requires situating Rawls' political liberalism in the context of communicative politics. In the remainder of this paper I shall reexamine the race school position in this reformulated context.

The race school would need to revise its conception of two important assumptions of liberal equality: (1) the ideal of non-discrimination, and (2) the ideal of treating people as individuals and not as members of groups. According to the principles of non-discrimination, no person should be disadvantaged on account of his or her race. And the way to ensure that this does not happen is through "color-blind" policies where persons would be judged solely on the basis of their performance or the choices they make rather than on their circumstances. However, this point of view is rendered problematic with the rejection of the state as the realm of neutrality and impartiality. Since "color-blind" policies would have the effect of privileging some perspectives over others, the only way to satisfy the ideal of nondiscrimination is to constitute a discursive public in which every individual or group of individuals enjoys equal opportunity to state their perspectives in an arena where others are willing to listen and to validate their claims. Clearly the acquired civility of society makes this possible.

The next issue to address is the liberal ideal of treating people as individuals and not as members of a group. Liberalism is an individualist based philosophy. Its main goal is to promote the freedom of individuals by ensuring that they could make autonomous choices unhindered. The ideal society for pursuing this objective, according to liberalism, is a homogeneous nation-state. However, this way of treating the individual citizen fails to take into account that individuals are carriers of culture. Where the national culture is defined by the values of a dominant cultural group which is both racist and sexist, individual members of despised national minorities would in essence be accommodating themselves to values and roles that are clearly inimical to their interests. It is thus clearly unjust to arbitrarily subordinate minority group interest for the sake of preserving national unity. Kymlicka is correct in arguing that liberals who see a tension between justice and national unity are mistaken since justice is a fundamental principle of national unity (Kymlicka [1990]). Far from yielding national unity, a policy of integration which disregards the just aspirations of national minorities sows disunity in the state.

239

From the standpoint of communicative politics, I shall propose two solutions to national integration: (1) that a racist society which commits itself to move to a discrimination-free society must acknowledge its cultural diversity, and (2) that since a racist culture defines roles and positions in such a way as to reflect its racial bias, it cannot become a discrimination-free society until the so-called racist institutions are dismantled and attitudes altered. These proposals, in my view, envision a developmental approach to democracy.

First, a racist society which decides to move to a discrimination-free society must acknowledge its cultural diversity. As we have seen, the problem with a polity of color blindness is that it fails to articulate how a dominant group's preference could come to be perceived as the universal impartial view. To repair this problem, a discourse-based approach would acknowledge all perspectives and through dialogue allow all voices to be listened to and interests validated. It is in this context that "affirmative action" is required to ensure that a groups' perspective is taken into account and its legitimate interests validated. This serves as a check on groups which may seek to use the power concentrated in their hands to dominate other groups. Only when there is no danger of people being discriminated against on grounds of their race (or gender) would ethnic or racial representation at the state

CAREW

level become unnecessary. This however is contingent on the development of civility and fellow-feeling in civil society.

The second argument highlights the structural impediments to freedom. Iris Young has observed that whites had fashioned institutions and defined roles without any input from blacks. With racism outlawed, blacks are now expected to accept norms and to play roles that had been devised to subjugate them in the first place. These are roles and norms they would have rejected had they participated in the design and definition of those functions. In this case, as in the last, "affirmative action" is required to ensure that white stereotypes of blacks and their control of the major avenues of communication would not be used to continue the subjugation of blacks. "affirmative action" would ensure that these institutions are dismantled.

The incoherence of the old politics of emancipation clearly highlights the paradox of using means which are in contradiction with one's goals. So long as racist tendencies had shaped the division of labor hierarchy, placing mostly whites at the top and blacks at the bottom, the racialization of poverty would not be eradicated by simply redistributing wealth, income and jobs to blacks. This is the point Boxill makes to class school advocates when he rejects the idea put forward by Booker T. Washington that skill acquisition would earn blacks respectability and economic freedom. The corrective to the injustice produced by uneven social power cannot be found in the redistribution of wealth. For as long as racism defines and redefines roles and functions, redistribution of wealth and positions would not produce a discrimination-free society.

The false hope skill acquisition would earn blacks social recognition and economic gains is based on the conflation of the virtue of the economic sphere (which is efficiency), with the virtue of the discourse sphere (which is justice). One's social standing as a moral agent ought not to rest on the acquisition of skills, but on the moral and social reciprocity required of the discourse public. Since discrimination against blacks is essentially a moral problem with economic and society ramifications, it is by creating solidarity in society that the root cause of the problem would be overcome. The task of the new politics of emancipation is to ensure that the connection between social institutions, which unduly privilege certain groups because of their race, and the influence and power this allows them to wield in the public sphere, is not maintained. The way to achieve this in the short run is through "affirmative action." In the long run, full emancipation would only come when civility and solidarity now characterize the activities of civil society. But until such time civil society has the responsibility of creating responsible citizenship.

CAREW

NOTES

1 For a precise statement of the controversy, see Bernard Boxill (1983): 107–16.

2 Contemporary theorists of the class school have a different problem to contend with, given that racism and slavery had been outlawed. They do not have to argue that they need to "prove themselves" worthy of white respect. They can only blame black disabilities on the lack of skills. What they have in common though with earlier class school advocates is acquisition of skills.

3 In addition to the works of Sowell and W.J. Wilson, see Fullinwider.

4 Kymlicka (unpublished) takes issue with the presumption implicit in Liberalism that there are common values in every political community. This approach does not take into account the historical origins of some states and therefore, cannot provide answers to the critical issues such as what needs to be done in nation-states where there are no shared values.

CAREW

CORNEL WEST AS PRAGMATIST AND EXISTENTIALIST[1]

Clarence Sholé Johnson

ALTHOUGH CORNEL WEST is generally acknowledged as a pragmatist, in light of his own very identification with that position, very little attempt has been made thus far to relate his pragmatism to his existentialist preoccupations.[2] It is precisely this task that I wish to undertake in the present study. In particular, I propose to show how West draws upon his concept of prophetic pragmatism to address the nihilistic threat to black America. To realize this goal, I will give a general but detailed overview of West's philosophical orientation in order to situate him within the pragmatist tradition. I will then elaborate his discussion of nihilism in black America and provide a critique of his philosophy of prophetic pragmatism as a viable strategy to resolve the nihilistic threat to black America.

A useful starting pointing for my discussion in West's own exemplary historical, if brief, account of the genealogy of pragmatism in his book

The American Evasion of Philosophy. In this work West delineates some of the most distinctive, perhaps even the defining, attributes of pragmatism. Essentially, he says, pragmatism, as a philosophical movement begun by Ralph Waldo Emerson, marked a radical departure from the dominant philosophy in Europe as reflected in the writings of the continental rationalists and the so-called British empiricists. The concern of rationalists and empiricists alike was epistemological; specifically, to subvert skepticism by providing a sound foundation for knowledge. This foundation was sought in the criterion of certainty. The point of deviance between these two competing schools, however, was over the method by which the purported certainty could be attained. For the rationalists it was through the employment of reason unaided by experience, whereas for the empiricists it was by means of sensation. What is significant is that this issue dogged philosophy with no sign of a resolution. Besides, there was also a metaphysical import to the whole enterprise in that the quest for certainty was a quest for apprehending (i.e., attaining knowledge of) the nature of reality. Thus, the issue between the rationalists and the empiricists was about the method by which knowledge of reality could be attained—through the employment of reason unaided by experience or through atomistic sensation.[3] According to West, it was this unresolvable issue, which had engaged the European philosophers, that provided, indeed constituted, the point of departure for pragmatism, the only authentic Western philosophy native to America. What then does pragmatism advocate?

Pragmatism, says West, in its historical evasion of epistemologically centered philosophy, is "a future-oriented instrumentalism that tries to deploy thought as a weapon to enable more effective action." Or, better still, pragmatism advances "a conception of philosophy as a form of cultural criticism in which the meaning of America is put forward by intellectuals in response to distinct social and cultural crises" ([1989]: 5).[4] It is this characteristic of pragmatism, namely, of its having as an end *knowledge as it relates to action*, that clearly distinguishes the doctrine from European philosophy, the latter of which was concerned either with knowledge as such or with being as an extrasensory phenomenon.

It is not my aim here to identify let alone discuss any of the crises in reaction to which pragmatism originated as response and/or tried to sidestep. I provide this background of the point of departure of pragmatism only to call attention to the following features of pragmatism: (1) that it is action-oriented; (2) that it is concerned with consequences; and (3) that as a social and cultural critique, it is a dynamic (as opposed to a static) philosophical position. This last point is of the utmost significance because it brings out very clearly the relevance of pragmatism to contemporary America. As society undergoes change—social, economic and cultural—so does pragmatism come to bear on the ongoing discussion about the nature of the change. It is in this connection that one sees clearly the rationale for West's identification of himself as a Deweyan rather than a Piercean or Jamesian pragmatist. As he tells us, "The thoroughgoing historical consciousness and empha-

sis on social and political matters found in John Dewey speaks more to my purpose than the preoccupations with logic in Pierce and the obsessions with individuality in James" (1989: 6). This remark immediately begs a central question of
the present study: What is Cornel West's purpose in his philosophy? In order to
answer this question I will have to answer yet another, even a more fundamental,
question: What, in West's view, is the nature of Dewey's pragmatism?

West characterizes Dewey as "the greatest of the American pragmatists" ([1989]:
69) because, among other things, Dewey's pragmatism expresses "a mode of historical consciousness that highlights the conditioned and circumstantial character
of human existence in terms of changing societies, cultures, and communities"
([1989]: 69–70). West goes on to elaborate his meaning in a note explaining the
difference between the pragmatism of William James and that of Dewey, saying that
Dewey's is concerned with "the social and historical forces that shape the creative
individual" ([1989]: 252). The central causal agents of change that help shape the
modern individual are the economic structures that had emerged in a nineteenth-
century society undergoing rapid industrialization. Inversely proportionate to the
tremendous economic success of the industrial capitalist investors was a sharp
decline in the living conditions of the new industrial working class who were
largely immigrants and African Americans. Put baldly, the industrial working class
experienced economic poverty and social misery at a time when the capitalist
investors and organizations were experiencing huge economic successes. West sums
up the socio-economic reality of the industrial underclass as "principally that of
economic deprivation, cultural dislocation, and personal disorientation" ([1989]:
80). It is directly to this crisis of the human condition that Dewey's pragmatism
speaks. Thus, in a sense, Dewey's pragmatism, in its bid to formulate strategies to
ameliorate the predicament thus described, is a from of social activism.

West lists three ways in which Dewey attempted to address the socio-economic crisis of nineteenth century America: (1) though journalism Dewey endeavored
to popularize critical intelligence (or critical thinking) so as to be able to educate
the masses; (2) Dewey affiliated himself with influential middle-class humanitarian
organizations that worked with the underclass in a bid "to assimilate and accultur-
ate immigrants into the American mainstream"; and (3) Dewey exercised leadership over a rapidly growing teaching profession both by practical examples and
through his writing ([1989]: 79–80).

It is arguable of course that Dewey succeeded in these ventures. For example,
West points out that while Dewey's commitment to cultivate critical intelligence,
especially in children, led him to set up a laboratory school in Chicago, popularly
known as the "Dewey School," his endeavor to take philosophy to the people
through the newspaper medium was scarcely helpful to this cause. Dewey not only
outraged the mainstream media which lampooned his idea, he also was unwilling
to engage them in any manner whatsoever. True, Dewey was directly involved with
humanitarian groups and organizations that were concerned about the social and

245

JOHNSON

economic condition of the industrial working class, as attested to by his participation in Hull House founded by Jane Addams. According to Richard J. Bernstein, "Dewey mixed with workers, union organizers, and political radicals of all sorts" (Bernstein). Yet Dewey's reluctance to engage the very core middle-class establishment from which his income and status as a professional originated seems to cast a shadow on his social activism. Thus, although he believed that social and economic redemption for the underclass could be obtained through a democratization process facilitated by education, he was most unwilling to invest the hard capital, using his professional career as collateral, for this end.

West contrasts Dewey's unwillingness to risk his professional career in support of his political beliefs with the willingness of his friend and former classmate Henry Carter Adams to do just that. Adams was dismissed from his teaching position at Cornell University because of his public support of the Knights of Labor. What is significant is that Adams had considerable difficulty securing a job because of his socialist beliefs ([1989]: 80). Yet he did not allow the thought of this difficulty obtaining a job to quell his desire to give expression to his political beliefs *after* he had landed a job. To be sure, Dewey did try to exercise leadership over his professional colleagues by even castigating them for their complacency, indolence, and ivory-tower mentality. As West puts it, "Dewey castigated the ivory-tower scholar frightened by the dirty world of politics and afraid of the consequences of active engagement" ([1989]: 92). But when one considers that Dewey was just not prepared to face the consequences of subscribing to a political belief, his criticism of his professional colleagues seems to ring hollow. Surprisingly, West describes as "quite understandable" ([1989]: 82) Dewey's unwillingness to risk his career in promoting and defending against press criticism his political beliefs, especially his belief of taking philosophy to the masses. And continuing his apology for Dewey, West says "Dewey practiced professional caution and political reticence. He remained deeply engaged in civic affairs, but shunned controversy" ([1989]: 82).[5] No doubt all of this is true. Yet it remains an open question whether or not Dewey was prepared to confront and engage the real culprits, the causes of the problems he was presumably working to resolve, namely, the very middle-class institutions and establishments that supported his economic and social life-style.

In any case, to sum up the key points of the discussion thus far, West regards the following as central to Dewey's pragmatism: (1) that it is action-oriented in endeavoring to provide strategies through education for the amelioration of the dismal socio-economic condition of the emergent underclass in nineteenth-century industrial America; (2) that it utilized existing middle-class institutions, such as universities and humanitarian organizations, to sound a note of urgency in its critique of social and economic injustice that was meted out to the underclass; and (3) that for Dewey philosophy has an instrumental rather than an intrinsic worth in that its value consists in its ability to be employed in the resolution of human problems rather than in its celebration of ideas as such à la the endeavors of the

European epistemologists. It is in this context that, for West, Dewey was as much a social reformer as he was a philosopher.

Drawing upon the foregoing, I now can attempt to answer the question raised earlier about West's purpose in his philosophy. Essentially, and in a similar Deweyan spirit, West's philosophy (or his pragmatism) is unquestionably a form of cultural criticism and social activism. His principal motivation in outlining his philosophical views in *The American Evasion of Philosophy* is, in his words, "my disenchantment with intellectual life in America and my own demoralization regarding the political and cultural state of the country." In the intellectual sphere, West is disenchanted by what he describes as "the transformation of highly intelligent liberal intellectuals into tendentious neoconservatives owing to crude ethnic identity-based allegiances and vulgar neo-nationalist sentiments." On the political sphere, West is concerned about and disappointed with "the professional incorporation of former New Left activists who now often thrive on a self-serving careerism while espousing rhetoric of oppositional politics of little serious integrity." And on the cultural domain, he is "depressed about the concrete nihilism in working-class and underclass American communities—the pervasive drug addiction, suicides, alcoholism, male violence against women, white violence against black, yellow, and brown people, and the black criminality against others, especially other black people" ([1989]: 7–8).

There can be do doubt but that these concerns about the human predicament in contemporary America situate West squarely within the pragmatist tradition of Emerson and Dewey. Some parallelisms are certainly in order. For example, West's avowed interest in the plight of the underclass parallels Dewey's concern with the new industrial underclass in nineteenth-century America. West's declared disappointment with intellectual colleagues is but a reflection or a replay of Dewey's indictment of Dewey's own professional colleagues. And West's membership in the Democratic Socialists of America is reminiscent of Dewey's affiliation with unions and organized labor.

As with Dewey, West gives a practical use to philosophy by deploying philosophy to resolving concrete issues that affect human beings in their day-to-day struggles. His aim in so doing is to effect change in the society through a reconfiguration of the structures that delimit or exclude individuals from participating in the political and economic systems of the society. He characterizes his philosophy as "prophetic pragmatism," a position he elaborates in a variety of ways of which the following is a succinct statement:

> Prophetic pragmatism understands the Emersonian swerve from epistemology...not as a wholesale rejection of philosophy but rather as a reconception of philosophy as a form of social, cultural, and political traditions for the purposes of increasing the scope of individual development and democratic operations...[It] conceives of philosophy as a historically circumscribed quest for

JOHNSON

wisdom that puts forward new interpretations of the world based on past traditions in order to promote existential sustenance and political relevance. Like
Emerson and earlier pragmatists, it views thought as a species of the good, as
that which enhances the flourishing of human progress. This does not mean
that philosophy ignores the ugly facts and unpleasant realities of life and history. Rather, it highlights these facts and realities precisely because they pro-
voke doubt, curiosity, outrage, or desperation that motivates efforts to overcome them. ([1989]: 230)[6]

West's pragmatism is "prophetic" precisely because West draws upon his
Christian background to articulate and engage the problems that confront the
powerless in contemporary America with a view to their amelioration as a spiritual vocation. Central to this vocation is an ethic of love of the kind expressed in the
Bible requiring us to love our neighbors as (we do) ourselves. As I will demonstrate
in the section that follows, this concept of love will play an important role in West's
discussion of the problem of black nihilism. But what I want to stress here is that
West, as both proponent and practitioner of prophetic pragmatism, envisions himself a modern day prophet, comparable to the biblical prophets, advocating on
behalf of "the wretched of the earth."

In sum, then, West, like Dewey in nineteenth-century America, is concerned
with the social, economic, cultural (in the broadest sense) and spiritual afflictions
of the powerless in modern day society. And like the biblical prophets, West sees
himself as bringing urgency to the conditions of the powerless, advocating their
amelioration, with honesty and integrity. With this in mind, prophetic pragmatism
may be characterized effectively as a philosophical position concerned with cultural criticism, imbued with a moral content and anchored in West's Christian
background. This characterization draws support from West's own very remark:

> I hold a religious conception of pragmatism. I have dubbed it "prophetic" in
> that it harks back to the Jewish and Christian tradition of prophets who
> brought urgent and compassionate critique to bear on the evils of their day.
> The mark of the prophet is to speak the truth in love with courage—come
> what may. Prophetic pragmatism proceeds from this impulse. It neither requires
> a religious foundation nor entails a religious perspective, yet prophetic prag-
> matism is compatible with religious outlooks." ([1989]: 233)

It scarcely needs any argument to show that West's primary objective in *Evasion*
is to contextualize prophetic pragmatism as an authentic variety of American pragmatism. He suggests as much in his concluding remarks in the introductory chapter of *Evasion*: "I began this work as an exercise in critical self-inventory, as a historical, social, and existential situating of my own work as an intellectual, activist,
and human being. I wanted to make clear to myself my own contradictions and

tensions, faults and foibles as one shaped by, in part, the tradition of American pragmatism." Or again: "I have written this text convinced that a thorough examination of American pragmatism, stripping it of its myths, caricatures, and stereotypes and viewing it as a component of a new and novel form of indigenous American oppositional thought and action, may be a first step toward fundamental change and transformation in America and the world" ([1989]: 8). These remarks, taken in light of the preceding discussion, validate further the point that West's philosophical concerns situate him squarely within the pragmatist tradition. I will now give an illustrative treatment of one specific issue about human existence that West interrogates from the perspective of an existentialist informed by the motivations of prophetic pragmatism. Specifically, I will consider his treatment of nihilism among African Americans in his book *Race Matters* (1994).

BLACK NIHILISM

One existentialist concern that West raises in *Race Matters* is the pervasive sense of utter meaninglessness, despondency, self-loathing and impotence that permeates Black America, especially its youth ([1994]: 22–3). It is this horrifying phenomenon that West characterizes as a nihilism in black America, for it is a life without hope that constitutes a severe threat to the very survival of black America. And it is precisely for this reason that, for West, such nihilism needs to be confronted.[7]

West identifies two main causes of this nihilism: (1) the preponderance of market morality in America and (2) the serious and deleterious crisis of leadership in the black community. Concerning the first, the preponderance of market morality, West contends that the market forces promote, even advocate, an ethic of consumerism which subordinates, instrumentalizes, or objectifies others as a means of pleasure for one's own profit. Another way of putting this point is to say that market morality commodifies human beings thereby treating them as a means to an end, the end being profit, rather than as (in Kant's terminology) ends in themselves. This morality construes bestial hedonism as a virtue, for it takes the end of life to be indulgence in the seductive transient pleasures of the body.

Furthermore, and more importantly, this market morality is transmitted through the airwaves and dominates popular culture—radio, television, movies, and so on— thereby creating a form of environmental and psychological pollution for all who breathe the American air or are exposed to the American environment. It is in this regard that the market morality is a partial cause of black nihilism. To the extent that blacks in America coexist with others in an environment whose atmosphere is overwhelmed by this pollution, their behavior is thus environmentally and psychologically determined by the influence of the market morality in question. In other words, there is a form of environmental and psychological determinism according to which the behavior of blacks, as with all others in the American atmosphere, is a direct consequence of the preponderance of market forces.

Among blacks, in particular, this determinism gives rise to either of two forms of behavior, depending on the economic (and hence social) stratum of society to which the individual belongs: (1) excessive, tasteless, and nauseating consumerism, if the individual belongs to the black middle class; or (2) drugs, crime, alcoholism, and violence, if the individual belongs to the underclass. Since the majority of blacks in American society occupy the lower stratum in the socio-economic ladder, it is among them that the nihilistic behavior is most virulent. The reason is that they cannot be active participants in the market forces that shape their lives and to which they nonetheless are constantly exposed. Thus they cannot enjoy the seeming benefits, albeit banal, that market morality glorifies and presents as the virtues of self-worth and personal success. The individual's perception of his or her failure to experience, via the market medium, the bodily titillations glorified and worshipped by market morality, occasions a sense of utter despair and meaninglessness, an existential anguish. And the net result of such anguish is crime, drugs, alcoholism, and violence. In sum, we have in the black community, particularly among the underclass, a self-destructiveness wrought on by a sense of utter powerlessness.

In saying this West is not excusing the immoral conduct of some blacks or attempting to absolve them from personal responsibility for their actions. He clearly states that "black murderers and rapists should go to jail" ([1994]: 25, cf. 85), a position that would be difficult to maintain if he subscribed to (because it is incompatible with) rigid determinism. On the other hand, he notes that failing to offer a causal explanation of the conduct of blacks in terms of the socio-economic forces that impinge upon their very being, forces that affect individual decisions, and yet condemn them, is to ascribe blame or responsibility to them unfairly. And it is this charge of unfairness that West brings against the new black conservatives for their uneven-handed indictment of black behavior, and for their argument in support of the wholesale dismantling of those social programs upon which individuals in the black underclass depend for sheer survival on the ground that such programs have bred nothing but a mentality of dependency. "It is imperative to steer a course between the Scylla of environmental determinism and the Charybdis of a blaming-the-victims perspective" ([1994]: 85).

The second partial cause of black nihilism, says West, is the absence of effective, in the sense of quality, leadership, both politically and intellectually, among blacks. Briefly stated, West's point here is that post–Civil Rights black leadership has failed to engage in a critical discussion of issues, actual and potential, affecting the black community with a view to putting forth concrete solutions, even in a preemptive way, to some of the ills that wreak havoc in the community. Among these ills are sexism and violence toward black women, homophobia, and xenophobia.

According to West, nowhere was this absence of black leadership voice more pronounced than in the 1992 Senate Confirmation Hearings of Clarence Thomas, President Bush's nominee for the Supreme Court. Among other things, West argues, the black leadership was silent on the issue of Thomas' (in)competence and hence (un)suitability to serve in the Supreme Court; they did not examine Thomas' proven track record in any of the offices in which he had served prior to being nominated; nor did they even discuss issues that had arisen about Thomas' character, especially in light of the charge of sexual harassment that Anita Hill had brought against him during the Confirmation Hearings, either to absolve him from or to convict him of wrongdoing.

West attributes this immoral silence of the black leadership to what he describes as racial reasoning, a black "closing-ranks mentality" ([1994]: 37–8) which demands that blacks should rally behind their fellow black in a racist society where the opportunity to serve in such a highly respected capacity is rare. Thus, even if the leadership had reservations about the suitability of Thomas to serve as the representative of the black intellectual leadership in matters of jurisprudence in the highest court of the land, they nevertheless allowed racial reasoning to override their better, honest, and truthful judgment about Thomas' very (un)qualification for the office. And this, says West, is "most disturbing," for it reflects a "failure of nerve of [the] black leadership" ([1994]: 35).

More generally, concerning black leadership in dealing with the threat of nihilism in the black community, West remarks that contemporary political leaders seem too anxious to call attention to themselves, in particular to their being successful in America, rather than to the afflictions of the less fortunate. And he deems this aspect of current black leadership a mark of moral degeneracy ([1994]: 54), since for such leadership politics functions instrumentally to the realization of *their* own individual selfish ends. Thus, contrasting contemporary black leadership with the leadership of the not-too-distant past, West states:

> Most present-day black political leaders appear too hungry for status to be angry, too eager for acceptance to be bold, too self-invested in advancement to be defiant. And when they do drop their masks and try to get mad (usually in the presence of black audiences), their bold rhetoric is more performance than personal, more play-acting than heartfelt. Malcolm, Martin, Ella, and Fannie made sense of the black plight in a poignant and powerful manner, whereas most contemporary political leaders' oratory appeals to black people's sense of the sentimental and sensational. ([1994]: 58)

It is in this context that West laments the non-existence of quality individuals of the likes of Frederick Douglass, Sojourner Truth, Martin Luther King, Jr., Malcolm X, and Fannie Lou Hamer among today's crop of black political leaders ([1994]: 53).

West proceeds to characterize contemporary black political leadership into the following three groups: race-effacing managerial leaders such as Wilson Goode and Thomas Bradley; race-identifying protest leaders such as Louis Farrakhan of the Nation of Islam and Marion Barry; and race-transcending prophetic leaders such as the late Harold Washington and, to some extent, at least in terms of effort, the "Jesse Jackson of 1988." Noting that "The first type is growing rapidly," West points out that, on the positive side, this group "survives on sheer political savvy and thrives on personal diplomacy." On the negative side, however, because this group's chief interest is "the practical mainstream as the only game in town," it "tends to stunt progressive development and silence the prophetic voices in the black community" ([1994]: 58–9).

In contrast, race-identifying protest leaders typically carve out a black turf over which they set themselves as warlords, "vowing to protect their leadership status over it, and serving as power brokers with powerful nonblack elites (usually white economic or political elites…to 'enhance' this black turf)." Continuing, West says that these leaders "function as figures who white Americans must appease *so that the plight of the black poor is overlooked and forgotten*" ([1994]: 60; emphasis added).

It is significant, however, that neither of these two groups can meet the challenge of the black nihilistic threat. The race-effacing leadership is too busy attempting to endear itself to the dominant (read white) establishment to have enough commitment to address the most urgent and burning ills afflicting the black community. Besides, it would not be *politically practical* to devote the time and commit the resources necessary to address such problems. For the race-identifying group, it would seem that the threat to black survival ceases to exist once the leadership has been appeased by the dominant establishment. And one could imagine such "appeasements" to occur regularly. Little wonder then that West says quite rightly that of the two types of leadership the former is the lesser evil where the alternative is a conservative, invariably a white, politician.

Finally, we turn to the race-transcending prophetic leadership. It is this group that West credits with the credentials, both political and moral, to avert black nihilism. He lists the following as the prerequisites for membership into this group: "personal integrity and political savvy, moral vision and prudential judgment, courageous defiance and organizational patience." But no sooner had he specified these attributes than West hastened to add that, "The present generation has yet to produce such a figure," i.e., one who would meet these requirements ([1994]: 61). Paradoxically, it is this type of leadership that has the authority to meet and hopefully resolve the existential crisis in the black community.

West's criticism of the lack of quality individuals among black political leadership extends also to black intellectuals. In a tone reminiscent of Dewey, West indicts contemporary black intellectuals with, among other things, mediocrity, narrow specialization, and a lack of engagement with "the battles of the streets" ([1994]: 62), meaning with concrete issues affecting black America. Among the reasons he gives for this phenomenon is that many black scholars isolate themselves from mainstream academy; they "distance themselves so far from the mainstream academy that they have little to sustain them as scholars" ([1994]: 63). And it is precise-

252

ly in this way that black scholars marginalize themselves, producing only work of mediocre quality.

Corresponding to the three categories of black politicians noted above, West draws a similar category of black intellectuals. These are the race-distancing elites, the race-embracing rebels, and the race-transcending prophets. The first, usually found in the most exclusive universities and colleges, view themselves as having a near monopoly on the knowledge of "what is wrong with black America." Further, says West, "They revel in severe denigration of much black behavior yet posit little potential or possibility in Afro-America." West's criticism of this group is particularly severe not because of their attack on black conduct as such, but because, as he says, their criticism, though trenchant, "often degenerates into a revealing self-hatred" ([1994]: 65). In other words, the virulence of their criticism reflects their self-hatred (at being black?) as it is a condemnation of black conduct. Race-embracing black intellectuals, says West, reject the white Academy with all its hierarchies only to reproduce similar hierarchies headed by themselves in the (black) institutions in which such individuals function. In such contexts, West continues, "rhetoric becomes a substitute for analysis, stimulatory rapping a replacement for serious reading, and uncreative publications an expression of existential catharsis" ([1994]: 65). And, finally, there are "the few race-transcending prophets" among whom West lists the late James Baldwin, noting however that "With the exception of Toni Morrison, the present generation has yet to produce such a figure" ([1994]: 66).

253

PROPHETIC PRAGMATISM AND THE RESOLUTION OF BLACK NIHILISM

Given this crisis of leadership in the black community, the question that arises is: What then needs to be done? This question is raised in at least three places in West's discussion of the aforementioned issue of black nihilism ([1994]: 11, 28, and 66). In this section, I will show that the question West puts forward to this existential *Angst* in the black community is grounded in both his philosophical orientation as a pragmatist of the Deweyan persuasion and in his Christian background. I begin with West's discussion of the crisis of leadership.

West laments the absence of credible (read quality) politically leadership in the black community, noting that, historically, such leadership functioned as custodians of traditional cultural (or institutional) pillars of strength and support in the community—churches, mosques, schools, etc. These institutions served as a source of empowerment, transmitting and reinforcing values in the community. Thus, it was in and through these institution that individuals drew support to affirm their self-worth. Both the centrality and vitality of these institutions in black communal life during trying times of economic deprivation and social anguish were owing to effective leadership. The erosion of the influence of these institutions in present-day black communal life, but particularly among the youth, added to the self-serving kind of political leadership in the black community, cannot but count as major factors for the moral crisis among black youth.

Thus, against this background, West calls for bold leadership in the spirit of Sojourner Truth, Martin Luther King, Jr., Malcolm X, Fannie Lou Hamer, and others. Not only must such leadership be genuinely angry about the plight of "the wretched of the earth," but it must also be provoked (in the Emersonian sense) to act on its anger so as to effect social change. In this context, it is worth noting West's insistence that effective leadership of the kind described must build race-transcending coalitions. The point here is not simply that West is invoking a historical accident of the kind witnessed in the social movement of Martin Luther King, Jr.; rather, and more importantly, he sees such a coalition as a pragmatic measure to anchor the moral crisis in the black community to the economic reality of American life that is its partial cause. Another way of putting this point is to say that, to the extent that the economic circumstances of the black community, felt more so by its youth, are determined directly or indirectly by white-owned corporate institutions over which such communities have no control, the only way to alter those economic circumstances, and hence partly to resolve the existential crisis in the black community, is by involving white and other (usually liberal) like-minded individuals concerned with justice and fairness to exert pressure on those corporate institutions to respond to the affliction they wrought on the powerless.

In the context of his philosophical position, West's proposal acknowledges a brute fact about America, namely, both its diversity and the logical connectedness of its various constitutive elements. Put otherwise, West's prophetic pragmatism recognizes that although America is diverse, no one group can exist atomistically— that is, logically independently of the others. Accordingly, no one group can address its own problems without the support and involvement of the others. It is in this spirit that West's prophetic pragmatism importunes progressive black political and intellectual leadership to be *race*-transcending in building coalitions to deal with nihilism among black youth. If West celebrates Martin Luther King, Jr.'s race-transcending strategy for social change (as he claims he does), it is precisely because that strategy exemplifies the idea he is articulating as central to prophetic pragmatism, even as he notes that King was not a prophetic pragmatist:

> The social movement led by Martin Luther King, Jr., represents the best of what the political dimension of prophetic pragmatism is all about. Like Sojourner Truth, Walter Rauschenbusch, Elizabeth Cady Stanton, and Dorothy Day, King was not a prophetic pragmatist. Yet like them he was a prophet, in which role he contributed mightily to the political project of prophetic pragmatism. *His all-embracing moral vision facilitated alliances and coalitions across racial, gender, class, and religious lines.* ([1989]: 235; emphasis added).

In addition to building race-transcending coalitions, West urges black political leadership to promote and practice "a politics of conversion." A politics of conversion is a mechanism that inspires people "to believe that there is a hope for the future and a meaning to the struggle" (1994: 29). More importantly, and central to this politics, says West, is "an affirmation of one's self-worth *fueled by the concern of others*" ([1994]: 29; emphasis added). In other words, one's self-worth is affirmed through and measured by one's concern about the predicament of others.

West's view of a politics of conversion echoes the biblical exhortation to love thy neighbor as thyself. I submit that it is to this exhortation that West is alluding in saying that an ethic of love is at the heart of a politics of conversion. Indeed, this ethic is unquestionably at the heart of West's own prophetic pragmatism. *Apropos* is West's already-noted unequivocal remark about the rootedness of his version of prophetic pragmatism in the Judeo-Christian tradition. Accordingly, West sees prophetic pragmatism, at least in terms of its advocacy of an ethic of love, as having a natural appeal to African-Americans because of their spirituality and their attachment to the cultural institutions in the community around which life centers: churches, schools, and similar organizations. Further, West believes that, given bold leadership of the prophetic kind he has described, these cultural institutions can be used effectively to stave off the self-hatred and self-devaluation that nihilism engenders in the psyche (or the souls) of black youth.

A similar insight about the need for prophetic voices among black intellectual leaders underlies West's criticism of the current black intellectual leadership. Indeed, West's criticism of the black intellectual leadership is no less a comment on what he deems to be the vocation and moral obligation of the intellectual to his/her community and of how effectively the intellectual will discharge these responsibilities. I believe that, again, as with his engagement of the political leadership, West is right in arguing that the vocation of black intellectuals is constantly to put forward and critique ideas about, among other things, issues affecting their communities. Among the issues in the black community are crime, drugs, violence, sexism, and intolerance toward "nontraditional" sexual orientation, and racial diversity. The black intellectual has a moral duty to his or her community to engage these issues. To treat these matters as "taboo subjects" is to acquiesce in the preposterous belief that they cannot be interrogated. Yet failure to interrogate *any* matter whatsoever is a grave moral crime an intellectual could commit both against his or her vocation and against his or her community. The reason is that, since an intellectual is obligated to investigate ideas, the view that some matters ought not to be investigated implies a contradiction, for it is logically at odds with the vocation of the intellectual. But, further, an intellectual who fails to engage in a critical discussion of the issues affecting his or her community is committing a crime against the community because there can be no solution to the ills that afflict the community in the absence of such discussion. It is for this reason that I think West is right in condemning those intellectuals who disengage themselves from "the battles of the streets" ([1994]: 62).

Yet, there is the often raised objection about the credentials of intellectuals to speak on behalf of the afflicted, especially since those intellectuals do not live in the communities and hence do not have the experiences of individuals whose interests they are supposed to be representing. Some may argue that the intellectuals do not have an appreciation of the complexity of the situation they are supposed to be criticizing in light of the fact that they are not members of the underclass. The thrust of such criticism is that intellectual leadership the absence of which West bemoans is empty without the actual underclass experiences on which to ground it. Thus, the discussion on which West engages and his call of intellectual leadership in the black community is purely academic.

This objection may even be reinforced by invoking West's own prescription for overcoming intellectual marginalization by blacks, namely, that black intellectuals should integrate themselves into mainstream and well-established (read "white and wealthy") institutions of learning both in order to have access to resources and to produce respectable material. The argument can then be advanced that, since these institutions are not in black communities and the experiences in them are foreign to black underclass experiences, those black academics who have been integrated into the culture of the mainstream institutions, thriving on the prestige and status conferred upon them, cannot therefore be effective representatives of "the wretched of the earth."

256

But this objection can be met easily. Besides that the objection is essentially an *ad hominem* against some advocates for the less fortunate in the black community, it commits the fallacy that one cannot appreciate the plight of any victim unless one also is a victim in similar circumstances. But does one need to be raped in order to appreciate the physical violence toward, the psycho-emotional trauma of, and moral transgression against a rape victim? Or, to take a different example, did the *white* abolitionists have to be transformed into black slaves and then experience the brutality, barbarity, and dehumanization of slavery in order to be legitimate antislavery advocates? Yet if the objection were sound it should answer these questions in the affirmative on pain of logical inconsistency.

It is true that some advocates of the plight of the underlcass, including West, are not themselves members of that class, nor do they live in underclass communities. But it does not follow that they cannot interrogate and then contribute substantively to the amelioration of the problems confronting the underclass, problems that culminate in despair, emptiness, and self-loathing. If anything, the contrary argument can be made that it is precisely because some advocates have acquired a certain status in the society, *especially those known to have personal moral integrity*, that their cry for social justice is heeded by the power structures which otherwise have a natural propensity to ignore the cries of the underclass.

In light of this view, then, I endorse West's contention that intellectuals, especially those who have access to mainstream institutions, like the prisoner in Plato's allegory of the cave who had escaped and symbolically apprehended reality, have a moral obligation to provide leadership in the black community by engaging the issues that plague the communities and putting forward ideas and strategies for social change. An implied moral judgment in West's view is that failure to do so is an egregious breach of a moral obligation to the community. And I take such judgment to be implicit further in West's condemnation both of the intellectual isolationism of the radical black intellectuals and of the philosophical detachment of those intellectuals who pontificate about "the problem *with* black America"—that is, those intellectuals whose penetrating criticisms of so-called black conduct, according to West, reflects only self-hatred.

This said, how effective is West's prophetic pragmatism in meeting the black nihilistic threat? Recall that nihilism, at least as it applies to black youths, is a state of mind that views life as meaningless. It is a state of mind that bespeaks self-loathing, despair, emptiness, and an utter loss of hope. The result of such existential predicament is senseless black-on-black violence, violence against black women, drugs, alcoholism, crime, and ultimately premature death. This is the mode of existence of the underclass black youth.

On my reading of West, there are two levels on which his prophetic pragmatism has attempted to meet this crisis: (1) the socio-psychological; and (2) the politico-economical. On the socio-psychological level, prophetic pragmatism has urged a rejuvenation of the traditional cultural pillars in black life—namely, families, churches, schools, and similar civic organizations—under moral leadership. I understand West as saying that these institutions should respond to the crisis in the community with a sense of urgency. Furthermore, as in previous times, these institutions should help instill in black youth positive self-valuation, a sense of self-worth, and in so doing inspire hope in life. In his essay, "Philosophy and the Urban Underclass," West makes this point indirectly in accounting for the existence and severity of the crisis in the black community:

257

> This level of self-destruction exists because for the first time there are now no longer viable institutions and structures in black America that can effectively transmit values such as hope, virtue, sacrifice, risk, and putting the needs of others higher or alongside one's own needs. In the past we've seen black colleges in which every Sunday they were forced to sit in those pews and Benjamin Mays would get up and say, "You must give service to the race," reminding these black, petit-bourgeois students that even as they went out into the world they had a cause, an obligation and a duty to do something beyond simply their own self-interest. What they did may have been narrow, myopic, and shortsighted, but the point is they had an institution that was transmitting that value. And it is not just the black school. We can talk about the black

church, fraternities, and whole hosts of other institutions in black civil society. We no longer have these to the degree we did in the past, and they are being eroded slowly but surely. This is what is most frightening. This is why we get the exponential increase in black suicides between eighteen and thirty-five, unprecedented in black history. This is why we get escalating black homicides in which you get some of the most cold-hearted, mean-spirited dispositions and attitudes displayed by black people against other black people as well as nonblacks. It is a breakdown in the moral fabric. ([1992]: 196)

I noted earlier that central to West's prophetic pragmatism is an ethic of love. I interpret West's conception of love to mean both a self-regarding and an other-regarding disposition in the individual. It is such a disposition that he expects the cultural apparatus to help cultivate in black youths. The need for cultivating such a disposition in the individual can easily be seen once it is realized that a condition of (say) my esteeming or showing respect toward others is that I respect or esteem myself. If I have a sense of self-worth, then I am more likely to value the person of others than if I do not. Conversely, if I lack a sense of self-worth then, similarly, I would devalue others. From this psychological point of view, an important remedy to the nihilistic threat to black America is to imbibe self-love, in the sense of self-esteem, in the youths. In this regard, I believe that, on the socio-psychological level, the recommendation West puts forward to meet the threat of nihilism among black youths cannot but be effective.

To some extent, West's recommendation compares with Jesse Jackson's well-known exhortation to black youths to value themselves, usually expressed in the chant, "I am somebody." This exhortation is Jackson's own attempt at instilling a sense of self-worth in the youths. Of course, there are significant differences between West's prophetic pragmatism and Jackson's endeavor in the search for a solution to the existential crisis in the black community. For example, West's prophetic pragmatism sees the importance of the traditional black cultural institutions in helping to delimit if not eliminate the threat to black survival. Furthermore, West presents a challenge to all forms of black leadership, but especially the political and intellectual, to engage the crisis. (I am not aware that Jackson, besides founding the civic organization Operation PUSH and his televisual exhortations, confronts the crisis with a sophisticated strategy for effecting profound long-term psychological change in the youth.)

On the politico-economical level, however, prophetic pragmatism is found wanting in the solution it proposes to the nihilistic threat to black America. To see this, recall that West sees the cause of the crisis as essentially economic. Accordingly, he reasons (correctly) that eliminating the cause is indeed eliminating the crisis itself. Unfortunately, however, West puts undue emphasis on coalition politics as the only viable source of eliminating the (economic) cause of the crisis. For one thing, critics may charge that West is naively optimistic in relying on such transracial coalitions to resolve the crisis in the black community. They may cite the current attempt by the dominant (white) race, white males in particular, and in complicity with some black conservatives, to dismantle the token gestures of the sixties, in the form of affirmative action programmes, that have served to redress some historical wrongdoings. In light of such endeavor, often referred to as "the angry white male syndrome," is it realistic to hope that the crisis in the black community will be resolved by a transracial alliance?

Besides, there is an inherent politicking in coalition groups, politicking of which West is fully aware, as he indicates elsewhere, but which he seems to gloss over in his treatment of the nihilistic crisis. Consider West's following observation in a discussion in which he elaborates some of the difficulties confronting black prophetic practices—or activities such as trade unionist, feminist, populist, socialist and political of whatever stripe—that attempt to bring to the center of American liberal discourse the concerns of black people:

> The design and operation of the American social system requires that this quest for democracy and self-realization be channeled into unfair competitive circumstances such that opportunistic results are unavoidable... *This "delivery prerequisite" usually forces even prophetic critics and actions to adopt opportunistic strategies and tactics in order to justify themselves to a disadvantaged and downtrodden constituency* ([1988]: 42; emphasis added).

I submit that West's observation in this passage accurately reflects his awareness of the difficulties inherent in race-transcendent strategies. In my view, these difficulties impose a severe constraint on his prophetic pragmatism especially in its attempt to address the nihilistic crisis under consideration.

The thrust of my criticism, then, is that simply because one is in a coalition does not mean that one necessarily wields power to address one's concerns. One may lack stature and hence influence within the coalition. Alternatively put, one may indeed be a partner in a coalition, but an *unequal* partner (see also E. Lott). And given such a situation, one always has to depend on the goodwill and generosity of other members in the coalition for support. As this is undoubtedly the case concerning blacks in such coalitions, West's undue emphasis on coalition politics to eliminate the economic cause of the nihilistic threat therefore at best is naive, especially since such goodwill has not been forthcoming lately.

Second, it can also be argued that such emphasis as West puts on race-transcending relations to meet a crisis that is peculiar to the black community smacks of a dependency syndrome. Granted, America is diverse and the various groups cannot live an atomistic existence. On the other hand, blacks have for too long been too dependent on governments and others for economic uplift in terms of providing investments in their communities. The consequence of such dependency is that, except only recently, politicians have either taken the black vote for

259

JOHNSON

granted or have simply dismissed it as inconsequential to the whole political process. It may be suggested, therefore, that perhaps if blacks, especially middle-class blacks, began to view themselves in entrepreneurial rather than consumerist terms, and act accordingly, they will gain the economic clout that invariably translates into political power. The argument here, in sum, is not that coalition politics is to be dismissed *per se*; rather, it is that blacks need not be overly dependent on the good-will of other races to solve a problem that, at least for now, is acknowledged to be peculiar to the black race in America.

The criticism in the above argument is all the more pertinent considering that even as West argues for the formation of race-transcending coalitions in order to exert pressure on the politico-economic structures so as to meet the economic issue that underlies the nihilism in black America, he fails to offer a protracted discussion on the need for economic leadership in the black community by blacks while correctly denouncing the consumerism of the black middle class. Surely, such leadership is just as critical to ameliorating the challenges, not the least of which is the nihilism being discussed, as is political and moral leadership.

To be sure, West's motivation for promoting coalition politics is the recognition that the underclass problem cuts across race and gender lines; therefore to meet it effectively requires that liberals from all races band together to exert pressure on the political and economic structures of the society. But, then, the nihilistic threat to black America is distinct and different from, even though related to, the problems confronting the underclass. To the extent that the underclass problem is transracial, coalition politics may be necessary for its resolution. However, a similar necessity cannot be claimed for the involvement of such politics in resolving the black nihilistic problem on pain of begging the question. Quite the contrary, the very fact that the nihilistic problem is peculiar to blacks would seem to suggest, if anything, that coalition politics may only be contingently relevant to its resolution. If I am correct, then West should not have emphasized coalition politics as he does in the removal of the economic cause of the black nihilistic crisis. Instead, his call for transracial coalitions should have been subordinate to race-based solutions.

On balance, then, prophetic pragmatism has advanced some very good suggestions on how to meet the nihilistic crisis in black America especially on the socio-psychological (including the moral) level. However, on the politico-economic level, the position is found wanting because of the greater emphasis that West places on coalition politics over race-based solutions to the problem.

CONCLUSION

My aim in the present study has been to establish a relation between Cornel West's existentialist concern about the black nihilistic threat and his prophetic pragmatism. To that end, I have situated West's philosophy within the pragmatist tradition while highlighting his own version of pragmatism, namely, prophetic pragmatism. I have shown that prophetic pragmatism is essentially concerned with social and cultural criticism with a strong moral emphasis. Against this background, I have demonstrated that West, drawing upon his philosophical orientation as a Deweyan pragmatist and viewing himself as a social and cultural critic, engages some of the burning issues of contemporary America as a spiritual vocation and with moral conviction. One such issue that he engages is the nihilistic threat to black America. The upshot of my discussion is that West's proposed solution to this existentialist crisis in the black community, particularly among black youths, though largely commendable, betrays a serious limitation because of the undue emphasis that he puts on coalition politics over race-based solutions to the problem.

NOTES

1 I thank Tina Johnson and George Carew for helpful comments on earlier versions of this paper.

2 For discussions of Cornel West's conception of pragmatism, among other things, and West's replies to his critics see, e.g., Kolenda; Spelman; Corrington; and Gooding-Williams (1991–2).

3 Besides these two philosophical movements which had reigned in Europe in the eighteenth century, in the nineteenth century there was Hegelian idealism in Germany, which spilled over into England and had engaged philosophers such as F.H. Bradley and J.E. McTaggart. In America, a leading proponent of idealism was Josiah Royce. Essentially, idealism is concerned with giving an account of the nature of reality.

4 All references are to West unless otherwise noted.

5 West's sympathy with Dewey could be seen in the context of his own political strategy of forming alliances and coalitions in order to address social issues. But as will be seen later, there are severe limitations on such a strategy. I take up this issue in my discussion of West's proposed solution to the afflictions of the black underclass later in this essay.

6 Elsewhere, West describes prophetic pragmatism as an attempt to revise "Emerson's concerns with power, provocation, and personality in light of Dewey's stress on historical consciousness and Du Bois' focus on the plight of the wretched of the earth" ([1989]: 212).

7 West's characterization of the problem confronting black youths, especially in the urban centers, as nihilistic has been challenged by Eric Lott (1994).

PSYCHOLOGICAL VIOLENCE, PHYSICAL VIOLENCE, AND RACIAL OPPRESSION

Howard McGary

STRONG PACIFISTS deny that violence is ever necessary in human affairs. Gandhi and Martin L. King, Jr. are seen as famous proponents of this position (Ansbro [1983]). Although Gandhi and King are well respected, most Americans reject the strong pacifist position. Most Americans believe that violence, under certain conditions, has its place. Americans disagree, however, over when it is morally appropriate to use violence in human affairs.

Violence for many theorists is evil and is only justified as a means to achieve some extremely important end. To do violence to someone is to injure that person, but persons can be injured in two basic ways: we can injure someone by physically abusing that person and we can injure someone by causing that person's psychological distress. Although Americans recognize both kinds of violence or injury, physical violence, as a response to injustice or wrongdoing is thought to require a stronger justification than the commission of an act that causes psychological violence. Psychological violence often results from the misuse of others through the manipulation of their emotions and feelings.

Even people who are weary of violence to achieve good ends are willing to accept violence if it is the only means to stop even greater physical violence. But many of these people reject using physical violence to halt psychological violence when it is the only means for doing so. Of course, we could debate whether physical violence is the only means available, in particular cases, but for the purposes of this paper, we shall assume that this is the case. If this is the case, are there moral reasons for opposing the use of physical violence to prevent psychological violence? I wish to explore this question in the context of the debate over what is morally appropriate in the battle to eliminate racial oppression. Our concern will be with the moral appropriateness of the use of physical violence to thwart psychological violence, not the tactics and the political wisdom of such use.

Let us begin to examine this question by considering the following hypothetical case: suppose large numbers of innocent African Americans are randomly seized by government authorities and hauled off to concentration camps. Would these African Americans or persons acting in their behalf be justified in using physical violence if nonviolent means have been tried and failed? Most people would think so. We tend to think that physical violence is justified as a kind of self-defense against violence provided that this self-defensive violence is proportionate in kind, unavoidable, and the threat that provokes the violence is imminent. In enumerating these conditions, I am not claiming that there is total agreement about the correct theory of self-defense, but only that most theorists believe physical violence can be used to prevent physical violence when the above conditions obtain.

What about the use of physical violence to prevent psychological violence caused by oppression? Many Americans cannot answer this question in the affirmative. Why is this so? Perhaps an important part of the answer lies in our lack of understanding about the serious detrimental consequences of psychological harms. Many people tend to underestimate their seriousness. These people are reluctant to justify physical violence to prevent what they take to be questionable harms. But even some of the people who acknowledge the severity of psychological harms are relevant to endorse the use of physical violence to prevent psychological violence. They question whether the conditions of proportionality, avoidability, and imminent danger are satisfied when we combat psychological violence with physical violence.

Juries, for example, have found it extremely difficult to acquit women who use self-defense to justify their use of physical violence against a psychologically (mentally) abusive husband. Jurors who have been interviewed in such cases often believe that the avoidability and imminent danger conditions have not been satisfied. In a number of cases, I think they are wrong in reaching this conclusion, but saying why they are wrong is no simple matter. The jurors rightfully draw a distinction in these cases between a woman who uses physical violence against a mentally abusive husband because of temporary insanity brought on by mental abuse and a self-defense plea. They recognize that it would be wrong to equate a temporary insanity plea with a self-defense plea. Logically speaking, a woman may use physical violence against a psychologically abusive husband without being insane or irrational. But given the circumstances of many abused women, the wherewithal and avenues of action available to these women are very circumscribed. So, in many cases, their violent response to abuse is rational given their circumscribed circumstances (see Bell [1993]).

Now I would like to return to the issue of racial oppression and the use of physical violence. In paper on violence and terrorism, the philosopher Kai Nielsen ask his readers to consider the following hypothetical case:

> Suppose that the members of a small, impoverished, ill-educated ethnic minority in some democratic society are treated as second-class citizens. They are grossly discriminated against in educational opportunities and jobs, segregated in specific and undesirable parts of the country, and not allowed to marry people from other ethnic groups or to mix socially with them. For years they have pleaded and argued their case but to no avail. Moreover, working through the courts has always been a dead end, and their desperate and despairing turn to nonviolent civil disobedience has been tolerated—as the powerful and arrogant can tolerate it—but utterly ignored. Their demonstrations have not been met with violence but, rather, have simply been on violently contained and then effectively ignored. And finally suppose this small, weak and desperately impoverished minority has no effective way of emigrating. (440)

Nielsen wonders whether members of this group are entitled to use violence to protect their human rights? Nielsen concludes that they are and that the telling reasons against their doing so are prudential and not moral. Is he right? Nielsen describes a case where a group of people are clearly oppressed, but it is not the case that the oppressors have used physical violence to oppress this group. Nonetheless, he rightfully concludes that the denial of important human rights can warrant self-defensive violence.

The human right that Nielsen focuses on is the right to equal opportunity. The denial of the right to equal opportunity is quite serious and according to Nielsen, may justify physical violence even when physical violence is not used to deny a group equal opportunities. Nielsen seems to believe that members of this group cannot avoid the harm caused to them and that the harm is so serious and direct to warrant the self-defensive physical violence.

But some people may be unconvinced that physical violence is the proper response is such cases because the very fact that this group lives in a democratic society means that their condition, at least in theory, can be addressed through democratic nonviolent means. The group should be patient and pursue all of the nonviolent means for changing their condition. Why is this not a correct response?

I think it fails because such a response does not appreciate the severe negative consequences that result from a denial of basic human rights. Nielsen's case focuses on a lack of opportunities, but by implication it points out that members of this group are not seen as moral equals. The kind of treatment described in Nielsen's example serves to undermine, damage, and destroy a person's sense of self. W.E.B. Du Bois spoke eloquently to what happens to the psyche of black people or any similarly oppressed people when they are not seen or treated as moral equals by the dominant society (see Du Bois[1969]). Frantz Fanon, the celebrated psychiatrist and revolutionary, graphically explains how a system of racial oppression constitutes psychological violence against the oppressed (Fanon [1967a]; [1968]). Both Du Bois and Fanon realized that a prolonged denial of a person's right as a human being to equal concern and respect leads to a depreciation of self and quite possibly to the destruction of the moral self. So in response to those who urge patience and tolerance, these virtues may come at too great a cost; namely, a loss of self (McGary [1992–93]: 283–5).

Earlier I claimed that there is a strong tendency to devalue the impact of psychological harm when it comes to the abuse of women. I also contend that this is the case with African Americans. There is plenty of evidence that shows that many whites ignore or underestimate the harms inflicted on African Americans (Hochschild and Herk [1990]: 310–6). Many of these harms have been physical, but there have also been serious and far-reaching psychological harms that accompany the denial of some basic human rights. These psychological harms, in some cases, are more damaging than physical harms. If this is true, then physical violence maybe a morally appropriate response to psychological violence.

If we assume that we can use physical violence to thwart physical violence under the conditions described above, then is it reasonable to think that serious psychological violence, under certain conditions, can warrant the use of physical violence? In the case of racial oppression in the United States, the harms that African Americans experienced were (and some would say still are) unavoidable because a system of racial oppression is constructed in ways that makes it next to impossible for oppressed groups to escape its damaging effects (McGary [1992–93]: 285–90). The use of physical violence to defend oneself against psychological harm in a racially oppressive system may be proportional and perhaps can be seen as such when we fully appreciate the serious destructive effects of a system of racial oppression. The threat of harm in such a system might be imminent because it is always present and pervasive, and it continues to get worse if not addressed.

I shall examine each of these conditions for when violence can be seen as self-defense in the context of racial oppression against African Americans. Hopefully, by doing so, I can shed some light on whether psychological violence brought on by a system of racial oppression can justify the use of physical violence by those who are oppressed by such a system. However, before I begin this examination, I will first explain why self-defense is the issue. One might think that a very psychologically oppressive system might cause its victims to be insane and thus their acts of violence are not acts of self-defense but merely the reactions of people who suffer from a form of socially induced mental illness.

For example, in the Colin Ferguson case in New York (the African-American male who was convicted of killing and wounding a number of people on the Long Island Railroad), Ferguson's original attorneys (before Ferguson decided to serve as his own attorney) proffered the so-called "black rage" defense. Drawing on the work of Cobbs and Grier on black rage (1969), they argued that Ferguson was not legally responsible for his conduct because he was acting out of compulsion brought on by the consuming nature of white racism. This is clearly a controversial claim. I will not discuss the merits of this claim here. I mention it only to point out one of the ways people have attempted to mitigate or excuse violent behavior associated with racial oppression.

The black rage defense, I think, should be distinguished from the classic defense of violence advanced by Frantz Fanon (See Fanon [1968]). Fanon argued that the Algerian native suffered from what he called "colonial neurosis." This neurosis resulted from Algerian peasants being treated as less than human by their French colonizers. This system of colonization caused the peasants to come to see themselves a less than human and thus not the moral equals of their colonizers. Fanon boldly asserted that violence was a necessary means for eliminating this neurosis. In a frequently quoted passage he wrote:

267

> At the level of individuals, violence is a cleansing force, it frees the colonized from his inferiority complex and from his despair and inaction; it makes him fearless and restores his self-respect. (Fanon [1968]: 94)

Fanon goes on to say:

> ...colonialism is not a thinking machine, nor a body endorsed with reasoning faculties. It is violence in its natural state and will only yield when confronted with greater violence. (Fanon [1968]: 61)

and

> Violence alone, violence committed by the people, violence *organized and education by its leaders*, make it possible for the masses to understand social truths and gives the key to them (Fanon [1968]: 147).

Clearly Fanon viewed revolutionary violence by the Algerian peasants as a cleansing force. For Fanon, it was the only way the colonialized peasant could

McGARY

restore his moral equality and self-respect. But, unfortunately, Fanon's definition of revolutionary violence is tautological in nature (Caute [1970]). He says that an action is revolutionary violence only if it rejuvenates and purifies the actor. This definition is not very helpful in our attempt to distinguish political or revolutionary violence from mere acts of violence. It is also unclear whether Fanon is offering a general theory of violence or whether he is only making contingent claims about the role of violence in the Algerian context. (I tend to think that the latter interpretation is probably what Fanon had in mind but, I will not argue for that here. However, a recent work by Lewis Gordon offers a thoughtful development of that issue[see Gordon (1995b)]. If we assume that this interpretation is correct, then colonial neurosis [which can only be cured by political violence] is specific to the Algerian situation.)

Fanon's views on the necessity of violence in the Algerian colonial context are intriguing, but very different from the black-rage defense offered in behalf of Colin Ferguson. According to the black-rage defense, Ferguson was driven by racism to a point where he snapped. He was, for all practical purposes, insane. However, for Fanon, the peasant who cures his colonial neurosis through an act of political violence makes a choice to regain his humanity through an act of political violence. The peasant is defending his humanity. So it is an act of self-defense for Fanon, not the compulsive behavior of an insane person.

I would like to make it clear that I am not claiming, as Frantz Fanon did, that physical violence is always necessary for freeing those who suffer from a system of racial oppression, but only that it may be morally permissible, under certain conditions, even when the system is not maintained through the use of physical violence. But in order to make such a view plausible we need to examine closely the conditions of valid claims to self-defense: avoidability, imminence, and proportionality.

A legitimate act of self-defense is not a preemptive strike against a dreaded aggressor or an act of retaliation against a successful aggressor. In the words of the legal scholar, George Fletcher, "self-defense must be neither too soon or too late" ([1988]: 20). In the case of an extremely racially oppressive system, the victims of this oppression cannot have the intention to act violently because they assume that some harmful event could happen when the event is not imminent. Nor can they have the intention of harming or punishing the aggressor if their action is to qualify as self-defense. The intention of the agent must be to thwart the assault or attack and not to harm the victim per se ([1988]: 19).

The case we are discussing is also complicated by the fact that we are talking about a group of people, namely African Americans. Given that our focus is a group, if self-defense is legitimate then it must be because each member of the group has acted with the appropriate intentions or that a subset of the group has the authority to act for the group. For example, a board of directors can have the legal and moral authority to act for an organization. But even if the subset is autho-

268

rized to act on behalf of the group, this subset must act with the appropriate intentions.

Let us now turn to the three conditions that are thought to be necessary and sufficient for an act of self-defense.

Avoidability

This condition requires that an actor not use violence or deadly force against someone who poses a threat to them if there is some other way to avoid the imminent harm without doing so. This requirement is most often understood in terms of the alternatives or lack of alternatives available to the actor. For example, if you threaten me with bodily harm, and I can avoid the harm by running away, I should do so. In such a case, if I choose to shoot you rather than run away, then I have failed to satisfy the avoidability condition on self-defense.

In our example involving an unyielding system of racial discrimination, the oppressed group cannot simply turn to the political process for relief because they are a discrete, despised minority in a majority-rule democracy. But what if there is a political mechanism that will allow these oppressed groups to mitigate the tyranny of the majority in democratic society? Perhaps proposals like the ones offered by Lani Guinier in her book, *The Tyranny of the Majority*, can make the system more responsive to the rights and interests of all, including a despised minority.

Guinier recommends the following: (1) Cumulative voting: "Voters get the same number of seats or options as to vote for, and they can then distribute their votes in combination to reflect their preferences. Like-minded voters can form a solid block, or instead form strategic cross-racial coalitions to gain mutual benefits" (Guinier: 15). (2) Race-Conscious Districting: legislative districts are constructed in a way such that certain groups who have historically not had their interests fairly represented can do so. It makes it possible for members of a discreet minority to elect representatives who are members of their group or to elect candidates that articulate their interests. Districts are based upon ensuring equal opportunity rather than geography (Guinier: 135). Guinier believes that when both of these proposals are combined together, we can achieve political procedures that are fair to all. In theory proposals like the ones offered by Guinier are instructive, and might solve the problem, but in reality her proposals have been met with strong opposition by some very powerful members of the majority. It is doubtful that her proposals in the present political climate will become law. The avoidability condition should focus on real alternatives, not alternatives that are just in theory possible.

Of course, Guinier's proposals are not the only ones offered to eliminate racial oppression. A frequent recommendation offered by some members of the majority is the proposal "love it or leave it." A generous interpretation of this recommendation is that the minority citizens are free to emigrate to other countries if they find this system so oppressive. Putting aside that this response is often just a

269

McGARY

polite way of expressing racial animosity, it fails to appreciate that the avoidability condition only requires people to take reasonable and practical alternatives that are available to them.

It is unreasonable and impractical to expect people with modest means who have lived all of their lives in this country to move to a foreign country where they have few, if any, prospects for securing a livelihood. Of course, wealthy African Americans might find this option more realistic, but wealthy African Americans are less likely to need to take such drastic measure because they are in a better position to ward off the damaging effects of systematic racial discrimination. The idea that the victims of racial oppression can eliminate this oppression by leaving the society or by forming their own separate communities within American society is not new. The reasonableness of these proposals have been vigorously debated for hundreds of years (McGary [1983]).

Whether an alternative open to the actor is reasonable is crucial in deciding whether or not the avoidability condition has been satisfied (Gillespie [1989]: 93). Is there some reasonable alternative to the use of physical violence to combat prolonged systematic racism? If the answer is yes, then morality would require that such an alternative be adopted. However, a reasonableness criteria is always culturally specific. Conduct that might be judged to be reasonable in one culture would not be so judged in a radically different culture. There are numerous examples that illustrate this point.

Certain legal scholars have also argued that what counts as reasonable can also be influenced by things like the gender of the actors. Cynthia K. Gillespie has pointed out that the courts still rely on "the reasonable man test." This is a standard for measuring what a reasonable person in like circumstances would do. But Gillespie argues that this test is unfair to women because it imposes, "a masculine standard against which to measure a woman's behavior" (Gillespie [1989]: 99). Gillespie's point is what the typical man might view as threatening is different from the typical woman given the norms in our society and the ways in which men and women are socialized. She argues that we need a culturally enlightened and gender sensitive standard for judging what is reasonable behavior (Gillespie [1989]: 100–22).

In a similar vein, scholars have argued that the experiences of black and white Americans are so different that generalizations based upon the experiences of the typical white American may not apply to the typical black American (Hochschild and Herk 1990). If this is so, what might be reasonable for a person who has experienced the alienation of the American-American experience might be different from a white person from the same economic background (see McGary [1992–93]). Therefore where physical violence might be viewed as unreasonable by mainstream white America, it might be viewed as clearly reasonable by African Americans who have experienced acute and prolonged alienation and racial oppression.

Imminent Danger

The word imminent means appearing as if about to happen, impending, menacing, and threatening. As a condition of justified self-defense, the imminent danger condition requires that an assault must be about to happen if a person is justified in using violence against his attacker. An apparent problem with claiming that a person can use violence as a form of self-defense against a pervasive system of racial discrimination is the identity of the source of the assault. In such a case, who qualifies as the agents of harms?

With more oppressive systems different people occupy varied roles. Some may be the architects of harm, some may execute the harmful acts, others may condone and encourage the harm, and some may be bystanders. Does the existence of these varied roles mean that self-defensive violence can never be justified in such cases?

I do not think so. Clearly the mere fact that people occupy different roles in an oppressive system does not mean that the victim of this oppression cannot identify the various sources of the assault. Nor does it imply that the source of the assault is not apparent, menacing or threatening. I reject the contention that prolonged oppressive institutions can operate without the existence of faulty agents. The idea that a pervasive system of racial oppression can be comprised of totally innocent persons is a bit farfetched. This is not to deny that it may be extremely difficulty in some cases to identify those who have acted in wrongful ways, but in theory and practice such identifications are possible.

The imminent danger condition is closely connected with the avoidability condition, but they are logically distinct. The close connection between the two conditions often means that when one condition is satisfied, so is the other condition. If it is true that a pervasive system of racial oppression is unavoidable for its victims, then there is a very good chance the dangers that these victims confront are imminent.

Proportionality

The proportionality condition requires that the self-defensive act must be only enough to stop or prevent the assault. For instance, you should not kill an aggressor when wounding him would stop the assault. The proportionality condition requires that we only use the minimal force necessary to stop or prevent an assault. This condition demands that we weigh the competing interests of the potential victim as well as the aggressor.

Given this condition, if the self-defense plea is used to justify the use of physical violence in our racial oppression case, then physical violence used to thwart the assault must be proportional to psychological violence used against the victims. Since the proportionality condition requires that we balance the interests of the victims as well as the aggressors, one might conclude that we can't properly balance these interests because we are dealing with apples and oranges. However, this belief is based upon the erroneous assumption that there is no adequate way to

271

McGARY

compare psychological and physical harms. But if we only reflect for a moment, we will see that this is a mistake. We often make such comparisons. For example, we judge that the pain caused by the death of a loved one is far less harmful than a serious cut on our finger. And many people would prefer to experience some physical harm than to be rejected by a love interest.

Psychological harms are real and people can cause them. Furthermore, these harms can be compared or balanced against physical harms. To claim otherwise is to raise a red herring. Acts of violence committed by members of a group who have experienced prolonged and acute systematic discrimination may be justifiable as a kind of self-defense, provided that their conduct satisfies the three conditions of justified self-defense.

Hopefully, in a preliminary way, I have offered some good reasons for thinking that these conditions can be satisfied. I am not arguing for violence. My task was to show that if violence can be justified on grounds of self-defense, then a pervasive system of racial oppression that causes serious psychological harms to its victims could warrant the use of physical violence.

THE FIGHT WITH COVEY

Bernard R. Boxill

chapter 21

I

FREDERICK DOUGLASS' reflections on the results of his fight with Covey are something of a puzzle. In his *Narrative of the Life of Frederick Douglass* he claims that the "battle with Mr. Covey" was the "turning-point" in his life as a slave, "recalled" his "departed self-confidence" and "inspired" him with "a determination to be free" ([1988]: 104).[1] This was in 1845. Yet until at least 1849 he was a faithful Garrisonian pacifist warning of the counterproductive consequences of violent slave resistance and calling instead for the peaceful conversion of the slaveholders. Did he not sense the tension between this pacifist stance and his celebration of the psychological and moral consequences of fighting Covey?

Of course after 1849 Douglass became an uncompromising advocate of slave resistance. But this still leaves it a mystery why he was ever a pacifist, given his account of the benefits he gained from resistance. One explanation of his change from pacifist to advocate of violent slave resistance is that while he was always clear that the slaves had a right to resist their masters violently, before 1849 he warned against violent slave resistance because he believed it would delay the abolition of slavery and have bad consequences overall: after 1849 he changed his mind and began urging violent slave resistance because he believed it would hasten the end of slavery. This explanation is suggested by some of Douglass' own remarks on violence and pacifism. In 1847, for example, he declared that he would "suffer rather than do any action of violence—rather than that the glorious day of liberty might be postponed" ([1950]: vol. 1; 277). And, when he began urging violent slave resistance in the 1850's he did so on the ground that it was both right and wise, right because it was justified by the right of self-defense, and wise because it would have the good consequence of discrediting the public's favorite justification of slavery, and in this way help to end slavery ([1950]: vol. 2; 284–9). But this explanation of Douglass' change from pacifist to advocate of violent resistance is not altogether satisfactory. In his account of his fight with Covey in the *Narrative*, Douglass extols the moral and psychological benefits he gained as a result of defending himself, claiming, in particular, that it inspired him with a "determination to be free" ([1988]: 104). Since this determination helped Douglass to win his freedom, and he gained it from fighting Covey, he should not have worried that slave resistance would "postpone" the day of liberty.

It may be argued that Douglass refrained from generalizing from his experience because he believed that his experience was exceptional and that he had gained the benefits of resistance only because of the unusual educational opportunities he had enjoyed while a slave. But his arguments runs into difficulties. It is true that Douglass' educational achievements were unusual for a slave. He had learned to read and write, and he had studied the dialogues and speeches against slavery in *The Columbian Orator* by the time that he fell into Covey's hands. And it is also true that his education informed and increased his hatred of slavery. But he never cited his education as any part of the reason why resistance was beneficial for him. And he never suggested that it was his education that enabled him to see the injustice of slavery. On the contrary, he often insisted that he was aware of the injustice of slavery before consulting any books or laws or authorities (see, e.g., [1993]: 50, 62, 138). Nor did he ever suggest that he was different from other slaves in this respect. He believed that all slaves came naturally to the conviction that they should be free. That was why the slaveholders tried to keep them from learning how to read and write, and from getting an education. Lack of book learning would not prevent the slaves from coming to believe that they should be free, but it would at least prevent them from knowing how to free themselves, and could therefore make them despair of ever gaining their freedom. The slaves' natural conviction that they should be free was also the reason why the slaveholders treated them so cruelly (e.g., [1950]: vol. 1; 157; [1993]: 128–33).

274

BOXILL

These considerations lead me to believe that Douglass was willing to suppose that slaves in general would gain the benefits from resistance that he gained. But, until 1849, he failed to endorse slave resistance because he had become convinced, by the arguments of William Lloyd Garrison and others of Garrison's school, that nonviolent moral suasion was *morally* preferable to slave resistance as a means to freeing the slaves. As he wrote in a letter to Francis Jackson in 1846, emphasizing the advantages of nonviolent moral suasion, "Thank God liberty is no longer to be contended for and gained by instruments of death. A higher, a nobler, a mightier than carnal weapon is placed into our hands—one which hurls defiance at all the improvements of carnal warfare. It is the righteous appeal to the understanding and the hear…" ([1950] vol. 1; 136).

This was a reasonable position. Other things equal, the means that can reach its end without bloodshed is morally preferable to the means that requires or is likely to involve bloodshed. Further, even if violent slaves resistance was morally defensible as a form of justifiable self-defense, moral suasion was not only morally defensible, but also, its advocates claimed, likely to end slavery by converting the slaveholders to the truth, and by making them into good citizens. If it could deliver what it promised, moral suasion would have more good consequences than slave resistance, which seemed likely to leave the slaveholders unregenerate, even if it forced them to give up their slaves.

As events unfolded, however, moral suasion failed both to free the slaves and to reform the slaveholders. Indeed it seemed to have the opposite effect for following the period when it was most vigorously pursued, the slaveholders were emboldened to propose, and managed to push through, the infamous Fugitive Slave Law of 1850. Frustrated by the ineffectiveness of nonviolent moral suasion, Douglass turned to endorsing slave uprisings. But then he came to a further and more radical conclusion: it was not only that violent slave resistance was both morally defensible, and likely to be more effective in ending slavery than nonviolent moral suasion. Violent slave resistance was also capable of producing the moral benefits that nonviolent moral suasion had promised, but failed to deliver—moral reform of slaveholders.[2] And it was not only the slavemasters who would benefit morally from slave resistance. The slave was also likely to grow in self-respect if he resisted his master. Of course, Douglass had already claimed in 1845 that he had benefitted morally from fighting Covey. After 1850, however, when he became converted to slave resistance, his remarks broadened and hardened. Before 1850 he had not argued that the slave had to resist to gain his self-respect. After 1850, however, he began to make precisely that claim.

Evidence for this development of Douglass' views are the striking additions to the account of the fight with Covey in the *Narrative* that Douglass made in his two subsequent autobiographies, *My Bondage and My Freedom*, first published in 1855, and *The Life and Times of Frederick Douglass*, first published in 1893. It is only in the

THE FIGHT WITH COVEY

two later books, for example, that Douglass concludes his acccount of the fight with Covey with the lines from Byron,

> Hereditary bondman, know ye not
> Who would be free, themselves must strike the blow?

Byron did not intend to make the palpably false claim that the bondman would not be free of physical constraints unless he resisted his enslaver. He meant, and Douglass took him to mean, that the bondman would not be free of mental constraints, that he would not know himself to the moral equal of others, unless he resisted his enslaver. And this view of the relation between self-defense and self-respect informed Douglass' discussion of his fight with Covey in the two later autobiographies. For example, in *My Bondage and My Freedom* Douglass noted in a manner similar to the *Narrative* that the fight with Covey had renewed his determination to be free. But then he added—a point not in the *Narrative*—that the fight had recalled to life his "crushed self-respect," and then appended this further comment: "A man, without force, is without the essential dignity of humanity. Human nature is so constituted that it cannot honor a helpless man, although it can pity him; and even this it cannot do long, if the signs of power do not arise" ([1969]: 247). Since these claims reappear verbatim in *The Life and Times of Frederick Douglass* published forty years later, we are safe in assuming that Douglass meant them to be taken seriously. The general and uncompromising claim that human nature *cannot* honor a person without power or force implies that Douglass was expressing the view that human beings, including presumably slaves, cannot honor themselves unless they possess power or force. Taken in isolation this can perhaps be read to mean that the slave need only be capable of defending himself against his master—not that he must actually do so—to be able to honor himself. I will undertake a detailed discussion of the point presently. For now, I note that Douglass broached it right after claiming that he had regained his self-respect from actually resisting Covey; that, and the fact that the lines he quoted from Byron say that the bondman "Must" strike the blow, strongly suggest that Douglass meant that the power or force necessary to gain self-respect was not merely a capacity to defend oneself, but also a willingness to do so.

The analysis of Douglass' account of the results of his fight with Covey that follows focuses on what I take to be the more mature presentation in *My Bondage and My Freedom* and in *The Life and Times of Frederick Douglass*. It will also rely to some extent on his claim that violent slave resistance could help to reform the slaveholders.

II

According to Douglass, one of the results of his fight with Covey was that he "had reached the point, at which I *was not afraid to die*" ([1969]: 247; emphasis in original). Douglass did not mean that Covey's mistreatment had made him weary of life, for then he should have attempted suicide instead of fighting Covey. His meaning is revealed by the immediately preceding comment that he "was not longer a coward trembling under the frown of a brother worm of the dust…" (Ibid). Since a coward fails to act as he ought to because he is afraid, and Douglass had just defended himself against Covey, I conclude that at least part of what Douglass meant by the claim that he had reached the point at which he was not afraid to die was that he had reached the point at which he would no longer fail to do his duty to defend himself because he was afraid to die. But we need to inquire more closely into the nature of the duty of self-defense than this discussion implies.

Douglass often suggested that slaves ought to be willing to imperil their lives for their freedom (e.g., [1950]: vol. 2; 287, 534). This argument suggests consequentialist considerations for resistance based on a nice weighing of the risks of attempts to escape against the great value of freedom. The slave should not throw away his life in a predictably vain attempt to gain freedom; life is too precious to justify that. Neither on the other hand should the slave play it altogether safe and refuse to take any chances to be free; freedom is too valuable for that. The slave should bide his time, but when the appropriate opportunity arises to gain his freedom he ought to seize it even if it was not a sure thing; he ought to be willing to imperil his life for his freedom. And in his two attempts to escape Douglass showed his allegiance to that argument, giving vivid accounts of how he canvassed and weighed the risks these attempts to escape involved, but he did not appeal to it when he made the case for duty of self-defense under discussion (e.g., [1969]: 281–90) When he defended himself against Covey he was not imperiling his life for his liberty. He was not trying to escape. He was simply defending himself from physical abuse. "I had brought my mind to the firm resolve," he notes, "to obey every order, however unreasonable, if it were possible, and, if Mr. Covey should then undertake to beat me, to defend and protect myself to the best of my ability" ([1969]: 241). It is true that Douglass arguably won his freedom as a result of the determination to be free that he gained from fighting Covey. But, he could not have foreseen that fighting Covey would result in such a determination, and consequently could not have fought Covey in order to acquire it.

If Douglass' fight with Covey was not a calculated periling of his life to gain his liberty, it was equally not a calculated periling of his life to put an end to his physical abuse. It is true that one of the results of the fight was that he was never beaten by a master again. From the time of the fight, Douglass reports, "I was never fairly whipped" ([1969]: 247). This was because he came to have the reputation of being a slave who could only be whipped if he was also killed ([1988]: 105). But, of course, Douglass had not anticipated this result when he undertook to fight Covey and consequently could not have fought Covey in order to gain it. It was not even the case that Douglass resisted Covey in order to avoid being whipped on that particular occasion. This would be a plausible possibility if he had antici-

277

BOXILL

pated *winning* the fight with Covey, or if he had even calculated his chances of doing so. But he never reports that he engaged in such forecasts or calculations on that occasion.

The other consequentialist consideration for slave resistance that Douglass often suggested—that such resistance would help establish the "manhood" of the race by wiping out the reproach that blacks were unwilling to suffer and sacrifice for their liberty and were therefore fit for slavery—is even less applicable to his reasons for fighting Covey. Douglass was not trying to impress Covey or anyone else with his "manhood" or his unfitness for slavery when he defended himself. I doubt that when he resolved to defend himself he was even thinking about how others would interpret his actions. According to his own report he resisted Covey because he had pledged to "stand up in my own defense" ([1969]: 242).

More generally, although Douglass insists that his fight with Covey restored his self-respect and manhood and helped him to gain eventually his freedom, he never said that he undertook it because he anticipated that doing so would help gain these good consequences. On the contrary he seems to have anticipated bad consequences for fighting Covey. As he noted he believed that he would "suffer for resistance," ([1969]: 248). This suggests that although Douglass came to the concluding that self-defense in his circumstances was a duty, he did not come to the conclusion by considering the good consequences of self-defense. I do not mean that he did not welcome the good consequences of fighting Covey when he became aware of them after the fight; but even then he never said that they justified the fight. He seemed to have viewed them as a bonus on an act that was justifiable on independent grounds.

It may seem that the fact that Douglass did not fight Covey for the good consequences of doing so, the fight must have been an act of desperation, that happily turned out to have good consequences. But although Douglass' fight was certainly undertaken in desperate circumstances, it was not an act of desperation if this means it was undertaken unthinkingly. In the first place the restrained manner in which he fought Covey did not have the typical earmarks of an unthinking conflict. He was, he said, "strictly on the defensive, preventing him from injuring me, rather than trying to injure him" ([1969]: 242). More important is the fact that the fight was undertaken only after the most careful consideration. The fight occurred on a Monday, that is, the day after the one day the slaves had time for reflection. And Douglass reports that he had spend the day pondering the situation and had resolved "during that Sunday's reflection," to defend himself if Covey tried to beat him ([1969]: 241).

The fact that Douglass resolved to fight Covey only after careful consideration, though not in order to gain the good consequences of self-defense, suggests that he must have resolved to defend himself "on principle." In his circumstances a principle supporting a resolution to fight Covey would probably involve the right not to be physically abused. But while such right justifies self-defense, it does not,

278

BOXILL

by itself, *require* self-defense, especially if one has reason to believe that self-defense may lead to worse abuse and even death. Somehow we need to derive a duty to act on the right of self-defense, even in apparently hopeless circumstances. Douglass' views on this issue are suggested by his comment that he was "not only ashamed to be contented in slavery, but ashamed to *seem* to be contented... ([1969]: 273; emphasis in original). Since shame necessarily involves a confession of failure, a fall from an acknowledged standard or duty, the clear implication is that the rights that slavery violates are so sacred and central a part of morality that one has a duty never to even *seem* to fail to be devoted to them, and that one should therefore always be ready to show one's allegiance to them by standing up for them, and fighting for them, when they are violated or even impugned.

This conclusion is too strong as it stands. It may be both wise and right to seem contented with slavery in order to make good one's escape. And in general Douglass did not think that we could be moral without carefully weighing the consequences of our actions. Such an implication would be far indeed from his views. His whole career shows a keen appreciation of the fact that in most circumstances the consequences of our actions help determine whether they are morally obligatory or not. The careful plans he made for his own escape, and his refusal to join John Brown in his attack on Harper's Ferry are only two of many examples that show this attitude.

Why then did he suppose that the duty to defend oneself against physical abuse was absolute, at least when one is in the circumstances he was in when he was with Covey? Why is this duty different from the duty to secure one's freedom? The answer to this question lies partly in the consequences of severe physical abuse. These consequences are of a greater and different order than the consequences of restrictions on freedom.[3]

According to Douglass, a person who is subjected to severe and continuous or unpredictable physical violence is liable to be "humbled, degraded, broken down, enslaved, and brutalized." This is the way Douglass depicted his own condition as a result of Covey's mistreatment ([1969]: 223). We need to get clearer on its exact nature to see why Douglass thought that avoiding it was so imperative. Describing the state of his mind when he was being brutalized by Covey, Douglass wrote, "When I was looking for the blow about to be inflicted on my head, I was not thinking of my liberty; it was my life." The implication is that severe and continuous pain is so imperious as to push all other thoughts out of one's mind, including thoughts of morality. It is not simply that one craves relief; one craves relief without indignation or resentment, without remembering that one's rights are being violated; one loses sight of, forgets, one's rights not to be physically abused, and simply pleads for relief—or life. His "continual prayer," when he was with Covey, Douglass reports, was, "Spare my life" ([1950]: vol. 1; 157).

By comparison, the condition of one who, though deprived of his freedom, is not physically abused, seems almost enviable. Such a person may, of course, long for

BOXILL

freedom. But she is not degraded. She can think about her moral status, her rights and duties, and her moral equality to others. Douglass supposed this to be generally true. Slaves, in particular, would think about their liberty and moral equality if they were not brutalized. No particular book learning was necessary. Ordinary experience, even one so intellectually impoverished as a slave's, could convince anyone of average intelligence that she should be her own master. Douglass came to this conclusion by generalizing from his own experience. He wrote: "When entombed at Covey's, shrouded in darkness and physical wretchedness, temporal well-being was the grand desideratum; but temporal wants supplied, the spirit puts in its claim. Beat and cuff your slave, keep him hungry and spiritless, and he will follow the chain of his master like a dog; but, feed and clothe him well, work him moderately—surround him with physical comfort—and dreams of freedom intrude. Give him a bad master, and he aspires to a good master; give him a good master and he wishes to become his own master. Such is human nature. You may hurl a man so low, beneath the level of his kind, that he loses all just ideas of his natural positiojn; but eleveate him a littel, and the clear conception of rights rises to life and power, and leads him onward" ([1969]: 263, 264).

If the preceding paragraphs correctly describe the conditions of persons subjected to physical abuse and to a depriviation of freedom, Douglass' position on the relative urgency of the duty to avoid to stop these evils is understandable. The person subjected to continuous or unpredictable physical abuse is liable to be broken, humbled, brutalized—in a word, degraded. If resistance is the only way to avoid or stop continuous or unpredictable physical abuse then perhaps we do have an absolute duty to resist such abuse. On the other hand, if Douglass is right that the consequences of being deprived of liberty are not as destructive to the soul as the consequences of severe and continuous physical abuse (though they are certainly serious) then the duty to resist deprivations of liberty probably need not be so unconditional.

It may be objected that the long passage from *My Bondage and My Freedom* just cited suggests that Douglass thought that severe physical abuse has its soul-destroying effects only while it lasts.[4] If this is indeed the case then—even if resistance is the only way to stop physical abuse—it is not clear that we have a duty to resist such abuse without regard to the consequences. Degradation, it seems, is not permanent. Death on the other hand is permanent. Since resistance can mean death, it may therefore seem wiser to resist only when doing so is reasonably safe. But then the duty to defend oneself against severe and continuous physical abuse when in Covey-like circumstances does not seem absolute. This difficulty cannot be met by emphasizing the evil of degradation. Degradation is evil, and it may be worse than death, but if it is as impermanent as Douglass seems to suggest, if we recover from it as soon as the physical abuse that causes it ceases, perhaps it should be endured if resistance may mean death. A man who was being subjected to degrading torture would act irrationally if he resisted his torturers without regard to the possibility that they could kill him for resisting.

Despite his optimistic remarks suggesting that degradation is transient, Douglass had to know that it could outlast physical abuse. The assumption that it could was the reason why his master sent him to Covey. As Douglass noted, Covey "enjoyed the execrated reputation, of being a first rate hand at breaking young negroes." Slavemasters sent Covey their "most fiery bloods" so as to get them back after a year or two, "well broken." All this would make no sense if the "fiery bloods" regained their fire as soon as they left Covey and returned to their masters. But if degradation can be permanent or even difficult to recover from once inculcated, the case for an absolute duty to resist physical abuse when in Covey-like circumstances seems more compelling. It may be irrational to choose death over impermanent degradation, but rational to choose death over permanent degradation.

Reinforcing this argument is the consideration that a person being subjected to severe and continuous physical abuse is normally not in a position to know if or when he will be rescued. Assuming that his tormentors want to break or degrade him they will want to keep him ignorant of his chances of being rescued, and will usually be in a position to do so. Further, his ability to weigh the consequences of his actions is likely to be impaired by the distractions of the pain he is enduring, and once he is degraded he will prefer even a permanently degraded life to resistance and death. These conditions seemed satisfied in Douglass' own case. He had been brutalized by Covey for six months and there was no relief in sight. He had appealed to his master to no avail. Perhaps in a few more months he too would be returned to his master, "well broken." In such, or like circumstances, his call for an absolute duty of self-defense seems plausible. To fail to resist, even to stop and weigh the consequences of resistance, could be to allow oneself to be reduced to a state in which one permanently lost a sense of one's equal moral standing.

These considerations indicate how important Douglass thought it was for a person to be self-consciously aware of her rights and her equal moral standing. But they do not quite show that we have an absolute duty to resist severe or continuous physical abuse. They rest on the assumption that resistance is the only way to avoid the abuse that leads to degradation. Is this assumption true? If it is not then even if physical abuse has the soul destroying effects that Douglass describes, and for that reason must be stopped, why must it be stopped by resistance? Why not some other way? Even a slave in "Covey-like" circumstances, with no reason to expect that he will be rescued, seems to have options for seeking relief from abuse less dangerous than resistance.

Perhaps, for example, he could appeal to the pity or the humanity of his enslavers. Douglass knew from his own bitter experience that this was not a viable option. After a particularly vicious beating from Covey he had appealed to his master for relief. "I presented," he wrote, "an appearance of wretchedness and woe, fitted to move any but a heart of stone. From the crown of my head to the sole of my feet, there were marks of blood...In this unhappy plight, I appeared before my professedly Christian master, humbly to invoke the interposition of his power and authority, to protect me from further abuse and violence" ([1969]: 228). And he carefully made his appeal in terms of his master's interests, rather than in terms of his own rights. He told his master that Covey was likely to kill him or "ruin" him "for future service" ([1969]: 230). But, as he reports, "I was disappointed." His master began by "finding excuses for Covey," and ended up "with a full justification of him, and a passionate condemnation of me" ([1969]: 229).

It is important not to misunderstand Douglass here. His rejection of appeals to the slaveholders' sense of pity was not meant as an indictment of pity per se. He did not believe that pity was inherently unreliable, nor did he hold, as many do, that it is suspect as a moral sentiment because the one who appeals for it necessarily demeans himself, or because the one who feels it necessarily feels superior to the one he pities. Douglass esteemed pity as a decent and worthy sentiment that is a natural part of human nature. He spoke of the "pity" in a glance his mother gave him, and recalled that he "pitied" the slave woman Esther when he saw her severely whipped, and that Miss Lucretia, his master's daughter, "pitied" him, clearly indicating in every instance that he felt that the sentiment reflected well on both those experiencing it and on those to whom it was directed ([1969]: 36, 88, 130). Douglass rejected appeals to the slaveholders sense of pity or humanity because he believed they were incapable of such sentiments. This is clear from his description of the way his master reacted to his appearance when he appealed to him for relief. As Douglass reports, "It was impossible—as I stood before him at the first—for him to seem indifferent. I distinctly saw his human nature asserting its conviction against the slave system, which made cases like mine possible; but, as I have said, humanity fell before the systematic tyranny of slavery" ([1969]: 229). There is no hint in this passage that it would have been inappropriate for his master to have feelings of pity or humanity for him. On the contrary Douglass obviously felt that it was a failing on the part of his master that his humanity fell before the tyranny of slavery.

It may be objected that Douglass had an exceptionally hard-hearted master; if he did his experience would not justify the conclusion that all appeals to the pity or humanity of slave masters are useless. But Douglass' own experience had taught him that most slaveholders were hard-hearted. He did not believe that they were naturally so; the passage just cited indicates that he believed that a capacity for humanity or pity was part of their human nature; it was having slaves that made them hard hearted. He had observed the process first hand. When he was ten years old his master's sister-in-law Sophia, a naturally kind woman new to having slaves, had been almost a mother to him and had even undertaken to teach him how to read. But, Douglass reports, "the fatal poison of irresponsible power, and the natural influence of slavery customs, were not long in making a suitable impression on the gentle and loving disposition of my excellent mistress." Eventually, "Her noble soul was overthrown…" ([1969]: 144, 153). Not that Douglass ever put all slave-holders in one bag morally. For example, on one occasion Douglass came to his master's brother, Hugh, after a beating somewhat similar to the one he got from Covey. Hugh showed himself, Douglass says, in "every way more humane" than his brother, and "gave many proofs of his strong indignation at what was done" ([1969]: 315). On this occasion too, he reports, the "heart" of his "once kind mistress, Sophia," was again "melted in pity" towards him ([1969]: 315). But Douglass was under no illusions about Hugh and Sophia. Sophia's "affectionate heart," was "not yet dead," but it had been "hardened." And, while Hugh's humanity might have been genuine his indignation was not. As Douglass understood, "it resulted from the thought that his rights of property, in my person, had not been respect-ed, more than from any sense of the outrage committed on me as man" ([1969]: 316). Had he believed, as his brother had, that "breaking" Douglass would improve him as property, he too would have suppressed his feelings of humanity.

It was therefore useless to appeal to the slaveholders' sense of pity and humani-ty as well as to their sense of justice. That too had been corrupted by having slaves ("Speech on John Brown" [1950]: 534). But what of the option of appealing to the pity or sense of justice of those who were not slaveholders? Since they did not hold slaves perhaps their capacity for pity and justice was still intact. Douglass could not dismiss this option altogether. Others had been touched by his condition and had helped him escape slavery, and more generally, the abolitionists and those operat-ing the Underground Railway seemed prepared to do what they could for the slave. But there were limits to the help that could be expected even from those who did not have slaves. Many of them had been corrupted by their proximity to slavery. And others, though opposed to slavery and perhaps as yet uncorrupted by it, could be frightened by the consequences of interfering. Douglass gave a vivid illustration of this point. On one occasion four men beat him bloody while fifty looked on, and "not a man of them all interposed a single word of mercy" ([1969]: 314). Douglass concedes that some of them might have "pitied" him. But if they did, he remarks, they "lacked the moral courage to come and volunteer their evi-dence. The slightest manifestation of sympathy or justice toward a person of color, was denounced as abolitionism; and the name of abolitionist, subjected its bearer to frightful liabilities" ([1969]: 317).

It seems then that Douglass felt that appeals to the pity or humanity or sense of justice of the enslavers or even uncorrupted bystanders were generally likely not to bring relief from the physical abuse slavery involved. But it does not follow that an absolute duty of self-defense in Covey-like circumstances can be derived from the good consequences of self-defense, for self-defense may be just as effective in bringing relief from physical abuse in such circumstances as appeals to pity, human-ity or the sense of justice. It may be objected that since self-defense necessarily involves the use of physical force, it is certain to end in either victory over the enslavers, escape, or death. But self-defense may end in defeat and further abuse,

283

not death, or escape. There may, in fact, be no way to avoid abuse. In such circumstances the absolute duty of self-defense cannot depend on its consequences, but on the fact that it is a way to show allegiance to the principles of morality. A final objection is that we can show allegiance to the principles of morality by protesting injustice rather than by violently resisting it, and consequently that there cannot be an absolute duty of self-defense even in Covey-like circumstances.[5] But this objection cannot be sustained. Some of the principles of morality entitle us to defend ourselves with force. We cannot show our allegiance to these principles if we steadfastly refuse to do what they entitle us to do.

I conclude that we if can have an absolute duty to defend ourselves against physical abuse in Covey-like circumstances, this duty must be based on the duty to show allegiance to the principles of morality, though acting on it can have good consequences, as is discussed in the next section.

III

Less obvious, and more philosophically interesting than the consequences of self-defense noted earlier (escape, victory, or death) is the possibility that Douglass describes. As we have seen, Douglass reports that his fight with Covey helped gain him the reputation of being a slave who could only be whipped if he was also killed, and as a result he was never again whipped. He also reports that the rewards he derived from resisting when well beyond being free of pain. No longer preoccupied with the thought of being beaten he could again turn his thoughts to his liberty, his rights, and his moral equality with others. So important did Douglass consider this consequence of resistance that he claimed that when a slave "cannot be flogged his is more than half free" ([1988]: 247).

This claim must now be considered more closely. One difficulty is that Douglass seems to have overlooked that the slave who resisted only gained a qualified protection from physical abuse, for, of course, such a slave could still be beaten, even if beating him would require killing him. It is not an adequate answer to this objection that the master would not beat such a slave since this would mean that he would have to kill the slave, and so, destroy his own property. Killing slaves was not uncommon. They were valuable as property but not so valuable as to reliably stop the master from killing them. And a master could have a powerful motive to kill a defiant slave. If this made the other slaves more compliant it would increase the value of the master's property. This difficulty is confirmed by Douglass' candid confession that he could not "fully explain" why Covey did not have him hanged for his defiance, as the law allowed, or at least publicly whipped as an example to other slaves ([1988]: 248).[6]

We should therefore remember that Douglass' experience with resistance was fortunate, though not altogether unprecedented or unique. Resistance was generally a very dangerous business. And this suggests a further difficulty. If continuous or unpredictable physical mistreatment can distract a man from thoughts of his

284

BOXILL

moral status, degrade him, and make him incapable of acting morally, then surely the fear of being suddenly cut off can have the same result, and perhaps even more effectively. But in that case resistance seems a bad bargain. Indeed it seems to be a way of jumping from the frying pan into the fire.

Douglass seems to have anticipated this difficulty. He had, he said, "reached the point at which he was not afraid to die" ([1988]: 247). Although life was precious to him, and he did not wish his death, since he was not afraid to die, he was not agitated and distracted by the thought that he could be killed because of his resistance. It was a settled point for him that he would die rather than fail to resist physical abuse. His mind was therefore free to reflect on his equal moral status. As Douglass reported, the spirit of not being afraid to die made him "a freeman in fact," while he "remained a slave in form" ([1988]: 247).

But Douglass' claim that he had reached the point at which he was not afraid to die raises questions of its own. If reaching such a point is a necessary condition for enjoying the benefits of being a slave who cannot be whipped, perhaps most slaves will never be able to enjoy these benefits for most people find it difficult not to be afraid to die. It may be suggested that this was why the early Douglass refrained from urging slave resistance; he was aware that only a few slaves could make themselves unafraid of death. But this suggestion runs into several difficulties. Douglass' claim that he had reached the point at which he was not afraid to die first appeared in *My Bondage and My Freedom* (1855) after Douglass had come out in favor of slave resistance. It does not appear in the *Narrative* first published in 1845, when Douglass was still advising against slave resistance. In any case the suggestion does not explain why Douglass changed his mind about slave resistance after 1849. Did he come to believe that most slaves would be able to overcome the fear of death? Douglass did seem to hold that belief. In *My Bondage and My Freedom* he wrote, "while slaves prefer their lives, with flogging, to instant death, they will always find Christians enough, like unto Covey, to accommodate that preference" ([1988]: 247). The intimation in this passage that slaves who are flogged are somehow partly responsible for their misfortune only makes sense if we suppose that such slaves have it in their power to stop being afraid and to come to prefer instant death to lives with flogging.[7] But is such a supposition at all plausible?

This question becomes more pressing when we notice that Douglass records that he reached the point at which he was not afraid to die after "resisting" Covey, as if his reaching that point was a result of his resisting Covey. It seems to make more sense that he resisted Covey because he had reached the point at which he was not afraid to die. The fact that Douglass wrote that he had resolved to defend himself the day before the fight seems to support this latter view. On the other hand, people often make apparently firm resolutions and then, when the moment to act arrives, fail to act as they had resolved. And Douglass was aware that there was a significant difference between making resolutions and acting on them. As we wrote, "I was resolved to fight, and, what was better still, I was actually hard at it"

([1988]: 242). We must therefore consider the possibility that Douglass reached the point at which he was not afraid to die because he resisted Covey.

It would be unreasonable to take Douglass to be saying that any fight, perhaps one undertaken on the spur of the moment, or without good reason, was "better" than resolving to fight. He meant that acting on his resolution to fight was better than his bare resolution to fight. To understand why this makes sense we must remember the nature of his resolution to defend himself. As I have argued he resolved to defend himself because he believed that his nature as a moral being required that he stand up for the principles of morality. But as I have said, people commonly make apparently firm resolutions and then fail to act as they had resolved. Such a failure is always disconcerting, but it is likely to be devastating when the resolution was based on principles that one had claimed to embrace as part of one's identity as a moral being. It is, as Douglass indicates, an occasion for being ashamed, for it is a kind of unmasking, showing that one's allegiance to morality is not as firm as one had tried to deceive oneself into believing, that one is not the person one claimed to be, and that one is a pretender and a hypocrite even to oneself. But now it shouldd be clear why acting on the resolution to fight and defend oneself is better than the bare resolution to fight. It provides the evidence that confirms that one is the person one claimed to be—one loyal to morality—the more so when self-defense is likely to lead to one's death.

These considerations provide some support for Douglass' claim that one of the results of resisting Covey was that he was no longer afraid to die. Before the fight he could not be sure that he would fight if Covey tried to beat him; he had resolved to fight, but he knew that he could back down when Covey, whip in hand, confronted him. Given the importance he placed on being the kind of person who stood up for his rights, he could therefore be *afraid* that he would back down when that moment of truth arrived. However, after the fight, when he had the strongest possible evidence that he was the kind of person he wanted and claimed to be, the kind of person who stood up for his rights, he would no longer be afraid that he would back down if Covey tried to beat him.

It will be objected that this conclusion falls short of the claim that he was not afraid to die; no longer being afraid that he would back down if Covey tried to beat him, and no longer being afraid to die seem different things. I argue, however, that Douglass could not have meant that resisting Covey made him unafraid to die, but that he must have meant instead that resisting Covey make him unafraid that he would fail to do his duty to stand up for the principles of morality if Covey tried to beat him.

Fear involves two parts: a wish that some harmful event not happen, and an uncertainty whether it will happen or whether it will not happen (Gordon [1980]: 560–78). Douglass accepts the first part of this account of fear. As I noted earlier he says that life is "precious" to all human beings, and not "lightly regarded by men of sane minds" ([1988]: 284). This suggests that all human beings wish not to die,

286

BOXILL

and that after the fight with Covey, Douglass too wished not to die, given that he did not think that at the time he was no longer of sane mind. Now consider the second part of the account of fear I proposed, that fear involves an uncertainty whether or not the harmful thing one wishes not to happen will happen. Supposing that Douglass accepts it implies that resisting Covey would have removed his fear of death only if it removed his uncertainty whether or not resisting Covey would lead to death. But it is difficult to see how resisting Covey could have had such an effect. Before the fight he was uncertain whether fighting Covey would mean his death or not. He compares his action to the act of someone who has "incurred something, hazarded something, to repel injustice ([1988]: 247). I do not see how resisting Covey could remove all uncertainty about the consequences of resisting him a second or third time. Douglass got off easily the first time, but this could not have reasonably led him to believe that he had become invulnerable. Douglass admits that he was never sure why Covey did not have him hanged. He could therefore not be certain that Covey would not have him hanged if he resisted again. I conclude that resisting Covey could not have made him unafraid to die. But, as I have indicated, it could have made him unafraid that he would back down if Covey tried to beat him.

This conclusion supports many of Douglass' claims about the results of his fight with Covey, most obviously that the fight have him courage and confidence. With courage and confidence he would also, as he reported, be more determined to be a "freeman" ([1988]: 246). The conclusion also provides one interpretation of Douglass claims about the relations between power and honor noted earlier. According to Douglass the slave who cannot be flogged is "a power on earth" ([1988]: 247). If such a slave is as I have described him, someone with a demonstrated willingness to stand up for the principles of morality, then, by power, Douglass can only mean here the demonstrated willingness to stand up for the principles of morality. This account of power provides plausible readings of Douglass' claims that force (or power) is part of the "essential dignity of humanity," and that human nature cannot honor a helpless man. The claims mean that a demonstrated willingness to stand up for the principles of morality is part of the essential dignity of humanity, and that human nature cannot honor a person who lacks such a willingness. Finally, if honor is close in meaning to respect, we have a justification of Douglass claim that the fight restored his "crushed self-respect." Before the fight he had not demonstrated a willingness to stand up for the principles of morality and therefore could not honor or respect himself; his self-respect was crushed. But the fight demonstrated that he was willing to stand up for the principles of morality and therefore restored his crushed self-respect.

IV

These conclusions, though sound, have serious limitations. At best they can be generalized to apply to slaves who, like Douglass, defend themselves because of a firm

287

BOXILL

resolution to act on the duty to show allegiance to the principles of morality. Such slaves, it says, will grow in self-knowledge, confidence, courage, and self-respect. But is it reasonable to expect that all or most slaves can be persuaded to defend themselves on Douglass' high standard? Douglass certainly seemed to think so. And other black abolitionists like Henry Highland Garnet called for resistance on a similar standard (Aptheker [1951]: 227–232). Still, it is useful to see that self-defense could be morally beneficial for the slave even if it was not undertaken on the uncompromising ground of a duty to show allegiance to the principles of morality.

The argument is somewhat indirect, relying on the morally beneficial effects resistance could have on the enslaver. As I have already noted Douglass often suggested that slaves ought to be willing to peril their lives for their liberty because this would wipe out the reproach that blacks were unwilling to make sacrifice for their liberty, and were therefore fit for slavery. Although Douglass did not fight Covey for the reason this argument suggests, the argument could still be sound. If it is, slaves would not have to resist on the high ground that resistance showed allegiance to the principles of morality in order to derive moral benefits from resistance. If they resisted to gain their liberty, the public would look on them more favorably, and this could support their self-respect and eventually help them to gain their freedom.

Unfortunately the argument is not sound, though it does point to interesting possibilities. The most obvious failing of the argument is that is seems to rest on the false assumption that persons who are unwilling to make sacrifices for their liberty are fit for slavery. Such people are certainly more likely to be enslaved than other people, and are also perhaps at fault, supposing that one ought to be willing to make sacrifices for one's liberty, but it does not follow that they are fittingly enslaved. It may be suggested that Douglass did not mean to endorse the assumption, but was only pointing out that it was the basis of the public's toleration of slavery. But this lets the public off too easily. The public may have had some vague belief that persons ought to be willing to risk something for their liberty, but it did not believe that they must be willing to risk almost certain death and torture for liberty—at least it does not apply this standard to its own members. But this is the standard Douglass' argument suggests that the public applies to the slaves; it demands that meet standards that it expects few to meet, and that they provide evidence for their humanity that it takes for granted in other people. This suggests that the public already had evidence of the slaves' humanity; but that it ignores or misinterpreted this evidence. But in that case, what reason was there to believe that it would take notice of, or correctly interpret any further evidence to that effect?

But slave resistance could have an effect on the public and the slaveholders, that would force them out of their dishonesty. That effect is fear. Douglass suggested this possibility in his "Speech on John Brown," where he claimed that the slaves could reach "the slaveholder's conscience though his fear of personal danger" ([1950]: vol.

2; 535). I have argued that the slaveholders ignore or overlook evidence of the slaves' rights to freedom. But, as Aristotle observes, "fear make people inclined to deliberation" (Aristotle [1991]: vol. 2; 141). Since we deliberate when we are not clear what we ought to do, and are reconsidering and reexamining the evidence to determine how we ought to act, the effect that fear has on us that Aristotle points to may be sufficient to make the slaveholders acknowledge the slaves' humanity, and consequently that they have rights to freedom. And fear has another effect that may make the deliberation it inclines us to especially effective: it tends to undermine the pride and avarice that can lead us to interpret evidence dishonestly and in a way that justifies or excuses our pride and avarice. If this is the case, then as I have argued in another essay, slave resistance that arouses the fear of the public and the slaveholders could put them in a position to acknowledge the slaves' humanity and equal rights to be free (see Boxill [1995]).

Douglass does not mention this argument in his discussion of his fight with Covey. But it is consistent with what he does say, and indeed provides additional support for some of the good results he claimed to derive from the fight. First Douglass reports that Covey was "frightened" by his resistance, "lost his usual strength and coolness," and "cried out lustily for help" ([1988]: 243, 244). If fear has the effects I suggested, Covey's fear could have moved him to see Douglass in a new light, as a human being with rights, and Douglass might have seen this new respect in Covey's eyes. Since our conception of ourselves is supported by the conception of ourselves that we see in others' eyes, this could help explain why the fight with Covey helped Douglass regain his crushed self-respect.

289

There is a final more speculative advantage of this line of argument. Douglass suggested that Covey did not have him hanged or publicly whipped because he was ashamed to admit that he had been "mastered by a boy of sixteen." Such an admission would also damage his reputation as a "negro breaker" and therefore hurt him financially because it was this reputation that enabled him to procure the use of other slaveholders' slaves for very trifling compensation.[8] But, as I have emphasized, Douglass only "ventured" this explanation and pointedly indicated that he was not fully satisfied with it. The present discussion may help fill it out. Perhaps Douglass reached Covey's conscience through arousing his fear of personal danger. Such fear could have, in the way I have suggested, led Covey to deliberate more honestly on the evidence of Douglass' humanity and consequently to see him as a human being with rights. This would not be a whole hearted respect, for in that case Covey would have released Douglass. But it could have been a kind of grudging respect that could combine with his pride and avarice, and deter him from having Douglass hanged or publicly whipped.

If this discussion is sound, the good results Douglass claimed to have derived from his fight with Covey depended in part on his having won that fight. If he had resisted Covey but had been easily beaten or had not frightened him, and had been easily beaten, perhaps he would have gained the important knowledge of himself

BOXILL

as a man who would stand up for the principles of morality. This is no small matter. But if some people's consciences can only be revealed by arousing their fear, he would not have wrung any respect from Covey, and there would have been no respect in Covey's eyes to support his own self-respect. If this is true to Douglass' meaning his remarks on power and its relation to honor and dignity bear a second interpretation. Power is not simply a demonstrated willingness to stand up for the principles of morality. It is also a capacity to arouse the fear of others. On this account Douglass would be an advocate of Black Power, though not perhaps in the manner of his great contemporary Martin Delany. For Delany, Black Power was necessary for blacks to avoid white oppression. For Douglass, Black Power was also necessary for blacks and whites to have any sense of morality.

NOTES

1 All references are to Douglass unless otherwise noted.

2 His argument that slave resistance would help to end slavery by discrediting the public's favorite argument for slavery suggests this view. It is made even more pointedly (in [1950]: vol. 2; 535) when he claimed that slave resistance would "reach the slaveholders' conscience through his fear of personal danger." See also his claim that the slavemaster has deprived "his victim of every means of reaching his sense of justice, except through his bodily fear" ([1950]: vol. 5; 213). I have tried to spell out the argument that slave violence could be morally persuasive in Boxill (1995).

3 This appeal to consequences does not contradict the position I have attributed to Douglass that the duty of self-defense when in Covey-like circumstances is absolute. The general rule justifying self-defense may be justified by its consequences, though the agent should follow the rule and defend herself without weighing the consequences. In other words I am giving a rule-utilitarian interpretation of Douglass' deontological view of the duty of self-defense against physical abuse when is Covey-like circumstances. The agent should simply follow the rule without weighing the consequences when she is in Covey-like circumstances because people in such circumstances are very likely to weigh the relevant circumstances so as to justify the morally wrong conclusion.

4 Consider also his claim that "as soon as the blow was not to be feared, then came the longing for liberty" ([1950]: vol. 1; 157).

5 I have myself presented protest in this way in Boxill [1983]: 190–8.

6 This was written more than twenty years after the incident. The same confession appears in *The Life and Times of Frederick Douglass* published more than fifty years after the incident.

7 This passage is deleted in the later biography.

8 I emphasize the tentative nature of Douglass' explanation. In the *Narrative* he conceded that it did not "entirely satisfy him" (105).

BIBLIOGRAPHY

Adell, S. 1994. *Double Consciousness/Double Blind: Theoretical Issues in Twentieth-Century Black Literature*. Urbana: University of Illinois.

Ahmad, A. 1992. *In Theory: Classes, Nations, Literatures*. London and NY: Verso.

Akst, H. and G. Clark. 1928. "Am I Blue." NY: ASCAP.

Alcoff, L., and E. Potter, eds. 1993. *Feminist Epistemologies*. NY: Routledge.

Alianzas In *Bridges of Power: Women's Multicultural Alliances*, ed. L. Albrecht and R. M. Brewer. Philadelphia: New Society.

Allen, D.C. 1964. "Donne's 'Sappho to Philaenis.'" *English Language Notes* 1, no. 3.

Allen, E., Jr. 1992. "Ever Feeling One's Twoness: 'Double Ideals' and 'Double Consciousness' in *The Souls of Black Folk*," *Contributions in Black Studies* 9/10.

Allen, N., ed. 1991. *African-American Humanism: An Anthology*. Buffalo, NY: Prometheus.

Anderson, B. 1983. *Imagined Communities: Reflections on the Origin and Spread of Nationalism*. NY: Verso.

Ansboro, J.J. 1983. *Martin Luther King, Jr.: The Making of a Mind*. NY: Orbis.

Anzaldúa, G. 1990. "Bridge, Drawbridge, Sandbar or Island: Lesbians-of-Color *Hacienda Alianzas*." in *Bridges of Power: Women's Multicultural Alliances*, ed. L. Albrecht and R.M. Brewer. Philadelphia: New Society.

Appiah, K. 1985. "The Uncompleted Argument: Du Bois and the Illusion of Race." in *"Race," Writing, Difference* (see Gates 1985).
———1992. *In My Father's House: Africa in the Philosophy of Culture*. NY: Oxford.
———1990. "Racisms." in *Anatomy of Racism* (see Goldberg 1995).

Aptheker, H., ed. 1951. *A Documentary History of the Negro People in the United States*. NY: Citadel.

Arendt, H. 1958. *The Human Condition*. Chicago and London: University of Chicago.
———1963. *On Revolution*. NY: Viking.
———1969. *On Violence*. NY: Harcourt Brace Jovanovich.

Aristotle 1941. *The Basic Works of Aristotle*, ed. intro. by Richard McKeon. NY: Random House.
———1991. *On Rhetoric*, trans. G.A. Kennedy. NY: Oxford.

Asante, M.K. 1988. *Afrocentricity*. Trenton, NJ: Africa World.
———1993a. "Racing to Leave Race: Black Postmodernists Off-Track," *The Black Scholar: The Multicultural Debate* 23 nos. 3 and 4.
———1993b. "Racism, Consciousness, and Afrocentricity." in *Lure and Loathing: Essays on Race, Identity, and the Ambivalence of Assimilation*. NY: Allen Lane.

Aschheim, S.E. 1992. *The Nietzsche Legacy in Germany: 1890–1990*. Berkeley: University of California.

Babbitt, S.E. 1994. "Identity, Knowledge, and Toni Morrison's *Beloved*: Questions about Understanding Racism." *Hypatia: A Journal of Feminist Philosophy* 9, no. 3.

Baker, H.A., Jr. 1993. *Black Studies, Rap, and the Academy*. Chicago: University of Chicago.

Baldwin, J. 1963. *The Fire Next Time*. NY: Dell Publishing Company.
———1955. *Notes of a Native Son*. Boston: Beacon.

Baltazar, E. 1973. *The Dark Center: A Process Theology of Blackness*. NY: Paulist.

Banton, M., and Harwood. 1975. *The Race Concept*. NY: Praeger.

Barrett, L. 1977. *The Rastafarians*. Boston: Beacon.

Bartky, S.L. 1990. *Femininity and Domination: Studies in the Phenomenology of Oppression*. NY: Routledge.

Bataille, G. 1994. *On Nietzsche*, trans. B. Boone, intro. by S. Lotringer. NY: Paragon.

Baudrillard, J. 1979. *Seduction*, trans. Brian Singer. NY: St. Martin's.

Beauvoir, S., de. 1947. *Pour une morale de l'ambiguïté*. Paris: Gallimard.
———1948. *The Ethics of Ambiguity*, trans. by B. Frechtman. Secaucus, NJ: The Citadel.
———1983. *The Second Sex*, trans. H.M. Parshley. NY: Alfred A. Knopf.

Bell, B.W. 1974. *The Folk Roots of Contemporary Afro-American Poetry*. Detroit: Broadside.

Bell, D. 1973. *The Coming of Post-Industrial Society*. NY: Basic Books.
———1976. *The Cultural Contradictions of Capitalism*. NY: Basic Books.

Bell, L. 1993. *Rethinking Ethics in the Midst of Violence: A Feminist Approach to Freedom*. Boston: Rowman and Littlefield.

Bendyshe, T. 1863-64. *The History of Anthropology*. Vol. 1: *Memoirs*. Anthropological Society of London.

Benhabib, S. 1994. "Deliberative Rationality and Models of Democratic Legitimacy." *Constellations* 1, no. 1.

Benson, P. 1994. "Free Agency and Self-Worth," *The Journal of Philosophy* XCI, no. 12.

Bergoffen, D. 1992. "Casting Shadows: The Body in Descartes, Sartre, de Beauvoir, and Lacan." *Bulletin de la Société Américaine de Philosophie de Langue Française* IV, nos. 2–3: 232–243.

Bernal, M. *Black Athena: The Afroasiatic Roots of Classical Civilization*. New Brunswick, NJ: Rutgers.

Bernstein, R. "John Dewey." *Encyclopedia of Philosophy*, Vol. 2. NY: Free.

Bhabha, H., ed. 1990. *Nation and Narration*. NY: Routledge.

Bisnauth, D. 1989. *History of Religions in the Caribbean*. Kingston, Jamaica: Kingston.

Blassingame, J. 1972. *The Slave Community: Plantation Life in the Ante-Bellum South*. NY: Oxford.

Bluestein, G. 1972. *The Voice of the Folk: Folklore and American Literary Theory*. Amherst, MA: University of Massachusetts.

293

Blumenbach. 1795. *On the Natural Variety of Mankind*. in Bendyshe, *Treatises of Blumenbach*.

Boorstin, D.J. 1970. "From News Gathering to News Making: A Flood of Pseudo-Events," *Freedom and Tyranny: Social Problems in a Technological Society*, ed. J.D. Douglas. NY: Alfred A. Knopf.

Boxill, B. 1983a. "The Race-Class Question." in *Philosophy Born of Struggle* (see Harris 1983).

———1983b. "Self-Respect and Protest." in *Philosophy Born of Struggle*.

———1984. *Blacks and Social Justice*. Totowa, NJ: Rowman and Allanheld.

———1992. "The Underclass and the Race-Class Issue." in *The Underclass Question* (see Lawson 1992).

———1992–3. "Two Traditions in African American Political Philosophy," *Philosophical Forum*, 24, no. 103.

———1995. "Fear and Shame as Forms of Moral Suasion in the Thought of Frederick Douglass." *The Charles S. Pierce Society Proceedings* 31, no. 4.

Bowman, E., and R. Stone. Forthcoming. *Sartre's Morality of Praxis: An Introduction to the Ethical Writings of the Mid-1960's*.

Bradbury, R. 1957. *Fahrenheit 451*. NY: Ballantine.

Broderick, F.L. 1958. "German Influence on the Scholarship of W.E.B. Du Bois," *Phylon* 19.

Brotz, H. 1970. *The Black Jews of Harlem: Negro Nationalism and the Dilemmas of Negro Leadership*. NY: Schocken.

———ed. 1992. *African-American Social and Political Thought, 1850–1920*. New Brunswick, NJ: Transaction.

Brown, D.A. 1984. *Bloods: An Oral History of the Vietnam War*, ed. T. Wallace. NY: Ballantine.

Buber, M. 1948. *Das Problem des Menschen*. Heidelberg: Verlag Lambert Schneider, 1948.

———1958. *I and Thou*. trans. Ronald Gregor Smith. NY: Scribner's Sons/Collier.

———1965. *Between Man and Man*. Translated by Ronald Gregor Smith, intro. by Maurice Friedman. NY: Collier.

Butler, J. *Bodies that Matter: On the Discursive Limits of "Sex."* NY: Routledge, 1993.

———1990. *Gender Trouble: Feminism and the Subversion of Identity*. NY: Routledge.

———1987. *Subjects of Desire: Hegelian Reflections in Twentieth-Century France*. NY: Columbia.

Cabral, A. 1969. *Revolution in Guinea: Selected Texts by Amilcar Cabral*. NY: Monthly Review.

Calhoun, J.C. 1963. "Speech on the Reception of Abolitionist Petitions." in *Slavery Defended: The Views of the Old South*, ed. E.L. McKitrick. Englewood Cliffs, NJ: Prentice-Hall.

Callinicos, A. 1989. *Against Postmodernism: A Marxist Critique*. Oxford: Blackwell/Polity.

Campbell, B.M. 1992. *Your Blues Ain't Like Mine*. NY: Ballantine.

Camus, A. 1942. *Le mythe de sisyphe*. Paris: Gallimard.
———1955. *"The Myth of Sisyphus" and Other Essays*, trans. J. O'Brien. NY: Vintage.

Carleton C. 1962. *The Origin of the Races*.

Carlyle, T. 1971. *The Nigger Question*. NY: Appleton-Century-Crofts

Cassinelli, C. W. 1976. *Total Revolution: A Comparative Study of Germany under Hitler, the Soviet Union under Stalin, and China under Mao*. Santa Barbara, CA: Clio.

Catalano, J. 1980. *A Commentary on Jean-Paul Sartre's "Being and Nothingness."* Chicago: University of Chicago.
———1986. *A Commentary on Jean-Paul Sartre's "Critique of Dialectical Reason," Volume 1, "Theory of Practical Ensembles."* Chicago: University of Chicago.

Caute, D. 1970. *Frantz Fanon*. NY: Viking.

Césaire, A. 1972. *Discourse on Colonialism*. NY: Monthly Review.

Charmé, S. 1991. *Vulgarity and Authenticity: Dimensions of Otherness in the World of Jean-Paul Sartre*. Amherst: University of Massachusetts.

Chopp, R.S. 1991. *The Power to Speak: Feminism, Language, God*. NY: Crossroad.

Collins, P.H. 1990. *Black Feminist Thought: Knowledge, Consciousness, and the Politics of Empowerment*. NY: Routledge.
———1993. "Setting Our Own Agenda." *The Black Scholar: The Multicultural Debate* 23 nos. 3 and 4.

Cone, J. 1969. *Black Theology and Black Power*. NY: Seabury.
———1970. *A Black Theology of Liberation*. Philadelphia: J.B. Lippencott.
———1975. *God of the Oppressed*. NY: Seabury.

Coon, C. 1962. *The Origin of the Races*. NY: Knopf.

Cooper, A.J. 1988. *A Voice from the South*, foreword H.L. Gates, Jr., intro. M.H. Washington. NY and Oxford: Oxford.

Cornell, D. 1991. *Beyond Accommodation: Ethical Feminism, Deconstruction, and the Law*. NY: Routledge.
———1992a. *Philosophy of the Limit*. NY: Routledge.
———(with M. Rosenfeld and D. Gray Carlson, eds.) 1992b. *Deconstruction and the Possibility of Justice*. NY: Routledge.

295

Corrington, R.S. 1991. "The Emancipation of American Philosophy," *American Philosophical Association Newsletter on Philosophy and the Black Experience* 90, no. 3.

Cose, E. 1993. *The Rage of a Privileged Class*. NY: Harper Collins.

Crosby, D.A. 1988. *The Specter of the Absurd: Sources and Criticisms of Modern Nihilism*. Albany: State University of New York.

Crummell, A. 1992a. *Destiny and Race: Selected Writings, 1948–1898*, ed. W.J. Moses. Amherst: University of Massachusetts.
————1992b. "The Race Problem in America." in *African-American Social and Political Thought, 1850–1920*, ed. H. Brotz. New Brunswick, NJ: Transaction.

Cruse, H. 1984. *The Crisis of the Negro Intellectual: A Historical Analysis of the Failure of Black Leadership*. NY: Quill.

Cullen, C. 1929. *"The Black Christ" and Other Poems*. NY: Harper and Brothers.
————1969. *Color*. NY: Arno Press and the *New York Times*.

Curry, G.E. 1994. "Farrakhan, Jesse and Jews, Part II," *Emerge* (September).

Davis, A.Y. 1983a. *Women, Race, and Class*. NY: Vintage.
————1983b. "Unfinished Lecture on Liberation." in *Philosophy Born of Struggle* (see Harris 1983).

Derrida, J. 1982. *The Margins of Philosophy*, trans. Alan Bass. Chicago: University of Chicago.
————1991. *A Derrida Reader: Between the Blinds*, ed. and with an intro. by Peggy Kamuf. NY: Columbia.
————1992. "Force of Law: The 'Mystical Foundation of Authority.'" in *Deconstruction and the Possibility of Justice*. (see Cornell, Rosenfeld, and Carlson.).
————1994. *Specters of Marx*, trans. P. Kamuf, intro. B. Magnus and S. Cullenberg. NY: Routledge.

Descartes, R. 1952. *Descartes' Philosophical Writings*, trans., and ed. N.K. Smith. London: Macmillan.

Dickens, C. 1903. *The Niger Expedition*. NY.

Donne, J., and W. Blake. 1941. *The Complete Poetry and Prose of John Donne and The Complete Poetry of William Blake*. NY: Random House.

Dostoyevsky, F. 1968. *Great Short Works of Fyodor Dostoyevsky*, ed. intro. by R. Hingley. NY: Harper & Row.

Douglas, J.D. 1970. *Freedom and Tyranny: Social Problems in a Technological Society*. NY: Alfred Knopf.

Douglass, F. 1950. *The Life and Writings of Frederick Douglass*, Vols. 1–5, ed. P. Foner. NY: International.

———1962. *Life and Times of Frederick Douglass: The Complete Autobiography*. intro. by R.W. Logan. NY: Crowell-Collier.

———1969. *My Bondage and My Freedom*. NY: Dover.

———1972. "I Denounce the So-called Emancipation as a Stupendous Fraud." in *The Voice of Black America*, ed. P.S. Foner. NY: Simon and Schuster.

———1988. *Narrative of the life of Frederick Douglass An American Slave*, ed. B. Charles. Cambridge: Harvard.

———1993. *The Life and Times of Frederick Douglass*. NY: Gramercy.

———1992. *Frederick Douglass on Women's Rights*, ed. P.S. Foner. NY: Da Capo.

Dubin, A., and H. Warren. 1934. *I Only Have Eyes for You*. NY: ASCAP.

Du Bois, W.E.B. 1897. "The Striving of the Negro People," *Atlantic Monthly* 80 (August).

———1898. "The Study of the Negro Problems," *Annals of the American Academy of Political and Social Sciences* XI (January). Reprinted in *The Black Sociologists: The First Half Century*, ed. J. Bracey, Jr., A. Meier, and E. Rudwick. Belmont, CA: Wadsworth.

———1899. *The Philadelphia Negro: A Social Study*. Philadelphia: University of Pennsylvania.

———1920. *Darkwater: Voices from within the Veil*. NY: Harcourt, Brace and Howe.

———1952. *In Battle for Peace: The Story of My 83rd Birthday*. NY: Masses & Mainstream.

———1965. *The World and Africa*. NY: International. [1947].

———1968a. *Dusk of Dawn: An Essay Towards an Autobiography of a Race Concept*. NY: Schocken.

———1968b. *The Autobiography of W.E.B. Du Bois: A Soliloquy on Viewing My Life from the Last Decade of Its First Century*, ed. H. Aptheker. NY: International.

———1969. *The Souls of Black Folk*. Intros. by N. Hare and A. Poussaint. NY: Signet Classics.

———1970a. "The Conservation of Races." in *Black Nationalism in America*, ed. J.H. Bracey, Jr., A. Meier, and E. Rudwick. Indianapolis: Bobbs-Merrill.

———1970b. "Criteria of Negro Art." in *Black Nationalism in America*.

———1975. *The Gift of Black Folk*. Millwood, NY: Kraus-Thompson.

———1985. *Against Racism: Unpublished Essays, Papers, Addresses, 1887–1961*, ed. H. Aptheker. Amherst: University of Massachusetts.

———1986. *W.E.B. Du Bois: Writings*, ed. N. Huggins. NY: Library of America.

———1995. *Du Bois*, ed. D.L. Lewis. NY: Henry Holt.

Eddy, J.H., Jr. 1977. "Buffon, Organic Change, and the Races of Man." Ph.D. diss. University of Oklahoma.

Einstein, A. 1946. *The Meaning of Relativity*. Princeton, NJ: Princeton.

———1961. *Relativity: The Special and the General Theory: A Clear Explanation that Anyone Can Understand*. NY: Crown.

Ellison, R. 1990. *Invisible Man*. NY: Vintage.

———1972. *Shadow and Act*. NY: Vintage.

297

Emerson, R.W. 1903. *Nature: Addresses and Lectures*. Boston: Houghton Mifflin.

———1904. *The Conduct of Life*. Boston: Houghton Mifflin.

———1938. *Young Emerson Speaks*, ed. A.C. McGiffert, Jr. Boston: Houghton Mifflin.

———1966. *The Early Lectures of Ralph Waldo Emerson*, Vol. I, ed. S.E. Wicher and R.E. Spiller. Cambridge: Harvard.

———1972. *The Early Lectures of Ralph Waldo Emerson*, Vol. 3, ed. S.E. Wicher and R.E. Spiller. Cambridge: Harvard.

Ergang, R.R. 1966. *Herder and the Foundations of German Nationalism*. NY: Octagon.

Estes-Hicks, O. 1985–6. "Jean Toomer and the Politics and Poetics of National Identity," *Contributions in Black Studies* 7.

Eze, E., ed. 1996. *African Philosophy in American Terrain*. Oxford: Blackwell.

Fanon, F. 1952. *Peau Noire, Masques Blancs*. Paris: Éditions de Seuil.

———1963. *The Wretched of the Earth*, preface by J-P Sartre, trans. C. Farrington. NY: Grove.

———1967a. *Black Skin, White Masks*, trans. C.L. Markmann. NY: Grove.

———1967b. *Toward the African Revolution*, trans. H. Chevalier. NY: Grove.

———1967c. *A Dying Colonialism*, trans. H. Chevalier intro. by A. Gilly. NY: Grove Weidenfield.

———1968. *Sociologie d'une Révolution*. Paris: François Maspero.

———1979. *Pour la Révolution Africaine: Écrits Politiques*. Paris: François Maspero.

———1991. *Les Damnés de la Terre*. Préface de J-P Sartre. Paris: Paris: Éditions Gallimard, 1991.

Fahrenheit 451 1966. Directed by F. Truffaut.

Faulkner, W. 1962. *Light in August*. intro. by C. Brooks. NY: Modern Library.

Fiedman, M., ed. 1991. *the Worlds of Existentialism: A Critical Reader*. Atlantic Highlands, NJ: Humanities.

Firestone, S. 1970. *The Dialectic of Sex: The Case for Feminist Revolution*. NY: William Morrow.

Fiss, O. "Groups and the Equal Protection Clause." in *Equality and Preferential Treatment*. Dover, MA: Case Publishing Co.

Fletcher, G.P. 1988. *A Crime of Self Defense: Bernard Goetz and the Law on Trial*. NY: Free Press.

Fortes, M. 1945. *The Dynamics of Clanship Among the Tellensi*. NY: Oxford.

———1959. *Oedipus and Job in West African Religion*. NY: Cambridge.

Foucault, M. 1967. *Nietzsche*. Paris: Minuit.

———1973. *The Order of Things: An Archaeology of the Human Sciences*. NY:Vintage.

———1979. *Discipline and Punish:The Birth of the Prison*, trans.A. Sheridan NY:Vintage.

———1980. *Power/Knowledge*, ed. C. Gordon, trans. C. Gordon, L. Marshall, J. Mehpam, and K. Soper. NY: Pantheon.

Frazer, N. 1986. "Toward a Discourse Ethics of Solidarity," *Praxis International* 5.

Frazier, E.F. 1925. "Durham: Capitol of the Black Middle Class." in *The New Negro:An Interpretation*, ed.A. Locke (see Locke 1970).

Freire, P. 1990. *Pedagogy of the Oppressed*, trans. M.B. Ramos. NY: Continuum.

Freud, S. 1953–74. *The Standard Edition of the Complete Psychological Works of Sigmund Freud*, ed. and trans. J. Strachey. London.

Fullinwider, R. 1981. *The AT&T Case and Affirmative Action*. Dover, MA: Case.

———1992. "Reverse Discrimination and Equal Opportunity." in *The Moral Life*, ed. S. Luper-toy and C. Brown. Orlando, FL: Harcourt Brace Jovanovich.

Fuss, D. 1989. *Essentially Speaking: Feminism, Nature and Difference*. NY: Routledge.

Garnet, H. 1951. "An Address to the Slaves of the United States of America." in *A Documentary History of the Negro People in the United States*, ed. H.Apthekes. NY: Citadel.

Gates, H.L., Jr., ed. 1985. *"Race," Writing, Difference*. Chicago: University of Chicago.

———1992. "Black Demagogues and Pseudo Scholars." in *New York Times* (July 20).

Gayle, A. 1980. *Richard Wright: Ordeal of a Native Son*. Garden City: Anchor Press/Doubleday.

Gergen, K.J. 1991. *The Saturated Self: Dilemmas of Identity in Contemporary Life*. NY: Basic.

Gillespie, C.K. 1989. *Justifiable Homicide: Battered Women, Self, Defense, and the Law*. Columbus, OH: Ohio State University.

Gilman, S. 1985. "Black Bodies, White Bodies." in *"Race," Writing, and Difference*, ed. H.L. Gates, Jr. Chicago: University of Chicago.

Gilroy, P. 1993. *The Black Atlantic: Modernity and Double Consciousness*. Cambridge: Harvard.

Glass, J.M. 1993. *Shattered Selves: Multiple Personality in a Postmodern World*. Ithaca, NY: Cornell.

Glisssant, E. 1992. *Caribbean Discourse*. Charlottesville: University of Virginia.

Goldberg, D.T. *Racist Culture: Philosophy and the Politics of Meaning*. Oxford: Blackwell, 1993.

———ed. 1990. *Anatomy of Racism*. Minneapolis: University of Minnesota.

Gooding-Williams, R. 1987. "Philosophy of History and Social Critique in *The Souls of Black Folk*." in *Social Science Information* 26, no. 1.

———1991–2. "Evading Narrative Myth, Evading Prophetic Pragmatism: Cornel West's *The American Evasion of Philosophy*." in *Massachusetts Review* 32.

———ed. 1993. *Reading Rodney King, Reading Urban Uprising*. NY: Routledge.

Gordon, L.R. 1993. "Racism as a Form of Bad Faith." in *American Philosophical Association Newsletter on Philosophy and the Black Experience* 92, no. 2.

———1994a. "Review of *Race Matters*," *Political Affairs* 73, no. 2.

———1994b. "Reflections on *Brown v. Board of Education*," *Political Affairs* 73, no. 11.

———1995a. *Bad Faith and Antiblack Racism*. Atlantic Highlands, NJ: Humanities.

———1995b. *Fanon and the Crisis of European Man: An Essay on Philosophy and the Human Sciences*. NY and London: Routledge.

———1995c. "Antirace Rhetoric and Other Misrepresentations of Racism in the Present Age." *Social Text*. no. 42.

———1995d. "Sartrean Bad Faith and Antiblack Racism." in *The Prism of the Self: Essays in Honor of Maurice Natanson*, ed. Steven Crowell. Dordrecht: Kluwer Academic.

———1995e. "'Critical' Mixed Race?" *Social Identities* 1, no. 2.

———1995f. "A Review Essay of Linda Bell's *Rethinking Ethics in the Midst of Violence: A Feminist Approach to Freedom*," *Sartre Studies International* 1, no. 1.

———(ed., with T.D. Sharpley-Whiting and R.T. White) 1996a. *Fanon: A Critical Reader*. Oxford: Blackwell.

———1996b. "The Black and Body Politics: Fanon's Existential Phenomenological Critique of Psychoanalysis." in *Fanon: A Critical Reader*.

———(ed., with R.T. White). Forthcoming [a]. *Black Texts and Textuality: Constructing and De-Constructing Blackness*. Lanham, MD: Rowman and Littlefield.

———Forthcoming [b]. *Her Majesty's Other Children: Philosophy, Racism, and Intellectualism in a Neocolonial Age*. Lanham, MD: Rowman and Littlefield.

Gordon, R. 1980. "Fear." in *Philosophical Review* LXXXIX, no. 4.

Gossett, T.F. 1965. *Race: The History of an Idea in America, 1900–1930*. Baton Rouge: Louisiana State University.

Graham, L.O. 1995. *Member of the Club*. NY: Harper Collins.

Gramsci, A. 1975. *Selections from "The Prison Notebooks."* trans., and ed. Q. Haoare and G.N. Smith. NY: International.

Grant, J. 1989. *White Women's Christ and Black Women's Jesus*. Atlanta: Scholars.

Grier, W.H., and P. Cobbs 1969. *Black Rage*. NY: Basic.

Griffith, E., and C. Bell. 1989. "Recent Trends in Suicide and Homicide among Blacks." *JAMA, The Journal of the American Medical Association* 262 (October 27th).

Guinier, L. 1994. *The Tyranny of the Majority.* NY: Free Press.

Hadden, J., and A. Shupe, eds. 1986. *Prophetic Religions and Politics.* NY: Paragon House.

Harris, L., ed. 1983. *Philosophy Born of Struggle: Afro-American Philosophy Since 1917.* Dubuque, IA: Kendall/Hunt.

———1993. "Postmodernism and Utopia, An Unholy Alliance." in *Racism, The City And The State*, ed. M. Cross and M. Keith. NY: Routledge.

Harris, W. 1995. *History, Fable and Myth.* Wellesley, MA: Calaloux.

Hartsock, N. 1987. "Rethinking Modernism: Minority vs. Majority Theories." *Culture Critique* 7.

———Forthcoming. "Theoretical Bases for Coalition Building: An Assessment of Postmodernism." in *Feminsim and Social Change: Bridging Theory and Practice*, ed. H. Gottfried. Urbana: University of Illinois.

Harwood, J. and Banton, M.P. 1975. *The Race Concept.* NY: Praeger.

Hayes, III, F. 1996. "Fanon, African–Americans, and Resentment." in *Frantz Fanon: A Critical Reader* (see Gordon 1996).

Hegel, G.F.W. 1955. *Die Vernunft in der Geschichte*, 5th ed. Hamburg: Felix Meiner.

———1956. *Philosophy of History*, trans. with an intro. by J. Sibree, preface by C. Hegel and a new intro. by C.J. Friedrich. NY: Dover.

———1967. *Philosophy of Right*, trans. T.M. Knox. Oxford: Clarendon.

———1977. *Phenomenology of Spirit*, trans. A.V. Miller, with foreword by J.N. Findlay. NY: Oxford.

Heidegger, M. 1977. *Martin Heidegger: Basic Writings from "Being and Time" (1928) to "The Task of Thinking" (1964)*, ed. intro. by D.F. Krell. San Francisco: HarperSanFrancisco.

Henry, P. 1985. *Peripheral Capitalism and Underdevelopment in Antigua.* New Brunswick, NJ: Transaction.

———1993. "C.L.R. James, African and Afro-Caribbean Philosophy," *The C.L.R. James Journal* 4, no. 1.

———1996. "Fanon, African and Afro-Caribbean Philosophy." in *Fanon: A Critical Reader* (see Gordon 1996a).

Herder, J.G. 1966. *Outline of a Philosophy of the History of Man.* NY: Berman.

———1968. *Reflections on the Philosophy of the History of Mankind.* Chicago: University of Chicago.

———1969. *J.G. Herder on Social and Political Culture*, trans. and ed. F.M. Baranard. London: Cambridge.

Higginbotham, E.B. 1992. "African-American Women's History and the Metalanguage of Race." *Signs: A Journal of Culture and Society* 17, no. 2.

High Noon 1954. Directed by F. Zinneman.

301

Hochschild, J.L., and M. Herk 1990. "'Yes, But…': Caveats in American Racial Attitudes," in *Majorities and Minorities: Nomos XXXII*, ed. by J.W. Chapman and A. Wertheimer. NY: New York University.

Homer 1962. *The Illiad*, trans. R. Lattimore. Chicago: University of Chicago.

hooks, b. 1981. *Ain't I A Woman: Black Women and Feminism*. Boston: South End.
———1984. *Feminist Theory from Margins to Center*. Boston: South End.
———1990. *Yearning: Race, Gender, and Cultural Politics*. Boston: South End.
———1992. *Black Looks: Race and Representation*. Boston: South End.

Horsman, R. 1981. *Race and Manifest Destiny: The Orignis of American Racial Anglo-Saxonism*.

Hughes, R. 1986. *The Fatal Shore: The Epic of Australia's Founding*. NY: Vintage.

Hull, G., P.B. Scott, and B. Smith, eds. 1982. *All the Women Are White, All the Blacks Are Men, but Some of Us Are Brave: Black Women's Studies*. NY: Feminist.

Hurst, F. 1933. *Imitation of Life*. NY: Harpers.

Hurtado, A. 1989. "Relating to Privilege: Seduction and Rejection in the Subordination of White Women and Women of Color," *Signs: A Journal of Women in Culture and Society* 14, no. 4.

Hutcheon, L. 1989. *The Politics of Postmodernism*. NY: Routledge.

Imitation of Life 1934. Directed by J. Stahl.

Irigaray, L. 1985a. *The Speculum of the Other Woman*, trans. G.C. Gill. Ithaca, NY: Cornell.
———1985b. *This Sex Which Is Not One*, trans. C. Porter with C. Burke. Ithaca, NY: Cornell.
———1987. "Sexual Difference," trans. reprinted in *French Feminist Thought: A Reader*, ed. Toril Moi. Oxford: Blackwell. Originally published as the opening chapter of *L'Ethique de la différence sexuelle*. Paris: Les Éditions de Minuit, 1984.
———1993. *An Ethic of Sexual Difference*. trans. C. Burke and G.C. Gill. Ithaca, NY: Cornell.

James, J.A., and F. Farmer, eds. 1993. *Spirit, Space, and Survival: Black Women in (White) Academe*. NY: Routledge.

James, J.A. 1996a. *Resisting State Violence in US Culture*. Minneapolis: University of Minnesota.
———1996b. *Radicalizing the Talented Tenth*. NY: Routledge.

James, W. 1890. *The Principles of Psychology*. NY: Henry Holt.

JanMohamed, A.R. 1985. "The Ecomomy of Manichaean Allegory: The Function of Racial Difference in Colonialist Literature." in *"Race," Writing, Difference* (see Gates 1985).

Jefferson, T. 1977. *The Portable Thomas Jefferson*, ed. M.D. Peterson. NY: Penguin.

Johnson, J.W. 1973. *Along this Way: The Autobiography of James Weldon Johnson*. NY: Viking. [1933].

Jones, J. 1981. *Bad Blood: The Tuskegee Syphilis Experiment*. NY: Free Press.

Jones, W. 1973. *Is God a White Racist?: A Preamble to Black Theology*. NY: Anchor/Doubleday.

Jordan, W. 1968. *White Over Black: American Attitudes toward the Negro, 1550–1812*. NY: W.W. Norton.

Judy, R.A.T. 1996. "Fanon's Body of Black Experience." in *Frantz Fanon: A Critical Reader* (see Gordon, 1996).

July, R. 1968. *The Origins of Modern African Thought*. London: Faber and Faber.

Kaufmann, W., ed. 1975. *Existentialism from Dostoyevsky to Sartre*. NY: Meridian.

Keil, C. 1966. *Urban Blues*. Chicago: University of Chicago.

Keneally, T. 1972. *The Chant of Jimmy Blacksmith*. NY: Penguin.

Kierkegaard, S. 1957. *The Concept of Dread*, trans. W. Lowrie. Princeton, NJ: Princeton.
———1980. *The Concept of Anxiety*. Princeton, NJ: Princeton.

King, D. 1988. "Multiple Jeopardy: The Context of a Black Feminist Ideology." in *Signs: A Journal of Women in Culture and Society* 14, no. 1.

King, M.L., Jr. 1991. *A Testament of Hope: The Essential Writings and Speeches of Martin Luther King, Jr.*, ed. J. Melvin Washington. San Francisco: HarperSanFrancisco.

Kirkland, H.T. 1984. *Bloods: An Oral History of the Vietnam War*, ed. Terry Wallace. NY: Ballantine.

Kolenda, K. 1991. "The (Cornel) West-Ward Vision for American Philosophy." *American Philospohical Association Newsletter on Philosophy and the Black Experience* 90, no. 3.

Kymlicka, W. 1990. *Contemporary Political Philosophy*. Oxford: Clarendon.
———Unpublished. "Ethnicity and the Law. ".

Laing, R.D. 1962. *The Divided Self*. NY: Pelican.
———1962. *Sanity, Madness, and the Family*. NY: Pelican.

La Strada. 1954. Directed by F. Fellini.

Lawson, L.A. 1971. "Cross Damon: Kierkegaardian Man of Dread," in *CLA Journal* 14: 291–8.

Lawson, B.(E.). 1989. "Locke and the Legal Obligations of Black Americans." *Public Affairs Quarterly* 3, no. 3.
———ed. 1992. *The Underclass Question*. Philadelphia: Temple.

Lehan, R. 1959. "Existentialism in Recent American Fiction: The Demonic Quest," in *Texas Studies in Literature and Language* 1.

Lerner, M., and C. West. 1995. *Jews and Blacks*. NY: G. P. Putnam.

Levin, D.M. 1988. *The Opening of Vision: Nihilism and the Postmodern Situation*. NY: Routledge, 1988.

Lévi-Strauss, C. 1965. "Race and History." in *Race, Science and Society*, ed. L. Kuper. NY: Columbia.

Lewis, D.L. 1993. *W.E.B. Du Bois: Biography of a Race*. NY: Henry Holt.

Lewis, R.F., and B.S. Walker. 1995. "*Why Should White Guys Have All the Fun?*" NY: John Wiley.

Lincoln, C.E. 1993. "The Du Boisian Dubiety and the American Dilemma: Two Levels of Lure and Loathing." in *Lure and Loathing: Essays on Race, Identity, and the Ambivalence of Assimilation*, ed. G. Early. NY: Allen Lane/Penguin.

Linneaus. 1863–4. *Systema Naturae*, trans. Thomas Bendyshe, in "The History of Anthropology," Anthropological Society of London, *Memoirs* 1.

Locke, A., ed. 1970. *The New Negro*, with new preface by R. Hayden. NY: Atheneum.
———1983. "The New Negro." in *Philosophy Born of Struggle*. (see Harris 1983.).
———1989. *The Philosophy of Alain Locke: Harlem Renaissance and Beyond*. ed. and intro. L. Harris. Philadelphia: Temple.

Locke, J. 1991. *Two Treatises of Government*, ed. P. Laslett. Cambridge, UK: Cambridge.

Lorde, A. 1984. *Sister Outsider*. Trumansburg, NY: Crossing.

Lott, E. 1994. "Cornel West in the Hour of Chaos: Culture and Politics in *Race Matters*," no. 41.

Lott, T. 1992–3. "Du Bois on the Invention of Race." *Philosophical Forum* 23, no. 103.

Loury, G. 1988. "Why Should We Care About Group Inequality," *Social Phyilosphy and Policy* 5, no. 1.

Lugones, M., and V. Spelman. 1990. "Have We Got A Theory For You! Feminist Theory, Cultural Imperialism, and The Demand for 'The Woman's Voice.' in *Hypatia Reborn: Essays in Feminist Philosophy.* ed. A.Y. al-Hibri and M.A. Simons. Bloomington: Indiana University.

Lynch, H.R. 1967. *Edward Wilmot Blyden: Pan-Negro Patriot, 1832–1912.* NY: Oxford.

Lyotard, J-F. 1984. *The Postmodern Condition: A Report on Knowledge,* trans. G. Bennington and B. Massumi, foreword by F. Jameson. Minneapolis: University of Minnesota.

Madhubuti, H.R. 1993–4. "Blacks, Jews and Henry Louis Gates, Jr.," *Black Books Bulletin: WordsWork* 16, nos. 1 and 2.

Maistre, J. de. 1994. *Coniderations on France,* trans., and ed. R. Lebrun, intro. by I. Berlin. Cambridge, UK: Cambridge.

Malouf, D. 1993. *Remembering Babylon.* NY: Pantheon.

Marcuse, H. 1964. *One-Dimensional Man.* Boston: Beacon.
———1969. *An Essay on Liberation.* Boston: Beacon.
———1972. *From Luther to Popper,* trans. J. de Bres. London: Verso.

Marable, M. 1981. *Black Water: Historical Studies in Race, Class Consciousness and Revolution.* Dayton: Black Praxis.

Marx, K., and F. Engels. *The Marx-Engels Reader,* 2nd Edition, ed. F. Tucker. NY: W.W. Norton.

Masolo, D.A. 1994. *African Philosophy in Search of Identity.* Bloomington: Indiana University.

Matustík, M. 1993. *Postnational Identity: Critical Theory and Existential Philosophy in Habermas, Kierkegaard, and Havel.* NY: The Guilford.

McGary, H. 1983. "Racial Integration and Racial Separatism: Conceptual Clarification." in *Philosophy Born of Struggle* (see Harris 1983).
———1992. "The Black Underclass and the Question of Values." in *The Underclass Question* (see Lawson 1992).
———1992–3. "Alienation and the African-American Experience," in *The Philosophical Forum* 24, nos. 1-3.
———and B.(E.). Lawson., eds. 1993. *Between Slavery and Freedom.* Bloomington: Indiana University.

McKitrick, E.L., ed. 1963. *Slavery Defended: The Views of the Old South.* Englewood Cliffs, NJ: Prentice-Hall.

McLuhan, M. 1969. *Counter Blast.* NY: Harcourt, Brace and World.

Memmi, A. 1968. *Dominated Man.* Boston: Beacon.

305

Merleau-Ponty, M. 1962. *Phenomenology of Perception*, trans. C. Smith. Atlantic Highlands, NJ: Humanities.

————1968. *The Visible and the Invisible: Followed by Working Notes*, ed. C. Lefort and trans. A. Lingis. Evanston: Northwestern University.

Millet, K. 1970. *Sexual Politics*. NY: Avon.

Moon, J.D. *Constructing Community*. Princeton, NJ: Princeton.

Moraga, C. 1993. "From A Long Line of Vendidas: Chicanas and Feminism." in *Feminist Frameworks: Alternative Theoretical Accounts of the Relations Between Women and Men*. 3rd Edition, ed. A.M. Jaggar and P.S. Rothenberg. NY: McGraw-Hill. Excerpted from, A Long Line of Vendidas. in *Loving in the War Years: Lo que nunca pasó por sus labios*. Boston: South End.

Morrison, R., II 1994. *Scienice, Theology and the Transcendental Horizon: Einstein, Kant and Tillich*. Atlanta: Scholars.

Morrison, T. 1970. *The Bluest Eye*. NY: Holt, Reinholt and Winston.

————1977. *Song of Solomon*. NY: New American Library.

————1987. *Beloved*. NY: Knopf.

————1990. "The Site of Memory." in *Out There: Marginalization and Contemporary Cultures*, ed. R. Ferguson, M. Gever, T.T. Minh-ha, and C. West. Cambridge: MIT.

————1992. *Playing in the Dark*. Cambridge: Harvard.

Mosco, V. 1982. *Pushbutton Fantasies*. Norwood, NJ: ABLEX.

Mosely, A. 1992. "Affirmative Action and the Urban Underclass." in *The Underclass Question* (see Lawson 1992).

Moses, W.J. 1992. *Alexander Crummell: A Study of Civilization and Discontent*. Amherst: University of Massachusetts.

Mouffe, C., ed. 1992. *Dimensions of Radical Democracy*. NY: Vessa.

Mulgan, G.J. 1991. *Communication and Control: Networks and the New Economies of Communications*. NY: Guilford.

Natanson, M. 1970. *The Journeying Self: A Study in Philosophy and Social Role*. Reading, MA: Addison-Wesley.

————1986. *Anonymity: A Study in the Philosophy of Alfred Schutz*. Bloomington: Indiana University.

National Association for the Advancement of Colored People (NAACP). 1919. *Thirty Years of Lynching in the United States: 1889–1918*. NY: NAACP.

Nei, M., and A.K. Roychoudhury. 1983. "Genetic Relatinshi and Evolution of Human Races." *Evolutionary Biolgy* 14.

Nicoloff, P.L. 1961. *Emerson on Race and History: An Examination of English Traits*. NY: Columbia.

Nietzsche, F. 1968a. *The Will to Power*, trans. W.F. Kaufmann and R.J. Hollingdale. NY: Vintage.
———1968b. *Beyond Good and Evil*, trans. with a preface by W. Kaufmann, in *Basic Writings of Nietzsche*. NY: Random House.
———1974. *The Gay Science*, trans. intro. by W. Kaufmann. NY: Vintage.
———1982. *Daybreak*, trans. R.J. Holingdale, intro. by M. Tanner. Cambridge, UK: Cambridge.
———1989a. *On the Genealogy of Morals*, trans. W. Kaufmann and R.J. Hollingdale, intro. by W. Kaufmann. NY: Vintage.
———1989b. *Ecce Homo*, trans. intro. by W. Kaufmann. NY: Vintage.

Oliver, K. 1993. "Importing 'The French Feminists' and Their Desires." in *Reading Kristeva: Unravelling the Double-bind*. Bloomington: Indiana University.

Omi, M., and H. Winant. 1994. *Racial Formation in the United States From the 1960s to the 1980s*. NY: Routledge.

Outlaw, L.T. 1990. "Toward a Critical Theory of 'Race.'" in *Anatomy of Racism* (see Goldberg 1990).
———1992–3. "Africana Philosophy." *Philosophical Forum* 24, no. 103.

Ovid 1914. *Heroides*. trans. G. Showerman. Cambridge: Harvard.

Owens, J. 1976. *Dread*. Kingston, Jamaica: Sangsters.

307

Patterson, O. 1972. "Toward a Future that Has No Past: Reflections on the Fate of Blacks in the Americas," *Public Interest*, no. 27.

Paynter, R. "W.E.B. Du Bois and the Material World of African-Americans in Great Barrington, Massachusetts." *Critique of Anthropology* 12, no. 3.

Phelan, S. 1993. "(Be)Coming Out: Lesbian Identity and Politics." *Signs: A Journal of Women in Culture and Society* 18, no. 4.

Philip, M.N. 1989. *She Tries Her Tongue*. Charlottetown: Ragweed.

Pieterse, J.N. 1992. *White on Black: Images of Africa and Blacks in Western Popular Culture*. New Haven: Yale.

Putt, K.A., and P. Valdes-Dapena, "Movin' Into the Fast Lane on the Information Superhighway," *Crisis* 102, no. 3.

Quarles, B. 1948. *Frederick Douglass*. Washington, D.C.: Associated.

Ramirez, M. 1986. "The Challenge of Alternative Communications." in *The Myth of the Information Revolution: The Social and Ethical Implications of Communication Technology*, ed. M. Traber. Newbury Park, CA: SAGE.

Rampersad, A. 1990. *The Art and Imagination of W.E.B. Du Bois*. NY: Schocken.

Rawls, J. 1971. *A Theory of Justice*. Cambridge: Harvard.
————1993. *Political Liberalism*. NY: Columbia.

Randolph, L. 1995. "Blacks in the Fast Lane of the Information Highway," *Ebony* (January).

Robinson, C. 1983. *Black Marxismm: The Making of the Black Radical Tradition*. London: Zed.

Rorty, R. 1989. *Contingency, Irony, and Solidarity*. NY: Cambridge.

Rose, T., and A. Ross, eds. 1995. "Race and Racism: A Symposium," *Social Text*, no. 42.

Rosenfeld, M. 1991. *Affirmative Action and Justice*. New Haven: Yale.

Rosenthal, A. 1935. *Nietzsches "Europäisches Rasse-Problem": "Der Kampf Um die Erdherrschaft."* Leiden: A.W. Sijthoff.

Rosenau, P.M. 1992. *Post-Modernism and the Social Sciences: Insights, Inroads, and Intrusions*. Princeton, NJ: Princeton.

Ruchames, L., ed. 1969. *Racial Thougt in America: From the Puritans to Abraham Linclon*. Amherst: University of Massachusetts.

Rushkoff, D. 1994. *Media Virus! Hidden Agendas in Popular Culture*. NY: Ballantine.

Sangari, K. 1987. "The Politics of the Possible." *Culture Critique* 7.

Sartre, J.-P. 1938. *Nausée*. Paris: Gallimard.
————1943. *L'être et le néant: essai d'ontologie phénoménologique*. Paris: Gallimard.
————1945. "Retour des Etats-Unis: ce que j'ai appris du problème noir." *Le Figaro*.
————1948. *Anti-Semite and Jew*, trans. G. Becker. NY: Schocken.
————1949. "Orphée noir," in *Situations*, III. Paris: Gallimard.
————1955. *"No Exit" and Three Other Plays*. NY: Vintage.
————1956b. *Being and Nothingness: A Phenomenological Essay on Ontology*, trans. intro. by H. Barnes. NY: Washington Square.
————1963. "Preface." *The Wretched of the Earth*. (see Fanon 1963).
————Unpublished. 19*64 Rome Lecture Notes*. Paris: Bibliothèque Nationale.
————1968. *Search for a Method*, trans. intro. by H. Barnes. NY: Vintage.
————1974a. "Black Presence." in *The Writings of Jean-Paul Sartre, Vol. 2, Selected Prose*. ed. M. Contat and M. Rybalka, trans. R. McCleary. Evanston: Northwestern.
————1976. *"No Exit" and Three Other Plays*. NY: Vintage.
————1982. *Cahiers pour une morale*. Paris: Gallimard.
————1988. *"What Is Literature?" and Other Essays*, ed. intro. by S. Ungar. Cambridge: Harvard.
————1991a. *Critique of Dialectical Reason, Volume I, Theory of Practical Ensembles*, trans. A. Sheridan-Smith and ed. J. Rée. London: Verso.

Sartre, J.-P (continued)

———1991b. "Kennedy and West Virginia," excerpt from unpublished *Morality and History*, trans. Bowman and Stone. in *Sartre, Alive!* (see Aronson and van den Hoven).

———1992. *Notebooks for an Ethics*, trans. D. Pellauer. Chicago: University of Chicago.

Schutz, A. 1962. *Collected Papers, Volume I, The Problem of Social Reality*, ed. intro. by M. Natanson, with preface by H.L. Van Breda. Boston: Martinus Nijhoff.

———1964. *Collected Papers, Volume II, Studies in Social Theory*, ed. with and intro. by Arvid Brodersen. The Hague: Martinus Nijhoff.

———1966. *Collected Papers, Volume III, Studies in Social Phenomenological Philosophy*. Ilse Schutz, ed. The Hague: Martinus Nijhoff.

———1967. *The Phenomenology of the Social World*, trans. G. Walsh and F. Lehnhert, intro. by G. Walsh. Evanston: Northwestern.

———1970. *Reflections on the Problem of Relevance*. ed. R.M. Zaner. New Haven and London: Yale.

———(with Thomas Luckmann.) 1973. *The Structures of the Life-World*. trans. R.M. Zaner and H.T. Engelhardt, Jr. Evanston: Northwestern.

———(with Thomas Luckmann.) 1989. *The Structures of the Life-World, Volume II*, trans. R.M. Zaner and D.J. Parent. Evanston: Northwestern.

Schweitzer, A. 1956. *The Mysticisim of Paul the Apostle*. NY: Macmillan.

Scott, M.S. 1995. "Tapping into the Telecommunications Industry," *Black Enterprise* (February).

Senghor, L. 1964. *Liberté I: Négritude et humanisme*. Paris: Édition de Seuil.

Sharpley-Whiting, T.D. 1996. "The Dawning of Racial-Sexual Science." *French Literature Series* 23.

———1997a. *Fanon and Feminisms: Theory, Thought, Praxis*. Lanham, MD: Rowman & Littlefield.

———1997b. *Black Venus: Sexualized Savages, Primal Fears and Primitive Narratives*. Durham: Duke.

Shaw, T., P. Sinclair, B. Andah, and A. Okpoko. (eds.) 1993. *The Archaeology of Africa: Food, Metals, and Towns*. London and NY: Routledge.

Simons, M. 1979. "Racism and Feminism: A Schism in the Sisterhood." *Feminist Studies* 5, no. 2.

Simpson, G. 1970. *Religious Cults of the Caribbean*. Rio Pedras: Institute of Caribbean Studies.

Slaughter, T.F., Jr., 1983. "Epidermalizing the World: A Basic Mode of Being Black." in *Philosophy Born of Struggle* (see Harris 1983).

Smith, B., ed. 1983. *Home Girls: A Black Feminist Anthology*. NY: Kitchen Table/Woman of Color.

———1985. "Toward a Black Feminist Criticism." in *Feminist Criticism and Social Change: Sex, Class and Race in Literature and Culture*, ed. J. Newton and D. Rosenfelt. NY: Methuen.

Soyinka, W. 1990. *Myth, Literature and the African World*. NY: Cambridge.

Sowell, T. 1984. *Civil Rights—Rhetoric or Reality*. NY: William Morrow.

Spelman, E. 1991. "Theodicy, Tragedy and Prophecy: Comments on Cornel West's *The American Evasion of Philosphoy*," *American Philosophical Association Newsletter on Philosophy and the Black Experience* 90, no. 3.

Spencer, J.M. 1993. "Trends of Opposition to Multiculturalism." *The Black Scholar* 23, no. 2.

Spillers, H.J. "Mama's Baby, Papa's Maybe: An American Grammar Book." *Diacritics* 17, No. 2.

Stabile, C.A. 1994. "Feminism without Guarantees: The Misalliances and Missed Alliances of Postmodern Social Theory." *Rethinking Marxism* 7, no. 1.

Stepto, R.B. 1991. *From Behind the Veil: A Study of Afro-American Narrative*, 2nd ed. Urbana, IL: University of Illinois.

Stephan, N. 1982. *The Idea of Race in Science: Great Britain 1800–1960*.

Stewart, M. 1987. *The Political Speeches of Maria Stewart*, ed. M. Richardson. Bloomington: Indiana University.

Stevens, D. 1988. *The Origins of Freemasonry: Scotland's Century, 1590–1710*. Cambridge, UK: Cambridge.

Stoll, C. 1995. *Silicone Snake Oil: Second Thoughts on the Information Highway* NY: Doubleday.

Tate, C. 1993. "Christian Existentialism in *The Outsider*." in *Richard Wright: Critical Perspectives Past and Present*, ed. H.L. Gates, Jr., and K.A. Appiah. NY: Amistad.

Taylor, C. 1992. *Multiculturalism and "The Politics of Recognition": An Essay by Charles Taylor*. Commentary by A. Gutmann, ed., S. Rockefeller, M. Walzer, and S. Wolf. Princeton, NJ: Princeton.

Tempels, P. 1959. *Bantu Philosophy*, trans. C. King with foreword by M. Read. Paris: Présence Africaine.

Tillich, P. 1952. *The Courage to Be*. New Haven: Yale.

Traber, M. 1986. *The Myth of the Information Revolution: The Social and Ethical Implications of Communication Technology*. Newbury Park, CA: SAGE.

Turner, H.M.T. 1971. *Respect Black: The Writings and Speeches of Henry McNeal Turner*, ed. E. Redkey. NY: Arno and the *New York Times*.

Turner, V. 1967. *The Forest of Symbolism*. Ithaca, NY: Cornell.

Tylor, E. 1871. *Primitive Culture*. Boston.

U.S. Supreme Court. 1976. *Runyon v. McCrary* 427.
————1987. *Saint Francis College v. Al-Khazraji* 107.
————1989. *Richmond v. Croson* 109.

Visions of Light—The Art of Cinematography. 1993. Directed by A. Glassman.

Wagner, J. 1974. *Black Poets of the United States: From Paul Laurence Dunbar to Langston Hughes*. Urbana: University of Illinois.

Wallace, M. 1979. *Black Macho and the Myth of the Superwoman*. NY: Dial.

Wallace, T. 1984. *Bloods: An Oral History of the Vietnam War*. NY: Ballantine.

Walker, D. *Appeal to All Colored Citizens of the World*.

Walker, M. 1988. *Richard Wright Daemonic Genius: A Portrait of the Man and a Critical Look at His Work*. NY: Warner.

Warren, M. 1988. *Nietzsche and Political Thought*. Cambridge: MIT.

Watts, J.G. 1993. "Reflections on the King Verdict." in *Reading Rodney King* (see Gooding-Williams 1993).

Webb, C. 1968. *Richard Wright: A Biography*. NY: G.P. Putnam.

Weinstein, M.A. 1991. "The Dark Night of the Liberal Spirit and the Dawn of the Savage." in *Ideology and Power in the Age of Lenin in Ruins*. NY: St. Martin's.

Wells-Barnett, I.B. 1969. *On Lynching: Southern Horrors, a Red Record, Mob Rule in New Orleans*. NY: Arno and the *New York Times*.
————1970. *Crusade for Justice: The Autobiography of Ida B. Wells*, ed. A. Barnett Duster. Chicago: University of Chicago.

West, C. 1982. *Prophesy, Deliverance!: An Afro-American Revolutionary Christianity*. Philadelphia: Westminster.
————1988. *Prophetic Fragments*. Trenton, NJ: Africa World.
————1989. *The American Evasion of Philosophy: A Genealogy of Pragmatism*. Madison: University of Wisconsin.
————1991. "Nihilism in Black America: A Danger that Corrodes from Within," *Dissent* (Spring).
————1992. "Philosophy and the Urban Underclass." in *The Underclass Question* (see Lawson 1992).

311

West, C. (continued)

———1993a. *Race Matters*. Boston: Beacon.

———1993b. *Keeping Faith*. NY: Routledge.

———1994. *Race Matters*. NY: Vintage.

———1995. (see Lerner 1995.).

Wheeler, D.L. 1995. "A Growing Number," *The Chronicle of Higher Education* (February 17th).

White, F. "'MultiQueer' Theory," *Radical America* 36.

Whitford, M. 1991. *Luce Irigaray: Philosophy in the Feminine*. NY: Routledge.

Williams, R. 1976. *Keywords: A Vocabulary of Culture and Society*. NY: Oxford.

Williams, R.C. 1983. "W.E.B. Du Bois: Afro-American Philosopher of Social Reality." in *Philosophy Born of Struggle* (see Harris 1983).

Williamson, J. 1984. *The Crucible of Race: Black-White Relations in the American South since Emancipation*. NY: Oxford.

Wilson, J. 1992. "Lifting 'the Veil': Henry O. Tanner's *The Banjo Lesson* and *The Thankful Poor*," *Contributions in Black Studies* 9/10.

Wilson, R.M. 1967. "Mani and Manichaeism." in *The Encyclopedia of Philosophy*, Volume 5. NY: Macmillan.

Wilson, W.J. 1987. *The Truly Disadvantaged*. Chicago: University of Chicago.

Wright, R. 1953. *The Outsider*. NY: Harper and Row.

———1972. "Blueprint for Negro Writing." in *The Black Aesthetic*, ed. A. Gayle. Garden City, NJ: Anchor/Doubleday.

———1977. *American Hunger*. NY: Harper and Row.

Young, I.M. 1990. *Justice and the Politics of Difference*. Princeton, NJ: Princeton.

Yovel, Y. 1994. "Nietzsche, the Jews, and *Ressentiment*." in *Nietzsche, Genealogy, Morality: Essays on Nietzsche's "Geneaology of Morals,"* ed. R. Schacht. Berkeley: University of California.

Zack, N. 1993. *Race and Mixed Race*. Philadelphia: Temple.

———1994. "Race and Philosophic Meaning," *American Philospohical Association Newsletter on Philosophy and the Black Experience* 91, no. 1.

———ed. 1995. *American Mixed Race*. Boston: Rowman and Littlefield.

———1996a. *Bachelors of Science: Seventeenth-Century Identity Then and Now*. Philadelphia: Temple.

———ed. 1997. *Race/Sex: Their Sameness, Difference, and Interplay*. NY and London: Routledge.

Zamir, S. 1995. *Dark Voices: W.E.B. Du Bois and American Thought, 1888–1903*. Chicago and London: University of Chicago.

312

INDEX

323